Archaeological Perspectives on the American Civil War

Florida A&M University, Tallahassee
Florida Atlantic University, Boca Raton
Florida Gulf Coast University, Ft. Myers
Florida International University, Miami
Florida State University, Tallahassee
University of Central Florida, Orlando
University of Florida, Gainesville
University of North Florida, Jacksonville
University of South Florida, Tampa
University of West Florida, Pensacola

Archaeological Perspectives on the American Civil War

edited by Clarence R. Geier and Stephen R. Potter

University Press of Florida

Gainesville · Tallahassee · Tampa · Boca Raton

Pensacola · Orlando · Miami · Jacksonville · Ft. Myers

08 07 06 05 04 03   6 5 4 3 2 1

Library of Congress Cataloging-in-Publication Data
Archaeological perspectives on the American Civil War / edited by
Clarence R. Geier and Stephen R. Potter.
p. cm.
Includes bibliographical references and index.
ISBN 0-8130-1834-X (cloth: alk. paper)
ISBN 0-8130-2651-2 (pbk.: alk. paper)
1. United States—History—Civil War, 1861–1865—Antiquities.
2. United States—History—Civil War, 1861–1865—Battlefields.
3. Excavations (Archaeology)—United States. I. Geier, Clarence R.
II. Potter, Stephen R.
E646.5 .A74 2001
973.7—dc21 00-047971

The University Press of Florida is the scholarly publishing agency
for the State University System of Florida, comprising Florida A&M
University, Florida Atlantic University, Florida Gulf Coast University,
Florida International University, Florida State University, University
of Central Florida, University of Florida, University of North Florida,
University of South Florida, and University of West Florida.

University Press of Florida
15 Northwest 15th Street
Gainesville, FL 32611–2079
http://www.upf.com

To Deane . . . with love. For twenty-nine years of tolerance, understanding, and support.
CRG

To the memory of my great-great-grandfather, Jesse W. Viar, private, Company H, 1st Virginia Infantry, C.S.A.
SRP

Contents

Figures

Tables

Foreword

Jim Lehrer

The story of the American Civil War will never have an ending. That's because there are new discoveries about what happened and insights on their meaning being uncovered every day. Much of that important work is being done by archaeologists and anthropologists who have made it their mission to keep the news and information coming. I salute them.

We ordinary mortals walk a piece of ground today where a Civil War battle was fought and hear birds singing or breezes blowing through the trees. Archaeologists and anthropologists hear cannon volleys and screams from one hundred and forty years ago. They examine bones and rusted belt buckles and read stories of life and death in horrific, bloody combat.

History applauds them. So should we all.

Introduction

My introduction to battlefield and site-related archaeology came more than twoscore years ago. In the summer of 1956, nine months after I joined the National Park Service (NPS) as park historian at Vicksburg National Military Park, I met Beverly M. DuBose, Jr.—insurance executive, collector, historian—whose one-of-a-kind collection of Civil War militaria is highlighted in the Atlanta History Center. This was during the years when battlefield archaeology was in the dark ages, and few, if any, NPS professionals knew of or appreciated the breakthrough in that discipline that metal detectors presaged.

DuBose, because of his Civil War knowledge, experience with metal detectors, and association with the service's chief curator, Harold Peterson, became an NPS collaborator. As such, DuBose was tasked with visiting battlefield parks and familiarizing the staff with the use of the first generation of metal detectors then coming on the market.

In January 1956, I had reconnoitered Grand Gulf, Mississippi, and had identified the sites of Forts Wade and Cobun, two Confederate river batteries. This area, since it had not been collected from, would be a good place for Beverly, his son "Bo," and me to study. Our visit was a success in confirming the locations of the forts. Objects pinpointed by the detectors and recovered from the Fort Wade site included several projectiles fired by Union rifled, 42-pounders and fragments from explosive 9-inch and 32-pound shells. More interesting were the elevating screw and several pieces of a burst, rifled 32-pounder gun.

Documentary research confirmed that the Eads City Series Ironclads, which dueled with the Grand Gulf forts on April 29, 1863, mounted rifled 42-pounders and smoothbore 9-inch and 32-pounders. The fort emplaced four cannon, including two rifled 32-pounders that were dismounted by the fire of the naval guns and subsequently spiked when the Confederates evacuated Grand Gulf on the night of May 2–3.

During the next nine years, before leaving Vicksburg in April 1966, I worked with several local collectors skilled in the use of metal detectors. Retired Lt. Col. Harold Hanisee and Dr. James Hyde, a microbiologist, ground-truthed battle positions I had identified from documentary sources at Chickasaw Bayou, Port Gibson, and Raymond. At Chickasaw Bayou, the Confederates emplaced two guns atop the Indian mound. After-action reports indicated that Company H, 1st Illinois Light Artillery, armed with 20-pounder Parrotts, shelled the mound. This was confirmed when Hanisee located and recovered a number of fired projectiles of that weight from the site. Hyde's Port Gibson and Raymond surveys, in addition to identifying Confederate battle lines, led to the excavation of an

Enfield rifle musket. An x-ray revealed that the bore contained a number of rounds, which confirmed that in the excitement of battle, soldiers would ram a round home and forget to cap the piece. At Raymond, near Fourteenmile Creek, Hyde found a partial skeleton, fragments of a cartridge box with a number of unfired .577-caliber Minié balls, and a "Lone Star" belt buckle, a discovery that confirmed the paper trail's location of the 7th Texas Infantry.

Meanwhile in Montana, Don Rickey, historian at Custer Battlefield National Monument—now Little Bighorn Battlefield National Monument—and archaeologist Robert T. Bray employed metal detectors to survey selected areas of the battlefield as well as Big Hole National Battlefield.

In the early 1960s—before the enactment of the National Historic Preservation Act of 1966 and the advent of Cultural Resources Management—interdisciplinary research was not commonly practiced in the NPS. The professionals, if they communicated, saw the other disciplines as rivals. Under these circumstances, it is not surprising that at Manassas National Battlefield Park, the superintendent, relying on the small-scale D. B. Harris Map of First Manassas as an infallible guide, made several errors in interpreting the battlefield and restoring the ground cover. The first of these involved the location of the 13 Confederate cannon on Henry Hill, which was done without any input from archaeology and then corrected by a subsequent superintendent. The reestablishment of a woodlot on Matthews Hill, where one did not exist, is more serious. The removal of these woods, now mature after more than twoscore years, will constitute a serious public relations problem with the environmentalists.

Fortunately, there has been a dramatic change in relationships among archaeologists, historians, and management. Broad professional relationships were established, new technologies adopted, and methodologies developed and honed in applying an interdisciplinary approach to investigation and interpretation of the nation's battlefields and related cultural resources. Between 1983 and 1989, major breakthroughs in the survey of historic battlefields occurred in which archaeologists made use of increasingly sophisticated metal detectors and employment and oversight of workforces composed of eager volunteers, many of whom were experienced with metal detectors.

The first challenge undertaken and mastered by battlefield archaeologists was at the Little Bighorn in 1984–85. An August 1983 grass fire that burned off sagebrush and deep-rooted prairie grasses provided opportunities to develop and implement a research design that has, with refinements, become a model for an interdisciplinary and cost-effective archaeological survey of battlefields and has enriched our knowledge and enhanced our interpretation of the battle. A vivid memory of the 1986 annual meeting of the Western History Association in Billings, Montana, was NPS archaeologist Douglas D. Scott's use of facial bones and forensic anthropology to reconstruct in his slide presentation the face of Mitch Boyer, Custer's mixed-race scout.

On October 13, 1980, President Jimmy Carter signed into law legislation expanding the boundary of Manassas National Battlefield Park to include the 312-acre Brawner Tract. A failure to agree on price with the owners stalled acquisition of the property until 1984. That year, relic collectors informed the NPS that friction primers used to fire cannon had been found in the position occupied by Col. Stephen D. Lee's artillery battalion on August 30, 1862, as well as an unmarked battlefield grave. This information galvanized NPS management into action, and a declaration of taking filed in October led to acquisition of the tract eight months later. Subsequent research by the NPS confirmed the location of four of Lee's cannon pinpointed through the recovery of the friction primers.

The Kansas Historical Society, taking measures to preserve and interpret the Mine Creek battlefield, called on staff archaeologist William Lees to survey the site. Lees employed metal detectors and volunteers to implement a research design similar to that employed by Scott and Richard A. Fox, Jr., at Little Bighorn. Once again the value of this approach was demonstrated while the written record was enhanced; Lees, by "peeling the land," located the ford where Fort Scott Road crossed Mine Creek, a center of battle actions, at a site different than that assumed by historians.

My years as the National Park Service's chief historian (1981–94) gave me the opportunity to work closely with NPS archaeologists Stephen R. Potter and Doug Scott and their colleagues within and outside the service. They were exciting years, as these young professionals employed technology and developed partnerships with relic collectors, historians, and forensic anthropologists to advance historical archaeology as pioneered by J. C. "Pinky" Harrington and John L. Cotter from individual sites onto the battlefield. Because of my appreciation and interest, I was enthused to be involved with and become a participant in the American Civil War session at the 24th Annual Meeting of the Society for Historical Archaeology in Richmond, Virginia, in January 1991. There I heard papers read by archaeologists who had interacted with NPS colleagues or worked on sites and battlefields that had piqued my curiosity.

Eight years later I was honored and excited when Clarence R. Geier and Stephen R. Potter asked me to read and prepare an introduction to *Archaeological Perspectives on the American Civil War*. The book they edited includes 18 essays. Two of the first five chapters focus on projects with which I am familiar, from close association with Stephen Potter and the Manassas and Antietam parks. The first centers on the epic firefight near the Brawner house between the Iron Brigade's 19th Indiana and the 4th Virginia of the Stonewall Brigade. Potter and his coauthors, using metal detectors to recover and identify a pattern of militaria, pinpoint the

Indianans' first firing line. The best that the documentary record could provide was the approximate position. Neither do they ignore the interpretive value of the remains found in a trash pit to enhance the written record.

"An Irishman Dies at Antietam. An Archaeology of the Individual" by Potter and Douglas W. Owsley is equal to a Sherlock Holmes mystery. It begins near Antietam's Bloody Lane with the discovery and reporting of a gravesite by Cleveland-area relic collectors. An archaeological investigation ensues with cooperation and input by a diverse constituency—the landowner, federal, state, and county officials, professionals, the Catholic Church, and the reenactor community. Partial remains of four soldiers of the Irish Brigade's 63rd New York Regiment, Catholic miraculous medals, New York buttons, and musket and Minié balls have been recovered. Analysis of these objects, together with forensic and documentary evidence, suggests the identity of one of the soldiers. The final scene in the drama closed on September 17, 1989, 127 years after the four died, when their partial remains were reinterred in Antietam National Cemetery.

The second and fifth essays address subjects commanding special interest. The discovery and archaeological survey of the long-lost Confederate submarine *H. L. Hunley,* appropriately identified as a Confederate icon, is Steven D. Smith's topic. Because of my association with the rediscovery, salvage, restoration, and display of the Union ironclad *Cairo* at Vicksburg National Military Park, I found the Smith essay especially relevant. The eager preservation community, particularly the South Carolina Hunley Commission, is urged to read Smith's essay to avoid pitfalls that plagued efforts to raise *Cairo, Jackson, Neuse, Chattahoochee,* and others. As I cautioned in introducing my talks on *Cairo,* "this is the story of how *not* to, not how to raise a Civil War vessel."

Chapter 5, "The Battle of Cool Spring, July 16–20, 1864," represents the ideal in the multidiscipline approach to battlefield archaeology and interpretation. Archaeologist Clarence R. Geier and historian Joseph W. A. Whitehorne collaborate to enhance our knowledge of the battle and its context. They augment the data compiled by Peter J. Meaney, Order of St. Benedict, in his monograph and the artifacts collected by Brother James on the grounds of the Holy Cross Abbey. During the last decade, I have led a number of tours of the Cool Spring battlefield and can vouch for the significance of the coauthors' efforts and the value of their maps.

Robert J. Fryman's monograph "Fortifying the Landscape. An Archaeological Study of Military Engineering and the Atlanta Campaign" is of significance to a broad audience—archaeologists, preservationists, historians, and Civil War buffs. As part of the visual environment, his analysis of fortifications and their "placement, construction, occupation, and armament . . . provides new insights into the cultural factors, such as perceptions of military engineering and tactics, by which these features were integrated into their surroundings."

The next four essays address the camp life of the soldier. Chapter 6 by W. Stephen McBride, Susan C. Andrews, and Sean P. Coughlin takes the reader to Camp Nelson, a Union camp of instruction and depot on the edge of Kentucky's Bluegrass Country. The Camp Nelson site possesses considerable significance because of the large number of U.S. Colored Troops mustered in, organized, and trained there. The coauthors' investigation and report involve archival and archaeological work on the Owens House/Post Office Complex. Their interdisciplinary approach provides a model in assessing diverse social status and rank implications derived from detailed study of artifacts found at the sites.

The studies on Fort C. F. Smith and the Winchester military hospital site open new ground. Information presented by Joseph Balicki on the fort and its associated garrison enriches interpretation of Arlington's newest park, within walking distance of the Rosslyn stop on the Washington, D.C., metrorail subway system. The questions raised and addressed by the multidisciplinary trio—Joseph Whitehorne, Clarence R. Geier, and Warren Hofstra—regarding the hospital complex enlighten and inform about a military activity and its interface with the local community that is novel and welcomed.

My association with Andersonville dates to the studies that led to its 1971 establishment as a national historic site. The project undertaken and described by Guy and Marie Prentice to ensure an accurate on-site reconstruction of the inner stockade's northeast corner and north gates is must reading. By peeling the land, the archaeologists ascertained what the documents did not tell that the logs used to enlarge the stockade as an emergency measure in late June 1864 were not squared as were the logs in the stockade built in the winter of 1863–64.

Chapters 10, 11, and 14 relate to the impact of battle and military occupations on civilians. Like the Winchester hospital essay, they provide a dimension to the Civil War story that, unfortunately, because of the reading public's interest, is too often placed on the back burner. Elise Manning-Sterling's contribution addresses the impact of the Antietam holocaust on a rural environment and the Alfred Poffenberger and Samuel Mumma families; Paul Shackel does the same by using archaeological evidence from digs at two Harpers Ferry sites to present "the other history" as experienced by the townspeople; and Erika Martin Seibert and Mia T. Parsons meld the talents of the historian, ethnographer, and archaeologist to interpret the free African American—"Gentleman Jim" Robinson and his family. The Robinsons resided on their Henry Hill tract from before the Battle of Manassas until its acquisition as part of Manassas Battlefield Park in 1937. The Robinson story, as reconstructed by the authors, has particular significance to me because in the early 1980s I was elated to tour the battlefield with "Gentleman Jim's" grandson and listen to his reminiscences.

Chapters 12 and 13 also highlight African Americans. Kenneth E. Koons, in the former, examines the place of the slave and the free African American in the Shenandoah Valley in the years immediately preceding emancipation and in the ensuing 15 years. The study, based on documentary sources, provides valuable insights into the place of African Americans and their significance to the economy and social structure of the breadbasket of Virginia. In Chapter 13, Laura Galke assesses evidence collected in recent archaeological projects at Manassas National Battlefield Park's Portici, Nash, and Brownsville sites. This information reveals that Virginia Piedmont slaves possessed and shared a subculture relating to their African heritage which has been found at other regional sites.

The final four essays demonstrate how the new approaches to battlefield archaeology, beginning in the early 1980s at Custer Battlefield National Monument and refined and enhanced during the next 15 years, have contributed to the identity of troops' positions and movements, to technology, and to enriching interpretation of sites. John Cornelison's focus in Chapter 15 is on information gleaned from the metal detector survey of the planned Highway 27 corridor bordering the western edge of Chickamauga and Chattanooga National Military Park. An analysis of the artifact patterns provided significant data pertaining to the tactical condition and behavioral pattern of Union troops as they withdrew from the battlefield, reinforcing the methods and set of techniques developed by Scott and Fox at Little Bighorn.

Chapters 17 and 18 flow from Chapter 16, coauthored by Bruce B. Sterling and Bernard W. Slaughter. They describe the systematic detector surveys undertaken in four areas of the Antietam battlefield—West Woods, North Woods, East Woods, and Piper Orchard—where significant combat ebbed and flowed. The project demonstrated that important archaeological artifacts can still be pinpointed in ground that had been disturbed and extensively collected from. Chapters 17 and 18 take the data found in the preceding essay and present analyses of the projectiles, both small arms and cannon, recovered from the four sites. Bruce Sterling addresses the former and Jeffrey Harbison the latter. The authors employ similar formats. Their discussions of weaponry, projectiles, and the technological revolution are succinct and informative, setting the stage for their effect on the battle's tactics. Documentary research, at which the authors are adept, yields information on unit armament too often overlooked by historians. Recovery of "a significant assemblage of quantifiable military artifacts," it is noted, provides the archaeologist and historian an "opportunity to examine a moment in time relevant" to the belligerents, arms, and ammunition.

Archaeological Perspectives on the American Civil War is must reading for professionals, collectors, and all people interested in battlefield archaeology, the material culture of the Civil War era, and the preservation of associated sites. Because of the popularity of Civil War literature and archaeology, this well-illustrated and well-written publication will appeal to the general public, as well as to the professional community.

Edwin C. Bearss
Historian Emeritus
National Park Service

"To Peel This Land"

Clarence R. Geier and Stephen R. Potter

As anyone who has become personally convinced of something of importance knows, the effort to convince others of that importance is often biased, subjective, and emotional. With respect to the American Civil War, the authors plead guilty on all counts. This text's editors and researchers share three core beliefs that motivated its compilation. First, much of the existing scholarly work and historic data pertinent to the Civil War needs to be reexamined from a more impartial, multidisciplinary, and anthropological-social historical perspective. Second, the historical status and place of the War between the States within the continuum of the 19th- and 20th-century history of our nation needs to be reassessed based on the results of that reexamination. And, third, the multidisciplinary field of historical archaeology must assume a leadership role in developing new data, methods, and theoretical premises useful in generating a historically accurate and complete evaluation of Civil War era events.

Historical archaeology is a relatively new discipline that is still in the throes of defining itself. It is a multidiscipline-based field that is principally a product of the increasingly shared interests of historians, anthropologists, and archaeologists as they seek to understand the human past. In this framework, historians provide a theoretical and methodological base built on the interpretation of written record, documents, and oral history. Archaeologists, in turn, add a theoretical and methodological expertise centered on the ability to identify and interpret the material byproducts of human behavior: artifacts, the spatial patterning of artifacts in archaeological sites, and the patterns of archaeological sites across landscapes. By joining these established areas of inquiry, researchers are able to broaden the available database to interpret and give voice to past human events as well as compensate for the limitations and gaps that are inherent in the historical and archaeological records.

Beyond the logical advantages of sharing methodological approaches, growing interest in social history unites many historians and anthropologically trained archaeologists in efforts to explain and understand factors that shaped particular events. Rather than being satisfied with simply generating sequences of events and providing descriptions of them, many historical archaeologists are interested in expanding their goals to an understanding of the environmental, social, political, ideological, economic, and human/cultural factors that caused the events to take place.

Like many new fields, historical archaeology is seeking to establish its identity and place within the subject matter and research interests that are part of the traditional areas of study of its parent disciplines. Similarly, as researchers come to understand the character and strengths of the new multidisciplinary field, they are developing new areas of inquiry and questioning. In 1991, the first full-day session dedicated to the application of historical archaeology to the study of the American Civil War was held at the Society for Historical Archaeology meetings in Richmond, Virginia. This, and other sessions held at those meetings, illustrated the growing interest and importance of historical archaeology in, and to the study of, the Civil War, and to the study of warfare in shaping our nation's history. Just as Richmond seemed to be an appropriate place to encourage the process of scholarly reawakening within our profession, the Civil War heritage of Atlanta made it an appropriate place to nurture that movement. As a result, in January 1998, at the Conference on Underwater and Historical Archaeology of the Society for Historical Archaeology meetings held in that city, a second full-day session dealing with the American Civil War was organized, the participants in which are also contributors to this text. At those meetings, the increased interest and activity in the study of the various military and cultural aspects of the war were indicated in numerous presentations made in other sessions as well.

As we assessed the work of our colleagues and contributors for the Atlanta meetings, and as we reflected on our own experiences in applying historical and archaeological method and theory to the examination and interpretation of Civil War sites and issues, we identified five areas of concern that we believe need to be addressed by historical archaeology as it defines its role relative to the historically significant events of the mid-19th century.

1. At a time when popular interest in the Civil War continues to grow, the priority given to this period of history by professional researchers in historical archaeology varies but is for the most part uninformed and tangential. For many of our colleagues, including some working in parts of the country where Civil War events were pivotal to local history, the sites and culture history of the period between 1861 and 1865 are often dealt with, of necessity, in the process of considering topics perceived to be of greater professional merit and historical significance. While many academic research institutions willingly take money to excavate Civil War sites, it is only recently that *some* have begun to identify the material and culture history of this period as legitimate and desirable areas of research and training for their students. In effect, the scholarly image and prestige assigned by many historical archaeologists to this time in the history of our nation is low and must be elevated.

It would be easy to justify a debate on the need to change the role and perception of historical archaeology in Civil War studies by enumerating the horror stories of the loss of significant domestic, industrial, and military sites to looting and the process of community development and growth. Similarly, the loss and dispersal of invaluable historic records, diaries, and letters as they are auctioned off to an insatiable collector's market could be used to rally action. However, most professional historical archaeologists could identify similar threats to the database of their particular areas of interest. The point is, however, that while the rapid and extensive development and growth of many of the key areas of Civil War history across the United States generates a real urgency to the increasing role of historical archaeology, meaningful change in the scholarly prestige of the period within our discipline will occur only through an informed awareness of the critical importance of this time of national trauma, both within the trajectory of American history and to those events of the modern era.

2. The place of the American Civil War relative to modern history is clear, though often given only lip service. Without question, there was no more violent time in the American experiment, yet having said that, the violence was neither contrived nor accidental. Rather, it was the unfortunate culmination of a process of enhanced conflict between the champions of established economic, political, and social ideologies, and those who perceived a new cultural order. While cloaked in violence and social disruption, the Civil War must be recognized as a time of critical transition that marked the end of one political and social reality and the birth of a process of cultural revitalization crossing the spectrum of American technology, economy, social order, and political authority that continues to this day. A sample of some of the significant issues includes the following:

- the end of slavery and the implications of that fact to an economy that was still labor intensive, as well as to a minority population whose status as "emancipated" presented it with new and additional ambiguities and challenges regarding the definition of its societal place;
- a military victory that clearly established the authority of a strong central government over the autonomy and independence of individual states;
- the onset of a period of reconstruction and political renewal in which the one-time Confederate states began the process of rebuilding and reestablishing their place within the new cultural reality of the United States;
- the emergence of a political and government structure that clearly favored the legislative and market agenda of an increasingly industrialized North with respect to the postwar domestic and international economy;
- the rampant growth of an industrialized economy and its demands

for social reform and immigrant labor in a society that had just undergone a tremendous bloodletting of its manpower;

- the dynamic nature of a reunified Union and the dream of a nation that saw its boundaries stretching from ocean to ocean; and
- the contrivance of "a splendid little war"—the Spanish-American—that furthered the country's reunification by focusing national attention on a foreign enemy while simultaneously catapulting the Reunited States of America onto the world stage as an international player.

Although varying in their character and impact locally and regionally, these and other areas of renewal, societal experimentation, and expansion are the result of decisions made, imposed, or made possible as outcomes of the Civil War.

3. We would join those who argue that the period of 1861 to 1865 and its events must undergo scrutiny from other than a traditional perspective of great men and battlefields. As David Madden, director of the U.S. Civil War Center, has written, "We Americans have missed the war by focusing too much and too long on battles and leaders. That focus distracts us from the deeper purpose: to trace back to Reconstruction, to the War itself, and to the Antebellum era the origins of the forces at work in our culture today" (Madden 1995).

We would avoid studies that romanticize the time, place, and personalities, just as we would discourage research that focuses on the period as one of only violence and cruelty. We would avoid studies which seek to apologize for one side or the other, which inappropriately celebrate those who are simply victorious, or which attempt to provide simplistic explanations for complex realities. The respect for this time and the people who lived it can be obtained only by a comprehensive, informed, and sincere effort to understand the real social and historical context in which they existed and acted. It is time to move from the images of all Southerners as racist slave owners living in patrician estates and of all Northerners as idealistic humanists or greedy, carpetbagging industrialists. It is perhaps time to rejuvenate the study of an anthropology of war that can be used to provide a theoretical basis for the study of armed conflict between nation states. Rather than focusing on "great men," the focus should shift to include the men and women of both sides who fought and feared, died or survived, benefited or lost everything as they participated, often through no choice of their own, in an event which they did not necessarily understand or support. Rather than focusing on war as a purely military activity in which competing armies and navies are moved across a passive game board, historical archaeologists need to reassert the image of a complex and active cultural landscape of working farms, small towns and cities, industrial centers, and the roads, railroads, canals, and waterways that joined them together. It is onto and within this environment that the movement, conflict, and mere presence of armies and navies has to be evaluated and assessed. Further, while a particular battle may or may not have had an impact on shaping the final outcome of the war, we must recognize that the effect of that battle on the cultural landscape over which it was fought can have a very significant impact on historic dynamics at the local and regional levels.

4. Within this anthropology of war, we must come to see an army, navy, or other military construct as a semiautonomous unit of culture, having its own unique social structure and organization, internal support systems, and rules of social order. It is a society in its own right, whose survival and success is dependent on the ability of those who comprise it to act as individuals and as part of the larger whole. It is an organic, living thing that is capable of violent action and prolonged periods of rest. It can be killed, and it can be affected by the presence of disease. It must be fed, and the inability to supply the necessary nourishment and resources bears directly on its ability to function. The need for supply, in fact, can be as much a stimulus to action as political agendas, battle tactics, and campaign strategies. As with any social unit, each army is different, even though it may be functionally joined under a single leadership or government. They are not constant in their character but change continuously over time, affecting their ability to act.

As social and cultural units, the interaction between armies and civilian populations should be a serious focus of study. In August of 1863, Daniel Snyder, with the 11th Virginia Cavalry stationed at Culpeper Courthouse, Virginia, wrote: "Of all the countries I ever got into this is the hardest and the people the meanest. If it were not wrong, I almost wish the Yankees could stay in here with such a class. We were better treated in Pennsylvania (Gettysburg) than by these stuck up Tuckahoes. The fact is they hate to see a soldier come near their houses. Seen them sell a man a corncake size of the bottom of a tin cup for $1. Oh they are just the meanest people you ever heard tell of. They would let a sick soldier lay and die in ten steps of their door and never give him a mouthfull to eat or assist him in any way. What I experienced I know to be true" (Snyder 1861–65: August 1863).

In another letter, Marion Epperly, who was with the 54th Virginia Infantry at Atlanta on August 12, 1864, made the following observations: "They [the Union] keep shelling the town studdy/ They have all most runed the plase with shells: they have kild and wounded a great many women and Children/ I can tell you they [the women and children] see very hard times and are in a grate deel of dainger/ I think if I was in thear plases I would leave the plase: but ther is so many it is hard for them to get any plase to Go Too/ I cannot tell what they doo for provision here/ the [Confederate] soldier has taken every thing out of the Gardens that they could Get" (Marion Epperly 1861–65: August 12, 1864).

In both cases, the examples are of Confederate soldiers acting in defense of Confederate land, yet the relations that exist between the army's soldiers and the resident domestic community, rather than being cordial, are strained and to some degree self-serving. When extended to consider the presence of an enemy army, the needs and interaction of the two cultures are even more polarized and hostile. Certainly the parasitic actions of armies during the Civil War are evident. The impact of Sheridan's victorious army of 35,000 to 40,000 Union troops as it moved and encamped across the Shenandoah Valley in the fall and winter of 1864 is an example (Heatwole 1998). Taking what provender it needed, and then burning and destroying the rest as it moved toward anticipated winter camps along Cedar Creek in the lower valley, had a devastating impact on the domestic economy of that region. At the same time, however, the requirement of the citizens of the upper Shenandoah Valley to supply the provender or support for the 13,000- to 20,000-man Confederate Army of the valley and for Lee's forces in Richmond also placed a severe economic drain on local productivity. While often perceived as the "breadbasket of the Confederacy," the Shenandoah Valley also had its productive limits as well as a substantial civilian population to support. As the war progressed and lines of supply to the Confederate Army in the valley and central Virginia were cut, demands on local productivity became severe. Local newspapers dating to that period reveal that this strain often resulted in finger-pointing toward those citizens perceived as not carrying their share of the load. This was particularly the case against pacifist Mennonites in the middle and upper valley, some of whom were accused of deliberately reducing their productivity to favor the Union cause.

5. As illustrated in the following presentations, any move toward an enhanced role for historical archaeology in the redefinition of the American Civil War, or any period of hostility, will require new initiatives in scholarship and education as well as developments in areas of field techniques and methods of analysis. For most professional archaeologists and historians, including many who have been active in the area of military history, the culture of an army is a huge black box. Few are knowledgeable concerning issues of chain of command, organizational structure, battlefield tactics and strategy, military technology and its applications, or in the construction of defensive fortifications. Issues of supply and support personnel and staff, the composition of military trains, and the character and development of field hospitals and medicine are poorly understood by many historians and archaeologists. In effect, a key problem for most of us is that we are profoundly ignorant of the structural character of an army at rest or in action. As a result, when studying military events we are prone to oversimplification of the circumstances and factors that are shaping or driving them.

In addition, and as will be illustrated subsequently, it is increasingly evident that while conventional archaeological methodologies may be appropriate to assess many domestic and industrial sites, new techniques of field investigation will be required to identify and assess military sites such as battlefields and encampments, or those present underwater. The character and sheer magnitude of many such sites have been repeatedly shown to respond poorly to the traditional strategies of archaeological site identification and assessment. For example, it is dangerous to limit field testing to the excavation of fixed-interval shovel test pits if the goal of the fieldwork is to identify tactical military positions on a battlefield. As will be illustrated, such positions are consistently missed by these established, standardized techniques but can often be identified when meaningful historic research is combined with field strategies implementing systematic metal detector surveys and subsequent archaeological sampling. Similarly, the identification of military encampments, particularly those that were not constructed as winter quarters, requires primary historical research coupled with a mixed field strategy combining thorough visual reconnaissance of the terrain surface with systematic and comprehensive metal detector surveys and archaeological testing.

Clearly, field researchers must develop an appropriate understanding of the character of the military phenomenon that they are seeking to identify and the form it might reasonably be expected to take as an archaeological feature within the complex terrain which comprises many battlefields and military activity areas. By understanding the purpose and associated activities of military unit formations on a battlefield, archaeologists can begin to recognize their distinctive signatures. For example, a battle line marks the place of deployment of a military unit from a marching column to a battle formation. In contrast, a firing line marks the place where a military unit has "gone to ground," for minutes or sometimes for hours, in order to fire upon the enemy. Translating these behaviors into their archaeological correlates, a preponderance of dropped or unfired bullets in a linear pattern might characterize the formation of a line of battle where soldiers loaded their weapons prior to advancing onto the battlefield. A firing line, however, might be identified by a linear pattern of dropped bullets *and* a wider range and higher frequency of militaria, such as buttons, finials, and roller buckles, that became detached from accoutrements and uniforms during the frenzied action of engagement.

Our collective, professional ignorance of Civil War military hardware, such as bullets and buttons, is highlighted by the fact that those who have written the bibles on the subject are not academically trained historical archaeologists. Rather, they are men and women who collect and study documents, images, and material culture of the Civil War era, passionately pursuing their interest "on the side" as their avocation. We have much to learn from these authors if we are to identify and correctly interpret the war's imprint upon the land and its present occupants. Further, it will be through alliances with such individuals that we will be able to ensure the protection and preservation of period cultural resources.

Because of the large size of many Civil War sites, it is also critical that we continue to experiment with and refine the use of geophysical prospecting, remote sensing, GPS/GIS, computer visualization, and other new technologies to aid in locating features of interest both on the land and beneath the water. While this introduction references land sites for the most part, the naval history of the era, as documented by numerous sites along the Mississippi River and in the bays and coastal waters of our nation, is every bit as important to understanding the historical events and dynamics of that time. As we look to the western theater of the war, the fortification of major river ports, such as St. Louis, Cairo, Memphis, Vicksburg, and New Orleans, and the major engagements fought at certain of them draw attention to significant military and domestic features, many of which are currently underwater. Efforts to control and blockade the James River in Virginia, as well as coastal ports such as Savannah, Charleston, and Pensacola, further attest to the significance of naval actions and the importance of underwater cultural resources. Add to these the near mythical events associated with the Confederate submersible *H. L. Hunley*, the contest between the ironclads *Monitor* and C.S.S. *Virginia* (Merrimack) at Hampton Roads, the sinking of the *Alabama* by the U.S.S. *Kearsarge* off the coast of France, and the fascinating stories associated with the coast and blockade runners in their efforts to supply the South, and the importance of underwater archaeology to Civil War history is fixed. Yet the environment in which these remains lie provides amazingly complex, varied, and often dangerous archaeological contexts which historical archaeologists must come to understand and learn to deal with. Underwater sites and the varied conditions that influence them pose a complex array of methodological and interpretive demands in which the development and refinement of remote sensing technologies, such as sidescan sonar and proton magnetometers, are of increasing importance to strategies of site identification and evaluation. In addition, the challenges posed to the processes of archaeological recovery, artifact preservation, and curation continually call for new solutions.

In yet another area, rapid advances in computer technology offer new possibilities for the analysis of Civil War photographs and sketches. The results of these analyses have profound implications for efforts of site identification and for the historical, archaeological, and architectural study and public interpretation of battlefields as cultural landscapes.

The Civil War is often called the first "modern," unlimited, or total war because of the involvement of and effect upon large segments of the civilian population. Perhaps historical archaeologists can learn something from one of the earliest practitioners of the "modern" art of total war, Gen. Philip Sheridan, whose Union Army torched the Shenandoah Valley of Virginia after defeating the Confederates under Gen. Jubal Early. "Previously the burning of supplies and outbuildings had been incidental to battles, but now the torch was applied deliberately and intentionally," wrote a Pennsylvania cavalryman (quoted in Catton 1965:322). A chaplain in Sheridan's 1st Rhode Island Cavalry described the purpose of "modern" warfare more metaphorically: "The time had fully come to peel this land and put an end to the long strife for its possession" (Catton 1965:321). If historical archaeologists are going to study modern or total wars, then they, too, must look beyond the battlefields to other aspects of the total cultural context of war. Within the evolving field of historical archaeology lies a multidisciplinary strength that merges, minimally, the theoretical, methodological, and databases of history, anthropology, and archaeology into a holistic study of the historic emergence of our nation. The application of this developing power is clearly challenged by the demands of the American Civil War as a cultural node in the continuum of our history. It is up to the members of the profession to determine the extent to which it will respond.

In addressing the above noted concerns, the following presentations are organized with respect to three areas of research: Part I, Tactics and the Conduct of Battle; Part II, The Home Front and Military Life; and Part III, New Methods and Techniques. Each section has a brief theoretical introduction followed by a series of essays that serve to illustrate current directions and opportunities for Civil War research within the discipline of historical archaeology.

Acknowledgments

The authors wish to gratefully thank Douglas Scott and Lawrence Babits for their support in this undertaking. The willingness of Babits to work with the authors in crafting the text has contributed significantly to its content and presentation. We also wish to thank Ginger Usry, Sunny Sanders, and Brenda Sutherland, who worked with the authors in compiling and editing the draft manuscripts. To Joe Balicki and Susannah L. Dean for their patience and help in crafting the bibliography we extend our most profound thanks. In addition, the support of the Department of Sociology and Anthropology and the Center for Instructional Technology at James Madison University was invaluable to meeting project goals. Thanks David, Craig, Linda, and Sharon.

1

Tactics and the Conduct of Battle

Four of the five chapters in this section examine the application of historical archaeology to the study of what might be considered traditional areas of military history and inquiry. The use of historic and archaeological data to reconstruct battlefield contexts, the cultural landscapes over which battles were fought, and an understanding of the natural settings that shaped the evolution of battles and battlefields are themes developed in chapters 1, 3, and 5. Chapter 2 enters the exciting world of underwater archaeology, considering its application in a recent controversial and historically significant find, the *H. L. Hunley*.

Chapter 4 deals with a military theme of a somewhat nontraditional sort. In this case, the effort is to use diverse databases in an effort to identify particular soldiers, members of the Irish Brigade, whose physical remains were recently discovered in shallow burials at Antietam Battlefield. Along with studies of material culture and historical records, analyses of the skeletal remains provide the information needed to propose identities.

Chapter 1 deals with the Battle of Brawner Farm, fought on August 28, 1862. Documents and archaeological remains are used to reveal the nature of the farm at the time of the battle and as modified after the Civil War. While reputed to have been heavily disturbed, the application of modern archaeological techniques identified artifact patterns that could be used to define troop positions during the engagement. In addition, artifacts attributed to post-battle events identified a Confederate encampment. Additional studies address the use of archaeological data gathered through systematic metal detecting to resolve controversial questions concerning the position of a key firing line held by Union forces.

In chapter 2, Steven Smith introduces the reader to the discovery of the Confederate submersible *H. L. Hunley*. Using this discovery as a vehicle, the author discusses the history of underwater innovation by the Confederate forces, ultimately presenting the events leading to the loss of the *Hunley*. While introducing the story of the *Hunley* and the events leading to its location, Smith also considers the political and legal controversies generated by its discovery.

In chapter 3, Robert Fryman reviews remnant structural remains and the historic record as it pertains to the construction of the defensive perimeter that surrounded Atlanta, Georgia, during the 1864 campaign. Analyses of the topographic placement of hastily built field fortifications are compared to the more carefully designed and executed fortifications around the city proper. The result is a new understanding or perception of certain cultural factors that influenced and guided their construction.

Chapter 5 is the story of a battle and the mobilization of armies leading to its resolution. Following Confederate Gen. Jubal Early's very successful march on Washington D.C., in July of 1864, General Grant created an army and assigned to its leader, Gen. Horatio G. Wright, the responsibility of removing the threat from northern Virginia. The progression of events that followed culminated in the Battle of Cool Spring, a day-long engagement fought on the banks of the Shenandoah River. Despite more than 800 casualties, both sides treated this battle as a relatively minor skirmish. Recent historical and archaeological studies combine to allow an understanding of the conduct of the engagement, the cultural environment in which it took place, and the manner in which local topography shaped its flow and the overall posturing of the two armies. In addition, important new information has been gathered concerning the composition and makeup of the Union Army that confronted Early's Confederates.

"No Maneuvering and Very Little Tactics"

Archaeology and the Battle of Brawner Farm

Stephen R. Potter, Robert C. Sonderman, Marian C. Creveling, and Susannah L. Dean

Late in the afternoon of August 28, 1862, on the Brawner farm near the First Manassas Battlefield, one of the fiercest firefights of the Civil War erupted between the Confederacy's Stonewall Brigade and the Union's Black Hat Brigade, later known as the Iron Brigade. The opposing infantry lines, only 70 to 80 yards apart, blasted away at one another for 90 minutes. One of the focal points of this bloody combat was a house known as Bachelor's Hall, rented by John Brawner.

After acquiring the Brawner farm in May 1985, the National Park Service needed to determine if portions of the existing house dated to the time of the battle. To do so, historical, archaeological, and architectural research was undertaken in 1987 through 1989. The discovery of *in situ* battle-related artifacts in the yard surrounding the house prompted additional archaeological investigations in 1994 to locate evidence of the firing lines.

The Brawner Farmhouse

History

About dawn on August 28, 1862, a squadron of Confederate cavalry was sent beyond the infantry pickets to give advance warning of the approach of Union Maj. Gen. John Pope's Army of Virginia. Shortly after daylight, cavalry videttes captured a Federal courier carrying plans of an attack on Manassas Junction. After forwarding the captured order to Confederate Maj. Gen. Thomas J. Jackson, Col. Bradley T. Johnson, with a small brigade guarding Jackson's left flank, carefully studied the terrain around the little crossroads village of Groveton. Johnson decided that the farm of Mr. John C. Brawner, located on a prominent ridge, was the key to his defense (fig. 1.1). The 319.5-acre farm consisted of a house, known as Bachelor's

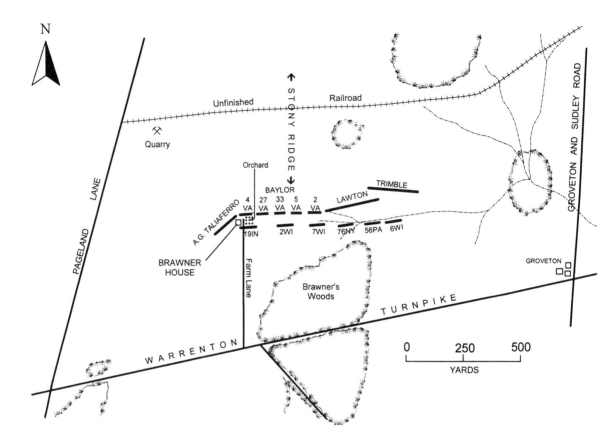

1.1. Map of the Battle of Brawner Farm (courtesy of the National Park Service, National Capital Region).

Hall, some outbuildings, and an orchard. Brawner rented the farm from the owner, Mrs. Augusta Douglass, for an annual fee of $150 plus two-thirds of the harvest (Gaff 1985:43–46; Parker 1989:2).

Writing about the events of that morning nine years later, Brawner (1871) recalled that "some officers came up and asked me why I did not leave as all the rest of the people had left. I told them I was a cripple and could not leave." Handicapped or not, the 64-year-old Brawner, his wife, and three daughters fled northward to a neighbor's home when Brawner (1871) matter-of-factly noted that the "battle commenced. House was shelled and balls passing through the house."

The Battle of Brawner Farm began late in the day when the Stonewall Brigade and five others from Jackson's left wing of the Army of Northern Virginia engaged Brig. Gen. John Gibbon's Black Hat Brigade and two additional regiments from Brig. Gen. Abner Doubleday's Brigade. The height of the battle was a 90-minute firefight between opposing infantry lines only 70 to 80 yards apart. When darkness finally put an end to the slaughter, Confederate casualties exceeded 1,250 men killed, wounded, and missing, while Union losses totaled 1,025. This action was a prelude to even greater events on August 29 and 30, when the Battle of Second Manassas raged to the east and south of Bachelor's Hall (Gaff 1985; Hennessy 1993:168–93).

The day after Second Manassas, John Brawner returned to survey the damage to his farm. The house, though riddled by bullets, was still standing and apparently habitable, but the vegetable garden was destroyed and the orchard damaged. Other losses suffered by the Brawners, for which they attempted to receive restitution from the U.S. government in 1871, included the destruction of all household and kitchen furniture, farm tools, food supplies, and livestock. For a family that led a hardscrabble existence before the war, life suddenly became even harder. Being poor, the Brawners had no choice but to sit out the war at Bachelor's Hall (Brawner 1871).

In the deposition she filed with her father's war claim, Brawner's daughter, Mary, laconically described what it was like being caught between opposing armies: "Part of the time we were within the Confederate lines. When the southern [*sic*] army fell back we were within the Union lines. That was in 1863. The Union army was passing backwards and forwards all the time after the southern army left. We were not able to cultivate the farm after the first year [of the war]. We raised a small crop in 1862 . . . [and that] was lost at the time of the battle [of Second Manassas]" (Brawner 1871). Because the Brawner family lived at Bachelor's Hall during Second Manassas, the property was referred to as Brawner farm (Parker 1989:2).

Archaeology and Architecture

Archaeologically, the devastation to the Brawners's meager way of life and the intensity of the combat around their home was apparent when the National Park Service, National Capital Region, Regional Archeology Program, began to collect information for use by a planning team drafting a Development Concept Plan for the newly acquired property. A key element of the planning concerned the Brawner farmhouse. Did the remodeled 1904–5 structure contain the original antebellum house within its walls or was it a later house built after the battle? In cooperation with National Park Service historical architects and structural preservationists, and aided by volunteers, we proceeded to uncover the archaeological and architectural history of the Brawner farmhouse.

Excavation units placed along the west, north, and east sides of the extant structure revealed a fairly consistent stratigraphic pattern across the site (fig. 1.2). The first layer consisted of a mixture of modern domestic trash and topsoil. Beneath this was a thin stratum of Virginia bluestone gravel and hard-packed clay deposited after the Brawners returned to their home following the Battle of Second Manassas. The source for the crushed

Virginia bluestone was a quarry located about 500 yards from the Brawner house. This quarry was associated with the construction of the unfinished Independent Line of the Manassas Gap Railroad and was the place "where rock for ballast probably was quarried, crushed, and transported to the site of the roadbed" (Neville et al. 1995:60, 78). Underlying this gravel was the antebellum grade upon which the Battle of Brawner Farm was fought—a hard-packed, bare-earth, swept yard that was swept because it was probably maintained as an outdoor workspace (Perry Wheelock, personal communication, August 23, 1999). Architectural features associated with this stratum included a set-stone walk, rubble from an outbuilding probably destroyed during the fighting, and, most important, the west, north, and east foundation walls of Brawner's antebellum house, Bachelor's Hall (Parker 1989:3–5).

This stone foundation, measuring 24 feet north-south by 31 feet east-west, was all that remained of Bachelor's Hall. The cut sandstone and fieldstone footers rested on the antebellum grade. Along the north foundation wall were two stone piers. The interior portions of the piers probably served as supports for floor joists, while the exteriors may have supported porch columns. Two chimney footings were found on the east side of the house and one on the west. A second chimney footing on the west side had been destroyed by extensive tree root activity and the removal of the stones for later rebuilding (Parker 1989:5).

These antebellum architectural features are indicative of a two-story house with four chimneys, two on each end, and a four-room floor plan. The size and symmetry of the circa 1820 structure are in keeping with the features and proportions of an early 19th-century Georgian-style house and are definitely not the remains of a log house, as previously thought (Gaff 1985:44; Moore 1910:115). They also reflect the type of house that would be referred to as a "hall" (Newlin 1987; Parker 1989:5).

The archaeological record clearly indicates that Bachelor's Hall was consolidated after the Battle of Second Manassas. The revised floor plan, approximately one-third smaller than the antebellum house, utilized the original south foundation wall and a portion of the east wall. Consolidation and reconstruction is also reflected in the 1868 Prince William County Land Tax Records. In 1857, the year John Brawner began renting Bachelor's Hall, the assessed value of the property was about $3,800. Due to the Civil War, there is a gap in the tax records for the property until 1866, when the assessed value was $639 less than its prewar value. By 1868, the assessed value had returned to its prewar level, which suggests that Augusta Douglass probably rebuilt Brawner's home around 1867–68 (Parker 1989:2).

The historical and archaeological research was supported by an architectural fabric investigation of the remodeled 1904–5, two-and-one-half-story, L-shaped Brawner farmhouse, conducted by the Williamsport Pres-

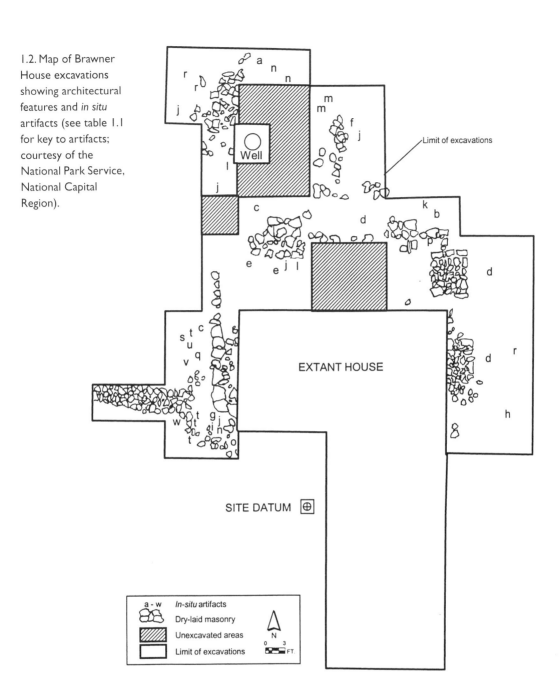

1.2. Map of Brawner House excavations showing architectural features and *in situ* artifacts (see table 1.1 for key to artifacts; courtesy of the National Park Service, National Capital Region).

Within the map:
- Well
- Limit of excavations
- EXTANT HOUSE
- SITE DATUM

Legend:
- a – w — *In-situ* artifacts
- Dry-laid masonry
- Unexcavated areas
- Limit of excavations
- N
- 0   3 FT.

ervation Training Center in 1987. Within the shorter leg of the L, running on an east-west axis, are the remnants of the circa 1868 house. It was hastily constructed using early-19th-century building techniques. From the second-floor plate down, the current structure is a braced timber frame of hand-hewn sill plates and corner posts with vertically sawn studs, joists, and knee braces, mortised-and-tenoned at the joints. Vertically sawn framing lumber was available between circa 1830–70, before the general use of circular sawn material in the area. Machine-cut nails of a type in general use after 1835 are found throughout the structural frame. Traces of mud and straw insulation remain in the spaces between studs. Significantly, neither bullet holes nor any fired or impacted Civil War–period bullets were discovered in the building's fabric (Newlin 1987).

Other physical evidence suggests the possibility that some materials were used from the antebellum house or from an off-site structure. The west exterior wall was built without knee braces at the corner posts. A through mortise is cut into the south exterior wall, second-floor plate, with no other framing member in evidence. On the east and west exterior walls, the sill plates are joined at midspan with a half-lap joint, suggesting reuse of materials (Newlin 1987).

Collectively, the architectural fabric indicates that the first floor of the east-west leg of the current structure was part of a post-battle, one-and-one-half-story, timber-framed house, with a chimney at either end. The exterior was sided and trimmed with cornice and soffit. Inside, the walls of the two first-floor rooms were plastered and the first-floor ceiling joists and the bottom of the second-floor flooring were exposed and whitewashed (Newlin 1987). It was in this cramped structure that the Brawners lived during the difficult years following the War between the States.

The Battle and the 19th Indiana

History

It is useful to begin this section by quoting an insightful comment about combat history by historian Carol Reardon (1997:2): "[one must start] with an acknowledgment that traditional research materials for battle studies should be accepted less as objective truth and more, as historian David Thelen suggests, as memories that were 'authentic for the person at the moment of construction.'" Reardon (1997:15) further observed that "historians have been slow to appreciate what . . . [the Civil War] . . . veterans understood"—each combatant's field of vision was limited in some way, whether the person was a private in the ranks or a field officer on horseback. No Civil War combat soldier, regardless of rank, knew all that was going on around him, much less 100 feet down the firing line, or in the next regiment or brigade. And, in the end, what they wrote was an account of the battle from their perspective.

It is the same with the histories and memories of the battle at Brawner farm. While most accounts of the engagement are in general agreement, they are occasionally at variance regarding specifics. For this reason, the brief history that follows is based on the battle's reconstruction as presented in the works of the two specialists on the subject, historians Alan Gaff (1985) and John Hennessy (1985, 1993), supplemented by primary sources when necessary. It is focused on those events that took place around the Brawner farmhouse and vicinity, or that involved the 19th Indiana Infantry Regiment.

The artillery shells and musket balls that fell around or passed through John Brawner's home, shortly after 10:00 A.M. on August 28, came from artillery and small arms skirmishing between Colonel Johnson's small command of Confederates and lead elements of Brig. Gen. John F. Reynolds's division. Johnson started the ruckus by having two 3-inch rifled guns open fire on the Union column as it trudged along, four abreast, heading east on the Warrenton Turnpike. The two guns, supported by the 21st Virginia Infantry, were posted on the ridge east of Brawner's house, with the 42nd Virginia deployed in and beyond Brawner's woods as skirmishers (U.S. War Department 1880–1905:12(2):665).

Capt. Dunbar Ransom's battery of 12-pounder, smoothbore Napoleons was called in to drive off the Confederates, but their range was not long enough to reach them. Frustrated, Reynolds ordered Capt. James H. Cooper's battery of 10-pounder rifled Parrott guns into action. They quickly found the range of the Rebel cannon and, along with six companies of infantry from Brig. Gen. George Meade's Pennsylvania Brigade, forced Johnson to pull back to the village of Groveton (Gaff 1985:48–49). In spite of this, Johnson succeeded in halting a column of 15,000 Yankees for more than an hour. Believing that Johnson's small force was merely fighting a delaying action to protect a Confederate wagon train, Reynolds withdrew his skirmishers—Companies B, D, and K of the 1st Pennsylvania Rifles (42nd Pennsylvania Volunteer Infantry)—and turned his division south on Pageland Lane toward Manassas Junction. It was about 1:00 P.M. (Hennessy 1993:149–50).

For a while, things remained relatively quiet on Brawner's farm until sometime after 5:00 P.M. As Brig. Gen. Rufus King's Division began passing in front of Brawner's fields, heading east on the turnpike, the commander of his lead brigade, Brig. Gen. John Hatch, prudently ordered the 14th Brooklyn Militia (84th New York Regiment) to fan out as skirmishers in the fields north of the turnpike. This movement took them across the front fields of Brawner's farm and perhaps as far north as the house. They discovered no Rebels in force, even though a mile to their north Jackson's 24,000 men were concealed in the woods near the earthen roadbed of the unfinished railroad (Hennessy 1993:164–67).

Continuing east on the turnpike toward Centreville, the head of Hatch's Brigade had passed Groveton when Jackson's artillery began firing on the Yankee columns, sending men scrambling for shelter. By 6:30 P.M., King's four brigades were under fire from three Confederate batteries posted on the high ground north of the turnpike (Gaff 1985:60–66). Union artillery went into battery to answer the Confederate guns while the brigades of Brigadier Generals Gibbon and Doubleday piled themselves along the sides of the turnpike. Needing more cover, Gibbon and Doubleday moved many of their troops into Brawner's woods (today's Gibbon's Woods) along the north side of the turnpike. Behind them, most of Brig. Gen. Marsena Patrick's Brigade followed suit and went into the woods south of the turnpike near Pageland Lane (Gaff 1985:60–66; Hennessy 1993:169–71).

Conferring with one another along the south side of Brawner's woods, Gibbon and Doubleday made the assumption that the Rebel batteries were horse artillery without infantry support, as the 14th Brooklyn had not run into any organized body of the enemy less than an hour before. Determined to drive off the Confederate artillery, Gibbon agreed to send in some of his men. He chose his only veteran regiment, the 430 Badgers of the 2nd Wisconsin Infantry (Hennessy 1993:172).

The 2nd Wisconsin Regiment, led by Col. Edgar O'Conner, followed a road (no longer extant) north through Brawner's woods. Emerging from the cover of the trees, skirmishers moved into the fields toward the Rebel battery near Brawner's house. Meanwhile, the main body of the regiment formed in line of battle and began its advance through the tall grass. Before the Yankee skirmishers could fire, Confederate skirmishers began peppering the 2nd Wisconsin, while the battery quickly limbered its guns and rode off. Suddenly, Rebel battle lines deployed a quarter mile to the north. With their flags in front, the five small regiments of the famous Stonewall Brigade, numbering about 800 men commanded by Col. William S. Baylor, advanced to engage the enemy (Hennessy 1993:173).

Expecting to drive off a Rebel battery, not to fight a brigade, the 2nd Wisconsin, nevertheless, stood its ground. When the Stonewall Brigade got within 150 yards, O'Conner ordered his men to fire. In spite of the effect of the 2nd Wisconsin's first volley, the Virginians returned the fire and moved forward to a rail fence (see fig. 1.1). Since neither side was willing to budge, they settled down to the grim business of dealing out death, with the firing lines only 70 to 80 yards apart (Hennessy 1993: 175–76).

To support the 2nd Wisconsin, Gibbon sent in the 423 officers and enlisted men of the 19th Indiana Regiment. Quickly, the Hoosiers moved to the aid of the Badgers engaged at the southern end of high ground known as Stony Ridge. Following Gibbon's directions, Col. "Long" Sol Meredith angled his men to the left of the 2nd Wisconsin and up the slope toward Brawner's house (Gaff 1985:72).

As the intensity of the musketry grew and daylight waned, both sides sent more troops into the fray. The rest of Gibbon's Brigade, the 6th and 7th Wisconsin, plus two of Doubleday's regiments, the 76th New York and the 56th Pennsylvania, went into action on the Union right flank. Opposing them were the Confederate brigades of Brig. Gens. Alexander Lawton and Isaac Trimble (see fig. 1.1; Hennessy 1993:177–81).

Over on the Union left flank, Meredith's 19th Indiana Regiment climbed over a rail fence, dressed their battle line, and advanced toward the crest of the hill. As they neared the rise, with their left flank resting on Brawner's house, the Hoosiers were stopped by a volley from the Stonewall Brigade's 4th Virginia Regiment, about 70 yards away (Gibbon 1978:54). In position behind a rail fence, with their right flank anchored around some of Brawner's outbuildings north of the house, the 4th Virginia held the Confederate's extreme right flank. To their left was another of the Stonewall Brigade's regiments, the 27th Virginia, also firing on the 19th Indiana (Gaff 1985:72; Hennessy 1993:175–76). To add to the 19th Indiana's woes, the Union line was being hit by two batteries behind the Stonewall Brigade—Lt. John Carpenter's Alleghany Artillery and Capt. William T. Poague's Rockbridge Artillery (Stuart 1947; Gaff 1985:189; U.S. War Department 1880–1905:12(2):643).

Sometime after 7:00 P.M., Stuart's Horse Artillery, under the command of Capt. John Pelham, approached the 19th Indiana's left flank. Seeing the Rebel artillery column heading their way, officers of the 19th Indiana pulled the two left companies out of line and deployed them as skirmishers. When the Confederates got within 50 yards, the Yankees fired. Unharmed by the volley, Pelham's men unlimbered their two 3-inch rifles a short distance away. Continued skirmish fire finally forced Pelham to retire to a less exposed position (U.S. War Department 1880–1905:12(2): 754; Dudley 1862; Gaff 1985:79).

While the 19th Indiana's flank companies took on Stuart's Horse Artillery, three Virginia regiments from Colonel Alexander Taliaferro's Brigade attempted to get between them and the exposed flank of the Hoosier's main line. To prevent this, Colonel Meredith ordered his men to fall back two rods (33 feet) to a rail fence. From this new position, the 19th Indiana repulsed Taliaferro's first attempt to gain the Brawner yard (see fig. 1.1). On their second try, the Virginians got into the yard as the 19th Indiana began a fighting withdrawal back to the edge of Brawner's woods. It was about 8:15 P.M. now and so dark that it was pointless to continue a battle in which neither side had gained a clear advantage (Gaff 1985:79–80; Hennessy 1993:185–86).

Sometime after 9:30 P.M., survivors of the 19th Indiana formed a party of about 100 men to return to the battlefield to collect their wounded comrades. It was a moonless night and exceedingly dark. William R. Moore (n.d.), veteran of the 19th Indiana, recalled that "when they had gotten nearly back to their former line of battle—the night was unusually a dark one, other than the shining stars, when there came a voice out of the darkness: 'Halt, who comes there?' Captain Williams answered and said: 'The ambulance corps.' 'Ambulance corps, hell,' and immediately we were fired upon by the [Confederate] pickets. Not caring to bring on another engagement that night we could do nothing else but return to our command."

The commander of King's 3rd Brigade, Brigadier General Patrick, recalled 16 years later that "it was in this ground, up to this house, and from about here [Douglass's house—this insertion is in the original testimony], during the night and until one o'clock perhaps—I could not say exactly—when we were engaged in caring for those that were wounded." Patrick had this information secondhand since he had gone to the head of the division's column to find King (U.S. Congress 1879:225–26).

The two regiments that Patrick said were aiding Gibbon's wounded men were the 21st and 23rd New York. A veteran of the 21st New York and the author of the regiment's history wrote, "and now comes a call for volunteers to help the wounded on our right. An hundred willing voices respond, and our little detachment hurries down the road" where they found wounded men "in plenty; and for a sad half hour are engaged in giving such assistance as we can" (Mills 1887:248–49).

Afterward, the 21st and 23rd New York regiments were "ordered to the right to relieve the wearied men of Gibbon and Doubleday upon the field" (Mills 1887:249). They moved in column up the turnpike until the 21st New York was opposite Brawner's woods where the 21st faced the woods and advanced through them to the north. Mills (1887:249) recalled that "at the front of the wood our line is formed, commanding the open ground in front. The arms are stacked, a picket detailed, and then . . . the rest lie down to seek a little forgetfulness in sleep."

The aid provided by the New Yorkers to Gibbon's men may not have been all it was touted to be. Pvt. J. H. Stine of Company C, 19th Indiana, had this to say about his experience: "I was badly wounded and I imagined that if I staid there twenty-four hours that would be the last of me. There were some New York troops coming along and my left arm was so palsied with the shot that I could not use it much. I took my hat down and took off the '19,' and I got a New York man to take care of me, under the impression that I was a New York man; each regiment took care of their own wounded. He met some of his comrades, who told him he was not very smart to carry off one of those broad-brimmed hat fellows for a New Yorker; and he threw me down across a log" (U.S. Congress 1879:595).

Samuel G. Hill, another private of Company C, 19th Indiana, was wounded in action and lay on the battlefield from the evening of August 28 until the following Thursday—seven days. He remained on the field so long because he was within the Confederate lines (U.S. Congress 1879:589).

Given these firsthand accounts from 19th Indiana veterans, it is most likely that Confederate pickets held Brawner's yard and house after the battle, since the Stonewall Brigade remained "on the ground it had occupied during the fight the previous evening" until dawn (Hennessy 1985: 86). Perhaps Private Hill was wounded at the 19th Indiana's first firing line, located at and east of the Brawner house. This would have put him behind the Confederate pickets—the ones who challenged William Moore's band of volunteers as they approached their former firing line, probably the second one behind the post-and-rail fence. It is also likely that Private Stine was wounded during the 19th Indiana's fighting retreat back to Brawner's woods because he did not encounter any opposition on his way toward the turnpike to the south.

Sometime after daylight on the morning of August 29, the Stonewall Brigade withdrew to the north end of Brawner's farm, behind the roadbed of the unfinished railroad. Later that morning, according to Brigadier General Reynolds, Captain Cooper's Battery, supported by the 4th Pennsylvania Reserves, was deployed "on the same ridge on which" the Confederate right flank was located the previous evening (quoted in Hennessy 1985:80). Cooper's Battery engaged the Confederates, possibly Captain Poague's Rockbridge Artillery, from about 10:00 until shortly after 10:30 A.M., when Cooper and his infantry support were withdrawn south of the turnpike (Hennessy 1985:111). Although the Battle of Second Manassas continued through August 30, and the Civil War raged on another two and a half years after the battles of Brawner Farm and Second Manassas, no other significant infantry engagements took place around the Brawner house and yard (Edwin C. Bearss, personal communication, August 31, 1999).

Archaeology

Warfare between state-level governments is, to quote a Civil War soldier, "systematic killing," done on a grand scale and with the states' blessings (Time-Life 1996a:112). Indeed, it is one of the most organized, premeditated, regimented, and patterned forms of human behavior. The actions of military units on a battlefield are based on the tactics of the prevailing military wisdom of the day; *they are not random.* Therefore, one should not expect the debris of battle to be distributed randomly over a battlefield. The tactics employed on a battlefield do leave their traces in the archaeological record. Subsequently, if natural forces or human activities do not significantly disturb, mix, or mask all or parts of the battlefield, it should be possible to identify and define artifact patterns created by the tactical positions and movements of individual military units.

Of importance is the fact that artifact patterns often remain in spite of the bias caused by the private collecting of Civil War relics. There are several reasons for this. Most metal detectorists search an area randomly, rather than covering it in a systematic manner. Even when collectors hit concentrations of artifacts or "hot spots" and search them intensively, the density of battle debris is often so great that it would be very difficult to remove all traces of combat. Even when archaeologists have systematically surveyed 100 percent of an area, 100 percent coverage does not result in 100 percent recovery. Soil and weather conditions, vegetative cover, past and current use of the land, the type of metal detector, and the experience and skill of the operator, to name some factors, all have an effect on the ability to successfully detect and recover metal artifacts. Sim-

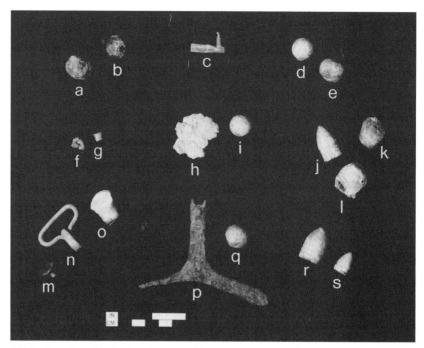

1.3. Artifacts found *in situ* from Brawner House excavations: (*a*) impacted iron case shot; (*b*) iron case shot; (*c*) fired friction primer; (*d*) lead case shot; (*e*) impacted lead case shot; (*f, g*) fired and unfired percussion caps; (*h, i*) impacted and unfired .69 cal. musket balls; (*j*) impacted .58 cal., 3-ring bullet; (*k*) impacted .54 cal., 3-ring bullet; (*l*) impacted .54 cal. Gardner bullet; (*m*) brad; (*n*) knapsack hook; (*o*) bullet carved as chess piece; (*p*) Austrian Lorenz rifle-musket gun tool; (*q*) impacted .70 cal. musket ball; (*r*) .69 cal., 3-ring unfired bullet; (*s*) unfired .44 cal. Colt pistol bullets (courtesy of the National Park Service, National Capital Region).

ply put, the random recovery of militaria over time by private collectors usually will not completely eliminate evidence of the archaeological patterns created by the activities and positions of military units on a battlefield (see Sterling and Slaughter, chapter 16 of this volume).

Archaeological evidence of the intense fighting around Brawner's home was recovered during the 1987 excavations that revealed the sandstone foundation of the antebellum house. More than 100 Civil War military artifacts were found, of which 40 were in their original historic context—the antebellum ground surface of the hard-packed, swept, bare-earth yard or the area that once was beneath the antebellum house (table 1.1; figs. 1.2, 1.3). It is also probable that these 40 artifacts came from the Battle of Brawner Farm or Second Manassas and *not* from some subsequent military event. Thirty-seven of them were found *beneath* the thin layer of crushed Virginia bluestone gravel and hard-packed clay that had been deposited after the Brawners returned to their home, perhaps to cover battle debris lying in the yard around the house in an attempt to reestablish a compacted surface for a swept, outdoor workspace (Perry Wheelock, personal communication, August 23, 1999). This gravel was easily

Table 1.1 Key to artifacts from Brawner yard

	Catalog no.(s)	Count	Object description
a	7682	1	.44 cal. 1-ring Colt pistol, bullet, unfired
b	6340	1	.54 cal. 3-ring conical bullet, unfired
c	5711, 7409	2	.54 cal. 3-ring conical bullet, impacted
d	6340, 7597, 6215	3	.58 cal. 3-ring conical bullet, unfired
e	7106, 7078	2	.58 cal. 3-ring conical bullet, impacted
f	6848	1	.58 cal. 2-ring Gardner conical bullet, impacted
g	5749	1	ind. cal. 3-ring conical bullet, impacted
h	6079	1	.69 cal. 3-ring conical bullet, unfired
i	5244	1	.69 cal. round ball, unfired
j	5480, 7077, 7832, 7142, 6823	5	.69 cal. round ball, impacted
k	7699	1	.70 cal round ball, impacted
l	7075, 7766	2	ind cal. round ball, impacted & chewed
m	6820, 6821	2	carved bullets, chess pieces
n	5245, 7683, 7684	3	lead case shot
o	5245	1	lead case shot, impacted
p	6663	1	iron case shot
q	5795	1	iron case shot, impacted
r	6217, 7250	3	friction primer, fired
s	5793	1	percussion cap, unfired
t	5486, 5792	4	percussion cap, fired
u	9653	1	Austrian gun tool
v	9652	1	Model 1816 bayonet
w	5488	1	knapsack hook

obtainable from the abandoned quarry site of the unfinished Independent Line of the Manassas Gap Railroad located on the Brawner farm about 500 yards from the house (Neville et al. 1995:60–65, 78). The remaining three military artifacts probably associated with the battle were found inside the antebellum house foundations. The additional 60-plus Civil War artifacts were found in the topsoil *above* the gravel and clay layer, indicating that they were deposited later in the war, since the house probably acted as a magnet, attracting troops who were, as Mary Brawner put it, "passing backwards and forwards all the time" (Brawner 1871). By analyzing the distribution and association of the 40 artifacts found on the antebellum ground surface, to each other and to the antebellum architectural features, patterns emerge of the military actions on this portion of the Brawner farm battlefield.

Fired Minié bullets and round balls, which hit something hard (impacted) such as wood or masonry, were found on the north and west sides of the house (table 1.1; fig. 1.2). Two impacted, 3-ring, .58-caliber Minié bullets were found inside the north foundation wall, indicating they penetrated the north wall of the house (fig. 1.3j). An impacted, 2-ring, .58-caliber Confederate-made Gardner bullet was also found north of the north foundation wall (fig. 1.3l). These bullets were fired toward the north face of Brawner's home from a position due north of the house, where historical records indicate the 4th Virginia Regiment had their right flank anchored on some outbuildings. The 4th Virginia was armed with a variety of different caliber weapons, including the .58-caliber U.S. Model 1855 "Harpers Ferry" rifles (Todd 1983:1275), as well as .54-caliber rifles, .577-caliber British-made Enfield rifle muskets, and .69-caliber muskets (Earl J. Coates, personal communication, March 2, 1999). It is likely that the impacted .58-caliber Minié bullets were fired from Confederate troops positioned north of the house.

Impacted .54-caliber Minié bullets and .69-caliber musket or round balls were found beside or near the northwest and west sides of the antebellum house (table 1.1; figs. 1.2, 1.3h, 1.3k). One impacted .69-caliber round ball was discovered inside the northwest corner of the foundation wall. Again, this indicates that it penetrated the north wall of Brawner's home. The direction of fire for these projectiles was from the west-northwest. It was from this direction that Colonel Taliaferro's three Virginia infantry regiments—the 10th, 23rd, and 37th—attacked the 19th Indiana's left flank. The 23rd Virginia was conspicuous in its efforts to take the Brawner house and yard. They, too, were armed with a combination of shoulder arms (Todd 1983:1276). Company H carried the .54-caliber U.S. Model 1841 "Mississippi" rifle and the remainder of the regiment used converted, .69-caliber smoothbore muskets (converted from a flintlock to a percussion ignition system). The impacted .54-caliber bullets and .69-caliber round balls were probably fired by members of the 23rd Virginia as they attacked from the west-northwest toward the Brawner yard and house, or some may have been fired by the 4th Virginia north of the house.

The presence of artillery in the Brawner yard is suggested by the discovery of two fired friction primers, one on the east side of the antebellum house and the other on the north (figs. 1.2, 1.3c; table 1.1). Friction primers, used to fire artillery pieces, consisted of a short metal tube filled with a powder charge that was ignited by friction when a twisted-wire pin was pulled from the tube. Perhaps these artifacts came from one of the Confederate batteries engaged on the evening of August 28 (Gaff 1985:62–69) or possibly from Union guns positioned north of the house on the morning of August 29.

The only possible indication of the 19th Indiana's presence in the Brawner yard came from three unfired, 3-ring, .58-caliber Minié bullets. They were found on the east and northeast sides of the antebellum house foundation (table 1.1; fig. 1.2). This is where one would expect to find them if they came from the Hoosiers, since the 19th Indiana was armed with .58-caliber Springfield rifle muskets (Todd 1983:785) and their initial firing line was east of Brawner's home.

Just north of the house foundation, two carved bullets were found close to each other (table 1.1; fig. 1.2). Judging by its shape, one bullet was probably a chess piece (fig. 1.3o). During the Civil War, it was common for soldiers on both sides to carve bullets as a way of alleviating boredom (Crouch 1995:109).

Encouraged by the discovery of *in situ*, battle-related artifacts around the Brawner house, we returned to the site in 1994 to determine if evidence of the firing lines still existed east of the house. Although the Brawner farm property had been searched by Civil War collectors before it became part of Manassas National Battlefield Park in 1985, prior experience at Civil War sites led us to believe that some evidence would be left to mark the units' positions because of the intensity of the 90-minute firefight and the fact that the firing lines moved little during the engagement. Brigadier General Gibbon (1978:54) described the action as "the most terrific musketry fire I have ever listened to." A year later, the effect of such concentrated small arms fire was still evident when Gibbon visited the battlefield and could easily trace his brigade's firing line by the thousands of paper cartridges littering the ground (Gaff 1985:178). Also, in spite of later troop movements and other military activities in the area, the linear artifact patterns of the earlier firing lines would remain because the later activities would leave different archaeological signatures that would neither completely mask nor eradicate the linear patterns.

Prior to selecting the area for archaeological investigation, Alan Gaff, John Hennessy, and Edwin Bearss, historians familiar with the Battle of Brawner Farm, were asked to choose, independently of one another, the place most likely to contain a segment of one of the 19th Indiana's firing lines. The spot picked by the historians was "the offset where the Hoosiers sought shelter" (Gaff 1985:17).

The systematic metal detector survey began in the area selected by the historians as the most promising location for one of the 19th Indiana's firing lines and proceeded northward toward the Stonewall Brigade's position. The field procedure consisted of placing a control grid over the area, 200 feet north-south by about 220 feet east-west at its widest. Then operators using metal detectors *completely* swept the area, marking the metal targets, carefully excavating and screening the soil to recover both metallic and nonmetallic artifacts, and mapping the positions where the objects were found.

Evidence of one of the 19th Indiana's firing lines was found almost due east from the northeast corner of the antebellum house foundation. It was in this vicinity that three unfired, 3-ring, .58-caliber Minié bullets were found. Not surprisingly, the firing line, too, was marked by unfired, 3-ring, .58-caliber Minié bullets from the 19th Indiana's .58-caliber Springfield rifle muskets (Todd 1983:785). In a linear pattern approximately 15 feet wide by 100 feet long, 13 unfired, 3-ring, .58-caliber Minié bullets, iron roller buckles of the type found on certain models of U.S. cartridge boxes, a brass finial from a U.S. cartridge box, an iron, canteen stopper loop, a steel musket sling loop, and other militaria defined one of the 19th Indiana's firing lines (fig. 1.4; table 1.2).

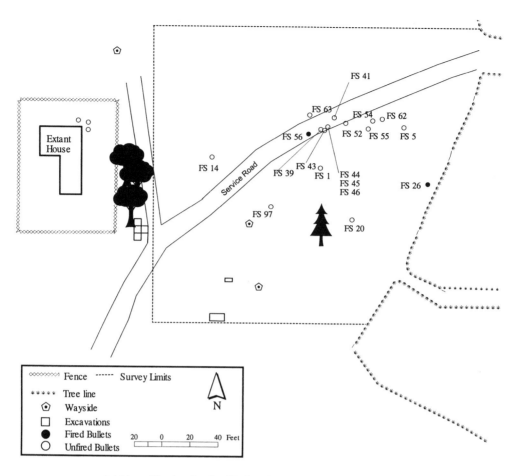

1.4. Map of fired and unfired bullets found during metal detector survey (courtesy of the National Park Service, National Capital Region).

The likelihood that this is one of the 19th Indiana's firing lines, and most probably the first one, is based on several pieces of evidence. First, the caliber of the unfired Minié bullets matches the caliber of the rifle muskets used by the Hoosiers. The 2nd Wisconsin, located to the east of the 19th Indiana, was armed with .54/.55-caliber Austrian Lorenz rifle muskets (Todd 1983:1307). The only other Union regiment engaged in a firefight near the Brawner house was the 4th Pennsylvania Reserves, who supported Captain Cooper's Battery on the morning of August 29. They were armed with .69-caliber smoothbore and rifled U.S. Model 1842 muskets (Todd 1983:1128).

Second, the artifact pattern and the types of militaria found support the interpretation that this is a firing line and not some other type of military formation (figs. 1.4, 1.5; table 1.2). It was common for soldiers on a firing line to drop unfired cartridges because of nervousness or haste, or because they were hit while reloading. Sometimes infantrymen discarded bullets because they were too large in diameter to fit easily in the rifle's bore

Table 1.2. Artifact inventory from the 19th Indiana firing line

Field specimen no.	Catalog no.	Object description
FS-01	19206	.58 cal., 3-ring, Minié ball, unfired, with star base
FS-05	19210	.58 cal., 3-ring, Minié ball, unfired
FS-08	19213	3-inch rifle shell, body frag.
FS-10	19215	3-inch rifle shell, nose frag.
FS-13	19218	3-inch Hotchkiss shell fragment, flame groove present
FS-14	19219	.58 cal., Minié ball, unfired, flattened
FS-15	19220	iron roller buckle of U.S. cartridge box
FS-17	19222	circular sheet brass disk
FS-19	19224	20-pdr. Parrott rifle shell frag.
FS-20	19225	.58 cal., 3-ring, Minié ball, unfired
FS-21	19226	3-inch Hotchkiss shell fragment, flame groove present
FS-22	19227	brass Enfield bayonet scabbard throat
FS-26	19231	.58 cal., 3-ring, Minié ball, fired
FS-30	19235	20-pdr. Parrott shell, nose frag.
FS-37	19242	3-inch rifle shell, nose frag.
FS-38	19243	20-pdr. Parrott shell, nose frag.
FS-39	19244	.58 cal., 3-ring, Minié ball, unfired
FS-40	19245	iron roller buckle of U.S. cartridge box
FS-41	19246	.58 cal., 3-ring, Minié ball, unfired
FS-43	19248	.58 cal., 3-ring, Minié ball, unfired
FS-44	19249	.58 cal., 3-ring, Minié ball, unfired
FS-45	19250	.58 cal., 3-ring, Minié ball, unfired
FS-46	19251	.58 cal., 3-ring, Minié ball, unfired
FS-52	19257	.58 cal., 3-ring, Minié ball, unfired
FS-54	19259	.58 cal., 3-ring, Minié ball, unfired
FS-55	19260	.58 cal., 3-ring, Minié ball, unfired
FS-56	19261	.58 cal., 3-ring, Minié ball, fired, impacted
FS-58	19263	20-pdr. Parrott shell frag.
FS-60	19265	1-inch iron canister shot
FS-62	19266	.58 cal., 3-ring, Minié ball, unfired
FS-63	19267	.58 cal., 3-ring, Minié ball, unfired
FS-67	19270	3-inch rifle shell, nose frag.
FS-68	19071	3-inch Reed rifle shell, sabot frag.
FS-71	19274	3-inch rifle shell, body frag.
FS-75	19278	3-inch rifle, case shot/shell body frag., poss. Confederate
FS-77	19280	3-inch rifle, case shot/shell body frag., poss. Confederate
FS-78	19281	iron canteen stopper loop
FS-79	19282	3-inch rifle, case shot/shell body frag., poss. Confederate
FS-81	19284	3-inch rifle, case shot/shell body frag., poss. Confederate
FS-82	19285	brass finial from U.S. cartridge box
FS-86	19289	iron musket sling loop
FS-87	19290	circular sheet brass disk
FS-92	19295	20-pdr. Parrott rifle shell frag.
FS-94	19297	20-pdr. Parrott rifle shell frag.
FS-95	19298	20-pdr. Parrott rifle shell, nose frag.
FS-96	19299	20-pdr. Parrott rifle case shot/shell, body/base frag.
FS-97	19300	.58 cal., 3-ring, Minié ball, unfired

(Babits 1995). This predicament made it especially difficult to reload when black-powder residue built up after firing several rounds. Other militaria, particularly objects that served as fasteners or were located at stress points, such as finials, buckles, canteen stoppers, and musket sling loops, became detached from accoutrements and clothing or were lost during the frenzied action on a firing line. Most important, it is the type, distribution, and density of these artifacts in combination with the type, distribution, and density of the unfired bullets that supports the interpretation that this is a firing line and *not* something as diffuse and ephemeral as a skirmish or picket line, or the position of troops being held in reserve (Slaughter and Sterling 1998).

Third, the distribution of iron fragments from Confederate-made or other 3-inch rifle artillery shells (figs. 1.6, 1.7; table 1.2) approximated the distribution of the unfired bullets and militaria marking the firing line. Although the area was completely surveyed with metal detectors, the shell fragments defined a broad, linear, east-west pattern, overlaying the linear pattern of artifacts from the infantry firing line. Most likely, the Confederate-made shells came from the rifled guns of Captain Poague's Rockbridge Artillery or Lieutenant Carpenter's Alleghany Artillery, which fired on the Union infantry line from positions behind the Stonewall Brigade. Carpenter's battery consisted of two 12-pounder, smoothbore Napoleons and two 3-inch rifles. These guns, along with their ammunition, had been captured the day before at the Union supply depot at Manassas Junction, replacing in kind Carpenter's worn-out guns and equipment (Gaff 1985: 25, 74, 189; Stuart 1947). This is intriguing because the Union normally fired Hotchkiss or Schenkl projectiles from 3-inch rifled guns (Peterson 1969:95). Thus, it is possible that the fragments of Union-made Hotchkiss shells that we found were fired from Carpenter's two 3-inch rifled guns. The fragments of Confederate-made and other 3-inch rifled shells could have come from either Carpenter's battery or Poague's two 10-pounder Parrotts (Gaff 1985:189).

The only artillery shell fragments that could not have come from Confederate guns were the 20-pounder rifled Parrott shell fragments (fig. 1.6; table 1.2). There were two 20-pounder Parrott guns at First Manassas, but they were deployed at Blackburn's Ford, far out of range of Brawner's farm. At Second Manassas, there were five Union batteries of 20-pounder Parrotts engaged in the battle. Of these five, Capt. Freeman McGilvery's battery of four 20-pounder Parrotts, posted approximately 660 yards north-northwest of John Dogan's house, was the *only* battery firing 20-pound rifled shells within the range and field of fire of this location (James M. Burgess, personal communication, July 20, 1999; Stuart 1947; Hennessy 1985: Map 11).

Fourth, historical accounts place the 19th Indiana Regiment's first firing line east of Brawner's home on the hillcrest, with their left flank at the

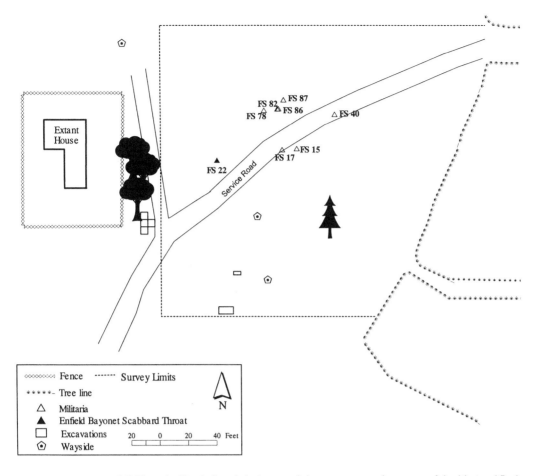

1.5. Map of militaria found during metal detector survey (courtesy of the National Park Service, National Capital Region).

house (Gibbon 1978:54; Dudley 1862:2; Meredith 1862:4). From this forward position, the 19th Indiana eventually retired to a second firing line behind a post-and-rail fence to the rear (Moore n.d.; Meredith 1862:4).

One artifact found south of the archaeological pattern of the firing line needs to be discussed—the brass throat to an Enfield bayonet scabbard (table 1.2; fig. 1.5). It has been suggested that this artifact could have been dropped by a soldier of the 23rd New York while on picket duty. According to Brigadier General Patrick (U.S. Congress 1879:225), "it was in this ground, up to this house, and from about here," meaning Brawner's house, that the 21st and 23rd New York Regiments gathered the wounded and later were on picket duty. In fact, the picket line of the 21st New York was several hundred yards southeast of Brawner's house, along the edge of a field at the north end of Brawner's woods (Mills 1887:249; in 1862, the northern edge of Brawner's woods was located south of the current wood-

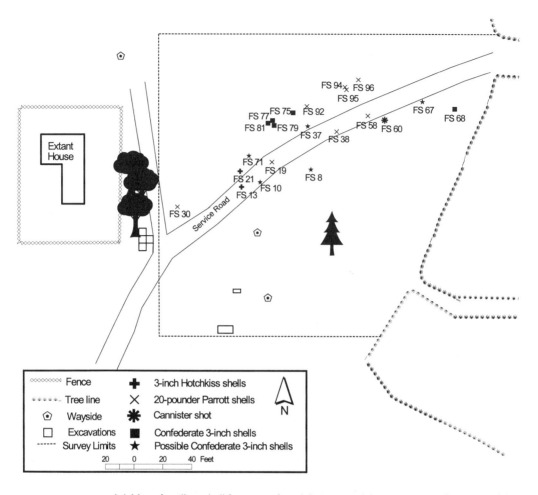

1.6. Map of artillery shell fragments found during metal detector survey (courtesy of the National Park Service, National Capital Region).

line). The exact position of the 23rd New York is not known. However, if the picket line of the 23rd New York Regiment was around Brawner's house it would have been some distance forward of the 21st New York's and in a dangerously exposed position. While the 23rd New York was armed with Enfield rifle muskets (Todd 1983:1038), some 4th Virginia soldiers were similarly equipped, as were many other Southern troops who passed through the farm on August 30 (Earl J. Coates, personal communication, March 2, 1999; James M. Burgess, personal communication, September 9, 1999). Finally, William Moore (n.d.), a veteran of the 19th Indiana, made it clear that Confederate pickets were posted around Brawner's house.

In the southeast corner of the Brawner yard, adjacent to the antebellum road trace, a large metallic contact was detected during the metal detector survey. As with other metal targets, the initial step was to excavate the sod in a divot (a clump of turf and soil) and then examine the hole and the divot for the metal object. Removal of the divot in this instance uncovered a large flat object. Excavation of additional sod and soil revealed a canteen associated with a number of nonmetallic items. Everything was left in place and a 5 x 5–foot excavation unit, tied to the grid, was placed over the objects. Systematic removal of the sod and soil overburden uncovered a shallow, roughly circular feature. Excavation of the surrounding soil revealed a Confederate pewter copy of a U.S. Model 1858 canteen (fig. 1.8; Sylvia and O'Donnell 1990:129). Still in their original context were the iron roller buckles from the canteen sling and stains from the iron chain that had held the stopper to the canteen.

The feature extended to the edge of the initial unit. As a result, three additional 5 x 5–foot units, one to the north, one to the east, and one to the south, were excavated to delineate the feature and to further investigate

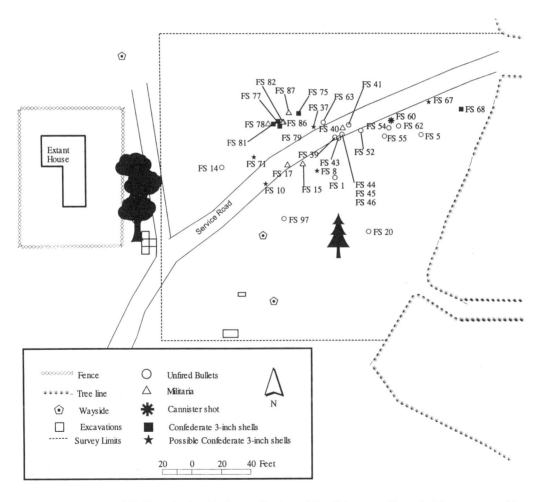

1.7. Map of unfired bullets, militaria, and Confederate artillery shell fragments marking the position of a firing line (courtesy of the National Park Service, National Capital Region).

the immediate area. The excavation exposed a shallow, basin-shaped fire pit less than 0.5 feet at its deepest point and with a maximum diameter of 2.5 feet. Such a small feature could be dug easily in several minutes with a bayonet and a tin cup or one's hands. Found in association with the canteen were fire-cracked rocks, burned fragments of brick and mortar, and animal bones (fig. 1.8; table 1.3).

The Confederate canteen was found at the top of the feature (fig. 1.8), indicating it was one of the last items to be tossed on the fire pit. The side of the canteen that faced upward was in perfect condition, while the downward face was partially crushed, as though it had been stepped on. That the damaged side of the canteen was face down was evidence that it was damaged before it was tossed on top of the feature by a Confederate soldier.

The animal bones and one tooth came from a minimum of one cow, one pig, and one horse (see Appendix, p. 26, for details). The 1871 claim for damages filed with the U.S. government by John Brawner (1871) included one cow and 22 hogs "killed and eaten," and one horse that was shot and died from its wounds. Most of the excavated cow bones came from meaty portions of the cow and several bore evidence of crude butchering. Other bones showed signs of burning. The horse bones, however, were elements located just above the hoof—a portion of the animal not usually considered an epicurean delicacy. Although the armies often drove herds of cattle to provide the troops with fresh meat, the fact that cow, pig, and horse remains were all found in the same shallow pit—which represented a single, short-term event—makes it more likely that these remains came from Brawner's animals killed during the battle of August 28. Thus, the feature probably represents a shallow cooking pit made by famished Confederates sometime after the departure of Union troops from Brawner's woods and fields around 1:00 A.M. on August 29 and before the return of the Brawner family on August 31.

Summary and Interpretations

When the Brawners fled their home on the morning of August 28, 1862, the structure they left was not "a neat log house," as described by Confederate artilleryman Edward Moore (1910:115). Rather, it was a circa 1820, two-story Georgian-style house called Bachelor's Hall, with double exterior chimneys at the east and west walls and a sandstone foundation measuring 24 x 31 feet. As a result of damage caused during the battle, the house was rebuilt circa 1867–68. The post-battle structure occupied a foundation about one-third smaller than the antebellum plan and was built directly on all of the south and a portion of the east foundation walls of the original structure. Incorporating some salvaged material, possibly from Bachelor's Hall, the new house was one and one-half stories, with two rooms on the first floor and a chimney on the east and west ends. It

1.8. Feature 2 showing Confederate pewter canteen, iron roller buckles from canteen sling, animal bones, and fire-cracked rock (courtesy of the National Park Service, National Capital Region).

was in this much smaller structure that John Brawner and his family continued to live during the hard times endured by many Virginians after the war.

Although the study area was reputed to have been heavily disturbed by earlier collectors, archaeological patterns remained of troop positions. Impacted .54- and .69-caliber bullets and musket balls, fired by Colonel Taliaferro's Virginians in their attempts to drive the 19th Indiana from the Brawner yard and house, were found on the west and northwest sides of the house. Around the northeast corner of the house and to the east, a portion of the 19th Indiana's first firing line remained. Marked by unfired .58-caliber Minié bullets and other infantry militaria, these artifacts were found in a linear pattern approximately 15 x 100 feet. Significantly, the distribution of iron fragments from exploded Confederate-made artillery shells approximated the linear pattern of the unfired bullets and militaria (see fig. 1.7), confirming the firing line's location. Finally, evidence of post-battle activities was discovered in the southeast corner of the Brawner yard, where a small roasting pit made by Confederate soldiers was excavated that contained, among other things, a Confederate pewter canteen and bones from a cow, pig, and horse—most likely some of the animals that Brawner reported killed and eaten as a consequence of the battle.

More important are the implications of this research for future efforts to define other tactical positions, particularly the 19th Indiana's second firing line behind the post-and-rail fence. The Hoosiers' first firing line was identified 110 feet north of a National Park Service interpretive marker. Yet, even though 100 percent of the survey area was searched with metal detectors, there was no archaeological pattern of a second firing line. Maybe William Moore's (n.d.) recollection that the rail fence they retreated to was "75 paces [about 150 feet] in the rear of our [first] line" is more accurate than Colonel Meredith's statement (1862:4) that they fell back "to a fence about two rods [33 feet] in the rear." Based on the archaeology, Meredith's account is suspect.

It is also unlikely that the firing line identified due east of the northeast corner of the antebellum house foundation is the 19th Indiana's second firing line—the one behind the rail fence. If that were so, then the Hoosier's first firing line would be north of Brawner's house, in the area of the outbuildings. By all historical accounts, the 4th Virginia Regiment held the outbuildings during the battle. Possibly, the 19th Indiana's second firing line awaits discovery a short distance south of the National Park Service interpretive marker.

Unlike most Civil War battlefields, where the bodies of the dead marked routes of attack, retreat, and counterattack, the static nature of the fighting at Brawner's farm imposed an unnatural order on the battlefield (Hennessy 1993:188). The morning after the battle, Confederate Capt. William Blackford remarked that "the positions of the two [firing] lines were about 70 yards apart and had not changed during the action. The lines were well marked by the dark rows of bodies . . . , lying just where they had fallen, with their heels on a well-defined line" (quoted in Hennessy 1993:188). Such a sight was mute testimony to Brig. Gen. William Booth Taliaferro's comment on the battle: "In this fight there was no maneuvering and very little tactics—it was a question of endurance, and both endured" (quoted in Gaff 1985:164).

Acknowledgments

The authors would like to thank the following persons for their assistance during various phases of this research: Ken Apschnikat, Edwin Bearss, James Burgess, Earl "Jerry" Coates, Karen Cucurullo, Craig Davis, Alan Gaff, Tara Goodrich, William Hanna, John Hennessy, John Imlay, Jeanne Lavelle, Barbara Little, Michael Lucas, Richard Maestas, Keith Newlin, Kathleen Parker, Claude "Pete" Petrone, Malcolm "Rich" Richardson, Carter Shields, Charles "Chip" Smith, Tammy Stidham, Michael Strutt, James Thompson, Jackie Volmer, and Perry Wheelock.

Appendix

Susannah L. Dean

There were many casualties of the Battle of Brawner Farm besides the fighting soldiers. As described by Alan Gaff: "All the farm animals left behind by the Brawner family were dead in their pens and out in the long grass were dead birds and rabbits, 'innocent victims of man's brutality'" (quoted in Gaff 1985:178). As described by both Mary and John Brawner (1871), all of their livestock were killed during the battle with the single exception of a colt that was later "taken by a scouting Party from Genl F. Sigel's Corps." The following testimony was sworn on June 15, 1871, by Mary B. Brawner:

> The cow was killed at [the time of the battle] in the barn-yard. She was found dead in the barn-yard, and of course she must have been killed. She was left there when we left the place. I don't know whether they used her for beef or not, because we left the place early the next morning before light—the battle was raging so furiously we could not stay.
>
> The hogs were killed at the same time. I don't remember how many there were. I saw some of them that had been butchered: after we went back to the house we saw where they had been butchered. [John Brawner's testimony specified "16 big hogs and 7 shoats."]
>
> The horse was shot and died from wounds at the same time. . . .
>
> The colt was taken at a later time from a gentleman's farm where it was put to pasture. It belonged to my father: one that he had raised. (Brawner 1871)

Faunal Analysis

Twenty-two bone fragments were recovered from the small feature containing the Confederate canteen (Feature 2; see table 1.3). All of these were from medium- to large-sized mammals. Three species were identified: cow, pig, and horse.

Six fragments of cattle bone were recovered, representing at least one adult cow. Identified elements include one left humerus, one right tibia, one metacarpal, and two left pelvic bones. The tibia and pelvic bones appear to have been hacked or crudely butchered. The tibia shows signs of carnivore scavenging, and the pelvic bones exhibit signs of both carnivore and rodent chewing. The metacarpal had been carnivore chewed and may have been burned.

The pig was represented by a single adult-sized incisor.

Four fragments of horse bone were recovered: a single phalange and three fragments of a right calcaneus (the latter have been identified as possibly horse). These bones were clearly from an adult animal—they could not have come from the previously mentioned colt.

Nine unidentified large mammal bones were also recovered from this pit. Some of these showed signs of having been burned.

Interpretations

While the number of identified bones is low, it is likely that these bones are the remains of John Brawner's livestock killed during the Battle of Brawner Farm. This interpretation is based not only on John Brawner's 1871 claims for restitution but on the stratigraphic context of the bones

Table 1.3 Inventory of material from Feature 2 excavations

Provenience	Catalog no.	Object description
N10W40.Fea.2	19303	fire-cracked rock
N10W40.Fea.2	19310	iron roller buckles from canteen sling
N10W40.Fea.2	19311	iron roller buckle from canteen sling
N10W40.Fea.2	19312	pewter Confederate copy of U.S. Model 1858 canteen
N10W40.Fea.2	19317	horse phalange, poss. burned
N10W40.Fea.2	19318	cow humerous
N10W40.Fea.2	19319	cow tibia, poss. butchered
N10W40.Fea.2	19320	cow pelvis, poss. butchered
N10W40.Fea.2	19321	horse calcaneous, poss.
N10W40.Fea.2	19322	large mammal
N10W40	19349	iron case shot
N5W40	19383	tinned-metal, 4-hole Federal trouser button
N5W40	19387	iron case shot
N10W35.2	19451	iron case shot

and associated artifacts. Cow humerus and pelvis are both meaty elements. The tibia can likewise be boiled for soups or stews or broken to release the calorie-rich marrow. Both the pelvis and tibia showed evidence of having been hacked or crudely butchered. Other large mammal bones showed evidence of having been burned, probably cooked. It is probable that these farm animals were killed during the battle and later eaten by the famished soldiers, after which the bones were simply discarded, some into the actual cook fire in which they had been roasted.

The livestock penned at Brawner farm most assuredly offered the foot soldiers a hearty meal after their intense fighting: "16 big hogs" (Brawner 1871) could yield a potential 1,600 pounds of pork. A single cow could yield 400 pounds of beef. Even the horse, if consumed, could yield more than 300 pounds of meat. It is likely that this feature was only one of many cook fires in use in and around the Brawner yard following the battle.

Some of the bones recovered showed evidence of being chewed by carnivores and rodents. Once the soldiers had their fill, it is likely that the surviving local fauna came into the yard area, picking out, and probably dragging away, remaining bits of meat and bone. This may account for the lack of small bones witnessed in this collection. Both Mary and John Brawner (1871) mentioned domestic fowl in their claim for restitution. It is likely that these animals were likewise consumed by soldiers and that any faunal evidence of this meal was eaten or carried away by other scavengers such as raccoons, rats, and crows.

2

The Submarine *H. L. Hunley*

Confederate Innovation and Southern Icon

Steven D. Smith

On a crisp, cloudless sundown in mid-February 1864, a long, thin, iron watercraft cleared Breach Inlet, South Carolina, and entered the open sea. Less than three miles dead ahead lay its objective, the Union sloop of war U.S.S. *Housatonic,* at anchor, but with a full head of steam. On board, the *Housatonic*'s crew was alert, keeping an eye out for a rumored Confederate torpedo boat seeking targets among the Union fleet blockading Charleston. In fact the iron vessel bearing down on them was the *H. L. Hunley,* a true submarine and a glimmering example of the South's innovative attempts to overcome the might of the Federal Navy.

About nine that evening, months of experimentation, failure, and re-experimentation came to an end. Yankee sailors aboard the *Housatonic* spotted the approaching dark shape some yards away and, while blazing away with rifles and pistols, attempted to bring to bear their larger guns. With the *Housatonic*'s confused crew watching, the *Hunley* rammed its spar-mounted torpedo into her side and backed away. There was a jarring explosion. The *Housatonic* quickly rolled to port and settled in thirty feet of water, its men seeking safety in the rigging. The era of submarine warfare had begun. The *Hunley* was the first submarine to sink an enemy vessel in combat (Kloeppel 1992:59–81; Ragan 1995:132–40; Schafer 1996:113–25). But for what would eventually become a weapon of shock and deadly efficiency in World Wars I and II, it was an unassuming dawn, for the *Hunley* failed to return to port (Ragan 1995:141).

The mystery of the *Hunley*'s fate has been the subject of debate by military historians, wreck salvors, and professional archaeologists practically since its loss. In early May 1995, the *Hunley* controversy radically changed when the submarine was discovered (Hall and Wilbanks 1995). Overnight, dispute concerning the *Hunley*'s fate was secondary to quarrels respecting its discovery, ownership, and future. These wrangles soon broadened to higher philosophical questions of states' rights and, ultimately, the vessel's ideological meaning. Now the *Hunley* is serious business, embroiling private citizens and citizens' groups, state governments, the U.S. Congress, the U.S. Navy, the media, and the literary elite, in a struggle for control over its destiny and especially its meaning. Although its archaeological significance is first on everyone's lips, it often seems from the clamor, alas, to be last in the struggle for its control. This chapter examines the *Hunley*'s past as a unique example of Confederate innovation, its discovery and recent assessment by the National Park Service and the South Carolina Institute of Archaeology and Anthropology, and its future as an icon of Southern culture. The *Hunley* is no mere historic underwater artifact, and its multilayered symbolism continues to grow while government agencies attempt to raise and display it.

Confederate Innovation

In creating an entirely new navy to challenge the Union, Confederate secretary of the navy Stephen Russell Mallory faced a daunting and ultimately insurmountable task. The South was rural and agrarian, while the North had a strong industrial infrastructure. Although there was a "Southern industry," it served the agricultural community and hardly could be described as diverse. In terms of capital alone, Northern industrial investment was nearly eight times as large as the South's (Genovese 1965; Luraghi 1996:34). Among Mallory's immediate industrial needs were shipyards. At the beginning of the war, the U.S. Navy had eight shipyards while the Confederacy captured only a small yard in Pensacola, Florida, and the prominent Norfolk, Virginia, yard. Both sides had numerous small private yards, but, overall, the South was decidedly at a disadvantage. Indeed, the South had no navy to begin with, while the U.S. fleet was ninety strong, and if most Federal vessels were old and aging, a few were the most modern steamers in the world. The rest could be repaired or at least used as floating batteries (Luraghi 1996:32). In his classic study of the Confederate Navy, French admiral Lepotier summed up the situation by noting that the Civil War was probably the only occasion in history when, as two ocean-facing nations prepared for conflict, one had total dominion of the seas (Luraghi 1996:61).

Essentially, Mallory had to build a navy from the keel up, while the North only had to rig for war. The Confederacy faced numerous challenges, but four stand out as decisive. The first was a decided lack of raw materials. Specifically, the South lacked pig iron. William Still stated that it "is nearly impossible to exaggerate the effect of iron production on the entire Confederate war effort" (Still 1987:47). Lacking both iron reserves and iron ore at the beginning of the war, the Confederacy could not even get started building an iron fleet. Second, while the South had abundant timber for wooden ship construction, there was no way to get the timber to its naval yards. Its transportation infrastructure was wholly inadequate—there were only a few railroads and dirt roads—and there was no means for rapid improvement of the situation. The critical demand for iron actually worked against the need to build up the transportation system as operational railroads were raided for their iron rails to construct armored vessels (Still 1987:50–51). The third critical need was skilled labor. The South had genius at the level of invention, but invention has to be engineered and such skills were scarce south of the Mason-Dixon Line. As Confederate naval historian Raimondo Luraghi noted, the South's lack of mechanics, technicians, and engineers—or the existence of a true industrial machine—was the basic reason for the South's defeat (Luraghi 1996:346). Finally, the Confederacy lacked time. The time to build a transportation system, cut timber, forge iron, and construct a Confederate Navy was simply not available (Still 1987:80–81).

Mallory did his best to meet these challenges. As he worked desperately to build a navy, he looked for any advantage. There were a few. First, there was hope that the Confederacy could purchase part of its navy from European powers. Second, there were its timber resources, both wood and resin products such as tar and pitch. If it could get these resources to its naval yards, wooden ship production could be sustained. Third was private investment. Southern patriotic fervor and the possibility of profit motivated Southern venture capitalists to invest in privateering and blockade running. The former was largely ineffective, the latter quite successful (Wise 1988). The Confederacy primed this investment fever with loans, giving the government some control over the required new industries and what they would produce (Luraghi 1996:39). Most critically, private investment provided the Confederacy with the fuel to sail its one ship of hope—the hope of technical innovation. Free from bureaucratic restraints faced by the Federal Navy (Wills 1998:23) and spurred by men of genius, Mallory looked to novel technological inventions to float the Confederate Navy.

Mallory's initial vision was "based on a four-fold technical surprise: armored ships, rifled naval guns, commerce destroying, and submarine weapons" (Luraghi 1996:69). It is important to understand that reliance on technical innovation was not simply a side issue in Mallory's overall strategy, but rather it was at its core. Mallory was well versed in the recent progress in maritime technology and, according to one contemporary, was responsible for the initiation of Confederate submarine warfare (Luraghi 1996:236). "To hold that this evolution influenced his strategy understates the case. In reality, technology affected Confederate naval strategy in its very bases and ground rules, in the cardinal point upon which the talented secretary built it: technology would be the tool that appeared to offer a breath of hope in facing a war that otherwise would be hopeless or lost before it began" (Luraghi 1996:61).

Although submarine weapons were one of Mallory's fourfold elements in his hope of technical surprise, his intentions lay with the development of torpedoes, or as we call them today, mines, rather than submersible boats. Clearly, Southern innovation is no better illustrated than in its development of torpedo warfare, through which these examples of "Rebel barbarity" were forged into a "formidable strategy" (Schafer 1996:3, 180). Even when they didn't cause havoc with vessel destruction, they caused the Union fleets to proceed with caution. In the end, torpedoes were remarkably successful, causing more destruction to Union vessels than did Confederate warships (Schafer 1996:12). But mines are largely passive instruments, drifting ambuscades. To wrest control of the seas, the Confederacy had to take the offensive, and this meant either self-propelled torpedoes in the modern sense or the delivery of the torpedo by a submersible vessel. The Confederacy worked to develop both.

The Union made the first attempt at a submarine, and although it developed the famed submersible the *Intelligent Whale,* Northern submarine development was thwarted by an indifference to underwater warfare induced by its domination of the surface (Luraghi 1996:251). Submarines were left to the South, and the South went at it at the Tredegar Iron Works in Richmond, Virginia, the Leed's Foundry in New Orleans, Louisiana, the Park & Lyon's Machine Shops in Mobile, Alabama, and the Confederate naval facilities at Selma, Alabama (Wills 1998:24).

The *Hunley* was the product of two earlier prototypes, the *Pioneer* and the *American Diver,* built by a team of machinists and businessmen who began their efforts at Leed's Yard in New Orleans, perhaps as early as August 1861. The machinists were Baxter Watson and James McClintock. These practical men were joined by entrepreneurs Horace L. Hunley, John K. Scott, Robert Ruffin Barrow, and Henry J. Leovy. The core of this group was McClintock and Hunley. They kept the dream of a fully submersible submarine alive after numerous failures. Their first attempt, the *Pioneer,* was made of quarter-inch iron plate, about 34 feet long, 4 feet at the beam, and 4 feet in depth. Shaped somewhat like a cigar, the main body, where four men propelled the vessel with a hand crank, was about 10 feet in length. From this 10-foot central section the vessel tapered to a conical bow and stern (Ragan 1995:20). The *Pioneer* gained notoriety and a Letter of Marque by successfully sinking a schooner and two target barges using a towed torpedo in Lake Pontchartrain in February 1862 (Wills 1998:24). Its potentially deadly future was cut short when New Orleans fell to the North and the vessel had to be abandoned. McClintock, Watson, and Hunley made their way to Mobile, Alabama. At Thomas Park and Thomas Lyons's machine shop, they met Lt. William Alexander, who was instructed by the Confederate Army to assist them in their next venture.

The second effort at a submersible was funded entirely by Horace Hunley. Using the success of the *Pioneer* as a starting point, the machinist innovators experimented with the propulsion system in the form of, amazingly, an electromagnetic engine. Though this engine did not work, it gives us a measure of their advanced thinking (Ragan 1995:22). Next they tried steam. Historian Mark Ragan points out that although many others criticized their attempts at steam propulsion in a submersible craft, these machinists were steam-gauge manufacturers by civilian trade and must have known something about their chances of success. Though their steam propulsion effort failed, they were eventually vindicated by the French, who successfully operated a steam submarine after the Civil War (Ragan 1995:24). Finally, the team settled on a hand-cranked propeller turned by four men. The vessel, known as either *Pioneer II* or the *American Diver,* was about 36 to 40 feet in length, 3.5 feet in the beam and 4 feet in depth (Wills 1998:25). This vessel had two major problems. First, four men could not crank hard enough to gain sufficient speed to maneuver against an enemy vessel. Second, its armament consisted of a towed torpedo similar to the *Pioneer.* The sub had to dive under an enemy vessel and hope that the towed torpedo would hit its victim. Before the inventors could find solutions to these problems, the *Pioneer* sunk in Mobile Bay and could not be recovered.

Undaunted (or at least only slightly daunted), the team looked for more funds for another attempt. At this time, Mobile, Alabama, saw the formation of a group of entrepreneurs seeking to take advantage of the Confederate government's offer of 50 percent of the value of all Federal vessels destroyed to the privateers who sank the vessels. The leader of this group was E. C. Singer, whose uncle was the inventor of the Singer sewing machine, and who himself was the innovator of the Singer underwater contact mine (Ragan 1995:26). The Singer Submarine Corps invested in the McClintock team's next adventure, with Hunley once again adding funds. The new vessel would eventually be named after its financier and champion, Horace Hunley.

Historical sources regarding the *Hunley*'s design are vague, but from what is known, it was the next logical step in the designs used previously, but it incorporated new innovations based on experiences with the two prototypes (fig. 2.1). Memories of the *Hunley* indicate that it was from 30 to 40 feet in length, between 4 and 3.5 feet at the beam, and between 4 and 5 feet in depth (Wills 1998:29). The 1996 assessment expedition found that it is 39 feet, 5 inches in length, 3 feet, 10 inches at the beam, and 4 feet, 3 inches in depth. Different from the previous two, the *Hunley* was built from a cylindrical steam boiler rather than plate metal. The inventors cut the boiler longitudinally, inserting two 12-inch boiler-iron strips in her sides. Both bow and stern tapered smoothly to wedge-shaped ends. Near each end, a bulkhead formed water-ballast tanks to raise and sink the vessel. The tanks were operated by opening sea-cocks that flooded them for diving. A force pump ejected the water for surfacing. Movement up

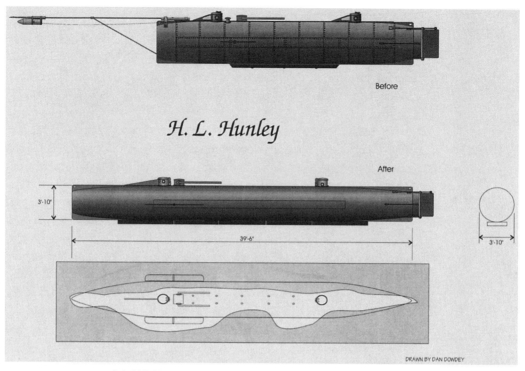

Before

H. L. Hunley

After

3'-10"

39'-6"

3'-10"

DRAWN BY DAN DOWDEY

2.1. *H. L. Hunley* drawn by Dan Dowdey (with permission of Dan Dowdey).

and down was performed by lateral diving planes, which pivoted like airplane flaps to direct the submerged vessel.

Propulsion, still a problem, was partially solved by a larger crew of eight that still hand-cranked an ordinary propeller. Men sat on the port side and cranked the shaft bracketed to the opposite wall. There was so little room inside that it was impossible to pass from fore to aft, so half the crew entered from a forward hatch and the other half from the rear. Outside, the propeller connection to the shaft was guarded by a wrought iron ring. The commander sat in the forward hatch, navigated using a compass, controlled the diving planes and rudder, and watched a mercury gauge that gave some general indication of depth below the surface. Just behind the fore hatch was a snorkel box, to allow some air from the surface while running submerged (Ragan 1995:26).

The team initially experimented with a towed torpedo, as this system had been somewhat successful in Mobile Bay. But in rough waters the torpedo became as dangerous to the *Hunley* as it was to its prey, so a new system was devised. Exactly how the new system worked is not known. A boom with a socket torpedo was used, though, attached somewhere on the bow (Wills 1998:30). With this configuration, the *Hunley* would ram, securing the torpedo in its victim, and then back away. The attached torpedo was then detonated by a lanyard.

The shallow waters of Mobile Bay were less than ideal hunting grounds for the *Hunley*, and permission was secured to move the vessel to Charleston, where Confederate general Pierre Gustave Toutant Beauregard welcomed its arrival on August 12, 1863 (Ragan 1995:35). At Charleston it underwent further testing. The history of the *Hunley* in Charleston is as fascinating and incredible as any human adventure. Twice during trials the vessel sunk. In the first instance, five crew members were lost, and the second claimed the life of Horace Hunley and many of the experienced mechanics who had been with the team in Mobile (Wills 1998:32). Since by this time the Confederate Army had full control of the *Hunley*, the new team was led by Lt. George Dixon, who would command the *Hunley* on its historic mission. Under Dixon's command, a new crew began a rigorous training program on Sullivan's Island, South Carolina, which was in fact the first submariner's school in the world (Luraghi 1996:256). The crew endured a physical training regimen and long hours in the sub. Once, the crew survived a two-hour-and-twenty-five-minute submersion at the bottom of Back Bay, South Carolina (Ragan 1995:120–22). By December 1863, they were ready, and General Beauregard issued orders for them to begin operations against the Federal fleet.

Discovery

Exactly what happened that night of February 17th, 1864, is clouded speculation, as documentary sources are contradictory, most being later reminiscences rather than contemporary records. The sheer genius of this vessel continues to be better appreciated as historians and archaeologists search tenaciously for new documents. The murky interpretations resulting from these documents could be clarified by the incontrovertible facts of archaeological excavation, as the *Hunley* has been found.

In May 1995, the *Hunley* was discovered, but controversy will probably continue as long as it exists. Several groups and individuals searched for the *Hunley* after its loss. The Union fleet dragged for it during the war while assessing the damage to the *Housatonic* (Ragan 1995:156). Again in 1872 and 1873, the U.S. government searched the area. Exactly who was the first in modern times to search for and discover the *Hunley* is one of many controversial issues that continue to be debated. One individual claims to have found it and/or the *Housatonic* in 1970 and filed for their discovery in federal court (Ragan 1995:204–3). Another person claims to have started his search in 1974 (*Hunley* Project Web Page:1997 http://members.aol.com/litespdcom/index.html). Fiction author Clive Cussler and the South Carolina Institute of Archaeology and Anthropology (SCIAA) jointly and unsuccessfully searched for it in 1980–81 and again in 1994. This set the stage for its confirmed discovery in 1995 by the National Underwater and Marine Agency (NUMA), Cussler's nonprofit foundation that searches for shipwrecks (Hall and Wilbanks 1995). Inevitably, with such intense interest by salvors, archaeologists, and adventurers, the sensational underwater discovery soon created a storm of charge and countercharge, which the media happily devoured.

During these exchanges, the SCIAA, the state agency responsible for South Carolina's underwater antiquities, was a highly visible target of much of the acrimony. Although often frustrating and sometimes amusing for its staff, the professional and legal responsibilities that kept the institute from entering the fray were played out in the press, on the Internet, and in various popular publications. The archaeological community was not always unaffected by this rancor either. In the confusing days immediately after the discovery, the institute attempted to organize a committee of experts into a "*Hunley* Project Working Group," its duties being to advise the institute regarding the vessel's protection and preservation. While some colleagues were genuinely concerned with the *Hunley* and were enthusiastic and helpful, others were hesitant and dissembling when asked to join the group. It was obvious that they did not wish to commit themselves until it was clear where the institute would emerge in the perceived political power struggle among various public and private factions.

Frankly, the SCIAA was momentarily caught flatfooted by the worldwide attention resulting from the announcement and the deep rancor developing among the various parties competing for discovery credit. The initial and immediate problem was determining legal responsibility, and that depended on the vessel's location, which was not known because Cussler refused to turn over coordinates to the institute. If the vessel was located in state waters as suspected, the underfunded institute was now the manager of what the media were calling the nation's most important underwater find of the decade, a find demanding the utmost in continual protection from rediscovery by looters.

To the institute at least, its responsibilities were clear, if widely misunderstood. Under national antiquity law, the vessel belonged to the U.S. government, specifically the General Services Administration. The Abandoned Shipwreck Act and the National Historic Preservation Act placed local responsibility with the State Historic Preservation Office (SHPO). In South Carolina, active management of underwater resources rested at that time with the institute, with SHPO oversight and cooperation as defined by the state's underwater act and a memorandum of agreement between the SHPO and the institute. Immediately after the announced discovery, the institute contacted the Naval Historical Center and began a collegial dialogue, including development of a draft memorandum for the vessel's security and possible recovery. Informed of the pending agreement, South Carolina's attorney general ordered the institute to cease negotiations with the navy and also to cease any further discussions with Cussler. Only ten days after the discovery, state representatives introduced a concurrent resolution in the state legislature to create the South Carolina *Hunley* Commission that would seek state ownership from the federal government and—critically for the institute—the commission was to become the ultimate state authority over the *Hunley*. When the bill passed later that month it left both the institute and the State Historic Preservation Office in a perplexing situation. Did a state resolution legally absolve state agencies with federal oversight of their federal preservation responsibilities? Amidst this great excitement and rapidly changing events, the subtle changes in authority were not clear to the stimulated public and concerned professional colleagues, who demanded action from the institute. Despite demands, all through the following year, the commission's authority solidified and the institute's duties became clearly defined when the state attorney general issued an informal opinion that the institute's role was *only* that which it was assigned by the commission (Cook 1996).

Throughout 1995 and into 1996, interest in the future of the *Hunley* continued to intensify. The state commission, with the assistance of South Carolina's national congressional representatives, vigorously sought ownership, and bills were introduced in the U.S. House and Senate to convey title to the state. Representatives from Alabama also sought to have the vessel displayed, when eventually raised, in Mobile (Neyland and Amer 1998:8). As federal interests were arranged, the Naval Historical Center became the lead organization acting on behalf of the General Services Administration. Naturally, they sought advice from an oversight committee consisting of the Advisory Council for Historic Preservation, the National Park Service, the National Oceanic and Atmospheric Administration, and the Smithsonian. Although the summer of 1995 saw negotiations breaking down between South Carolina and the federal government, the fall brought increased cooperation. In October, Cussler released the coordinates of his find to the Naval Historical Center.

With the location known, in November 1995 the commission and the Naval Historical Center decided to jointly oversee an expedition to verify the discovery and assess the vessel's condition. This project was jointly led by the institute on behalf of the state commission and the Submerged Cultural Resources Unit of the National Park Service on behalf of the federal government. One year after the vessel's discovery, the institute and the Park Service made the first scientific assessment of it (Murphy et al. 1998). The expedition partially uncovered the *Hunley*, providing an initial look at this long-sought artifact. One important finding was recognition of its advanced hydrodynamic design. Drawings of the *Hunley* indicated a rather blocky, blunt crude design, but the expedition revealed a sleek, thin, tubular vessel designed for submerged running. Hatch portholes were found only on the port side and deadlights ran along the top between the hatches. The only damage seen was at the forward hatch; a hole was found where there should have been a forward-facing viewport. The ragged hole adds fuel to the continuing debate about the *Hunley*'s demise.

Cooperation between the National Park Service and the institute in the field, with joint oversight by the state commission and the U.S. Navy, resulted in a successful expedition in spite of intense media scrutiny, and vocal naysayers. This effort went a long way toward ironing out misunderstandings between federal and state interests. Eventually, in August 1996, the commission and the navy signed a Programmatic Memorandum of Agreement (PMOA), giving title to the federal government, while the state had control over the *Hunley*'s fate, including its future interpretation (Memorandum 1996). The final PMOA was remarkably similar in overall content to that initially drafted by the institute and the navy.

Confederate Icon

Control of the *Hunley*'s future now rests in the hands of South Carolina's *Hunley* Commission and the federal government's Naval Historical Center. These two agencies, but especially the commission, exert a powerful control over the vessel's recovery, conservation, and display. The navy's mission is clear—to make sure that recovery and conservation are done correctly. The commission shares that responsibility and desire, but it has another concern which goes far beyond the *Hunley* as an archaeological artifact. Indeed, the controversy surrounding the *Hunley*'s discovery and the commission's actions must be understood in a much broader sense. The *Hunley* is no mere sensational archaeological find. Yes, it is a unique example of military engineering and an invaluable artifact of naval history and military technology. It is apparently in excellent condition—literally a time capsule encased in shell and sand—and our knowledge of submarine history will be greatly enhanced by its conservation and display. These facts alone make it a national treasure. But while significant, these facts may be secondary to its meaning to the modern South and the struggle for the *Hunley*'s interpretation. This struggle will bring to practical application all realms of political and philosophical discourse concerning who owns and who controls the past, since the *Hunley* may become the new icon of Southern heritage.

The historiography of Southern history is as fascinating as the history of the South. Through each generation, historians of the South have sought to define and explain Southern history and, by extension, its ultimate expression in the Confederacy. The question of how we interpret the South and the interrelated question of how we interpret the Civil War have been at the core of historical scholarship since 1865. The changing responses to these questions go far in defining each succeeding generation (Pressly 1965). Even the appellations used for the war of 1861–65 are demonstrative of these changing meanings. The war of the rebellion, the

War between the States, the needless war, the irrepressible war, and now, most often, the Civil War—all these epithets offer sometimes subtle but more often distinctly different interpretations of the "late unpleasantness." Today it is safe to say that the dominant paradigm, in academia at least, emphasizes the issues of slavery and race. Today the Civil War is interpreted as the war to end slavery, a perspective supported by noted historians such as James McPherson, Richard H. Sewell, David M. Potter, and William J. Copper (Toplin 1996:29). Indeed, regardless of initial causes, it cannot be debated that from the moment of Lincoln's Emancipation Proclamation, the war became the war to end slavery in America (Steven Smith 1994:5). This perspective was not always dominant but gained strength as the civil rights movement informed political and social change beginning in the 1950s. Today in academia, the slavery issue and the African American experience are manifest in almost all aspects of historical and social study disciplines. In archaeology, this focus is expressed in studies of slave life, plantations, and the whole issue now being labeled as the African Diaspora (*vide* McDavid and Babson 1997). Based on paper and symposium titles from the 1998 Society for Historical Archaeology annual meeting, for instance, 85 of the 396 papers presented, or 21 percent, dealt with African Americans, Diaspora, race, or slavery. The effect of this focus is, naturally, a decided avoidance of any aspects defined as traditional Southern culture, and of things Confederate. Back in 1969, Frank E. Vandiver wrote, "Currently the tide of historical interpretation is running against the Confederacy," pointing to scholars' avoidance of defending the Confederacy and especially its position on the institution of slavery. Vandiver added, "even Southern historians have shied away from a positive approach" (Vandiver 1969:148). Certainly this is even more apropos today.

Today academe seeks to project its paradigms into the public arena. Regarding the current paradigm, it does so by revising educational materials, by controlling government-sponsored research through revision of the requirements of grants-in-aid, by revising national historical contexts, and by revising the focus of federal and state park battlefield interpretation. Curiously, while there are numerous examples of academe's success, there is also a public countermovement diverging from academe's interpretations of the past. The war, as Shelby Foote has so well stated, is for Americans at "the crossroads of our being" (Cullen 1995:2), and with its multilayered complexity, it is difficult for the public's interest to be completely channeled. Spurred by Ken Burns's monumental film, public interest in the Civil War is at a peak not seen since the centennial. This interest seems—at least in South Carolina and, I would venture, throughout the South—focused on the war itself rather than on its ideological causes and effects. Contrary to academe, this perspective largely avoids divisive racial issues. Public interest is focused on the fate of the common man, both black and white, during the Civil War. The most visible manifestation of this interest is the rapid growth of black and white reenactor organizations. It is heartening to see black and white men and women work side by side to preserve a "memory" of the war that acknowledges but does not exploit or focus on the race issue. This public does not deny slavery or the horrors of racism but rather appears to want to focus on understanding what happened to *people,* not their underlying hatreds. The result is a healing and an interaction worthy of encouragement. There are other manifestations of this movement that can be easily gleaned on the Internet from an increasing number of institutions focusing on the Civil War, such as the U.S. Civil War Center at Louisiana State University, which proclaims a "pro-truth, anti-agenda" philosophy (http://www.cwc.lsu.edu). Further, Civil War magazines, roundtables, and discussion groups are stronger than ever. This renewed interest has also strengthened an undercurrent of renewed defense of Southern cultural traditions, again both black and white, and within the latter, strongly figures the Confederate traditions of honor and chivalry. Evidence of this is seen in the sustaining of Southern fraternal organizations such as the Sons and Daughters of Confederate Veterans.

Public interest in the war and its military aspects also runs counter to academe's growing bias against military history. The study of military history has "always been something of a pariah in U.S. Universities," and it faces an increasingly "hostile environment" (Lynn 1997:777–78). From a peak around 1970, interest in academic military history continues to drop, and "two major universities—Michigan and Wisconsin—have recently virtually abandoned the field" (Coffman 1997:775). This attitude "ignore[s] a literate lay audience that consistently has manifested an interest in the Civil War" (Gallagher 1996:42). Yet military aspects of the war (especially the experiences of the common soldier) continue to attract the public, and again the interest extends into studies of the Confederate Army. It would be wrong to state that this interest is totally ignored by universities. University presses today actively compete for and publish new works on the Civil War, especially diaries and war reminiscences. But when the Confederacy is discussed, it is usually about its military aspects. Also, as often as not, the authors of these works are outside academe. Regardless of source, these books are rapidly and avidly purchased by the public. It is virtually impossible to keep up with the literature as one peruses specialty book catalogs. Recent works on the *Hunley* or works including chapters on the *Hunley* are perfect examples of this trend (Campbell 1996; Kloeppel 1992; Ragan 1995; Schafer 1996).

It is within this context of divergent interests that the *Hunley*'s interpretation will be debated and its iconography will be established in the future, for the *Hunley* has been found at a unique period in South Carolina's history. It is widely known that South Carolina had the distinction of flying the Confederate battle flag over its state house. The public—stirred by media, politicians, and academics—is increasingly divided about its symbolism and meaning, some seeing it as a symbol of racism, others seeing it as a symbol honoring Confederate dead. The pro-flag forces, many of whom are active in Civil War reenactments, are decidedly in the minority and at a disadvantage on this ideological battlefield. Tagged with a flag whose former noble symbolism has been superseded by a history of Jim Crow and KKK hatred, the flag came down in July of 2000. In war, the battleground must be chosen to one's advantage, and this battleground was an undefendable position.

Upon this scene of tension and ideological conflict, comes the *Hunley*. The *Hunley* represents some of the few positive aspects of the Confederacy that can be proudly touted in a world dominated by a growing dogmatic, decidedly anti-Confederate, intelligentsia. The *Hunley* represents the underdog against a formidable foe. It represents Confederate innovation and invention. It represents youthful independent American ingenuity against the old established order of Northeastern industrialism. Indeed, it *is* a shining example of human bravery in the face of overwhelming odds. No matter what one's ideological stripe, one has to stand in awe of the courage it took to enter a tiny 3-feet-10-inch-by-4-feet iron tube—a tube that had already cost the lives of at least 13 people—and sail out on an open sea with little hope of return. The *Hunley* is an icon of the Confederacy that the battle flag can no longer be. Those defending the flag, the South, and the Confederacy need the *Hunley*. The *Hunley* Commission, made up mostly of Sons of Confederate Veterans, understands its importance. For this reason, they have repeatedly made it clear that they want total control over the interpretive displays for the *Hunley*. What they fear most is a Smithsonian revision of the Confederacy reminiscent of recent controversies surrounding the *Enola Gay* display (Harwit 1996; minutes, October 11, South Carolina *Hunley* Commission).

The *Hunley*'s iconography is much broader than Confederate innovation and bravery, and it includes just about all aspects of Confederate dialectic. Foremost is the issue of states' rights. During the year-long negotiations with the federal government, this issue was at the heart of negotiations over the question of *Hunley* ownership. At one point, a commission member stated in a semi-serious tone that South Carolina had once before gone to war over the issue and would do so again. Although the senator's statement was taken as the humorous *bon mot* that was intended, the senator was wrong. South Carolina twice has gone to "war" over the issue. The second time was in April 1961 during the commemoration of the Civil War centennial at Fort Sumter in Charleston, South Carolina. The U.S. Civil War Centennial Commission, established by Congress, arranged a ceremony at Fort Sumter. Among the "national assembly" was an African American representative from New Jersey who reported that she was denied a room at a Charleston hotel. State commissions from several Northern states said they would not take part in the ceremonies in protest of this treatment, and the president of the United States announced that the ceremonies would take place at the nonsegregated U.S. Naval Yard. On cue, the South Carolina Centennial Commission seceded from the national commission, and Charleston became the host of two centennial meetings (Pressly 1965:8). With regard to the *Hunley*, it is extremely doubtful that South Carolina would actually secede. It was clear from the negotiations, however, that the situation was serious, and both U.S. senators and at least one house representative worked behind the scenes to ensure that the state and the commission became full partners with the Naval Historical Center in shaping the *Hunley*'s future.

Beyond states' rights and Confederate symbols, the *Hunley* will continue to swirl in controversial waters. As this is being written, archaeologists working for the commission and the navy are diving on the 6.67-ton *Hunley* in preparation for its raising. By the time this chapter is read, the *Hunley* may be in its conservation tank, awash in a mixture of chemicals designed to preserve it forever. If so, the commission and the navy are to be congratulated. They would be the first to raise a whole Civil War vessel successfully, and their efforts would go a long way toward erasing the memory of the broken *Cairo*, a gunboat that collapssed during its raising from the Mississippi River (Bearss 1980). Another issue is the *Hunley*'s contents. It is possible that it contains not only valuable archaeological information but also human remains. The *Hunley* is a war grave. Reburial and repatriation concerns have not been at the forefront of the debate, but they are an undercurrent that could add to the tension surrounding the vessel's future.

Still another problem will be keeping public interest in the project while conservation drags on. The conservation process is estimated to take up to ten years. This brings us back to the control of the *Hunley*'s meaning. Can the commission keep its iconography alive long enough for its second raising—the one that will take it out of the conservation tank and into the display room? Will they be able to control its interpretation in a world increasingly hostile to all things Confederate? What is the future of Confederate history? Luraghi, in his exhaustive study of the Confederate Navy, concluded that "the Confederates showed an outstanding sagacity not only in creating new war tools but in using them in exceptional and creative ways so as to transform them from technical curiosities into tested elements that would change radically and forever the conduct of war at sea" (1996:346). This much can be said of the commission: it too has the sagacity displayed by the Confederate naval program and the tools to succeed in raising and conserving the vessel. But the ultimate question is how their *Hunley* will be remembered. Can a submarine become what a battle flag cannot—the icon of Southern heritage?

3

Fortifying the Landscape

An Archaeological Study of Military Engineering and the Atlanta Campaign

Robert J. Fryman

Throughout the Atlanta Campaign from May 7, 1864, to September 2, 1864, the construction of field fortifications had become an integral part of the military strategy employed by the armies of both the United States and Confederacy. These works ranged from temporary, hastily constructed rifle pits and entrenchments, such as those found at Pickett's Mill, to the more carefully planned and executed permanent fortifications and defensive lines surrounding the city of Atlanta.

Fortifications constitute a dominant feature found on the majority of archaeological sites associated with the Atlanta Campaign that have been subject to archaeological investigation. Defensive structures represent a component of the built environment reflecting the cultural contexts underlying their construction (Abrams 1989:47–87; Shackel 1994; Winter 1994). Analysis of the placement, construction, occupation, and armaments placed in the fortifications provides new insights into the cultural factors, such as perceptions of military engineering and tactics, by which these features were integrated into their surroundings. Interpretations drawn from the analysis of fortifications can also provide valuable insights into the military worldview of the engineers charged with their construction. Such insights serve to reflect both the engineer's prewar experience and his understanding of the military ordnance used by the opposing forces. This chapter will provide an archaeological perspective of the military engineering used to design and construct the fortifications surrounding the city of Atlanta and the insights provided by such perspectives on the military worldview of the Confederate engineers responsible for their design.

Antebellum Training in Military Engineering
and the Art of Fortification

Military engineering, with its emphasis on fortification design, dominated the curriculum at the U.S. Military Academy at West Point in antebellum America. Emphasis on engineering skills ensured that the graduates "had a solid grounding in mathematics and military engineering" (Griffith 1986; 1989:124). Under the direction of Maj. Sylvanus Thayer, the academy's curriculum was redesigned in 1817 following the course of study used by the École Polytechnique, the premier French military engineering school. The revised curriculum continued its emphasis on engineering, but the course of study was extended over a period of four years with the first three years devoted primarily to the study of mathematics and physics. Civil and military engineering, along with military theory and tactics, were extensively studied during the cadet's fourth year (Jones 1992:263–65).

One of the most influential instructors at West Point in the antebellum era was Dennis Hart Mahan, whose perceptions on military tactics and engineering influenced generations of graduates (Jones 1992:265–67). Mahan stressed the importance of topography as "among the most important modern addition to the military art, . . . the study of the natural features of position with a view to turn them to account in the first disposition for battle and its various succeeding phases" (Mahan 1861:63). Careful examination of the topography, particularly for the purposes of tactical defense, formed the core of Mahan's theories on military tactics and engineering. The influence of Mahan's views on West Point's graduates is illustrated by the topographic observations made in 1844 by William T. Sherman while on military duty in north and central Georgia. Riding on horseback from Rome, Georgia, to Atlanta and then to Augusta, Georgia, Sherman had the opportunity to study the topography of the area that he would cross in 1864. The nature of the terrain and its suitability for tactical defensive impressed Sherman, as shown in the following excerpt from his memoirs: "Thus by a mere accident I was enabled to traverse on horseback the very ground where in after-years I had to conduct vast armies and fight great battles. That the knowledge thus acquired was of infinite use to me, and consequently to the Government, I have always felt and stated" (Sherman 1885:32).

Another military tenet that Mahan stressed was that in order "to select a position understandingly, an officer must possess a thorough practical knowledge of the tactical combination of the different arms; their respective qualifications for the offensive and defensive; and of the adaptation of ground to their particular manoeuvres" (Mahan 1861:64). Knowledge of tactics and the different types of weaponry used by the infantry, cavalry, and artillery were integral to viewing the landscape from a military perspective. The curriculum at the U.S. Military Academy exposed cadets to all three branches of the army and, it was hoped, an understanding of how to combine them into a successful military campaign.

In the areas of military tactics and exposure to the weaponry used by the three branches of the army, West Point's engineering curriculum differed from that of other educational institutions. Comparison of the mathematics, physics, and civil engineering courses offered in the antebellum period by Western University, located in Pittsburgh, Pennsylvania (Alberts 1986:23–27), with those given at the U.S. Military Academy demonstrate no differences in content. As a result, the graduates of both West Point and the Western University were capable of viewing the landscape from the perspective of a civil engineer. However, only the West Point graduate received the indoctrination in tactics and armament that enabled him to perceive the topography as a potential weapon. In particular, the lack of training in combined arms and familiarity with improvements in the effective ranges of shoulder arms and artillery posed a potential problem for the civil engineers charged with the construction of fortifications during the war. Herman Hattaway has aptly noted that by 1861, "warfare, like everything else in [American] society [had] become more complex" (1998:3). In the 13 years following the Mexican War (1846–48), the United States' last major military conflict using conventional tactics prior to 1861, technological innovations in rifled shoulder arms, artillery, and munitions significantly increased the effective ranges of the tools of warfare. The development and adoption of the rifled musket drastically increased the lethal range of the common infantryman's shoulder arm such that bodies of opposing infantry could be hit at ranges greater than 300 yards (Coates and Thomas 1990; Edwards 1962; Thomas 1981; Todd 1978). Similarly, the development of the rifled cannon, such as the Parrott rifle and 3-inch ordnance rifle, vastly increased the effective range of the artillery, twice what it had been during the Mexican War (Dickey and George 1993; Ripley 1970; Time-Life 1987, 1998). Unfamiliarity with the potential effective range of the diverse types and calibers of artillery could affect the way in which a civil engineer would view the landscape for the purposes of constructing fortifications. This would appear to be one factor that influenced the placement of Atlanta's fortifications.

Military Engineering during the Atlanta Campaign

By the time of the Civil War, numerous books had been written on the siting and construction of earthworks, of which Mahan's *A Treatise on Field Fortifications* (1860) was the most widely referenced text on the types and construction methods used by military engineers in both the U.S. and Confederate armies. Mahan (1860:11–12) lists eight basic configurations which could be combined to construct a variety of different entrenchment plans (fig. 3.1). These basic forms are: (1) the Right Line, (2)

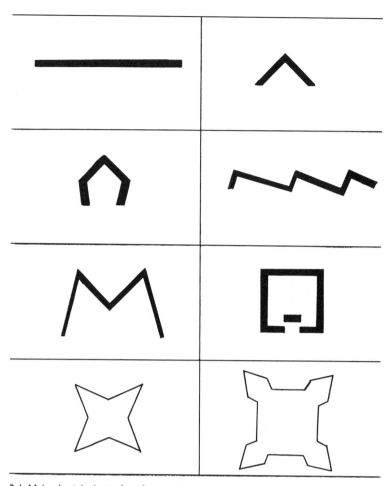

3.1. Mahan's eight basic fortification designs.

the Redan, (3) the Lunette, (4) the Indented Line (or Crémaillière), (5) the "Priest-Cap," (6) the Redoubt, (7) the Star Fort, and (8) the Bastion Fort. Definitions and examples of these basic fortification types were presented in Henry Scott's *Military Dictionary* (1861, reprint 1984), which was also widely available to the volunteer personnel in the U.S. Army during the war.

By 1864, fortifications had become a constant feature of the daily military routine in both the U.S. and Confederate armies. Construction of fortifications was not a new concept to the military; however, in the antebellum era their use had been confined largely to the preparation of coastal defenses. The high casualty rates experienced in the first year of the war brought about the erection of field fortifications under a wider array of military situations, ranging from the preparation of massive entrenchments to defend vital military installations and population centers to rifle pits and entrenchments constructed at the end of a day's march. Henry Dwight (1982:939–43) presents one of the most informative descriptions of the techniques employed by Federal troops to erect a line of infantry entrenchments. According to Dwight, a strong line could be constructed within a matter of five minutes which could easily be strengthened. The widespread use of fieldworks led Gen. William T. Sherman to remark that "these field intrenchments are peculiar to America, though I am convinced they were employed by the Romans in Gaul in the days of Caesar" (Sherman 1885:248).

Analysis of the fortification types constructed by the opposing armies during the Atlanta Campaign reveals a distinct cognitive pattern in the selection of fortification types constructed in the field as opposed to those built to defend the city of Atlanta. Archaeological investigations conducted at Pickett's Mill (Dickens and Worthy 1984), Gilgal Church (Braley 1987), Latimer's Farm (Wood and Wood 1990), Hardee's Salient (Fryman 1993c), and Johnston's Chattahoochee River Defense Line (Fryman 1993b) indicate a preference for use of the right line, redan, lunette, and redoubt in constructing field fortifications. All of these forms are easily adapted to the contingencies of active campaigning and could be built within a moderately short period of time.

The selective use of this limited number of fortification types throughout the opening of the Atlanta Campaign on May 5, 1864, to the investment of the city on July 20, 1864, by the Federal Army, was not dictated by the amount of time available for their construction. The preparations of defensive positions, such as Hardee's Salient, the Kennesaw Mountain Line, and the Chattahoochee River Defense Line, were all constructed in advance of their occupation by the Confederate Army of Tennessee but combine the limited number of fortification types into formidable defensive positions.

Accounts by participants in the battles for Atlanta attest to the strength of the Confederate fortifications throughout the campaign. Jacob Cox, commanding the 3rd Division of the Army of the Ohio (XXIII Corps), stated that the Confederates "had always confronted them with impregnable fortifications," and the works surrounding Atlanta were no exception (Cox 1895:148). Similar opinions were expressed by Capt. Orlando Poe, chief engineer of Sherman's Federal Armies. In his report of October 8, 1865, Poe described the Atlanta fortifications as follows:

> They completely encircled the city at a distance of about one and a half miles from the center and consisted of a system of batteries open to the rear and connected by infantry parapet, with complete abatis, in some places in three and four rows, with rows of pointed stakes, and long lines of chevaux-de-frise. In many places rows of palisading were planted along the foot of the exterior slope of the infantry parapet with sufficient opening between the timbers to permit the infantry fire. . . . The ground in front of these palisades or stockades was always completely swept by the fire from the adjacent batteries, which enabled a very small force to hold them. (Poe 1874:131–32)

Observations by Poe that Atlanta's defenses were designed so as to be held by a small force underscores a feature that appears to be characteristic of Confederate fortifications defending other Southern cities. Richard Sommers noted in his study on the 1864–65 Petersburg Campaign that the extensive fortifications ringing Richmond were never meant by the Confederates to be extensively garrisoned, "rather, they built unmanned works to meet every contingency and then counted on occupying them with mobile reserves, tactical or strategic, to meet specific threats. They were confident that the foe could no more attack the entire line simultaneously than they could defend it" (Sommers 1982:15). This observation is also applicable to the fortifications constructed to defend Vicksburg, Mississippi, in 1862 and 1863, where the resulting 12-mile line of entrenchments were manned by a force of approximately 21,000 men. It is therefore probable that while the effective manpower available to the Confederate Army of Tennessee in 1863 may have been a consideration in the design of Atlanta's fortifications, it most likely was not the determining factor in either the length of the defenses or its positioning relative to the city's core.

Poe also mentions in his report that after reconnoitering the Confederate defenses after the military engagement on July 22, 1864, General Sherman decided against any major assaults on Atlanta's fortification line, given the strength of its construction and positioning. Apart from the ill-fated Federal attack on the Confederate entrenchments situated on Kennesaw Mountain on June 27, 1864, the strategy adopted by General Sherman throughout the campaign was to attempt to force the Army of Tennessee out of its well-prepared fortifications by flanking movements. These tactics were largely influenced by the effective fortification of the landscape by the Confederate Corps of Engineers.

Although military engineering and fortifying the landscape were well developed by the Atlanta Campaign of 1864, there was a serious shortage of trained military engineers in both the U.S. and Confederate Corps of Engineers. At the outbreak of the war, the engineer troops of the United States consisted of a single company of men and officers. Because of the shortage of trained military engineers, the Federal government was forced to accept the services of civilian engineers and volunteer engineering companies (Lord 1950:81–84). A similar situation existed within the ranks of the Confederacy, which was faced with the equally daunting task of establishing a Corps of Engineers. Throughout the war, the Confederacy was forced to accept the services of civilian-trained engineers working under the command of the few Confederate military engineers and often entrusted with the responsibility for the fortification of major urban centers (Wynne and Taylor 1993). While lacking formal military training, the civilian engineers were able to adapt to Mahan's basic tenets. Construction of Atlanta's fortifications provides one such example. Incorporating indented lines, redans, and lunettes into the final design of the fortifications, the city's fortifications posed a formidable obstacle to the attacking Federal armies. However, the implicit assumptions engendered by the military/civilian worldview of the Confederate engineers, which influenced the positioning of Atlanta's defenses, compromised the safety of the city and the effectiveness of the fortifications.

Preparing Atlanta's Fortifications

The summer campaign of 1863 witnessed the further advance of Federal forces into central and eastern Tennessee. Gen. William S. Rosecrans, commanding the U.S. Army of the Cumberland, began to move on Chattanooga, while the Federal cavalry undertook a series of raids into northern Alabama and Georgia. These actions, combined with the surrender of the Confederate garrison at Vicksburg and the defeat of the Army of Northern Virginia at Gettysburg, prompted Confederate authorities to begin preparations for the construction of fortifications around key manufacturing and transportation points in Georgia and Alabama. Erection of the earthen redoubt, later christened Fort Tyler, in West Point, Georgia, was undertaken as a direct result of the Federal occupation of central Tennessee and northern Alabama in early 1863 (Fryman 1993a).

In July of 1863, Capt. Lemuel P. Grant, of the Confederate Corps of Engineers, was assigned the task of designing and constructing a series of fortifications around the city of Atlanta and its vital manufacturing and rail facilities. By July 22, 1863, Grant and Col. M. H. Wright had begun the survey and mapping of the area west of the city, including the various crossings of the Chattahoochee River, preparatory to developing a plan of fortification (Garrett 1954:567; Singer 1973:208).

Grant's biography indicates that he had no military training or experience prior to his being commissioned as a captain of engineers in the Confederate Army on November 1, 1862. Originally trained as a civil engineer, Grant was instrumental in the construction of the Georgia Railroad and the Western and Atlantic Railroad (Grant 1863–64:n.p.). From 1845 to 1848 he served as the chief engineer and superintendent of the Montgomery and West Point Railroad, following which he accepted a position as the resident engineer for the Georgia Railroad. Grant's lack of military experience did not hinder his initial assignments within the Confederate Corps of Engineers, which were primarily concerned with the rebuilding of rail lines following their destruction by Federal raiding parties. However, his lack of familiarity with both the prevailing military views on the construction of fortifications and the nature of the artillery used in both armies would have consequences in the defense of Atlanta in July 1864. As a result, the fortifications constructed to defend Atlanta reflected a civilian's perspective of the military landscape.

Grant's lack of previous military engineering experience most likely underscored the advice given to him by Col. J. F. Gilmer, chief of the Confederate Engineer Bureau. In his August 11, 1863, orders to Grant, Gilmer specifically stated that "the order of work on the general defenses for Atlanta should be to occupy the favorable points in the circuit around the place (far enough from the town to prevent the enemy coming within bombarding distance) by suitable detached works, closed towards the town with stockades. The intermediate spaces to be filled up afterward by rifle-pits or lines of infantry cover. The works to be earthworks, with such obstructions as abatis, pits, felled timber, etc." (Gilmer 1890b:489).

Grant's design for Atlanta's defenses lacks the sophistication so noticeable in the fortifications surrounding Vicksburg and Richmond. Both of the latter skillfully blend redoubts, redans, lunettes, and indented lines into their designs, providing for overlapping fields of fire. This in turn enabled the various parts of the fortification line to support another in the event of an enemy assault. The lethalness of Vicksburg's fortification lines is particularly witnessed by the May 22, 1863, repulse of the Federal columns during the assault on the stockade redan. Richmond's defenses possessed an even greater degree of sophistication in the design and placement of the earthworks. Protected by essentially three lines of earthworks, Richmond's fortifications possessed overlapping fields of fire, while their placement would have prevented the Federal army from using common field artillery to bombard the city.

Grant was well aware of the task facing him, as indicated in his August 4, 1863, report to Colonel Gilmer in which he stated that "the fortification of the city would be a problem second only to the fortification of Richmond" (Grant 1863–64: n.p.; Garrett 1954:567). In the same report, he submitted his preliminary design for Atlanta's defenses, which called for the construction of 12 to 15 enclosed works (that is, redans, lunettes, and/or redoubts) (fig. 3.2) on prominent landforms surrounding Atlanta at a distance of approximately 1.25 miles from the center of the city. The enclosed works would be connected by rifle pits and entrenchments.

While the Confederate Engineer Bureau approved Grant's initial plan, Colonel Gilmer wrote to Col. M. H. Wright, commander of the Atlanta Arsenal and the city garrison, on October 21, 1863, providing him with explicit instructions for the preparation of the areas in front of the earthworks. In his dispatch, Gilmer stated that "in order to make the works constructed for the defense of Atlanta effective, the timber must be cut down in front of the lines for a distance of, say, 900 to 1,000 cubic yards and the cutting should be continuous. The true rule should be to clear away as far as our own guns can command the ground well and no farther, as the ranges of the enemy's artillery are generally greater than ours (1890a:575).

By October 30, 1863, Grant reported to the Confederate Engineer Bureau that Atlanta's fortifications were nearly completed (Grant 1863–64:

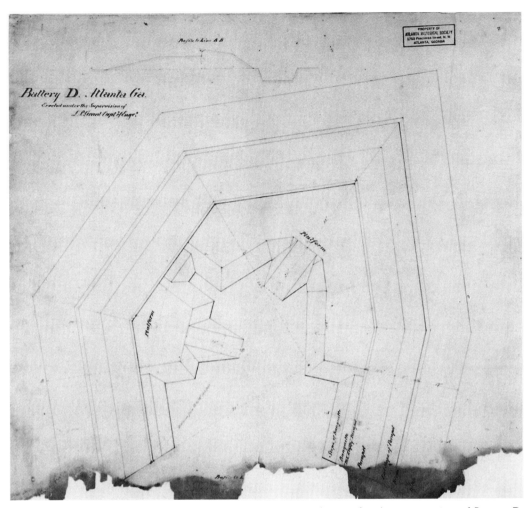

3.2. Grant's plan view and cross-section diagram for the construction of Battery D, located in the western perimeter of Atlanta's defenses (with permission of the Atlanta History Center).

n.p.; Garrett 1954:368). Colonel Gilmer inspected the works on December 1, 1863, approving of the earthworks and their plan. Completion of the fortifications occurred by April 12, 1864, when Grant submitted his report and final drawings of the artillery positions (Grant 1863–64: n.p.; Time-Life 1996b:27). In his report, Grant stated that "the length of the line . . . is 10 2080/5280 miles. To fully man this line will require Fifty five thousand (55,000) Troops" (Time-Life 1996b:27).

Archaeological Analysis and Interpretation of Atlanta's Defenses

As previously noted, defensive structures represent a component of the built environment, and their examination can provide insights into the cognitive structures and cultural contexts underlying their construction. In 1997, a study was initiated by the author to investigate the relationship between prevailing doctrines of defense and offensive held by the Confederate engineering officers and the armament used by the Confederate Army of Tennessee. This is the first report of findings from that research. The purpose of this study was to determine the influence, if any, that perceptions of the military landscape and the armament in use by the army had on the means by which fortifications surrounding Atlanta were positioned and constructed. During the course of the study, a combined archaeological and geographical analysis of the defenses constructed around Atlanta was conducted. Of the two data sets examined, the information on the geographical positioning of Atlanta's fortifications proved to be more complete than the existing archaeological data.

Compilation of the geographical data was facilitated by the large collection of Lemuel Grant's original drawings and specifications for Atlanta's fortifications that is maintained by the Atlanta Historical Society. Among the various engineering drawings in the Grant collection is the original drafting illustrating the final appearance of the defensive perimeter as developed by Grant (fig. 3.3). This drawing served as one of the base maps for the campaign maps, produced by the U.S. Army Corps of Engineers after the capture of the city in 1864, providing the locations of both the Federal and Confederate entrenchments (see Elkins and Lamont 1874; Ruger 1983). Equally important, the Grant map illustrates Atlanta's 1864 street pattern. Comparison of the 1864 street pattern with that shown on aerial photographs and U.S.G.S. quadrangles since 1950 clearly demonstrated very little deviation in the street pattern and railroad beds in the intervening 96 years. A series of 15 similar geographical points, consisting primarily of street intersections, appearing on both the 1864 map and the 1993 U.S.G.S. 7.5-minute series quadrangles for Atlanta were identified. Each of these points was field visited and their exact geographical position determined through hand-held GPS units. As a result, it was possible to superimpose Grant's 1864 drawing on a variety of aerial photographs and maps with a high degree of accuracy. In turn, it was now possible to more accurately examine the relationship of the fortifications to topographic features and landforms that no longer exist, given the rapid growth and expansion of Atlanta since 1960. The resulting drawings also facilitated comparison of distances between the center of the city and the Confederate and Federal entrenchments.

Compilation of the archaeological data on Atlanta's fortifications proved far more difficult. While remnants of Atlanta's Civil War fortifications were highly visible into the 20th century, the ensuing urban growth of Atlanta in the post–World War II era steadily obliterated many of the fieldworks. Prior to this study, all of the archaeological inquiries on Civil War sites within Atlanta were undertaken as part of cultural resource management (CRM) projects. Of these CRM projects, the most notable was the investigation conducted by Roy Dickens and Timothy Crimmins

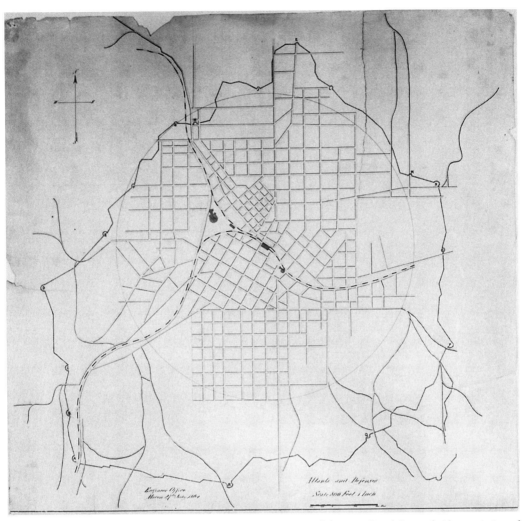

3.3. Capt. Lemuel Grant's final map showing Atlanta and its defenses (with permission of the Atlanta History Center).

(1982:105–13) on the site of the July 22, 1864, battlefield as part of the MARTA commuter rail line survey. Although Dickens and Crimmins did not identify any remnants of fortifications, their study did demonstrate the presence of archaeological deposits reflecting the military activities within the area.

The only surviving remnant of Grant's fortification line surrounding Atlanta is represented by Fort Walker, located at the southeast corner of the city's Grant Park. Originally constructed as an outlying separate four-gun redan, the position was later incorporated by Grant into the main defensive line. Apart from the placement of flagging stone on the ramparts, as a 1930s Works Progress Administration project, to protect against erosion, Fort Walker retains much of its integrity.

Examination of Grant's drawings of the Atlanta fortifications, along with the photographic record made of the city and its defenses by George N. Barnard (Barnard 1864), a photographer accompanying Sherman's armies during the Atlanta campaign, provides insights into the construction and placement of these features. The insights have implications for future archaeological investigations of the subsurface remnants of Atlanta's fortifications. Grant's drawings provide detailed measurements of both the infantry entrenchments and the more substantial enclosed works (fig. 3.3). According to his drawings, the infantry entrenchments, which consisted of the right-angle lines and indented lines, were constructed with a parapet approximately 10 feet in width, rising to a height of approximately 3 feet above the ground surface. The trench immediately behind the parapet is shown as measuring 8 feet in width by 4 feet in depth with a firing step cut into the parapet. Examination of the Barnard photographs, taken shortly after the capture of Atlanta, suggests that the dimensions recorded on Grant's construction drawing were strictly followed.

Comparison of Grant's specifications with the dimensions on the infantry entrenchments from archaeological investigations of Johnston's Lost Mountain Line, Gilgal Church, and the Chattahoochee River Line demonstrates similarity with the morphology of the Atlanta entrenchments. The archaeological data recovered from the Lost Mountain Line and the surviving remnants of the parapets at the Chattahoochee River Line indicate that the parapets would have been approximately 9 to 10 feet in width, rising approximately 3 feet from the original ground surface (Fryman 1993b:48), which is similar to Grant's designs. Measurements taken on the trench width at both sites again are comparable with the Atlanta drawings, allowing for erosion, measuring 6.26 feet and 6.5 feet, respectively (Fryman 1993b:48–49).

Measurements taken on the dimensions of Fort Walker's parapet were compared with the specifications given in Scott's *Military Dictionary* (1861, reprint 1984) and Laidley's *Ordnance Manual for the Use of the Officers of the United States Army* (1861). This comparison demonstrated a number of similarities between the recommended physical characteristics of a "typical" field fortification and those of Fort Walker, whose parapet width would have been sufficient to withstand the impact of 12-pounder artillery pieces and common musketry or rifle fire.

This same comparison aids in delineating other behavioral perceptions that influenced the placement of the Atlanta defenses, namely the distance at which they were built in relationship to the heart of the city. Larry J. Daniel's (1991:49–50) study of the Confederate Army of Tennessee demonstrates a preference for smoothbore artillery, primarily the bronze Model 1857 12-pounder Napoleon field gun (Confederate States Ordnance Bureau 1862–64). The maximum ranges for this gun firing solid shot and shell are 1,680 yards (0.95 miles) and 1,300 yards (0.74 miles), respectively (Laidley 1861:385; Ripley 1970:366; Scott 1984:66). The construction of Atlanta's defensive perimeter at an average distance of 1.25 miles would have provided more than adequate protection for the city's buildings and infrastructure had the opposing Federal forces been armed with identical field artillery.

Artillery returns for General Sherman's combined forces of the Armies of the Cumberland, Tennessee, and Ohio during the Atlanta Campaign reveal an overwhelming predominance of rifled artillery, firing a total of 90,135 projectiles of various types throughout the campaign. Sherman's rifled artillery consisted primarily of the 3-inch ordnance rifle, 10-pounder and 20-pounder Parrott rifles, and eight 4.5-inch rifled siege guns (Barry 1874:119–23). The maximum ranges for these guns firing shell were 3,972 yards (2.25 miles), 5,000 yards (2.84 miles), 4,400 yards (2.5 miles), and 3,265 yards (1.86 miles), respectively (Ripley 1970:370–74). Given the maximum ranges of the Federal artillery, Sherman was able to effectively bombard Atlanta with common field guns from distances beyond the Confederate defensive lines, both avoiding the threat posed by the fortifications to a direct assault and reducing its psychological comfort to both the citizens of Atlanta and the soldiers manning the works.

Summary and Conclusions

The archaeological examination of the defensive structures erected during the Atlanta Campaign of 1864 has provided insights into the contexts influencing the placement and construction of these components of the built environment. Far from being static monuments on the battlefields, the fortifications are reflections of the dynamic processes underlying their design and construction. Analysis of the geographical placement and construction of the hastily built fieldworks and the more carefully designed and executed fortifications around the city proper has allowed for new perspectives to be developed regarding the antebellum training and experience of the engineers that influenced and guided their construction. Further analysis of these under-exploited architectural features by anthropological archaeologists will enhance our understanding of them and the means by which they were integrated into their physical and cultural environments.

4

An Irishman Dies at Antietam

An Archaeology of the Individual

Stephen R. Potter and Douglas W. Owsley

One hundred and twenty-six years after the Battle of Antietam, three Civil War collectors looking for artifacts on private land near the Maryland battlefield discovered several unmarked human burials. Subsequent excavation by the National Park Service and the Smithsonian Institution revealed the partially disinterred graves of four Union soldiers, each represented by less than a dozen bone fragments. Yet these sparse remains, along with their artifacts and their location on the battlefield, provided enough clues to associate the men with a specific unit—the Irish Brigade. Through a combination of forensics, military history, and research into documentary archives, it was possible to place one soldier in his probable regiment and even to suggest his name. This archaeology of the individual can bring a human face out of the grids and charts that are an essential part of scientific research.

The History

About 5:30 A.M. on September 17, 1862, between the town of Sharpsburg, Maryland, and Antietam Creek, Maj. Gen. George B. McClellan's Army of the Potomac attacked Gen. Robert E. Lee's Army of Northern Virginia. After four hours of fierce fighting on Lee's left, the battle drifted to his center, where Brig. Gen. William French's Division attacked Southerners occupying a defensive position in a sunken road. When French's attack stalled, Maj. Gen. Israel Richardson's Division—composed of three brigades led by Brig. Gens. Thomas Francis Meagher and John C. Caldwell and Col. John R. Brooke—was sent in to carry the enemy position. "Relying on the impetuosity and recklessness of Irish soldiers in a charge" (U.S. War Department 1880–1905:19(1):294), Richardson chose Meagher's Irish Brigade to spearhead the attack against the right of the Confederate center (Sears 1983:235–42; Murfin 1965:245–56).

Moving at the double quick, the Irish Brigade filed into a swale northeast of William Roulette's house, where they halted to remove excess gear. Then they formed in line of battle, two ranks deep, stretched out over a quarter-mile front, along the edge of a cornfield. On the brigade's right flank was the 69th New York Regiment, followed by the 29th Massachusetts, then the 63rd New York, and finally the 88th New York on the brigade's left flank (fig. 4.1). The three New York regiments consisted of Irish Catholics recruited by Meagher from New York City. The 29th Massachusetts Regiment was composed of Protestants. They had been added to Meagher's Brigade that spring during the Peninsula Campaign in Virginia as substitutes when the 28th Massachusetts was ordered to the South Carolina coast (Sears 1983:242–43).

Once deployed, Meagher ordered the brigade forward through the tall corn. At the opposite side of the field, members of the brigade took down a worm fence that separated the cornfield from a recently harvested hayfield dotted with large haystacks. About 50 yards into the hayfield, Meagher halted the brigade and ordered the men to dress their lines. Then he called for volunteers to take down the next worm fence separating the hayfield from two large open fields—one in grass and the other plowed—that dipped and rolled toward a rise paralleling the Sunken Road. Confederate skirmishers on top of the rise shot about half the volunteers before the fence was down (O'Neill 1997:15–17).

While Meagher and his staff sat on their horses waiting for the second worm fence to be dismantled, the brigade's two chaplains, Catholic priests Father William Corby and Father Thomas Ouellet, rode across the brigade's front shouting conditional absolution to those who were about to die. Afterward, the chaplains dismounted and followed in the rear of the Irish Brigade's attack, administering the Last Rites to the dead and dying (Priest 1989:160). Meantime, the senior brigade surgeon, Doctor Laurence Reynolds, picked one of the large haystacks in the hayfield as the site for his hospital (O'Neill 1997:18).

Meagher stayed on the brigade's right flank with the 69th New York as they marched over some troops from French's Division lying in reserve behind the brow of a hill (Carman 1997:53). Opposite the brigade's left flank, Confederate reinforcements from Brig. Gen. William S. Featherston's Mississippi Brigade, led by Col. Carnot Posey, came out of the Sunken Road and attacked the flank of the 63rd New York, delivering "a volley which collapsed the whole left wing of the 63rd in a heap" (Bilby 1998:55). In advancing, Posey's men exposed their own flank to the approaching 88th New York Regiment, which they apparently did not see until it was too late. Fire from the 88th New York was so heavy that one of Posey's units, the 16th Mississippi, "disappeared as if it had gone into the earth" (Carman 1997:56). The routed Confederates retreated back to the dubious safety of the Sunken Road.

With the 88th New York back in line with the other regiments, the Irish

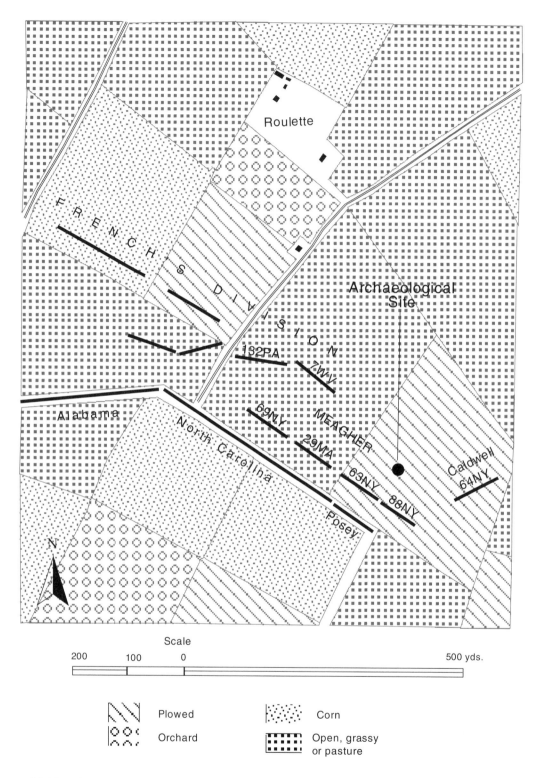

Roulette

Archaeological
Site

FRENCH'S DIVISION

132PA

7W'Y'

69MY

29MA

MEAGHER

63N.Y. 88N.Y

Caldwell
64N.Y.

Alabama

North Carolina

Posey

N

Scale

200   100   0   500 yds.

Plowed   Corn

Orchard   Open, grassy
                  or pasture

4.1. Map of Irish Brigade's attack at the Battle of Antietam, September 17, 1862, with location of the archaeological site inserted (courtesy of the National Park Service, National Capital Region).

Brigade surged up the remaining yards to the crest above the Sunken Road. Below them in the deeply worn lane, Brig. Gen. George B. Anderson's Brigade of North Carolinians waited, reinforced by Brig. Gen. Ambrose "Rans" Wright's Brigade and the survivors of Posey's command. When Meagher's men reached the crest, the Confederates rose up and delivered a devastating volley into their front rank, sending every regimental color bearer to the ground (Priest 1989:157–60).

The intense Confederate fire hit scores of men from the Irish Brigade, and the attack fell apart. The brigade's remnants went to ground and established a firing line on the forward slope of the crest. From this close position, between 30 and 50 yards, the New York regiments' .69-caliber buck-and-ball rounds—the equivalent of a combat shotgun—had a disastrous effect on Southern troops crowded in the Sunken Road (Priest 1989:160–62; O'Neill 1997:22–23). As one Union soldier later wrote, "we were shooting them like sheep in a pen" (Time-Life 1996a:114).

The 29th Massachusetts, armed with .577-caliber British Enfield rifle muskets, went to ground in a hollow in the rise between the 69th and 63rd New York Regiments. From this sheltered position they were able to hit Confederate reserves waiting in the Piper cornfield south of the Sunken Road (Goble 1997:64; Carman 1997:55; O'Neill 1997:23).

About 11:30 A.M., their cartridges almost spent, the Irish Brigade was finally relieved by Caldwell's troops and ordered to the rear to replenish their ammunition. The 63rd and 69th New York Regiments had suffered 60 percent casualties. Most of these losses were incurred in just a few minutes of combat on the crest above the Sunken Road. All told, 540 men of the Irish Brigade were dead, wounded, or missing (Priest 1989:180–82, 335; Sears 1983:243).

The Discovery

In March 1988, three Civil War collectors were searching for relics on what was then the privately owned, historic Roulette farm, adjacent to lands owned in fee by the National Park Service. During their search, they found what they initially assumed were only the contents of a disintegrated Civil War knapsack—until they unearthed some bone fragments and other artifacts. Excited by the potential significance of their discovery, the men notified the landowner and, later, the National Park Service. More than the location of a discarded knapsack, they had discovered the site of four battlefield burials. Because the graves were in a cultivated field, the property owner wanted the area systematically investigated for any other human remains. With the additional permission of the Maryland States' Attorney for Washington County, Maryland, an excavation team of National Park Service archaeologists, physical anthropologists from the Smithsonian Institution, and volunteers spent ten days at the site in

August 1988. (Through a generous donation by The Conservation Fund, the National Park Service assumed title to the historic Roulette farm on September 1, 1998.)

The Archaeology

The burial site lies in an agricultural field north of the Sunken Road or Bloody Lane (fig. 4.2), at the eastern base of an embankment created by a ridge of limestone jutting from the field. The Union burial detail may have chosen this area so that the graves would be located off to the side of the then-cultivated area, thereby increasing the chance that the remains might be left undisturbed until they could be properly buried elsewhere.

Two late 19th-century, permanent structures at Bloody Lane—the stone observation tower and the Maj. Gen. Israel Richardson mortuary cannon—provided fixed reference points for the archaeological fieldwork. From these points, a transit traverse carried the horizontal controls across the open field to the burials. At the site, a baseline was established along the east edge of a limestone outcropping, just west of the graves. This line became the grid's north-south baseline and was designated the E500 line. Individual excavation units were designated by reference to the southwest corner of grid coordinates. An absolute elevation of 480 feet was assigned using the closest contour line shown on the U.S. Geological Survey Keedysville quadrangle.

The area excavated was 15 feet, at its widest, by 40 feet long, most of which was dug to the heavily mottled clay subsoil of decayed bedrock (fig. 4.2). Excavation units were usually 5 by 5 feet, although several 3-by-5-feet units and one 10-by-10-feet unit were excavated. All soil was screened through 1/4-inch hardware mesh. Artifacts were bagged according to excavation unit and were assigned individual field specimen numbers. Site stratigraphy consisted of a plow zone, 0.7–0.8 feet deep, covering the eastern two-thirds of the excavation area. A layer of unplowed sheet wash or colluvium was observed at various depths as it sloped from west to east. Along the E500 baseline, or west edge of the site, the colluvium averaged about one foot deep. The depth of this deposit helped preserve the remnants of the partially disinterred burials, particularly in the west half of the site. It also protected some evidence of the digging done by the Civil War collectors, even though a tenant farmer cultivated the site twice between March and August 1988.

Soil stratigraphy was important to reconstructing the burial site. Although the collectors who first discovered the site disturbed most traces of the 1862 excavations and the later disinterment of the graves, enough signs remained of their March activities to be correlated with the teams' excavations. To their credit, the collectors' field notes and artifact inventory provided critical links necessary for a detailed site reconstruction.

The archaeological and forensic investigations revealed the partial remains of four individuals, likely buried in separate graves (see fig. 4.2). These were hastily dug, shallow pits, originally no deeper than 1.6 feet. Graves 1, 3, and 4 were spaced about 2.5–3.5 feet apart. Steven Stotelmyer (1992:4) described the manner in which these graves were probably prepared: "Once the bodies were collected at the grave site, a shallow hole was dug, usually 18 to 24 inches deep, and the body rolled in and another hole dug beside it. The second hole provided the dirt to fill the first, and this procedure was repeated as needed."

Oddly enough, Grave 2 was separated from the cluster of Graves 1, 3, and 4 by more than 13 feet (fig. 4.2). This disparity may indicate that other, shallower graves had once been located between Graves 1 and 2. Given the variation in the depth of the colluvium over the site, subsequent plowing could have obliterated evidence of some disinterred graves while leaving remnants of others.

It is probable that just after the war, in 1866 or 1867, these four soldiers were dug up by civilian laborers contracted by the federal government to exhume Union dead for reburial in the nearby national cemetery. Presumably, their collected skeletal remains were reinterred, probably as four of the 1,792 unknown Union dead buried in the cemetery (Stotelmyer 1992:21, 25). Considering the disagreeable nature and large scale of the task that confronted the civilian burial corps, it should not be surprising that some skeletal elements were missed.

The men in Graves 2, 3, and 4 were buried with their heads to the west, as indicated by the distribution of skeletal elements and associated artifacts. This placement suggests that they were given a Christian burial, facing east toward the Second Coming (Matthew 24:27, King James Bible, AV). The man in Grave 1 was probably buried in a similar manner, but there was not enough evidence to be certain.

Various buttons were found with the soldiers (table 4.1), including large brass coat buttons embossed with a plain-shield eagle, and small brass cuff buttons embossed with the New York State seal or a plain-shield eagle (Crouch 1995:178–79). Although called cuff buttons, they were used on vests and to secure shoulder straps and attach leather chin straps to the band of forage caps, or kepis, as well as to fasten cuffs. The New York State cuff buttons and the number of eagle coat buttons found in the graves indicated they were probably worn on New York soldiers' State Pattern fatigue jackets (Time-Life 1998:125). Other buttons from the graves included ones made from tinned-metal or white porcelain. Most of the tinned-metal four-hole buttons were probably worn on Federal-issue trousers, while the porcelain four-hole buttons were worn on shirts (Time-Life 1998:126–27).

The soldier in the first grave was buried with his knapsack as indicated by a knapsack hook and four small and one large iron roller buckles (table

Table 4.1. Artifact inventory by grave

Quantity	Description
Grave 1	
79	.30 cal. buckshot, unfired
20	.64/.65 cal. round balls, unfired
81	percussion caps, unfired
1	bullet worm
11	plain-shield eagle coat buttons
1	New York State cuff button
12	tinned-metal, 4-hole buttons
4	small iron roller buckles
1	large iron roller buckle
1	knapsack hook
1	Miraculous Medal
1	.58 cal. C.S.A. Gardner bullet, fired
Grave 2	
8	.30 cal. buckshot, unfired
4	.64/.65 cal. round balls, unfired
4	percussion caps, unfired
5	plain-shield eagle coat buttons
17	tinned-metal, 4-hole buttons
2	white porcelain, 4-hole buttons
2	brass suspender clasps w/ leather
1	.577 cal. Enfield bullet, fired
Grave 3	
9	.30 cal. buckshot, unfired
6	.64/.65 cal. round balls, unfired
1	percussion cap, unfired
8	plain shield eagle coat buttons
1	plain shield eagle cuff button
15	tinned-metal 4-hole buttons
1	white porcelain, 4-hole button
1	white metal button back
1	brass rivet
1	white clay tobacco pipe
1	leather parts to a right, square-toed, wooden-pegged shoe
1	Miraculous Medal nearby in plow zone
Grave 4	
11	30 cal. buckshot, unfired
3	.64/.65 cal. round balls, unfired
13	percussion caps, unfired
5	plain-shield eagle coat buttons
1	New York State cuff button
10	tinned-metal, 4-hole buttons
1	white porcelain, 4-hole button
1	small iron roller buckle
1	knapsack hook
1	brass, cap box finial
1	brass, bayonet scabbard tip
1	clasp knife
1	Miraculous Medal
1	crucifix with 5 wooden rosary beads
1	.58 cal. C.S.A. Gardner bullet, fired
2	.577 cal. Enfield bullets, fired

4.1). Apparently contained within the knapsack of Grave 1 were 20 of the soldier's .69-caliber buck-and-ball cartridges, each made up of a .64- or .65-caliber round ball and three .30-caliber buckshot. Also found in Grave 1 was a bullet worm used for extracting soft-lead bullets from the bore of the musket.

Only one of the man's personal belongings was left in the grave—his Roman Catholic Miraculous Medal. Also found among his remains was a fired, .58-caliber Gardner-patent bullet made at the Richmond Laboratory in Richmond, Virginia (Thomas and Thomas 1996:44–45). Quite possibly this is the slug that killed him.

The soldier in the second grave had several (at least four) unfired rounds of buck-and-ball ammunition, which he was probably carrying in a trouser pocket (table 4.1). His trousers were supported by a privately purchased pair of suspenders, judging by the fancy suspender clasps. One fired .577-caliber Enfield-pattern bullet found in the grave struck and, probably, killed him (Thomas and Thomas 1996:37–38). This conical-shaped, hollow-base bullet, along with the conical-shaped, hollow-base, .58-caliber Gardner bullet found in Grave 1, indicates that some Confederate soldiers opposing the Irish Brigade were armed with rifle muskets.

In addition to six or so unfired .69-caliber buck-and-ball cartridges, Grave 3 held three other interesting items (table 4.1). A heavily used, white clay tobacco pipe, marked "TK" on the base of the spur, was found in the area of the soldier's chest. Originally the pipe's stem would have been at least four inches long. Through use, breakage, and abrading, the stem was worn down to less than two inches (Russell 1996:30–31). It is evident from the carefully abraded bit end that the pipe was still serving faithfully as the soldier's "comfort" until his death. Also preserved in Grave 3 were leather remnants of the soldier's right shoe, along with four of his right foot bones. The shoe was a Federal-issue, pegged, square-toed brogan of the kind called mud scows and gunboats by Union soldiers (Time-Life 1998:191). A Miraculous Medal also was found in the plow zone near Grave 3 and may have been associated with it.

The soldier in the fourth grave is the most interesting because there is more to interpret. He had both a Miraculous Medal and a Rosary (fig. 4.3; table 4.1). The lower length of the Rosary, consisting of two larger Our Father beads and three smaller Hail Mary beads and a small brass crucifix, was discovered in the area of the upper torso and neck. Near the infantryman's right shoulder blade was a clasp knife, apparently once tucked in his breast pocket. A knapsack hook and a roller buckle indicate this soldier was carrying his knapsack as was his comrade in the first grave. A brass finial from a cap box and a brass bayonet scabbard tip suggest that he was wearing his waist belt when he was buried. Both the cap box and bayonet scabbard were hung from the waist belt, and it is unlikely that they would have been removed from the belt at the time of burial and placed separately into the grave (Time-Life 1998:198–99, 202).

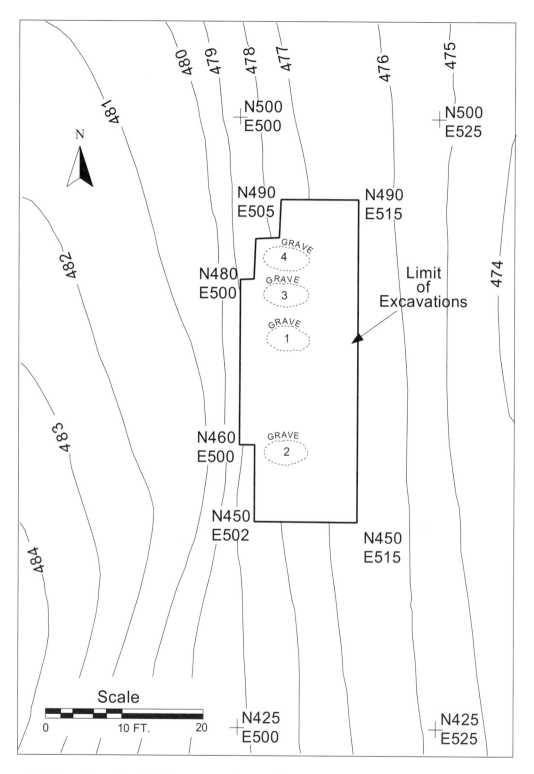

4.2. Map of the archaeological excavations, showing the positions of the graves (courtesy of the National Park Service, National Capital Region).

4.3. A miraculous medal, a brass crucifix, and three Hail Mary beads from Grave 4 (courtesy of the Smithsonian Institution).

Elsewhere in the fourth grave were three unfired .69-caliber buck-and-ball rounds. Most startling of all was the discovery of three fired bullets in the area of the soldier's chest (fig. 4.4). All of the soft-lead bullets—one .58-caliber Gardner and two .577-caliber Enfields (Thomas and Thomas 1996:37–38, 44–45)—struck bone, causing marked deformation in two of the slugs. It is very likely that these bullets caused the man's death.

4.4. An impacted .58 cal. Gardner bullet (*left*) and two impacted .577 cal. Enfield bullets (*right*) from Grave 4 (courtesy of the Smithsonian Institution).

The Forensics

By matching broken bones and the staining on some bones, it was possible to associate skeletal remains found by the collectors with those from the archaeological excavations. Even though the bones ranged from portions of the skull to the feet, very little was recovered from any individual (table 4.2). Out of 206 bones in an adult skeleton, only 8 to 11 bones were represented by the fragments found in each grave.

Burial 1 was especially fragmentary and incomplete. The only complete bone was from a finger on the left hand. The remaining fragments were bones from the right side of the skull, left hand, spine, ribs, left knee, left foot, and a left toe (table 4.2). A tooth, the second left premolar from the lower jaw (mandible), showed green staining from contact with either brass buttons or copper percussion caps found in the grave (see table 4.1). Green staining also was observed on one finger bone from the left hand (middle phalanx) and on the left foot bone (metatarsal). As limited as the skeletal elements were, they pointed to a small-featured adult. The best indicator of age was dental wear on the premolar which was consistent with someone between 25 and 40 years of age.

The individual in the second grave was represented by bone fragments from the left shoulder, right arm, a right rib, lower spine, both hips, the lower legs, and a right toe (table 4.2). Examination of the nearly complete right humerus (the upper arm bone), the sciatic notches of the innominates (part of the hip bones), and other skeletal elements indicated this soldier was a 20- to 30-year-old male with a small-to-medium build.

Burial 3 was also fragmentary and very incomplete (table 4.2). Along with a tooth, parts of bones were recovered from the right side of the skull, upper spine, right hand and finger, a left finger, one right rib, left knee, and right foot. All skeletal elements showed pronounced postmortem erosion, suggesting that the skeleton, or portions of it, may have been exposed after burial. This individual was probably 20 to 29 years old at death, based on very compact inner (cancellous) tissue in the medullary cavity of the right rib and the left knee cap (patella), as well as the absence of enamel loss on the upper left incisor.

The person in the fourth grave was represented by one left lateral incisor from the upper jaw (maxilla) and fragments of bones from the right shoulder, left lower arm, spine, right and left ribs, and right thigh and knee (table 4.2). Unlike the other three soldiers, this man was older than most of his comrades. The arthritic changes visible in his right shoulder blade, or scapula, suggested changes associated with age rather than acute trauma (fig. 4.5). Analysis of the scapula, femur, patella, and incisor pointed to someone more than 40 years old at death.

Table 4.2. Skeletal elements by burial

Sex	Age	Skeletal elements	Comments
Burial 1			
M	25–40	right temporal	small individual
		1 left mandibular tooth (P_2)	copper/brass stained; slight wear
		left hand proximal phalanx	
		1 left hand middle phalanx	
		1 thoracic vertebra (neural arch)	
		3 ribs[a]	
		left patella	
		1 left metatarsal	
		1 left foot middle phalanx	
Burial 2			
M	25–29	left clavicle	small- to medium-sized individual
		right humerus	
		right proximal radius	
		right proximal ulna	
		1 right rib	
		1 lumbar vertebra[a]	
		left and right innominates[a]	
		2 tibia	
		1 right foot proximal phalanx	
Burial 3			
M	25–29	right mastoid process (temporal)	
		1 cervical vertebra (atlas)	
		1 right first metacarpal	
		left and right hand phalanges	
		1 right rib[a]	
		left patella	
		right foot bones	
Burial 4			
M	40–49	1 left maxillary tooth (I^1)	moderate dental wear
		right scapula	arthritic changes (periarticular osteophyte development on the glenoid margin of the scapula)
		left proximal ulna	
		1 thoracic vertebra (neural arch)	
		1 right first rib	
		1 left rib[a]	
		right proximal femur	
		right patella	

a. fragment(s)

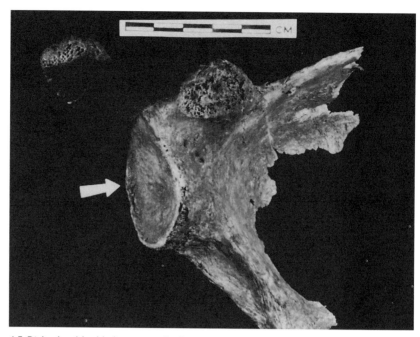

4.5. Right shoulder blade, or scapula, showing arthritic changes, from the soldier in Grave 4 (courtesy of the Smithsonian Institution).

Summary and Interpretations

The four shallow graves discovered on the Roulette farm contained the fragmentary and incomplete remains of infantrymen of the Irish Brigade killed attacking Confederate positions at the Battle of Antietam, Maryland. Sometime during 1866 or 1867, most of the four bodies were disinterred by day laborers for reburial in Antietam National Cemetery at Sharpsburg (Stotelmyer 1992:21). Four factors led to the conclusion that the soldiers in these graves were members of the Irish Brigade.

First, the burials were located along the axis of the Irish Brigade's attack (fig. 4.1). The 69th New York Regiment was on the brigade's right flank, near the Roulette farm lane, with the 29th Massachusetts to their left, then the 63rd New York, and finally the 88th New York on the brigade's left flank. The burials were found in the path of either the 63rd or 88th New York Regiments.

Second, two of the four burials had standard issue, U.S. eagle coat buttons and New York State cuff buttons. The presence of New York State cuff buttons with two burials eliminates the possibility that those two men were from the 29th Massachusetts Regiment.

Third, all four graves contained unfired .69-caliber buck-and-ball ammunition. This type of ammunition was used with the U.S. Model 1842 .69-caliber smoothbore muskets carried by the three New York regiments of the Irish Brigade (Goble 1997:61, 63). The 29th Massachusetts was armed with .577-caliber British-made Enfield rifle muskets, which eliminates all four men as soldiers in the Bay State regiment. The only Union units engaged on this part of the Antietam Battlefield *and* armed with .69-caliber smoothbore muskets were the three New York regiments of the Irish Brigade (Todd 1983).

And fourth, Roman Catholic religious artifacts, three Miraculous Medals and part of a Rosary, were found with the burials. The Rosary, consisting of two Our Father and three Hail Mary beads and a crucifix, was discovered in the area of the upper torso and neck of the soldier who was more than 40 when he died. These artifacts also eliminate Protestant soldiers of the 29th Massachusetts from further consideration.

It is interesting to note that the discovery in Graves 1 and 4 of metal parts from knapsacks contradicts the after-action report on the Battle of Antietam written by the Irish Brigade's commander, Brigadier General Meagher. In an often-quoted passage, Meagher wrote that before the attack, "Maj. Gen. Richardson ordered that everything but cartouch-boxes should be thrown off. The men of the Irish Brigade instantly obeyed this order with a hartiness [*sic*] and enthusiasm which it was rare to expect from men who had been wearied and worn by a [*sic*] unremitting 9 months' campaign" (U.S. War Department 1880–1905:19(1):293). It should not be surprising that some of the Irish Brigade disobeyed this order "since these packs were valuable to the soldier, and no one liked to consign them to the uncertain chances of war" (Griffith 1986:32).

An Individual's Archaeology

In September 1862, the Union Army was still all-volunteer, and most enlisted men were young, in their late teens and twenties. Since enlisted men in their forties were very much in the minority, it seemed possible to identify the 40-to-50-year-old in Grave 4. There was little doubt the middle-aged Irishman was an enlisted man. Plain-shield eagle coat buttons with no gold gilt and buck-and-ball ammunition for a .69-caliber smoothbore musket make it unlikely that he was an officer (normally, officers did not carry muskets or other shoulder arms).

In an effort to identify this enlisted man, compiled service records, medical records, and muster rolls and regimental papers in the National Archives, along with the State of New York registers of the 63rd and 88th Regiments of Infantry, were searched for all enlisted men who were more than 40 at the time of their deaths and who were killed in action at Antietam. This seemingly straightforward approach revealed some interesting quirks in the historical records.

Take for example the case of Pvt. Patrick Kinsella of Company F, 88th New York Infantry (New York State 1902a:85). The confusion started with multiple spellings of Patrick's last name. Over time, different copyists misspelled it until Kinsella became Kurler. A casualty sheet filled out on May 4, 1875, lists a Pvt. Patrick Kurler of Company F, 88th New York, as killed in action. This information was obtained from the original List of Casualties for the 88th New York Regiment, where the name Patrick Kensler appears as a private in Company F, "killed September 17, 62" (U.S. National Archives 1861–1917:Record Group 94). On the original casualty list, there is no mention of Kensler being killed in action.

The Company Muster Roll for June 30 to October 31, 1862, mentions a Pvt. Patrick Kinsella of Company F, 88th New York Infantry, "killed at the battle of Antietam, September 17, 1862" (U.S. National Archives 1861–1917:Record Group 94). The copyist first wrote "killed *in* the battle of Antietam" and then changed "in" to "at." The change in word choice made sense when a regimental hospital slip for the 88th New York Infantry was discovered for Pvt. Patrick Kensela of Company F. This slip indicates that he was seen by a surgeon at the regimental hospital where he died of "*Vulnus sclopeticum,*" a gunshot wound, on September 17, 1862 (U.S. National Archives 1861–1917:Record Group 94). In other words, Pvt. Patrick Kinsella (or Kensela) was not killed in action, so he can be eliminated from the list of possible candidates for the 40-something Irishman.

Patrick Kinsella's case pales beside the convoluted confusion surrounding three of the six John Gallaghers listed in the State of New York Register for the 63rd Regiment of Infantry. Quoting in full from the New York State register (1902b:61), the three John Gallaghers of interest are:

> Gallagher, John, 1st—Age, 21 years. Enlisted at New York city, to serve three years; and mustered in as private, Co. G, September 24, 1861; wounded in action, December 11 to 15, 1862, at Fredericksburg, Va.; deserted, no date; also borne as Galligar.
>
> Gallagher, John, 2d—Age—years. Enlisted at New York city, to serve three years, and mustered in as private, Co. G, March 10, 1862; lost about September 12, 1862, at Frederick City, Md.
>
> Gallagher, John—Age, 43 years. Enlisted, March 10, 1862, at New York city, to serve three years; mustered in as private, Co. C, April 13, 1862; killed in action, September 17, 1862, at Antietam, Md.

To begin, it is worth noting that the second and third John Gallaghers enlisted on the same day, the same place, and at the same rank; one in Company G and the other in Company C. The handwritten script "G" and "C" are easily confused on the original documents in the National Archives. Next, there is *no* individual service record for a 43-year-old John Gallagher in Company C of the 63rd New York. There is, however, a volunteer enlistment paper for a 43-year-old John Gallagher who enlisted in New York City on March 10, 1862, by making his "X" mark. This same John Gallagher of Company "G," not "C," 63rd New York Volunteers, made the following statement in front of witnesses on September 9, 1864 (U.S. National Archives 1861–1917:Record Group 94):

I enlisted March 10, 1862 at New York City. I left the regiment before the Battle of Antietam, Md about 15th Sept. [not 12th] 1862. I was not able to march I was so crippled by Rheumatism. Went to Frederick City Md where I worked on a farm while I was able. I was arrested in citizens clothes in Frederick City Md sometime in June 1864.

Sd John Gallagher, his "X" mark

Considering all the evidence presented above, it is quite probable that the New York State Register listings for the second and third John Gallaghers refer to the same man.

With that in mind, what about the first John Gallagher on the list, who was 21 years old when he supposedly enlisted in Company G? The 21-year-old John Gallagher was mustered in by Capt. John C. Lynch, who was the commander of Company C, not G, of the 63rd New York (U.S. National Archives 1861–1917:Record Group 94; not to be confused with a 2nd Lieut. George Lynch of Company G, see Carman 1997:54). This John Gallagher survived the Battle of Antietam, only to be seriously wounded in the hand at the Battle of Fredericksburg three months later. Thus, an 1870s medical card listing a Pvt. John Gallagher of Company C as "killed Sept. 17, 1862" is most likely a fiction—an agglomeration of bits and pieces of confusing information (like that discussed previously) gleaned from records for at least two different John Gallaghers (U.S. National Archives 1861–1917:Record Group 94). Combining the results of this analysis with the previous one, it is very probable that there was no 43-year-old John Gallagher of Company C, 63rd New York Regiment, killed on September 17, 1862, at Antietam.

Through detailed research such as that outlined above, it was possible to eliminate all but three men killed in action at Antietam and who were more than 40 at the time of their deaths. These soldiers, all Ireland born, were Pvt. James McGarrigan, 44, Company A, 63rd New York; Pvt. Martin McMahon, 49, Company I, 63rd New York; and Pvt. James Gallagher, 50, Company C, 63rd New York.

Considering the three Confederate bullets found in his chest region and the location of his grave on the battlefield, which is well behind the crest above the Sunken Road, it is likely that the 40-plus Irishman was killed during the attack against the 63rd New York Regiment by Posey's Mississippi Brigade. According to Stephan O'Neill (1997:19), "the Rebels attacked the left side of the regiment, firing a volley that decimated the Irish companies."

An infantry regiment was composed of ten companies, with each company led by a captain. A company's position in the regiment's line depended on the seniority of their captain. According to Casey's *Infantry Tactics,* the standard tactical manual used by Union troops, a regiment's order of battle, from right to left, was Company A, F, D, I, C, H, E, K, G, and B (to avoid confusion with the letter "I," there was no Company "J").

Company C, the fifth company from the right, was assigned as the color company, with the color party stationed to its left, in the center of a regiment's battle line (the color party consisted of two color sergeants, who carried the national and regimental flags, and ten corporals, one from each company, who served as the color guard). "This order could be changed when officer casualties revamped the seniority of the company commanders. Thus, any company could be rotated as the color company" (Sauers 1987:19; Paul Chiles, personal communication, August 30, 1999).

At Antietam, Company H was the 63rd New York's color company (O'Neill 1997:24). This departure from regulations means companies C and H would have switched positions. Assuming there were no other changes, the 63rd's order of battle was Company A, F, D, I, H, C, E, K, G, and B. If that was so, then Company C would have been on the 63rd New York's left, thereby increasing the chances that it suffered more casualties from the Mississippians' volley than the companies on the right. Of the three most probable candidates for the middle-aged Irishman, one was in Company A and another in Company I—both, ostensibly, on the 63rd New York's right flank. Only Pvt. James Gallagher, of Company C, was apparently on the left flank of the 63rd's formation. Perhaps, he was the unfortunate soldier who was hit by the three Confederate bullets.

Although it is not certain who the older enlisted man was, this research demonstrates that it is possible to construct an archaeology of the individual—even when there are, literally, only a handful of bones to analyze. Such an experience tends to personalize the past and to increase the public's interest in the study of the past. This interest was very apparent when hundreds of people came to pay their respects as the partial remains of the four Irish Brigade soldiers were reinterred in Antietam National Cemetery on September 17, 1989, 127 years after they died.

Acknowledgments

The authors would like to thank the following persons for their assistance during various phases of this research: Charles "Ted" Alexander, Edwin Bearss, David Bebenroth, Malcolm Brooker, Paul Chiles, Marian Creveling, Susannah Dean, Dennis Frye, Victor Krantz, Robert Mann, Robert McLernon, Howard Miller, Jr., Richard Rambur, John Ravenhorst, George Rees, Carter Shields, Robert Sonderman, Tammy Stidham, Susan Winter Trail, and Cari YoungRavenhorst.

5

The Battle of Cool Spring, July 16–20, 1864

Joseph W. A. Whitehorne and Clarence R. Geier

The Civil War Battle of Cool Spring, fought on July 18, 1864, was part of a sequence of events occurring between July 16 and 20. A total of 822 casualties (Meaney 1979:54) marked Cool Spring as the ninth bloodiest battle fought in the Shenandoah Valley yet the competing armies regarded the engagement as a minor skirmish. Despite this, the battle marked the end of Gen. Jubal Early's daring raid against Washington, D.C., in July 1864 (Cooling 1989), and the beginning of a transition in Lt. Gen. Ulysses S. Grant's perception of the strategic place held by the Shenandoah Valley to the conduct of the war. Early's Washington raid proved politically embarrassing, necessitating a realignment of the Union Armies in the east. Some of the hesitancy and interplay of Union field commanders at Cool Spring reflected a level of disarray resolved by the establishment, in August 1864, of the Middle Military Division with Maj. Gen. Philip Sheridan as its commander.

Previous studies of the five days that culminated in a battle at Cool Spring Plantation (fig. 5.1; Meaney 1979; Wert 1978) on July 18 have presented an analysis of the flow of the battle but provide little information on the historical, natural, cultural, and military contexts in which it took place. Even the official military accounts of the battle provide little insight into the complex character of the terrain over which the battle was fought and across which the opposing armies staged and postured for five days. In fact, the single map available for the battle (fig. 5.2) understates the natural and cultural context and, in the absence of a scale, dramatically downplays the size of the landscape involved. Further, historical simplifications of the Union command situation create a misleading portrayal of the tactical skills and capabilities of the overall Union commander, Maj. Gen. Horatio Wright.

In 1994, in an effort to more accurately assess the significance of the Battle of Cool Spring to the Civil War history of the Shenandoah Valley, the Clarke County Historical Association, with support from the National Park Service, initiated a historical-archaeological study of the engagement. In this study, field archaeologists walked the battlefield and military support areas searching for historic sites occupied at the time of the battle.

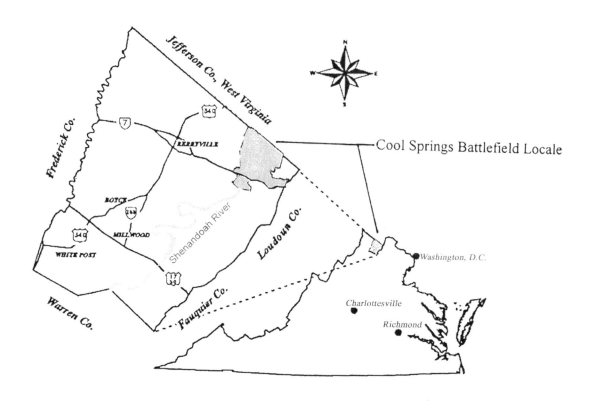

Cool Springs Battlefield Locale

Above: 5.1. Cool Spring battlefield locale, Clarke County, Virginia (courtesy of Clarke County, Virginia; prepared by Gordon Russell).

Right: 5.2. Jed Hotchkiss historical battlefield map of Cool Spring (Davis, Perry, and Kirkley 1978:pl. 84, map 20).

In addition, terrain and environmental features that might have influenced the flow of the battle and the dynamics of the larger five-day engagement were identified. Architectural historians visited standing structures dated to the period and gathered data of use in interpreting contemporary sites identified by field archaeologists. To cap the project, a comprehensive study was made of historic records dealing with the events prior to and during the engagement. As a result of this interdisciplinary study, new information was obtained on the structure and composition of the Confederate and Union armies that confronted each other and on the military events that influenced the confrontation of July 16 through 20, 1864. This information provided insight into the nature of Major General Wright's Union Army as it was thrown together in an almost desperate effort to drive Early's Confederates from the outskirts of Washington, D.C., and northern Virginia. In addition, the studies provided a previously undocumented delineation of the cultural landscape affected by the flow of the armies and an assessment of the strategic significance of the terrain over which the armies moved and fought (Geier, Whitehorne, and McCleary 1995). This chapter presents the findings of that study.

The Terrain

While the actual area of conflict took place on the agricultural fields enclosing Cool Spring Plantation north of Castleman's Ferry in northeastern Clarke County, Virginia (figs. 5.1, 5.3), the larger area of engagement encompassed a three-mile length of the northeast flow of the Shenandoah River and the landforms to the east and west. Within this area, wide, heavily dissected valley uplands bound the relatively narrow bottomlands of the Shenandoah River on the west. East of the river, sharply angled slopes rise toward the spine of the Blue Ridge Mountains (figs. 5.1, 5.3). Converging, deeply entrenched, commonly west-flowing ravines sculpt the interior of the mountain wall producing, narrow, moderate to sharply angled descending ridges which typically terminate in a series of elevated knobs above the trench of the Shenandoah. A significant exception to this pattern is Joe Bell Run (fig. 5.3, area 6), which drains southwest from the vicinity of Snicker's Gap (fig. 5.3, area 7). To the west of Joe Bell Run is a high ridge, Big River Mountain (fig. 5.3, area 8), which shields a weathered, dissected, interior mountain valley through which the stream flows. This interior valley was frequently used by Union and Confederate forces for encampment and played a key role in support activities involved with the Battle of Cool Spring.

West of the Shenandoah River, the valley floor consists of wide, weathered, flat to moderately sloping ridges dissected by east-flowing tributary streams (fig. 5.3). Primary streams draining the battlefield locale include Wheat Spring Branch and Long Marsh Run. These streams tend to be slow

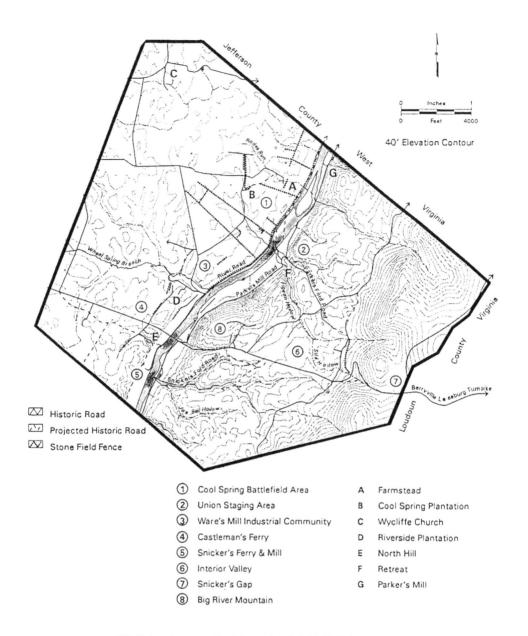

①	Cool Spring Battlefield Area	A	Farmstead
②	Union Staging Area	B	Cool Spring Plantation
③	Ware's Mill Industrial Community	C	Wycliffe Church
④	Castleman's Ferry	D	Riverside Plantation
⑤	Snicker's Ferry & Mill	E	North Hill
⑥	Interior Valley	F	Retreat
⑦	Snicker's Gap	G	Parker's Mill
⑧	Big River Mountain		

5.3. Cultural setting, Cool Spring battlefield, 1864 (courtesy of Clarke County, Virginia; prepared by Gordon Russell).

running within narrow U-shaped valleys. Associated bottomland features vary, but floodplain is the typical terrain feature. Lesser, spring-fed tributaries, Cool Spring Run and Rodes's Run (our name), bracket the immediate battlefield area and further shape local valley topography.

Within the battlefield area, the Shenandoah River lies within a narrow trench, typically less than one-half-mile wide. On the east, steep to bluff-like mountain walls, broken and weathered by entering tributary streams, rise abruptly from low, narrow terraces or, more typically, floodplain. On the west, upland valley features exhibit greater weathering, though bluff-like to markedly sloping walls are not uncommon. Low terraces occur along the river's flow, though floodplain is the more common landform. High, weathered upland knobs or ridge endlobes frequently overlook the valley floor (fig. 5.3). The river itself lies within a vertically sided trench, the river bed typically 10 to 20 feet or more below the floodplain. Limestone bedrock, which crosses the width of the river bed, is often exposed or lies within a couple of feet of the surface during periods of low water.

July 1864: The Cultural Landscape

Despite the limited information provided by military records, architectural and archaeological studies conducted in 1994 (Geier, Whitehorne, and McCleary 1995) indicate that the battle took place across a prosperous residential, agricultural, and industrial community (fig. 5.3). The small settlement of Castleman's Ferry, situated on the Shenandoah River's west bank at the Winchester-Leesburg Pike crossing, was an important transportation center in northeastern Clarke County. The turnpike was one of the most popular routes over the Blue Ridge Mountains, passing through Winchester, Berryville, Castleman's Ferry, and Snicker's Gap in the Blue Ridge, eastward toward Leesburg and Alexandria in northern Virginia. Crossing roads at or near Castleman's Ferry led to valley market centers at Harpers Ferry and Charlestown.

A small, rural industrial community known as Ware's Mill (fig. 5.3) was prospering along Wheat Springs Run, one-half mile north of Castleman's Ferry. In addition to several residences, at least one and possibly more grist mills and a tannery were operating in the community. Additional merchant mills stood on the west bank of the Shenandoah, just above Castleman's Ferry, and another stood on the east bank at what is now the West Virginia state line.

Other community centers were somewhat removed from the river. The Wycliffe Episcopal Church was the center of a group of modest farms and houses west of the Cool Spring Plantation (fig. 5.3c). Similarly, Tattletown or Pine Grove, consisting principally of log homes, was in place along the Winchester-Leesburg turnpike west of Snicker's Gap along Joe Bell Hollow.

In 1864 (Schmitt 1946:122), the valley land within the study area had been substantially cleared, creating vistas of open farms planted largely in wheat. Union soldiers at the time of the battle report watching Confederate soldiers harvest grain in distant fields (Storey 1907:112). Large, slave-based plantations dominated the landscape along the river. West of the Shenandoah, Francis McCormick lived at Cool Spring Plantation north of Wheat Springs Branch. Dr. J. M. G. McGuire resided at Riverside (fig. 5.3d) above the industrial community at Wheat Springs. James Castleman, of the Castleman Ferry Company, was living in a newly renovated plantation house at North Hill (fig. 5.3e) west and south of the ferry site. East of the Shenandoah, Richard E. Parker, presiding judge at John Brown's trial, lived at Retreat (fig. 5.3f), the family home situated opposite Cool Spring (Geier, Whitehorne, and McCleary 1995).

Preliminaries to the Battle and the Evolution of Wright's Union Army

Following his repulse at Lynchburg in June of 1864, Union Maj. Gen. David Hunter broke contact with Confederate forces commanded by Maj. Gen. Jubal Early and withdrew across West Virginia to the Kanawha Valley. His force eventually reappeared at Harpers Ferry after a roundabout trek by way of Parkersburg and Martinsburg. Hunter's prolonged absence allowed General Early to move his force down the Shenandoah Valley. Following a series of clashes, Early's army arrived at Silver Spring, Maryland, on the outskirts of Washington, on July 11. His approach to the Federal capital generated all the panic that could be expected. President Lincoln pressed General Grant to send reinforcements to augment the militia and convalescents who had been rushed into the city's defenses. Grant saw Early's move as intended to divert strength from the Union's main effort at Richmond-Petersburg. Accordingly, he was at first reluctant to weaken his own force to reinforce the defenses at Washington. At the last possible moment, Grant recognized the psychological and political ramifications of Confederate entry into the national capital and diverted the forces necessary to prevent it. In doing so, Grant was obliged to literally create an army to respond, the evolving composition of which would play a key role in General Wright's ability to effectively confront the well-organized and highly motivated army of Jubal Early.

In response to Early's advance toward Washington, Brig. Gen. James B. Ricketts's 3rd Division, VI Corps, which had been posted in defense of the capital, had been sent to Monocacy, Maryland, to fight in Maj. Gen. Lew Wallace's delaying action. Maj. Gen. Horatio G. Wright's 2nd Division, VI Corps, arrived at Washington by boat from Petersburg on July 11, a few hours after Early's arrival on the northwest side of Washington. Amidst great confusion and late in the evening, Wright's men reached Ft. Stevens, on the Washington defensive perimeter. Still later during the evening of July 11, Ricketts's returning division joined that of Wright. When Early realized he was confronting a formidable force, he began withdrawal that night.

At Grant's command, General Wright was reinforced by Maj. Gen. William H. Emory's 1st Division, XIX Corps. This was one of two divisions sent east from the four division corps that sailed from Louisiana to reinforce Grant's forces fighting around Richmond-Petersburg. Instead, given the emergency created by Early's raid, on reaching Hampton Roads, some XIX Corps elements were diverted to Washington.

Regiments from Emory's Division began landing at Washington at noon on July 13. Subject to the orders of excited Military Department of Washington staff officers, they were sent on unnecessarily long marches around the District. Eventually, most of Emory's men, confused, exhausted, and with no logistical support, staggered into camps around Tenallytown. The corps elements were unorganized, senior officers were still en route, and there was considerable confusion getting the regiments coordinated and aligned with some kind of trains and artillery. Still getting organized, the XIX Corps elements followed the VI Corps toward the Potomac and the withdrawing Confederates (Gould 1871:464–65; Irwin 1985:358).

General Wright initially understood his mission to be to shove Early away from Washington and back across the Potomac. He and Grant assumed that the Confederates would rejoin Lee around Richmond-Petersburg. This, in part, accounts for the apparent lack of Federal aggressiveness. A greater reason for Wright's slowness was the quality and condition of his improvised trains. Composed of a mix of inexperienced drivers and teams gathered during the crisis of Early's threat to Washington, neither men nor animals were trained (Bowen 1884:357).

Jubal Early's forces crossed the Potomac by July 14 and camped around Leesburg. They rested there throughout July 15, while Wright's force slowly pressed to the banks of the Potomac (Nichols 1898:174; Wellman 1956:174). Gen. David Hunter's command, after its anabasis from Lynchburg by way of Charleston and Parkersburg, reached Harpers Ferry on July 14. There, Hunter received a wire from General Grant ordering him to pressure Early with the troops he had on hand (Osborne 1992:298). While Hunter was getting organized, he received a message from Wright with instructions to effect a rendezvous at Leesburg. Hunter sent Brig. Gen. Jeremiah Sullivan's 7,000 infantry and Brig. Gen. Alfred Duffié's 2,000 cavalry in response, but he ordered them to march in the direction of Hillsborough and Purcellville, Virginia, rather than to Leesburg so as to have a better chance to intercept Early (Cooling 1989:193).

Early was aware of the converging Union forces and began withdrawing his men westward toward the Blue Ridge Mountain gaps on the night of July 15. The Federal generals, who had yet to establish direct contact, missed a golden opportunity to do serious harm to Early because of their lack of coordination. Brig. Gen. George Crook relieved Sullivan at noon on July 16 and energized his command (Schmitt 1946:121; Pond 1883:81; Cooling 1989:193).

The Confederate forces headed rapidly for the Shenandoah Valley. The main Confederate force left the Leesburg area on the morning of the 16th. The divisions of Maj. Gen. John B. Gordon and Brig. Gen. Gabriel C.

Wharton preceded the remaining trains ahead of the divisions of Maj. Gen. Robert E. Rodes and Maj. Gen. Steven Dodson Ramseur.

When Union General Crook assumed command of Sullivan's force, he immediately ordered Duffié's Cavalry to harass the moving columns (Cooling 1989:195; Pond 1883:81–82). Upon news of the cavalry's contact, Crook ordered his infantry into motion (Wildes 1884:128; Lincoln 1879:332). While this was going on, Wright's force crossed the Potomac and camped (Bowen 1884:361). The Federal infantry rested throughout July 17, while their rear elements continued to straggle in (Haines 1883:229; Bowen 1884:362). When the two officers met on the 16th, General Wright ordered Crook to maintain contact with the withdrawing Confederates. The next day, Crook dispatched Duffié's Cavalry and Brig. Gen. James A. Mulligan's Infantry Brigade to Snicker's Gap even as the remainder of his force gathered at Purcellville (Wildes 1884:128; Schmitt 1946:121; Pond 1883:81).

The Confederates crossed Snicker's Gap on the evening of July 16. That night, Breckinridge's command of Gordon's and Wharton's Divisions deployed on the western side of the Shenandoah River in the vicinity of Castleman's Ferry and North Hill Plantation. Rodes's Division camped east of the river, along Joe Bell Hollow, in the valley east of Big River Mountain. Ramseur's Division established itself on the crest of the Blue Ridge in Snicker's Gap and down the east slope toward Snickersville. Brig. Gen. John McCausland's Cavalry Brigade guarded Ashby's Gap to the south (Geier, Whitehorne, and McCleary 1995).

On the morning of the 17th (fig. 5.4), the entire Confederate command shifted west of the Shenandoah River, with Early setting up headquarters near Berryville on the Charlestown Road. Breckinridge stayed near Castleman's Ferry. Gordon was deployed along the river north and south of the ferry crossing, and Wharton was at Webbtown, two miles west on the Berryville Pike. Rodes's Division occupied a line from Wycliffe Church to Parker's (Rock's) Ford on the Shenandoah. Ramseur was on the Charlestown Road near Gaylord, well west and north of the future battlefield. McCausland's Cavalry screened Ashby's Gap well to the south, while Brig. Gen. William L. Jackson's and Bradley T. Johnson's Cavalry Brigades screened toward Charlestown and Martinsburg, respectively. Brig. Gen. John Imboden's horsemen covered the west (McDonald 1973:216; Cooling 1989:195; Wert 1978:37; Evans 1987:485). Early intended to cover all approaches through the Blue Ridge and from Harpers Ferry and Martinsburg while he determined Federal intentions (Early 1867:396).

General Duffié's force reached Snicker's Gap a few hours after the Confederates withdrew (Holcombe 1916:385). When Union cavalrymen moved down the rough turnpike to Castleman's Ferry (Meaney 1979:13, 14), they immediately came under fire from 62nd Virginia Infantry skirmishers placed behind a stone wall west of the river. Two Confederate

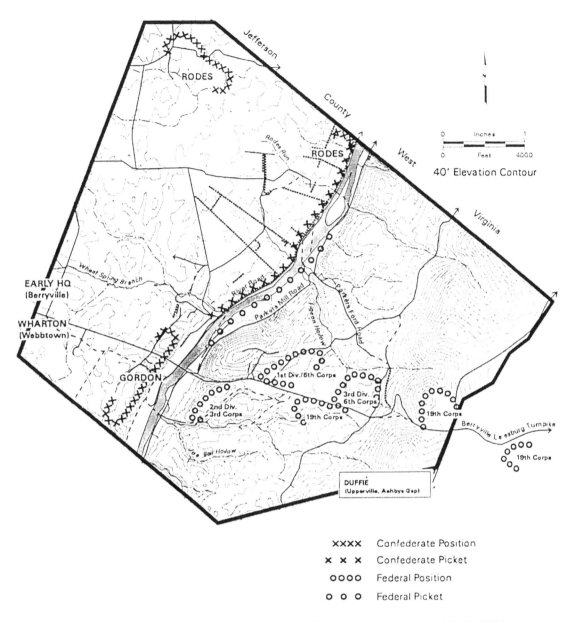

5.4. Confederate unit locations, July 17–18, Federal positions, July 18–19, 1864 (courtesy of Clarke County, Virginia; prepared by Gordon Russell).

cannon, placed on high ground further west in the vicinity of North Hill, added to the resistance (Wert 1978:38; U.S. War Department 1880–1905 [OR]: 37, I: 320).

General Duffié ordered an immediate assault on the Confederate defenders. Dismounted cavalry and their infantry support tried to rush across the drought-lowered river and establish a bridgehead but were repulsed with losses of two killed and fifteen wounded. General Crook arrived with his advance party about 2:00 P.M., just as fighting settled into vigorous skirmishing. About 6:00 P.M., Crook ordered another try, which ended quickly because of heavy Confederate fire. While lighter probing continued, all the cavalry, except the 21st New York, on vedette, withdrew to camp at Snickersville, east of Snicker's Gap.

Early on the morning of the 18th, the 21st New York Cavalry, supported by infantry, tried a third attack on the Confederate position at Castleman's Ferry. The small force of 75 attackers formed into separate groups and assaulted three different points. After they were forced back, they were replaced by infantry along the river line (OR37, I: 320; Matheny 1963:94). This stiff Confederate resistance caused Crook to look for alternative river crossings. He relieved Duffié of his responsibility for Snicker's Gap and ordered him to march to Ashby's Gap to the south to see if a crossing could be made at Berry's Ferry (OR37, I: 321).

Most Federal infantry did not begin to march toward Snicker's Gap until July 18. Crook's men, known as "Army of West Virginia" or VIII Corps, took the lead from their camps at Purcellville. Leaving their camps as early as 3:00 A.M., the lead units filed through Snicker's Gap about noon and were clearly visible to the Confederates west of the Shenandoah (Lincoln 1879:333; Pond 1883:82).

While the Federals descended the Berryville Turnpike, or what they called a "rocky track" (fig. 5.4), General Wright joined Crook to discuss the situation. Both officers assumed Castleman's Ferry was held by a Confederate rear guard. From their position on Big River Mountain, 200 feet above Castleman's Ferry, Confederate pickets could be seen at North Hill Plantation on the high ground south of the ferry crossing and at Riverside Plantation, one-half mile to the north (Schmitt 1946:122). Lt. Gulian V. Weir's L Battery, 5th U.S. Artillery, unlimbered on the Big River Mountain high ground adjacent to the generals' observation point.

At 2:00 P.M., at Wright's command, Crook ordered Col. Joseph Thoburn to take his 1st Division, reinforced with Col. Daniel Frost's 3rd Brigade, 2nd Division, to Parker's (Rock's) Ford about two miles north of Castleman's Ferry, cross there, and attempt to flank the Confederate defenders at Castleman's. Both generals presumed the enemy's rear guard would have to decamp when challenged by a strong force on its side of the river.

The Cool Spring Battlefield

The convenience of an established crossing attracted Union forces to Parker's Ford, but that crossing proved to be the setting's only advantage. While the intent had been to flank what were believed to be Confederate pickets at Castleman's Ferry, Thoburn's force found itself boxed in by natural features which limited his tactical options and entrapped his enlarged division. The principal battlefield (fig. 5.5) was a rectangular area,

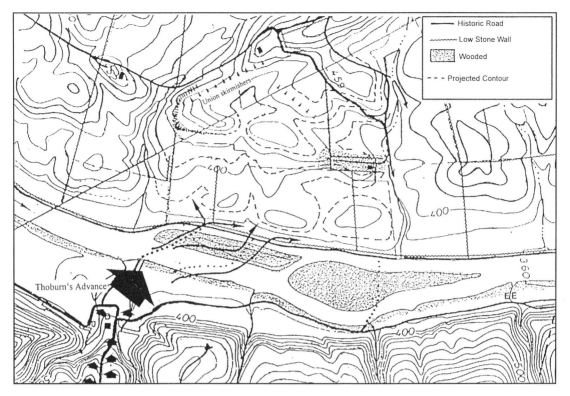

5.5. Battlefield locale, Federal approach, July 18, 1864 (courtesy of Clarke County, Virginia).

4,000 feet northeast-southwest by 5,000 feet northwest-southeast, including bottomland features east and west of the Shenandoah and its immediately adjoining uplands. West of the river, Cool Spring Run served as a southern boundary for the infantry engagement of July 18 and an unnamed stream, identified as Rodes's Run for this discussion, was the northern boundary. On the west, activity would extend to a second line of upland ridges about 2,500 feet west of the banks of the Shenandoah. To the east, staging activities involving Thoburn's force took place on the floodplain and terrace features west, and in front of Judge Parker's home, "Retreat" (fig. 5.5).

As Thoburn prepared to cross the Shenandoah, he confronted lands that were topographically complex and restricting. A narrow floodplain, 80 to 150 feet in width (fig. 5.5), lay below a weathered first terrace dissected into four knobs 20 to 40 feet high. Each knob was separated from its neighbor by moderate to steeply walled ravines. The northernmost ravine isolated a large domed knob that controlled the northeast corner of the battlefield.

The western margin of the battlefield included a series of upland ridges extending between Rodes's and Cool Spring Runs (fig. 5.5). These ridges are heavily eroded, with rock outcrops on the ridge faces being substantial features in some areas. Converging drainage patterns shape an initial, narrow, linear set of ridges paralleling the line of weathered terrace knobs and the Shenandoah. These ridges rise 80 to 100 feet above the floodplain and are approximately 40 feet higher than the terrace knobs. Midway along its length, the ridge complex is broken by a ravine passing east from the upland interior. South of the middle ravine, slopes rise at a moderate angle toward the upland ridge to confront a nearly vertical "bluff" of limestone (fig. 5.5) extending from Cool Spring Run nearly 600 feet northeast.

The battlefield area west of the first upland ridge line was shaped by the interior drainage nets of Rodes's and Cool Spring Run and by an intermediary system that heads up in a sink hole east of Cool Spring Mansion (fig. 5.5). As a composite, these drainages set off a second, north trending upland ridge that bounds Rodes's Run on the south. Cool Spring Mansion is situated at the midpoint of this ridge.

Cool Spring Run, which defines the battlefield on the south, flows through a very narrow, deeply entrenched (30+ feet), V-shaped valley where Confederate infantry from Wharton's Division would stage out of the line of sight of Union troops in the fields below. It also offered protection from Union artillery fire from east of the Shenandoah.

On the north side of the battlefield, the more developed flow of Rodes's Run was of key tactical importance. This stream is more U-shaped in character with a narrow but distinctly developed bottomland. An erosional scar that originates east of the McCormick Mansion flows northeast and creates a relatively wide, gently to moderately walled valley between the north ends of the first and second upland ridges (fig. 5.5). This locale provided a setting where Rodes's Confederate Division staged, unseen by Thoburn's Infantry and in relative security from Union artillery fire.

While the bottomland east of the Shenandoah does not lie within the immediate battle zone, it shaped the opportunities available to the Union advance and subsequent retreat. Unlike the west bank, east-side bottomland features (fig. 5.5) include extensive floodplain, with weathered, low, and narrow first terraces in some areas. These low-relief features were as much as 20+ feet lower than the terrace remnants west of the river. Except in areas where narrow mountain streams entered, the eastern valley wall was bluff-like in character, slopes rising as much as 60+ feet on the north, to as much as 200–300 feet on the south, below Big River Mountain (fig. 5.5).

Given the above, troops massing along the narrow eastern bottomlands could be observed by Confederate pickets west of the river. More importantly, the bluff-like character of the valley walls created a vertical wall severely restricting movement into or out of the bottomland. Tributary ravines entering from the east allowed human passage, but these narrow, deeply entrenched valleys were totally unsuitable for any rapid movements of a sizable military force (fig. 5.5). The only reasonable access into the valley for Thoburn's expanded division was a narrow, moderately sloping weathered ridge immediately east of "Retreat" and down a narrow trace that joined Retreat to the Winchester-Leesburg Pike (fig. 5.5). At best, this route was only minimally acceptable for a force interested in rapid forward movement, but it was all that was available. For an army in retreat, it could be a disastrous bottleneck.

At two points on Big River Mountain (figs. 5.4, 5.5) and on a series of upland ridge endlobes northeast of "Retreat," high (100–200 feet), flat-topped ridges were in place. These knobs, which *may* have been deforested and used as pasture at the time, served as positions for Union batteries and for observation posts used to monitor the flow of the battle.

The last feature of note is the Shenandoah itself. Within the battlefield, the river changes from a single stream about 250 feet wide to two streams separated by intervening islands (fig. 5.5). The average depth of the river is uncertain, but during the drought of 1864, it was fordable by men in most places. An exception to this is Parker's Hole, a deep pit east of the lower Parker's Island. West of the river, the bank rises as a near vertical bluff 15 to 20 feet above the flow of the stream. On the east, the bank is slightly less high and is more eroded.

In July of 1864, the lower fields west of the Shenandoah were in wheat, and scattered woodlands were on the uplands (Meaney 1979). One of these scattered woodlands included the northernmost of the first upland ridges west of the river, a factor that played a significant role in shaping the initial Confederate success. This area of oak woods was found by archaeologists to have contained a small farmstead associated with Cool Spring Plantation and that would have been occupied at the time of the battle.

On the east bank, the knob on Big River Mountain and those between "Retreat" and Rocky Branch had been significantly deforested. The east bank bottomlands were cleared for planting. Upper and lower Parker's Islands and the edges of both river banks were wooded (Meaney 1979). This is a significant point because such tree lines, in the middle of summer, would have significantly impaired direct observation of the west bank by Union infantry or artillery on the bottomlands east of the river. Similarly, Union troop movements on the east bank would have been blocked to some degree from the eyes of Confederates occupying the west bank.

The Battle at Cool Spring, July 18, 1864

Guided by a deserter from the Clarke Rifles (2nd Virginia Cavalry) named John P. Corrigan, Thoburn's Federals reached Judge Parker's house, "Retreat," massed on the terrace in front of the house, then along the floodplain east of the Shenandoah River (fig. 5.6). Trees and brush along the river helped conceal the men. The Federals were surprised to find the first crossing at Island Ford well defended and moved to a second ford farther north, over which they moved under covering fire from Weir's Union Bat-

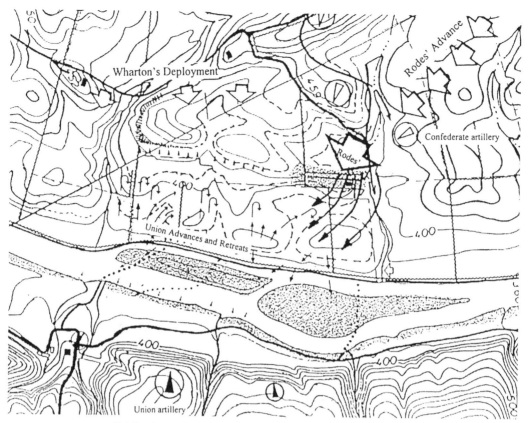

5.6. Deployment of Wharton's and Rodes's divisions and first Confederate attacks (courtesy of Clarke County, Virginia).

tery on Big River Mountain. Captured prisoners revealed that instead of advancing up the Shenandoah Valley, Early's whole command was still in the vicinity. This put the Union maneuver into a new perspective, and, rather than advancing toward Castleman's Ferry, Thoburn formed a defended bridgehead (fig. 5.6). He sent the information back to General Crook with a request for further instructions and reinforcements (Pond 1883:83; Matheny 1963:94; Cooling 1989:200).

Colonel Thoburn formed two lines across the fields east of the Cool Spring Mansion. His main line was established along a low stone wall constructed on the west side of a road that passed along the edge of the floodplain from Castleman's Ferry toward Harpers Ferry. A second line, approximately 100 yards further inland, was formed across the tops of the line of remnant terrace knobs. This area had been planted in wheat and was subdivided by low stone field walls set perpendicular to that along the River Road (fig. 5.6). As Federal skirmishers pressed west onto the first line of upland ridges and moved toward the road to Cool Spring Mansion (Gold 1914:115), they took shelter behind limestone outcroppings prevalent in the area. The Federal line formed a shallow crescent anchored at Cool Spring Run on the south and Rodes's Run to the north. Col. George

Wells's 1st Brigade held the Federal left. Next to it was Col. Daniel Frost's 3rd Brigade, 2nd Division. Thoburn's own 2nd Brigade extended the line north to Col. Samuel B. M. Young's Dismounted Provisional Cavalry Brigade, which held the extreme right (Pond 1883:83).

In response to Thoburn's threat, Confederate General Gordon's rear elements and Wharton's Division, encamped at Webbtown, were ordered to advance and attack the Federals. This move was intended to buy time for General Rodes, near Wycliffe Church, to advance his division against Thoburn's right. Wharton's men moved east and joined with Gordon's left flank. The latter extended his line from North Hill to the south edge of Cool Spring Farm. Wharton's Division extended along the second set of weathered upland ridges (fig. 5.7) on the west side of the battlefield to just past the Cool Spring Mansion, looking down on the Federal skirmishers (Meaney 1979:25).

In less than an hour, Union and Confederate forces were hotly engaged. Each side was supported by increasing numbers of artillery pieces. Lt. Jacob H. Lamb's Battery C, 1st Rhode Island Light Artillery, set up on the upland ridge, north of "Retreat" Mansion (fig. 5.7). Confederate Maj. William McLoughlin's Artillery Battalion of three batteries moved into

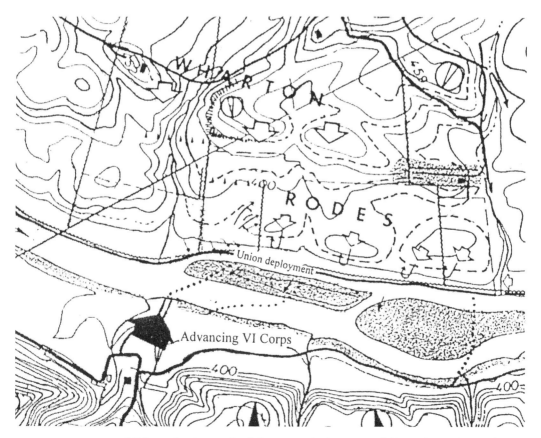

5.7. Second and third Confederate attacks (courtesy of Clarke County, Virginia).

Wharton's lines in search of good firing positions to help check the Federal advance. Concurrently, Confederate infantry burst out of a woods-line and hit the Union left. They were twice repulsed, but these actions distracted Federal attention from events transpiring beyond their right flank.

While the initial actions were under way, Rodes's Division advanced unobserved from the vicinity of Wycliffe Church through the valley of Rodes's Run (fig. 5.7; Park 1877:268). The 45th North Carolina Infantry Regiment slipped down to the Shenandoah, taking position near the point where Rodes's Run entered the river north of the Federal right flank. The rest of Rodes's Division staged in the ravine that entered Rodes's Run northeast of Cool Spring Mansion out of sight of Thoburn's force or observers east of the river. Once aligned, the greater part of Rodes's Division advanced through the grove of oak trees and the farmstead on the upland ridge to their east. As they moved into the open field in front of Col. Samuel B. M. Young's dismounted cavalry on the Union right, Federal artillery east of the Shenandoah (fig. 5.7) reacted with increased fire. Confederate batteries responded from positions on high ground northeast of the Cool Spring Mansion (Meaney 1979:32).

Young's cavalrymen, made up of casuals and convalescents impressed from 17 different regiments during the crisis created by Early's raid (Beavins n.d.), and Rodes's veteran infantry spotted each other simultaneously. Both sides recognized that success or failure depended on securing a low stone wall extending perpendicular to the river across the irregular floodplain and terrace (fig. 5.7). Thus, the first phase of their fight was a mutual dash for the wall that the Confederates won. Chaos quickly ensued among the Union cavalrymen. Their skirmish line collapsed within 15 minutes, and all the troopers rushed back to the protection of the stone wall and the road along the river, many retreating across the Shenandoah (Beavins n.d.).

The collapse of the Union right flank prompted Colonel Thoburn to shift the 116th Ohio Infantry from the less endangered southern flank along the narrow terrace road to plug the gap (fig. 5.8). The 116th Ohio stopped Rodes's advance and built a barrier of stones and logs to block a second Confederate try at dislodging the Union force. Rodes then pulled his men back to their start line behind the ridge at the north end of the battlefield. This withdrawal coincided with increased artillery and small arms fire coming from the newly arrived 3rd Division, VI Corps, east of the Shenandoah (Wildes 1884:131).

The presence of the VI Corps troops was a result of Wright's reaction to Thoburn's report about the size of the Confederate force he encountered. General Crook wanted to pull Thoburn's Division back as soon as the information was received, but General Wright disagreed. Instead, he said he would commit Ricketts's 3rd Division, VI Corps, which had just arrived. As understanding of Thoburn's situation improved, Ricketts felt that intervention would be impossible, and he refused to take his men across to join the fight, saying Thoburn should do his best to get out of the situation. Crook protested, but Wright supported Ricketts, and Thoburn was on his own (Schmitt 1946:122).

By this time, a third Confederate advance resulted in their assuming control of the terrace knobs west of the Shenandoah (fig. 5.8). Thoburn's embattled force was pressed back to the stone wall and road extending along the river bank (Wildes 1884:131). As presented in previous discussions of the battle (Meaney 1979), the superior position held by the Confederates should have placed Thoburn in an untenable position. Surprisingly, despite having lost the high ground to their front, the Federals held a good defensive position (fig. 5.8). Archaeological investigations found that the stone wall and road cut made it very difficult for Confederate artillery or musket fire to harm them. As constructed, the low stone wall was found to be placed on the immediate edge of the floodplain. The River Road, in turn, had been cut into the river bank, in many areas creating a 20-foot-wide bench situated 10 feet above the river and 6 to 15 feet below the stone wall and the edge of the floodplain. In effect, the combination of the road and wall provided an excellent defensive position behind which a large number of men could be stationed. Despite occupying higher ground, the Confederates could not bring effective rifle fire on the Union line. Further, a charge against that line would cause a huge loss of life and probable failure because of Union artillery fire. Confederate artillery on the western upland ridges could only interdict the fords. Federal artillery on the upland ridges east of the river, on the other hand, could sweep the open areas across which the Confederates would have to attack. Federal protective fire came so close to Thoburn's positions that it endangered his troops. It was sufficiently effective that after a third vigorous probe with heavy losses, Early called off any more offensive action (Wildes 1884: 131).

The Federals held their position behind the stone wall along the Shenandoah until twilight, when they retreated across the river to safety. Many of Thoburn's troops were lost in the crossing, some drowning in Parker's Hole. Once over, they had to traverse "a large open field" swept by Confederate rifle and artillery fire before they were safe and could move into camps on the slopes along Joe Bell Hollow (Lynch 1915:101). As darkness arrived, the fighting settled down into small arms exchanges as VI Corps troops took position on the wooded edge of the east bank of the river (Tyler 1912:246).

Elsewhere and Beyond

The poor organization of the evolving Union Army was a key factor in the lack of support provided by General Wright for Thoburn's Infantry at Cool Spring and his subsequent hesitation in moving against Early. In addition, military initiatives in the valley ordered by Gen. David Hunter, without the knowledge of General Wright, would contribute to the end of the standoff between the two armies on July 21.

Maj. Gen. David A. Russell's 1st Division was the second VI Corps unit to arrive in the Snicker's Gap locale. Russell had left Leesburg early on the morning of the 18th of July and marched steadily throughout the day. The division passed through Snicker's Gap, descended the narrow road toward Parker's Ford, and deployed along the eastern edge of the Shenandoah about 6:00 P.M. in anticipated support of Thoburn. The battle across the river was already at climax as the VI Corps troops began firing in support of Thoburn's men. Ricketts's command, already present, was relieved by Russell and withdrew with Thoburn's men as they moved into protected upland valley camps (Haynes 1870:98) along Joe Bell Hollow. Other elements of the VI Corps continued arriving throughout the evening of the 18th (Haines 1883:229).

Elements of XIX Corps reached the contested area even later. Still plagued by organizational problems, the XIX Corps lead elements did not reach Snicker's Gap until 9:00 P.M. on the 18th, after 17 hours on the road. Although artillery fire could be heard in the distance, the men were so exhausted that they gratefully halted for the night on a "level plateau" adjacent to the "rocky and steep" road (Winchester-Leesburg Pike) descending the west side of the Blue Ridge (Gould 1871:466; Beecher 1866:383).

Ohio militia, guarding the improvised XIX Corps trains, arrived still later and established camp west of Snicker's Gap, where they could see and hear gunfire in the valley below them. The army cattle were led to a cornfield close to the bivouac and within an hour had devoured the entire crop. The militia guarded trains at this location for two days with little idea of what was going on. Finally, at 9:00 P.M. on the 20th, they were pulled in from their guard posts, issued more ammunition, and told to get the trains moving east, away from the Shenandoah Valley at the double quick (Perkins 1911:25–26).

Following the climax of the Cool Spring engagement and after surveying the battlefield, General Early returned to his headquarters and directed that it be shifted to a point on the Winchester-Leesburg Pike 1.5 miles from Berryville (McDonald 1973:216; Park 1877:239). While he was concerned about repeated probes of his line made by Wright, he was also aware of Hunter's Union force to his north. In response, he sent Jackson's Cavalry west to screen toward Martinsburg, West Virginia, and ordered Ramseur to take his division north of Winchester to secure that flank (Runge 1991:89). Rodes's Division remained in place between Cool Spring and Wycliffe Church. Throughout the 19th, some of Rodes's men helped the wounded while others foraged (Hale 1986:82), but the bulk of the division remained in line of battle shifting its focus northward.

At Harpers Ferry, General Hunter recognized an opportunity in Early's deployment. Hunter knew that Crook and Wright were advancing toward Snicker's Gap. Consequently, on July 18, he ordered Brig. Gen. William W. Averill to advance south from Martinsburg, West Virginia, along the Valley Pike toward Winchester, and Col. Rutherford B. Hayes to march from near Halltown, West Virginia, to Keyes Gap. Hayes was to add Col. Isaac H. Duval's two regiments to his command and move up the Shenandoah River to Snicker's Ferry to assist Wright and Crook (Pond 1883:84). Unfortunately, Hunter did not explain to Hayes what he might expect nor how urgent his mission was. Consequently, when Hayes encountered stiff opposition and heard the sounds of fighting at Cool Spring he became very cautious. He held his command at Kabletown, West Virginia, and sent back to Hunter for instructions (Osborne 1992:301).

Hunter responded with a full explanation and ordered Hayes forward posthaste. Hayes tried to advance south early on the 19th, however, the Federals at Snicker's Gap held their position. Consequently, Rodes's men were able to devote their full attention to Hayes's small force. Heavy skirmishing went on for several hours. Hayes determined he was dealing with at least a Confederate division, and, since no help seemed forthcoming, he withdrew to Kabletown and held there until the morning of July 20. That day, he moved his force to Keyes Gap, then, on July 21, to Charlestown, West Virginia, where Hunter hoped he could assist Averill, who was approaching Winchester (Williams 1965:213–15). This activity north of the Cool Spring battlefield area caused Early to prepare to withdraw.

Wright's main body remained west of Snicker's Gap (Lynch 1915:101). In the distance, ambulance trains were observed, and columns of dust in the direction of Winchester intimated that Early's force was executing some kind of redeployment. Sounds of fighting were heard periodically from the direction of Ashby's Gap (General Duffié's Cavalry) to the south and Kabletown (Hayes's Infantry) to the north, the latter especially heavy (Lincoln 1879:334; Fiske 1983:243). Skirmishing along the riverbank continued all day at variable levels (Storey 1907:112). By 10:00 A.M., columns of dust to the north indicated Confederate movement toward Kabletown, but Wright's command remained in place.

Federal activity on his flanks north at Kabletown and south at Ashby's Gap alerted Early to the vulnerability of his position if Federal efforts were synchronized. Consequently, he ordered a shift deeper into the valley. Ramseur's Division completed its move northwest to the Valley Pike above Winchester to protect against Federal probes from Martinsburg. On the afternoon of the 19th, Confederate trains began to move toward Middletown and Newtown (Stephens City), accounting for the increased movement observed by the Union troops watching from Snicker's Gap (Hale 1986:384; McDonald 1973:217).

Most of Early's combat forces remained in the vicinity of Castleman's Ferry throughout daylight of the 19th. Rodes's Division left its position in the evening and marched through Berryville and then to Newtown (Stephens City) (Park 1877:381). About the same time, Early's headquarters began moving toward the same goal (McDonald 1973:217). McCausland's Cavalry guided Gordon's and Wharton's Divisions out of their positions through Millwood to Cedarville. By the 21st, the whole Confederate force had shifted to Cedar Creek and would be on Fishers Hill the next day (Evans 1987:485).

Early on the morning of the 20th, Wright's force was alerted to prepare for a river crossing to ascertain the meaning of the Confederate activities observed on the 19th. The VI Corps led the advance, crossing at Parker's Ford west of "Retreat." After their crossing, they moved unopposed over the Cool Spring Battlefield (Bowen 1884:363; Rhodes 1985:173; Tyler 1912:246). Other elements of the VI Corps crossed at Castleman's Ferry and joined their advanced element for a slow march, punctuated by frequent thunderstorms, toward Berryville. After going about three miles, they halted in battle order for the rest of the day (Haynes 1870:99; Haines 1883:232; Bowen 1884:364).

General Crook's VIII Corps followed the VI Corps, crossing at Castleman's Ferry. The corps then marched down the west bank of the Shenandoah to the Cool Spring battle area. Distant firing could be heard in the direction of Winchester, marking Averill's defeat of Ramseur at Rutherford's farm. The VIII Corps remained in the area throughout the 20th and most of the 21st. Its last unit left for Winchester at 6:00 A.M. on the 22nd (Lincoln 1879:335; Walker 1885:288; Lynch 1915:102; Keyes 1874:81; Storey 1907:112).

A part of the XIX Corps crossed at Ware's Mill north of Castleman's Ferry, while its trains remained encamped in Snicker's Gap. The men waded the river, then marched to Webbtown, where they sheltered in the woods and used some lean-tos left by the Confederates to protect themselves from the heavy rain and lightning (Hewitt 1892:160; Gould 1871:468; Beecher 1866:384).

Wright briefly contemplated pursuing Early in coordination with Hunter's forces from the north. But he reasoned that he had carried out his mission and should return his men as quickly as possible to Grant's command around Richmond-Petersburg. He presumed Early was headed there as well. Consequently, he judged Crook's battle-weary force to be sufficient to secure the lower valley. As darkness set in, he ordered the VI and XIX Corps to reverse direction and begin a speed march back to Washington (Pond 1883:84). The march began about 8:00 P.M., and by midnight most of the forces were on the road east. The command reached the District of Columbia by July 23, the day before General Early defeated General Crook at the Second Battle of Kernstown, and a new phase of the valley's military history began.

Conclusion

A combination of archaeological survey of the battlefield locale and architectural and historical research has led to a much more thorough and accurate understanding of the small but important Battle of Cool Spring. The multiplier effect of various disciplines working together has enriched knowledge of this battle, adding significant new information concerning the organization and character of the respective armies, the nature of the cultural landscape over which the battle was fought, and contemporary military actions taking place within the Shenandoah Valley that influenced the outcome. While previous studies have provided detailed and accurate information on the conduct of the actual battle at Cool Spring Plantation on July 18, analyses of the topography of the battlefield have provided a far better appreciation of the role played by terrain and the challenges it imposed on the decisions of the generals of both sides.

Acknowledgments

The research for this project was carried out under a contract provided by the National Park Service to the County of Clarke, Virginia. Gordon Russell, GIS Manager, Information Systems Administrator for Clarke County, used his GIS wizardry to compile interpretive maps of the larger battlefield area. Thanks go to numerous students from James Madison University who volunteered their time to ensure a successful project. Ann McCleary is recognized for her efforts in gathering the information available concerning the cultural landscape of the battlefield. To the monks at Cool Spring monastery, to whom care of the battlefield has fallen, we extend our thanks for their support and courtesy. Special recognition is extended to Brother James Sommers.

II

The Home Front and Military Life

Questions increasingly asked by Civil War historians concern the nature of military life for both Union and Confederate soldiers as part of their daily routine. In addition, as communities become committed to exploring their local histories, interest in Civil War events turns from simple discussions of military events to efforts to understand the impact of battles and military presences on the domestic and economic life of their citizens. The following nine chapters deal with such issues.

Chapters 6, 7, 8, and 9 deal with issues of military life. W. Stephen McBride, Susan C. Andrews, and Sean P. Coughlin begin the discussion with detailed considerations of recent archaeology at Camp Nelson, a U.S. Army Depot in Jessamine County, Kentucky. In this chapter, the military depot is compared to a small city with numerous civilian employees and soldiers interacting in a setting complete with social stratification based on real and perceived wealth and authority. Such centers often had commercial districts consisting of private businesses offering a wide variety of foods and services. Given this model, functional and social status/rank implications of artifacts found at the Owens' House/Post Office Complex component of the depot are presented.

In chapter 7, Joseph Balicki introduces fieldwork to research carried out at Fort C.F. Smith, a fort in the Washington, D.C., defenses occupied from 1863 to 1865. With reference to artifacts from refuse dumps and support buildings, insights are provided to the day-to-day behavior of the men living within a regimented, military setting. Comparing site remains to other Union military camps reveals distinct differences between camp types; these differences are often a result of things such as location, function or purpose, access to urban markets, and garrison composition.

In chapter 8, Joseph W. A. Whitehorne, Clarence R. Geier, and Warren R. Hofstra address questions of developing medical support networks in their discussion of Sheridan's mobile tent hospital constructed at Winchester, Virginia, following the Third Battle of Winchester in September 1864. Building from coincidental discoveries of a remnant of this massive, temporary, military complex, the authors introduce readers to a brief history of relevant military support systems. Specifically, however, the discussion considers the medical support network established by Gen. Philip Sheridan upon taking control of the Union Army in the Shenandoah Valley. It further describes how the hospital at Winchester was constructed and served the wounded from a sequence of battles conducted against the army of Confederate Gen. Jubal Early in September and October of 1864. As part of this presentation, the critical role of the town's citizens is considered as the Union doctors sought to meet the needs of the wounded who were in private facilities throughout the town.

Perhaps one of the most feared destinations for Union prisoners of war was Andersonville Prison. Excavations at that site allow an accurate reconstruction of a portion of the prison's inner stockade and north gate. In chapter 9, Guy and Marie Prentice discuss the history of past and recent excavations at the site, interpreting them within the context of existing written records and maps pertaining to the site, its construction, and prison life.

Chapters 10, 11, and 14 address the impact of battle and warfare on the civilian population. In chapter 10, Elise Manning-Sterling recounts the horrors of war brought to a rural farm community as a result of the Battle of Antietam. In the context of graphic descriptions of the events prior to, during, and following the battle, archaeology at two sites—the Locher cabin and Mumma house—is interpreted relative to the impact of the battle on two families.

In a similar vein, Erika K. Martin-Seibert and Mia T. Parsons (chapter 13) present interpretations of the James Robinson house, the home of a free, African American family residing on the lands encompassed by the Battles of First and Second Manassas. As the house was a prominent feature on the battlefield landscape during the second battle, research into historical records and oral history interviews enabled researchers to compile a social history of the Robinson family. Archaeological data excavated from the site supported Civil War accounts of the use of the structure but also provided insight into the continuity of site occupation of this free, African American family through the antebellum and postbellum periods.

At a different level, Paul A. Shackel (chapter 11) considers the impact of the war on Harpers Ferry, and in particular the everyday life of its residents. Although the town is best known for its military history and personalities such as John Brown, "Stonewall" Jackson, and Philip Sheridan, Shackel takes archaeological evidence from excavations at Mrs. Stipes's boardinghouse and Dr. Marmion's office and interprets it within Civil War history to present what he describes as "the other history" of the everyday citizen of the town.

The Civil War fosters an interest in the changing social place of African Americans. The social and economic place of freed slaves in the postwar United States is just beginning to be considered. To that end, Kenneth E. Koons (chapter 12) considers the role of slaves and free African Americans within the middle and upper Shenandoah Valley. This is not an archaeological study, but the use of historical records is consistent with that of historical archaeology and contributes significant new insights into the economic place of African Americans in the society and economy of a part of Virginia traditionally linked to the industry of yeomen farmers of Scots-Irish and German ancestry. Koons not only documents the place of African Americans in prewar economies but discusses their continuing importance to the valley's rural economy as agricultural laborers rather than as semi-independent tenants or fully independent owner-operators.

Using data gathered from recent excavations at Manassas National Battlefield Park, Laura J. Galke (chapter 13) draws attention to the fact that battlefields often contain cultural remains that have historic significance for reasons other than battle-related events. With reference to the sites of Portici and Stuart's Hill, Galke provides evidence that African Americans living in the Virginia Piedmont during the Civil War era possessed and shared a subculture that is evident in the archaeological remains from their sites.

6

"For the Convenience and Comforts of the Soldiers and Employees at the Depot"

Archaeology of the Owens' House/Post Office Complex, Camp Nelson, Kentucky

W. Stephen McBride, Susan C. Andrews, and Sean P. Coughlin

Permanent military depots of the Civil War era were complex settlements. They often contained a wide variety of functional components including storage, manufacturing, residential, and subsistence-oriented buildings or areas. Depots were also demographically and socially complex and contained numerous civilian employees and soldiers in a setting complete with social stratification based on real and perceived wealth and authority. In fact, many larger depots were small cities, albeit under military rules and regulations. They could even have commercial districts full of private businesses offering a wide variety of goods and services. Common establishments included shoe and clothing shops, sutler stores, and eating houses, all of which operated under army contracts or licenses.

Through a combination of archival and archaeological research, a business district was identified and investigated within Camp Nelson, a large U.S. Army Civil War depot in Jessamine County, Kentucky. The district contained eleven structures according to maps drawn at the time of occupation, but only two structures were identified by name—the Owens' House and the post office. The district was designated the Owens' House/Post Office Complex (15Js97), since these were the only named buildings within the site area.

In this chapter, we will combine archaeological data and primary historical documents in what James Deetz refers to as a "multidirectional approach" to investigate and describe functional and social status/rank differences at the Owens' House/Post Office Complex (15Js97). Deetz defines the "multidirectional approach" as "working back and forth between the documents and what the site has produced [i.e., artifacts and features], constantly refining and reformulating questions raised by one set of data looking at it against the background of the other" (1993:159). This approach makes better use of each data source and leads to the formulation of new questions and new research. We used these two different data sources to investigate such questions as settlement complexity, status, segregation, and consumption patterns at the Owens' House/Post Office Complex. Archaeological data from more than 50 Civil War features and a large body of archival material, particularly from the National Archives, are the basis of this study. The interplay of these two sources provided a more rewarding and rich analysis of life at Camp Nelson.

History of Camp Nelson

In June 1863, Maj. Gen. Ambrose Burnside, commander of the Army of the Ohio, ordered construction of a new camp to be used as the supply center for his planned East Tennessee campaign (Bartnik 1976:1). The selected site was along the Lexington-Danville Turnpike, about six miles south of Nicholasville (fig. 6.1). The total encampment, which contained approximately 4,000 acres, was named Camp Nelson after Maj. Gen. William Nelson, who established nearby Camp Dick Robinson, the first Union camp in Kentucky. Because of its strategic location on a major transportation route between the Ohio Valley and Tennessee, Camp Nelson soon became a major supply depot, recruitment center, and hospital for Federal armies operating in Kentucky and East Tennessee.

Within the camp, numerous structures were erected to house activities associated with quartermaster and recruitment functions. These buildings included numerous warehouses, stables, sheds, workshops, barracks, offices, and mess halls, as well as a sawmill, a machine shop, a prison, a post office, and the camp headquarters. Most buildings, including the headquarters and post office, were identified on maps drawn in 1864 and 1866 (Simpson 1864; Miller 1866) (figs. 6.1, 6.2). A large hospital and convalescent facility was established on the camp's south side. By the end of the war, as many as 300 buildings were located within the camp (Bartnik 1976:3; Hall 1865). A number of preexisting domestic structures and businesses situated within the camp boundaries were commandeered and used by the army during the war years.

During Camp Nelson's existence, it garrisoned many different regiments. Initially, these regiments were part of the IX Corps and came from the northeastern states. Later, all the troops belonged to the XXIII Corps and hailed from Kentucky, Tennessee, and midwestern states. Several regiments or companies were organized and trained at Camp Nelson, including two Kentucky and two Tennessee infantry regiments, one Kentucky and one Tennessee artillery battery, and one Tennessee cavalry regiment (Dyer 1959). The majority of regiments formed at the camp, however, were U.S. colored regiments. Eight U.S.C.T. regiments were founded at Camp Nelson, and three others were trained there. This made the camp the largest African American recruitment and training camp in Kentucky and the third largest in the United States (Dyer 1959). The U.S. colored regiments also were stationed at the camp for longer periods of time than most other regiments.

African American recruits often brought their families to Camp Nelson as well. Families came for many reasons, including fear of retaliation by angry slaveholders and anticipation of better opportunities or even emancipation for the entire family (Lucas 1989; Sears 1986). The army, with the assistance of the American Missionary Association and the U.S. Sanitary Commission, built a refugee camp for these people, which eventually housed 3,060 people, primarily women and children (Sears 1987:40).

After the war ended, military officials began preparing to close Camp Nelson. Inventories of serviceable and unserviceable equipment, supplies, and buildings were made between spring 1865 and winter 1866, and decisions were made about whether to keep, sell, or dispose of these (Meigs 1865, 1866; Resticaux 1865). After the spring of 1865, the majority of troops occupying Camp Nelson were African Americans. In fact, the families of the African American troops continued to enter Camp Nelson to attain emancipation until December 1865, when the 13th Amendment was passed. In June 1866, the army abandoned Camp Nelson, thus ending its military occupation.

The Owens' House/Post Office Complex

Figure 6.3 shows the location of the Owens' House/Post Office Complex with respect to the road and the rest of the camp. Our initial archival research on this site was simply directed toward identifying building functions and occupational history. Unfortunately, neither of the Camp Nelson maps—the 1864 Simpson map and the 1866 Miller map—identified many of the illustrated buildings at our site. Of the three buildings shown on the 1864 map, only the post office is identified. The 1866 map illustrates eleven buildings, but only the post office and the Owens' House are labeled (fig. 6.3).

Although the omissions of the 1864 map were not unexpected, given that few buildings are labeled on this map, the lack of labeling within the complex area on the 1866 map was surprising, since most buildings in other areas on this map (for example, machine shop, headquarters) are labeled. While this was disappointing, it actually was a clue to the function, or at least ownership, of other buildings at this complex.

No photographs of the Owens' House Complex were found in the 45 extant Civil War photographs of the camp. An elevation drawing of the post office was found, however, that shows it as a one-story building with glazed windows and identifies it as "the Adams Express Office" (U.S. National Archives Record Group 92, 1863–66, Entry 225, Box 720). Like most buildings in the camp, the post office was a frame building, probably of board and batten construction.

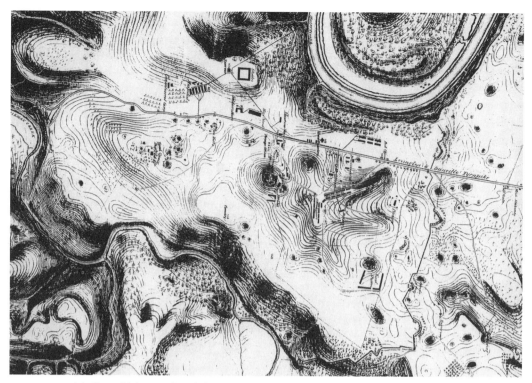

6.1. Camp Nelson and its defenses after Simpson 1864 (courtesy of the National Archives, Cartographic Division, College Park, Maryland).

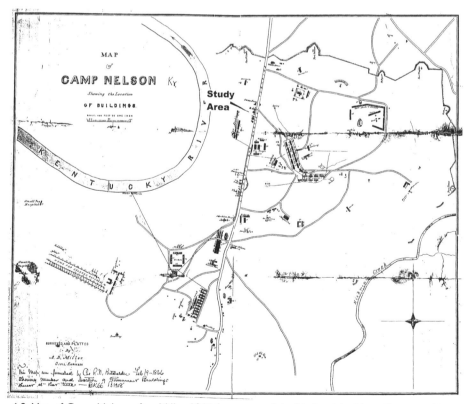

6.2. Map of Camp Nelson after Miller 1866 (courtesy of the National Archives, Cartographic Division, College Park, Maryland).

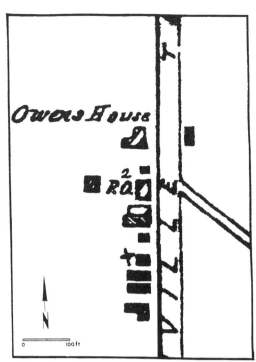

6.3. The Owens' House/Post Office Complex (15Js97) site map (courtesy of Wilbur Smith Associates).

Although no Civil War era drawings of the Owens' House have been located, an 1816 sketch illustrates it as a two-story building with a one-story addition (Jessamine County Will Book B:287–89). County deed and court files show that this dwelling was built before 1805 and continued as an owner-occupied residence until the 1850s, when it was rented to David Owens, a tavern keeper (Jessamine County Order Book M:20). Evidently, Owens operated this building as a tavern during the 1850s and early 1860s. It is not known exactly what function(s) the Owens' House performed during the Civil War.

Archival research on the military occupation of Camp Nelson uncovered four references to the Owens' House. The most informative one states: "notify proprietors of the Owens House and the sutlers on the west side of the pike and in the vicinity of the Owens House that they must police the grounds in the rear of their buildings. The filth will be removed and covered in earth, so as not to endanger the health of the camp" (Clark 1864a). The mention of the "proprietors of the Owens House" suggests that it was a privately run business. As the citation also mentions "the sutlers . . . in the vicinity of the Owens House," we can infer a function for some of the other nearby buildings. Sutlers were general goods merchants licensed to operate stores within army camps or posts (Lord 1969; Spear 1970).

Additional insights into the nature of the site and the general nature of the north side of Camp Nelson were attained from two other records, as follows: "Mr. William Berkely Post sutler has two stores, one in the convalescent Camp and the other nearly opposite the Owens House" (Hanaford 1864); and, "All hucksters coming in to sell fruits and vegetables, do it at these locations: North side of camp—on the hill opposite the Owens House. South side of camp—south side of pond below Nelson House" (Fry 1864a). These citations identify the Berkely Sutler Store across the pike from the Owens' House (fig. 6.3) and other commercial activity close to the Owens' House. Another record states that a lieutenant was ordered to "get the government pack saddle in the room over the Owens' House kitchen" (Clark 1864b). This statement tells us that the Owens' House had a kitchen, with at least a loft above it, and also that the army frowned on its property being left in private establishments.

These documents imply that the whole Owens' House Complex was a separate commercial section. Further proof of this was found on the back of a photograph, which stated "Wm. W. Rodecker, Photograph Gallery, Near the Post Office, Camp Nelson, Ky" (William Gladstone, personal communication). The nonmilitary and commercial nature of these buildings may explain why they were not numbered on the 1866 Miller map.

Archaeological Investigations at Camp Nelson

Between October 1994 and August 1995, the Owens' House Complex of Camp Nelson was excavated for the Kentucky Transportation Cabinet. At the time of the investigation, the site was in grass and possessed no surface evidence of the Civil War occupation. Excavation resulted in the discovery of two major concentrations of Civil War era features and refuse. At the north end of the complex, we identified four limestone chimney pads and a cellar foundation surrounded by numerous antebellum and Civil War refuse-filled features (fig. 6.4). The stone cellar and chimney pads represent the remains of the Owens' House shown on the 1866 Miller map. South of the Owens' House area, we found a large concentration of Civil War era features, midden, and artifacts. These appear to relate to two square buildings of unknown function shown on the Miller map. The area between these two concentrations contained fewer artifacts, particularly fewer kitchen items, and no features (fig. 6.5).

The abundance of architectural and domestic artifacts and refuse features in the Owens' House and the South Area strongly suggests that domestic activities such as eating and drinking occurred there (fig. 6.6). Civil War refuse features found near the Owens' House included seven rectangular privies, two root cellars, and five refuse pits or middens. Refuse features in the South Area included five privies, two refuse pits or privies, three root cellars, and one sub-floor cellar. Because of the South Area's continuous midden and the difficulty of clearly associating its features with one or the other of its two buildings, this area was treated as a single site.

The lack of similar artifact and feature concentrations between the north and south areas suggests that the three to four buildings located here

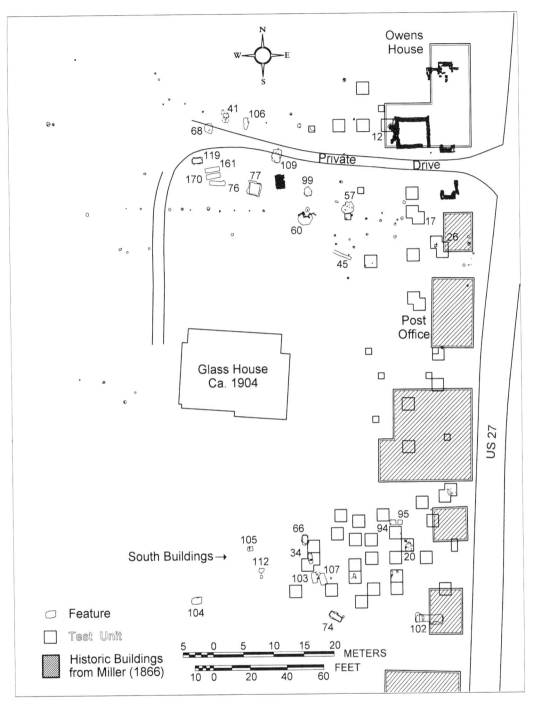

6.4. Buildings at 15Js97, 1866 (courtesy of Wilbur Smith Associates).

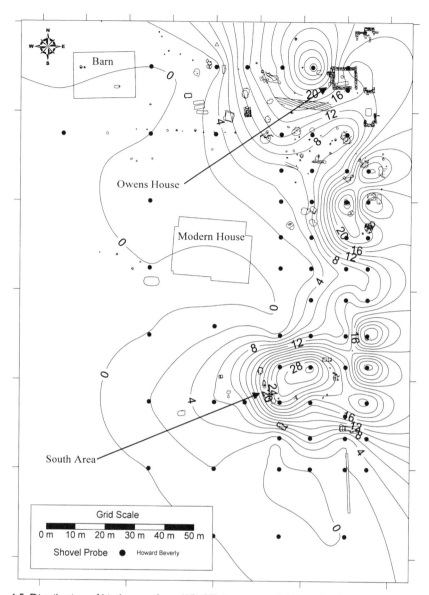

6.5. Distribution of kitchen artifacts (15Js97) (courtesy of Wilbur Smith Associates).

did not have domestic or food serving functions. They may have been specialized shops, such as the photographic studio, or more general sutler or merchandise stores.

Documentary research and preliminary fieldwork therefore suggest that the Owens' House and South Area buildings were involved in food and drink preparation, service, and consumption. The Owens' House was likely a tavern, while the South Area buildings were probably eating establishments of some sort. But little is known of the details of these establishments. For instance, what foods and drinks were served and to whom did they cater? What was the range in variability of eating establishments within Camp Nelson? Clearly more research was needed, first documentary and then archaeological.

Taverns, Saloons, and Sutler Stores

As a background to the questions of function and clientele, it is necessary to understand the nature of 19th-century public houses and their variability within Civil War camps and society in general. Taverns were among the most important social, political, and economic institutions in early American life. Tavern activities included eating, drinking, tobacco smoking, gaming, informal information exchange, formal meetings, business dealing, banquets, and overnight accommodations (Coleman 1935; Rockman and Rothschild 1984; Yoder 1969). To get a license, taverns had to provide overnight accommodations, normally for four or more people (Wagner and McCorvie 1992; Yoder 1969). This separated taverns—or, as they were sometimes called, inns or hotels—from more lowly saloons. The latter establishments provided drinks and, usually, some food.

According to Coleman (1935), little variability existed between Kentucky taverns during the 18th to early 19th centuries. By the mid-19th century, however, more towns and cities developed and the variability in quality between different establishments increased greatly. Fare might consist of a variety of meats (wild and domesticated), fish and fowl, breads, vegetables, and fruits. In fancier taverns, food would be prepared and presented according to the latest recipes and fashions (Hooker 1981). Fancy mixed drinks and foreign beverages were also offered at the expensive taverns (Coleman 1935; Hooker 1981).

A typical tavern might have two to four rooms on the first floor and sleeping accommodations upstairs. Downstairs rooms often included the taproom (bar), dining room, sitting or newsroom, and an attached (or detached) kitchen (Coleman 1935:65). Some taverns were less elaborate, with one or two multipurpose rooms downstairs, such as a combination kitchen, dining room, and taproom (McBride and Fenton 1996). Saloons, on the other hand, were typically one-story structures with one or two rooms.

Documentary research on the Owens' House uncovered evidence of a type of establishment common to Civil War camps, the sutler store. Sutlers were merchants who followed the army and sold a wide range of items, such as provisions, tobacco, merchandise, and often liquor and beer (Lord 1969:17). Union Army regulations dictated that each regiment have one sutler, although permanent camps might have many individually licensed sutlers (Lord 1969:17; Spears 1970:123).

Regimental sutlers typically set up a wide board shelf serving as a counter behind which a barman served food and drink (Lord 1969:67). In more permanent camps, they might construct log structures or board shanties or even occupy more permanent buildings (Spears 1970:123). The more substantial buildings often had stools, tables, and other furniture (Spears 1970:123). The sutler's establishment often became the social center of a camp, where soldiers lounged, gambled, and drank.

As an independent operator, the sutler could provide a broader range of food and drink than was available elsewhere. These products included dried and fresh fruit and vegetables (especially onions and potatoes), canned fruit and vegetables, dairy products such as canned condensed milk and butter, canned and bottled condiments, crackers (hard tack), cookies, fried pies, canned meats and oysters, dried beef, smoked tongue, Bologna sausages, dried and salted fish, sardines, eggs, flour, soda water, coffee and tea, beer, wine, and whiskey (Lord 1969; Spears 1970). Although the sale of alcoholic beverages was often restricted or forbidden, sutlers sold them anyway because of the great demand and poor enforcement of army regulations (Clark 1864c; Fry 1864b, 1864c; Spears 1970:125). Beer, wine, and whiskey were sold either by the glass or by the bottle.

Research on Camp Nelson uncovered references to at least 13 sutlers' stores within the camp, of which less than half were attached to regiments (Davis 1865). The proliferation of sutlers was criticized by commanding officers, many of whom tried to reduce the number to 2 or 3, apparently with little success (Davis 1865; Fry 1864c; Hammond 1865).

Archival records also mention other private establishments at Camp Nelson, including "hotels," "eating houses," "eating saloons," a shoe shop, a billiard hall, "peddlers," and fruit and vegetable "hucksters" (Carpenter 1865; Edgerly 1864; Fry 1864a; Griffin 1863). Moss' Eating House was located near the Refugee Home, and the Camp Nelson House, a possible tavern/hotel, was located in the center of camp (Gibson 1864). These were the only other named non-sutler businesses other than the Owens' House. Both the peddlers and hucksters set up their stands north of the Owens' House, and some of the above-mentioned establishments may be identified with the South Area buildings.

The differences between hotels, eating houses, and eating saloons can be speculated on. A hotel certainly would have had overnight accommodations and was probably equivalent to a tavern. The two terms are in fact never found in the same archival document. The Owens' House and Camp Nelson House probably fell under this category. Eating houses and saloons likely did not have overnight accommodations. These two eating establishments may not have been different since they were also never mentioned together in one order, but it is possible that the saloons were less formal and offered less variety of prepared foods than eating houses. The hotels/taverns, eating houses, eating saloons, and sutler stores were all in competition for the sale of alcoholic beverages and probably for the sale of foodstuffs as well. The different establishments may have had different clientele by rank or economic status, but the documents do not address this.

The above discussion gives us insights into the range of private businesses in camp and the possibilities for the Owens' House/Post Office Complex. The archaeological analysis presented below focuses on what further insights could be learned about the Owens' House and South Area buildings, especially what types of establishments they most closely resembled and who their clientele were. Some anticipated artifact patterning for taverns and eating houses include ceramic and glassware assemblages that are more standardized, plain or minimally decorated, and an overall greater frequency of drinking glasses and alcoholic beverage bottles. Taverns or eating houses serving higher-status clients will likely have more expensive ceramics and table glass and a greater variety of vessel forms. Wine and whiskey, as opposed to beer, should dominate the better establishments. Saloons and sutlers' establishments would likely have had fewer ceramics overall and less variety of vessels, particularly flatware and serving vessels. However, they should have a large assemblage of drinking glasses, alcohol bottles, and perhaps canned foods. The sutler stores might also have some artifactual evidence of other merchandise, although this would probably be minimal unless the items were consumed on site.

Artifact Analysis

In order to characterize the functions and activities of the Owens' House and South Area and the status of their respective clientele, a detailed analysis was conducted of artifacts known to be sensitive indicators of foodways activities, the main activity thought to take place at these areas, and social status. The artifacts chosen were ceramic vessels, drinking glasses, beverage and food containers, faunal remains, and military clothing and accoutrements. All of these artifact groups, except for the military items, relate to what could broadly be called foodways and therefore can be informative as to the types of foods and beverages consumed. They can also be sensitive indicators of social status, since the cost of these artifacts is known to have varied dramatically by type, quality, decoration, or contents. This is especially the case with refined ceramics, but it is also true for table glass, beverages, condiments, and cuts of meat. These artifacts, therefore, should provide evidence of what food and drinks were served and consumed at these establishments and how they were served. They should also indicate what class of clientele (that is, officers or enlisted men) each was catering to. Finally, examination of military uniform remains serves as an independent line of evidence to examine this clientele.

Ceramic artifacts were classified by vessel form, paste, and decoration so that price variability and purchasing behavior could be examined. Vessel identification was also conducted on table glass and bottle glass so that

Table 6.1. Ceramic refined ware and decorative types (vessels)

Description	Owens' House		South area	
	#	%	#	%
Plain whiteware	15	13	46	51
Molded whiteware	4	3	16	18
Slipped whiteware	-	-	2	2
Edged whiteware	4	3	1	1
Sponged whiteware	1	1	1	1
Painted whiteware	3	3	1	1
Printed whiteware	20	17	2	2
Total whiteware	47	40	69	76
Plain ironstone	26	22	14	15
Molded ironstone	34	29	4	4
Slipped ironstone	2	2	-	-
Painted ironstone	1	1	-	-
Printed ironstone	-	-	-	-
Total ironstone	63	54	18	19
Bone china	6	5	1	1
Hard porcelain	2	2	3	3
Total	118	101	91	100

form, function, and contents could be identified. To further examine the quality of meals served, faunal material from the two site areas was identified by species, element, and cut of meat.

The Ceramic Assemblage

The entire Owens' House/Post Office Complex produced 238 ceramic vessels, of which 137 were found at the Owens' House and 101 were recovered from the South Area. These ceramic vessels include refined wares such as whiteware, ironstone, and porcelain as well as coarse wares such as yellowware and stoneware.

At the Owens' House, over 80 percent of the vessels are refined wares, and the majority of these, or 53 percent, are ironstone (table 6.1). The ironstone assemblage contains a majority of molded vessels, followed by fewer plain vessels, and only three color decorated (two slipped and one painted) vessels. The whiteware vessels, which make up 40 percent of the refined wares, are most commonly color decorated, especially transfer printed, although molded and plain were also recovered. Only 7 percent of these refined vessels are porcelain.

The high proportion of ironstone (53 percent) and transfer printed whiteware (17 percent) from the Owens' House is in direct contrast to the South Area assemblage, where 76 percent of the refined wares are white-

Table 6.2. Refined ceramic vessel forms

Function	Owens' House		South area	
	#	%	#	%
Cups	24	20	35	38
Saucers	20	17	16	18
Bowls	3	3	4	4
Plates	57	48	30	33
Serving	10	8	5	5
Decorative	2	2	-	-
Sanitary	1	1	1	1
Unknown	1	1	-	-
Total	118	100	91	99

ware, 20 percent are ironstone, and only 4 percent are porcelain (table 6.1). Of the whiteware recovered, two-thirds are undecorated, and only 2 percent are transfer printed. Given the fact that ironstone and transfer printed whitewares were the most expensive refined earthenwares commonly available in the middle of the 19th century (Miller 1980, 1991; Miller et al. 1994), the Owens' House clearly has a much more expensive assemblage than the South Area.

Differences between the two areas are also evident when vessel forms are examined. The Owens' House refined ceramic assemblage includes 94 table setting (eating and drinking) vessels (88 percent), 10 table service vessels (8 percent), and 2 decorative vessels (table 6.2). The table setting vessels include 57 plates, 44 cups and saucers, 3 bowls, and 1 plate/saucer. The serving vessels include 2 platters, 6 serving bowls, 1 tureen, and 1 sugar.

The South Area vessels consist of an even greater proportion (93 percent) of table setting forms and fewer table service forms (only 5 percent; table 6.2). The service forms are also distinct and include only hollowware and no platters, suggesting that stews, soups, and beans, rather than large cuts of meat, were served in the South Area. The higher proportion of cups, with few saucers, and lower proportion of plates from the South Area are consistent with a less formal bar or saloon type of establishment.

A higher proportion of serving vessels is often linked to higher economic or social status (Fitts 1999; McBride and Esarey 1995; Otto 1977, 1980; Wall 1994a, 1994b, 1999). For instance, George L. Miller's (1980) indices indicate that platters were 50 percent more expensive than plates. The presence of large serving vessels such as platters and tureens at the Owens' House are indicative of more formal dining, entertaining, or display (Fitts 1999; Wall 1994a, 1994b, 1999).

The table setting assemblages from the two areas also show variability in forms. In the South Area, only 33 percent of the refined wares are flatware, while at the Owens' House 50 percent are flatware. Also, the

Owens' House assemblage includes four decorated sets of molded ironstone cups, saucers, and plates in the Prairie, Hyacinth, Double Wheat, and Wheat patterns (Wetherbee 1981). The South Area has no examples of tea sets and flatware being purchased together as matching sets. The presence of matching tea sets and tableware has been shown at other domestic sites to be indicative of genteel or formal dining (Fitts 1999; Wall 1999). According to Miller et al. (1994) and Williams (1987), matching tea sets and tableware were expensive and usually a mark of the middle and upper classes.

The high number of flatware and presence of sets at the Owens' House, indicative of more expensive purchasing behavior and higher-status individuals, is suggestive of the tavern's clientele. This pattern, along with the greater proportion of ironstone and service vessels, suggests that higher-paying customers, perhaps officers or higher-status (middle-class) civilians, frequented this establishment for more formal dining. The South Area establishments appear to have served cheaper fare in a simple, less formal manner using less expensive ceramics. They perhaps fit the "eating house" or "eating saloon" designation. The Miller Ceramic Price Index Values also support these conclusions. An index of 1.90 was calculated for the Owens' House while an index of 1.29 was calculated for the South Area.

The coarseware vessels and ware types from the two site areas were much the same. Both areas produced stoneware crocks and yellowware bowls. The main difference between the two areas was in the quantity of stoneware produced, with 20 vessels coming from the Owens' House and only two coming from the South Area. The much higher number of these food storage vessels at the Owens' House possibly points to a greater variety of foods and condiments served at this establishment, consistent with more formal dining activity with multiple dishes and courses of food.

The Glassware Assemblage

Given the likely tavern, saloon, or sutler store functions of the two site areas, the consumption of alcohol and other beverages was probably a major activity at each. But were there any differences in the consumption and service of beverages? Fortunately, large table glass and bottle glass assemblages were recovered from each site area so that beverage consumption can be investigated.

The table glass from the Owens' House area totals 36 vessels, including 29 drinking glasses, 4 large hollowware serving vessels, 2 small hollowware vessels, and an ointment jar (table 6.3). The drinking glasses consist of 18 tumblers, 2 footed tumblers, 5 shot glasses, 2 ale glasses, a beer mug, and a stemmed wine glass. The tumblers are simply decorated (geometric) or plain and held six ounces of fluid. These drinking vessels are consistent with a tavern, where a variety of alcoholic beverages and mixed drinks

Table 6.3. Table glass vessels

Function	Owens' House		South area	
	#	%	#	%
Tumbler	18	49	14	47
Footed tumbler	2	6	1	3
Shot glass	5	13	-	-
Wine glass	1	3	1	3
Ale glass	2	6	8	27
Beer mug	1	3	-	-
Decanter	-	-	1	3
Large holloware	4	11	1	3
Small holloware	2	6	2	7
Ointment dish	1	3	-	-
Lamp	-	-	2	7
Total	36	100	30	100

would have been served. However, the presence of only one stemware glass is at odds with other higher-status (officers) assemblages from the middle or late 19th century (Andrews and Mullins 1989; Scott 1989). Perhaps wine or sherry was not popular at this establishment or it was consumed from tumblers.

In the South Area, 30 table glass vessels were recovered, including 24 drinking glasses, 1 compote or bowl, 1 salt server, 1 mustard server, and 1 decanter (table 6.3). The drinking glasses include 14 tumblers, 1 footed tumbler, 8 ale glasses, and 1 small stemmed glass. Although the most common vessel from this area, as at the Owens' House, is the six-ounce tumbler, the presence of 8 ale glasses and the absence of any shot glasses clearly distinguishes the two areas. These ale glasses are footed and press-molded and held a beverage commonly, although not exclusively, associated with the working class during the 19th century (Hooker 1981:132). So, while both establishments served whiskey, which carried no class distinction (Hooker 1981:136), the South Area served much more beer. Apparently, neither area served much wine. According to food and drink historians, wine had a limited following in the United States and seemed to be consumed mostly on festive occasions (Hooker 1981:133).

An examination of the beverage bottle glass from the two areas tends to confirm this pattern. Both site areas produced large assemblages of bottle glass. The Owens' House assemblage includes 26 alcoholic beverage bottles and 1 soda water bottle, while the South Area produced 49 alcoholic beverage bottles and 5 soda water bottles. Both site areas produced similar numbers of whiskey and wine bottles, but with beer they sharply diverge. The South Area has 16 beer bottles and the Owens' House has only 1 (table 6.4). This supports the table glass pattern of much higher beer consumption in the South Area and, when combined with the lower-quality

Table 6.4. Bottle types

Function	Owens' House		South area	
	#	%	#	%
Whiskey	3	3	4	3
Gin	-	-	3	2
Wine	5	5	6	5
Beer	1	1	16	12
Unidentifiable alcohol	17	18	20	16
Food/condiment	32	34	35	27
Prescription/chemical	16	17	6	5
Patent medicine/bitters	6	6	17	13
Soda water	1	1	5	4
Toiletry	5	5	1	1
Ink	4	4	4	3
Unknown	5	5	12	9
Total	95	99	129	100

ceramics, suggests that the southern buildings and the Owens' House offered different atmospheres and probably served different clients.

Other bottles from the two site areas give further insights into their functions and activities. Both areas produced a large number of food/condiment and medicine bottles as well as smaller numbers of toiletry and ink bottles (table 6.4). Food containers from each area include pickle or preserve bottles, sauce bottles, mustard bottles, and olive oil bottles. It appears that condiments were an important part of meals at both areas.

Medicine bottles, including bitters, make up the third most common category from each area. The similarity ends here, however, as the Owens' House assemblage is dominated by prescription/chemical bottles while the South Area is dominated by patent medicine/bitters bottles (table 6.4). The prescription medicine bottles from the Owens' House may relate to having overnight guests and residents. It is unlikely that prescription bottles were served or sold to guests but rather that they were used by individuals accommodated at the tavern. The greater number of toiletry bottles at the Owens' House also supports this conclusion.

The number of patent medicine and bitters bottles from the South Area suggests that more typical sutler merchandise was provided in this area. Significantly, most (15 of 17) of these bottles were from three features (74, 102, and 104) on the southern edge of this area, suggesting an association with the more southerly building. Perhaps this building combined eating and sutler store functions.

Tin Cans

Further evidence for less formal dining and mercantile activities in the South Area is provided by the tin can assemblage from the site. While both

Table 6.5. Tin cans

| Function | Owens' House | | South area | |
#	%	#	%	
Rectangular food	3	25	42	53
Round food	3	25	21	27
Sardine	4	33	9	11
Personal	2	17	7	9
Total	12	100	79	100

the Owens' House and South Area produced tin food cans, the South Area assemblage was dramatically larger. It yielded 72 food cans, while the Owens' House yielded only 10 (table 6.5). This disparity suggests that there was a fundamental difference between the Owens' House and the southern establishments. The South Area is dominated by 63 round and

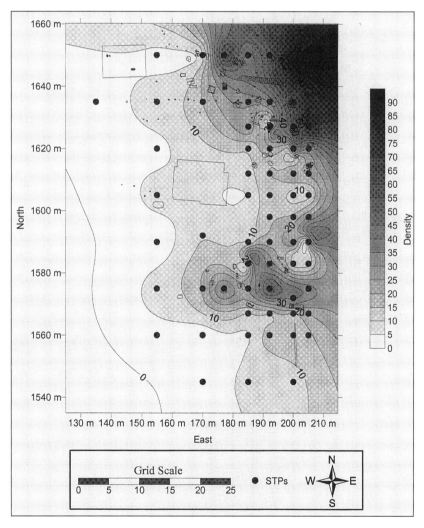

6.6. Distribution of architectural artifacts (15Js97) (courtesy of Wilbur Smith Associates).

rectangular hole-in-the-top cans that contained vegetable or fruit and meats or seafood, respectively. An additional 9 cans contained sardines. All of these cans were found in large numbers behind both South Area buildings.

These cans suggest that food service in the South Area relied on commercially prepared or convenience foods that would have taken little preparation before serving. These foods could have been eaten on the premises, following simple preparation, or taken elsewhere to be consumed. The can assemblage certainly supports conclusions drawn from ceramics and glassware that the South Area establishments were less formal.

Faunal Material

Evidence from ceramics, glassware, and tin cans indicates significant behavioral differences between the Owens' House and the South Area buildings. Given this, we also expect significant differences in the kinds of foods served at each establishment. While we have examined this issue somewhat with other artifacts, the remains of the food itself, particularly in the form of animal bones, is the most direct way to address this. Foodways are affected by many factors, including economic, ethnic, and functional ones, and these can be examined through faunal analysis. For instance, serving soups or stews is suggested by smaller and lower-ranked cuts of meat. Soups and stews are considered communal food and are often a less expensive food choice. They also have been associated with certain ethnic groups (see Otto 1980). Specific foodways could also be functionally related in that commercial establishments such as saloons might serve soups or stews to guests, as they can be prepared easily for large numbers. Fortunately, we have a large faunal assemblage from this site which will be investigated by using three standard analytical techniques: (1) taxonomic (usually species) identification, (2) element or body part identification, and (3) meat cut identification.

The faunal analysis began with a classification in terms of taxa and specific elements. The number of identified specimens (NISP) served as the unit of analysis for the assemblage. Questions concerning diet and social status were examined by identification of taxa and element, representative cuts of meat, butchering or serving methods (cuts and cut marks), and overall diversity of taxa and meat cut choices. Faunal remains were well preserved and abundant in refuse pits, cellars, and privy pits on the site. In this analysis, the faunal remains from two rectangular privy pits (Features 74 and 109) were examined. Feature 74 was located in the South Area and Feature 109 was located behind the Owens' House.

Taxonomic Representation

The assemblages from both site areas are dominated by mammals, but they do show some significant differences in taxa. The Owens' House

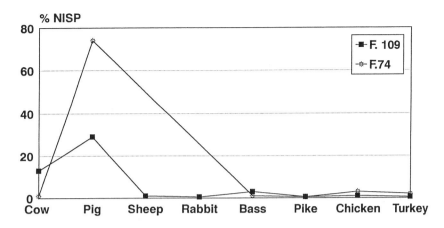

6.7. Identified taxa (15Js97) (courtesy of Wilbur Smith Associates).

(Feature 109) assemblage is much more diverse, with pig, cow, sheep, rabbit, fish (bass and pike), chicken, and turkey being present in descending order of frequency. In the South Area (Feature 74), pig dominates all other species at 75 percent of the total assemblage, although a small quantity of cow, chicken, turkey, and fish were recovered. No sheep or rabbit and much less cow were found in the South Area. Another striking difference in the two assemblages is in the amount of eggshell recovered. The Owens' House feature contained 20 grams of eggshell, while the South Area contained an astounding 2.5 kilograms.

An examination of the taxa from both areas reveals that pork and beef were the dominant meats, although pork was much more prevalent in the South Area. In both areas, fairly similar amounts of fowl were utilized with the exception of eggshell, which was much more common in the South Area. Only the Owens' House contained additional taxa representing meat sources, sheep and rabbit, as well as a slightly larger number of fish. In simply examining the taxa, subtle differences between the two features and site areas begin to emerge.

Element and Meat Cut Distribution

For analysis, the elements or anatomical parts of the mammal remains were identified as head, upper forelimb, lower forelimb, vertebrae, ribs, pelvis, upper hindlimb, lower hindlimb, and indeterminate lower limb. The distribution of pig elements from both areas shows a definite preference for hind and lower forelimb elements (fig. 6.7). The Owens' House feature has a high proportion of pig upper and lower hindlimb and less skull, upper and lower forelimb, vertebrae, and pelvic elements (fig 6.8). The pig elements from the South Area show similar trends, with no vertebrae elements identified and only a few head, upper forelimb, and hindlimb, or pelvis elements. The lower forelimbs and hindlimbs dominate the South Area (fig. 6.8).

In terms of standard 19th-century cuts of meat, these pig elements translate into jaw, hock, loin, ham, and feet (fig. 6.9). Both site areas are dominated by pigs' feet, and the South Area especially so. Hams and jaw cuts follow at the Owens' House. Hams were served in the South Area as well, although they account for only 7 percent of the pig remains (fig. 6.9). Interestingly, pig femurs recovered from the Owens' House exhibit regularly spaced cut marks running down the shaft of the bone perpendicular to its axis. This suggests that the proprietors of the Owens' House provided whole hams served in slices to customers of the tavern. Only one pig femur from the South Area exhibited cut marks indicative of slicing.

Turning to the cow elements, at the Owens' House these include vertebrae, ribs, pelvis, and upper hindlimb. Vertebrae are the most common cow elements followed by a moderate amount of upper hindlimbs and ribs (fig. 6.10). Only a few pelvic elements were recovered. The South Area has the same cow element groups represented, but its assemblage is dominated

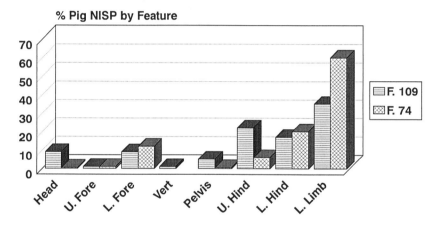

6.8. Pig element distribution (courtesy of Wilbur Smith Associates).

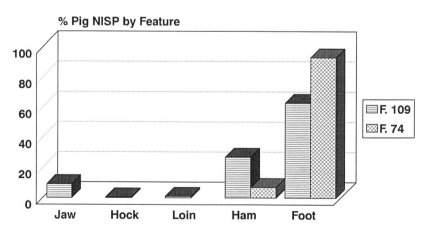

6.9. Pork cuts by feature (courtesy of Wilbur Smith Associates).

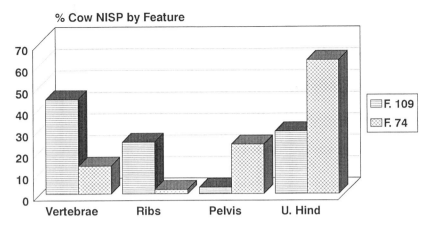

6.10. Cow element distribution (courtesy of Wilbur Smith Associates).

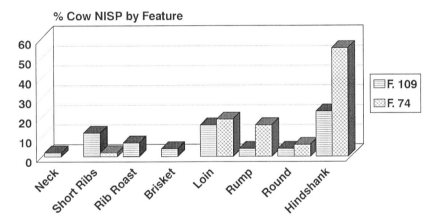

6.11. Beef cut distribution by feature (courtesy of Wilbur Smith Associates).

by upper hindlimb elements (fig. 6.10). These are followed by a moderate amount of pelvic elements and vertebrae and a sparse amount of ribs.

In terms of meat cuts, the cow remains show somewhat different patterns for the two site areas. A much wider range of meat cuts is present at the Owens' House and includes a large percentage of hindshank and loin cuts, a moderate amount of short ribs, and a small proportion of neck cuts, briskets, rump cuts, and round cuts (fig. 6.11). The South Area has a much higher proportion of hindshank and rump cuts and similar proportions of loin cuts, round cuts, and short ribs (fig. 6.11).

Overall, the cow remains suggest a diverse beef diet at the Owens' House, which included stews, roasts, steaks, and ribs. The South Area is dominated by hindshanks, which most likely were used in stews or soups. It should also be remembered that in terms of overall quantity, the Owens' House has a much larger cow assemblage.

Interestingly, a common factor between both features is the presence of articulated cow ankle joints. The Owens' House feature contains elements for two ankle units and the South Area feature contains three. All five joints would be from the least meaty portion of the shank and may have been used in the preparation of soups, stews, or stock.

Sheep elements from the Owens' House represent the upper hindlimb, upper forelimb, and lower forelimb. No sheep elements were found in the South Area. Unlike the cow or the pig materials, the sheep assemblage does contain upper forelimb material, but like the cow and pig, it lacks head elements.

Interestingly, even the mammal bones that are not identifiable at the species level are informative about diet. These are classified as large, medium, or medium-large mammals. These cuts represent sawn cross-sectioned long bones and other elements cut into steaks or chops or what are referred to as sliced meats.

At the Owens' House, sliced meats account for 22 percent of the medium- to large-mammal assemblage, and identifiable sawed elements include pelvic, femur, and tibia sections. Fourteen percent of this assemblage from Feature 109 consist of sternum cartilage associated with the brisket cut. The remaining medium- to large-mammal material consists of rib, vertebrae, and tibia fragments. Most of this material is probably pig, but the sternal cartilage is probably cow. The South Area had a low frequency of sliced meats, at 3 percent of the mammal assemblage, and identifiable sawed elements include pelvis, femur, and tibia sections. The remaining medium- to large-mammal material consists of a small percentage of rib fragments.

The chicken and turkey specimens from both features are restricted to wing, body, and leg elements. Like the cow, pig, and sheep elements, no cranial material was identified. Also no elements from the feet were recovered nor were any tarsometatarsi. The tarsometatarsus is a nonmeat-bearing bone below the tibiotarsus or drumstick that is commonly removed from dressed birds. This material probably represents the remains of whole dressed birds. The main difference between the two site areas in terms of bird products is the disproportional amount of eggshell, 2.5 kilograms, recovered from the South Area.

The identified fish material represents elements of bass and pike. Both sites produced indeterminate vertebrae of varying sizes and bass and pike cranial elements. This combination of cranial and vertebrae elements implies that whole fish were being utilized at these locations.

Faunal Discussion

What does the distribution of species, elements, and meat cuts between the two features tell us about camp life in these two distinct sections of the study area? First, there is no evidence for nonhuman taphonomic agents, including carnivores or rodents, and the bones appear to be unweathered.

This implies that the fauna in these features represents a quickly filled pit that did not remain open long and that element distributions are not products of differential destruction.

The lack or paucity of upper forelimbs in the cattle and pig material and the presence of whole dressed poultry suggests that meat being served at all of these establishments was brought in as butchered units, not as whole animals or whole dressed carcasses. None of these specimens represent typical hooves and heads butchering refuse. The overabundance of pigs' feet, especially in the South Area, suggests that feet were an acquisition unit and proprietors were intentionally acquiring and serving these cuts. The presence of the hindquarters and the articulated beef ankles at both site areas implies that possibly hindquarters were preferred over forequarters because they could be hung more easily for storage or transport than the front quarters.

Specifically, the Owens' House feature (Feature 109) appears to contain a higher-status faunal assemblage than the South Area (Feature 74). The Owens' House feature is distinguished by a greater taxonomic diversity of typical food mammals, with the addition of sheep and rabbit. Also a higher percentage of beef is present in the assemblage. In terms of meat cuts, a greater diversity of both pork and beef cuts are present, including loin and ribs. Not only were a variety of meat cuts served at this tavern, but it also has a higher frequency of sliced meats and femurs with patterned cut marks. The faunal assemblage, taken in concert with the ceramic analysis, suggests that cuts of meat were placed on platters and were sliced and served at table. The variety of meat cuts suggests more elaborate preparation and service in the Owens' House. These differences imply that the Owens' House tavern served a greater variety of food than did the South Area and that it served similar foods differently.

The assemblage from the South Area feature shows not only the reverse of the high-status trends—that is a lower diversity of food taxa and meat cuts—but the cuts present show an almost "portable" quality. This area is characterized by an overabundance of eggshell and pigs' feet. The amount of eggshell is phenomenal, and if it were being served or cooked fresh would represent intense cooking labor. To estimate the number of eggs present, an eggshell of a medium to large chicken egg was weighed. The eggshell weighed approximately 6 grams. Dividing the total eggshell weight, approximately 400 eggs can be accounted from half of Feature 74 at the South Area. Only 4 eggs are estimated from Feature 109 at the Owens' House. It is possible that eggs were served hard boiled or pickled or used in baking. During the early and mid-19th century, baking powder had not been invented, so eggs in large quantities were used as leavening. Another, almost astounding aspect of the South Area feature assemblage is the minimum number of pigs' feet. Here at least 135 individual pigs' feet were deposited. The Owens' House feature contains minimally the remains of only 8 pigs' feet. Pigs' feet were served pickled or boiled with potatoes and beans or used to flavor stews, soups, and stock. Taken together, the assemblage from Feature 74 suggests that soups, stews, beans, or other inexpensive foods that have an almost communal nature were served from establishments in the South Area. Soups, stews, or beans would have been served simply from a large pot or other vessel. Individuals, whether enlisted men or civilian laborers, would have used bowls or tin plates and might even have taken the food elsewhere on the premises to consume. The pickled pigs' feet and eggs have a pronounced "portable" quality and are the types of foods served in bars or diners even today.

In conclusion, there are differences in the faunal assemblages from the South Area and the Owens' House area indicative of higher-status and lower-status eating establishments. These differences persist despite similarities in the way each establishment was supplied and probably stored food. The main differences are seen in terms of how these similar foods were prepared and served. The Owens' House represents more variety in meat cuts and is more suggestive of elaborate meals served in a dining atmosphere, while the assemblage from the South Area is indicative of an establishment serving cheaper fare consisting of a narrower selection of cuts served in a communal atmosphere. The presence of portable/mobile bar foods such as pickled pigs' feet and pickled eggs in the South Area, which are largely absent from the Owens' House tavern, seems to underscore the status and functional differences apparent between these establishments and site areas.

Military Artifacts

An independent line of evidence to identify clientele, particularly to identify the presence of officers or enlisted men, is from their clothing, especially coat buttons and hat or coat insignia. According to Civil War regulations, enlisted men wore general service brass eagle buttons with the flag pattern on the shield (U.S. War Department 1861). They also had hat insignia consisting of plain stamped brass infantry (bugle), cavalry (crossed swords), or artillery (crossed cannons) symbols. Officers wore gilded brass eagle buttons with the service insignia within the shield—"I" for infantry, "C" for cavalry, and "A" for artillery—unless they were a general or on a general's staff (U.S. War Department 1861). General staff buttons were gilded and had a circle of stars surrounding the eagle. Officers' uniforms also had a shoulder rank insignia of metal or cloth and braided brass service branch insignia for their hats.

Although only a few military uniform items were recovered at the Owens' House/Post Office Complex, they indicate a strong difference between the north and south ends of the site. Two out of four eagle buttons found at the Owens' House were officers' buttons and the other two were enlisted men's buttons. In contrast, at the South Area twelve enlisted men's eagle buttons and only one officer's eagle button were recovered.

The four hat insignia illustrate a similar pattern for the site. The two insignia found in the South Area (one cavalry and one artillery) are from enlisted men's hats, while both hat insignia from the Owens' House (also one cavalry and one artillery) are from officers' hats. The Owens' House area also produced another clear officers' artifact, a gold-plated brass sword scabbard guide.

While the number of these military artifacts is small, their patterning is strong. The South Area military clients were overwhelmingly enlisted men, while those of the Owens' House were mostly officers.

Summary and Discussion

At Camp Nelson the preparation, serving, and consumption of food was not confined to the mess hall or the campsite. The reality was far more diverse in terms of location, complexity of the meal, and service. Numerous hotels or taverns, eating houses, saloons, sutler stores, and produce vendors were located in camp which offered officers, soldiers, and civilian employees a variety of dining and drinking experiences. Soldiers also foraged for food outside of camp and even purchased meals from surrounding farmers (Hunt 1966:17). A selection of foods and beverages was available from a variety of locales. At Camp Nelson, the meals were not what one soldier described in his diary, "Dinner and breakfast are alike, only sometimes the meat and potatoes are cut up and cooked together. Supper is the same, minus the meat and potatoes" (Wiley 1952). Meals could be complex affairs with multiple courses in one establishment, a bowl of beans in another, or rations consumed at a soldier's tent.

Thus one could argue that at least two foodways systems were working (sometimes independently) at Camp Nelson. One was the military foodways system that procured, prepared, and distributed food to soldiers, employees, and refugees. This system actually consisted of three separate subsystems: (1) the distribution of rations to enlisted men who prepared this themselves, (2) the sale of foodstuffs to officers by the camp or regimental commissary, and (3) the communal preparation and service of food in mess halls to employees and refugees. This system also controlled discard through military regulation.

The second system was somewhat independent of the military system and consisted of local peddlers, businessmen, or hucksters who procured, prepared, and distributed food within the limited market economy in the camp. Even this almost free-enterprise system was controlled by the military, which specified where (in camp) they could do business, thus affecting distribution and where refuse could be discarded. Beverages, particularly alcohol, were served by these entrepreneurs. The sale of alcoholic beverages was regulated by the military as well. Vendors and their establishments could restrict or control their clientele by charging higher prices. A combination of archaeological and documentary data suggests that consumption behavior within the free-enterprise system at Camp Nelson was regulated in this way.

The archaeological and historical investigations of the Owens' House/Post Office Complex have added considerably to our understanding of the second foodways system at Camp Nelson, particularly in the variety of dining situations and in the economic stratification or segregation of the different establishments. Archaeological and archival documentation on the Owens' House suggests that it was a tavern or hotel offering meals and overnight accommodations to middle- or upper-class clients such as officers and supervisory employees. It served more expensive cuts of meat and perhaps a variety of vegetables and desserts in multiple courses, in a more refined setting. Expensive molded ironstone and serving ware were used to set an elaborate table where middle- and upper-class officers and employees could engage in genteel dining.

The South Area eating establishments served liquor and beer by the drink, commercially packaged convenience foods, and simple snack-like meals in a less formal setting. These foods and conditions were not as genteel or expensive as those of the Owens' House, and their primary clientele was of a lower class, including enlisted men and laborers. Of the two south-end establishments, one appears to have been an eating house/saloon with sutlers store services and merchandise, while the other was a saloon serving food and drinks.

No documentation was found which suggested that private establishments were segregated by military rank through official orders. It is most likely that this separation was economic (that is, because of expense) and social. The result was an additional and unofficial (in the military sense) reinforcement of the military order which separates officers (traditionally gentlemen) and enlisted men (traditionally the working class or small farmers).

7

Defending the Capital

The Civil War Garrison at Fort C.F. Smith

Joseph Balicki

> If there had been a thousand years of life before us and we had no defi-
> nite plans in living, the stay in these forts might have been enjoyed. As
> it was there was a dull succession of inspections, parades of all sorts
> and the make-believe guard-duty that was hardly creditable to any one
> concerned. The constant query with us was, "What are we here for?"
> **Roe (1899:268)**

Civil War battles, regimental histories, military and political leaders, and
social issues have inspired public discussions and interest for more than
130 years. The dynamic flow of the war resulted in the creation of large
numbers of archaeological sites and the discard of countless artifacts. The
collection of war relics, begun by the soldiers themselves, continues in
earnest. Until recently, archaeologists focused primarily on battlefields or
fortifications. At the same time, soldiers' camps and material culture remained among the least known, in terms of archaeology, of any site type.
But camps have been the prime focus of relic collectors. Archaeological
attention began to shift in the 1980s, as an outgrowth of Cultural Resources Management studies, but the majority of data from Civil War
encampment sites remains inaccessible and poorly reported.

Military camp types vary from large permanent installations to short-
term field camps. Fort C.F. Smith, an earthwork in the defenses of Washington, D.C., was a permanent installation, occupied from 1863 to 1865.
Archaeological investigations at Fort C.F. Smith sampled deposits from
Civil War refuse dumps and from the location of the fort's support buildings. Comparing C.F. Smith's artifact assemblage with other Union encampments reveals that distinct differences between camp types exist.
Further, comparison allows for an examination of camp similarities and
differences based upon location, function, access to urban markets, and
garrison composition. Archaeological assemblages at campsites reflect
choices made both by the military and by individual soldiers, and the
material culture documents day-to-day behavior of men living within a

regimented, military social setting. Additionally, some artifacts are expressions of the soldiers' nonmilitary identity.

Military regulations defined social identities within a garrison. By directing hierarchical rank relationships, daily schedule, dress code, activities, weapons, and daily behavior, a bond was formed between soldiers that created a social entity, the army lifestyle. At the same time, non-issue items (some weapons, ceramics, clothing, and food) and personal items offer insight into expressions of individual identity and preference.

Military regulations also dictated how camps were to be set up (U.S. War Department 1980:74–80). The army's adherence to regulations governing arrangement of camps has been noted archaeologically (Legg and Smith 1989:130–31; Higgins et al. 1995:82–83). Permanent camps do not appear to be arranged in the same fashion as field camps. However, examining spatial artifact distribution within camps offers an opportunity to examine adherence to regulations.

In a general sense, military encampments exist to establish a household for soldiers. Here, the term household encompasses an aggregate group of individuals sharing space, activities associated with nonwork-related activities (for example, cooking, sleeping, personal interaction, family structure), and in the case of the military, work. Within a military encampment, military doctrine penetrated all aspects of the daily experience. The household was not separate from the workplace. Further, the household was primarily male. In some cases, notably at permanent installations, officers were permitted to have their families with them, and at many posts non-military personnel resided within camps. Viewing military encampments as a specific type of household broadens the context within which they can be examined.

Prior to the Civil War, the Federal Army's role was restricted to coastal defenses and suppression of Native American and Mormon insurrections on the western frontier. In times of crisis, state militias and private organizations were called upon to increase the size of the army. The different state and local militias had varying uniforms, arms, and training. Although many aspects of the military were dictated by tradition and doctrine, it was not until the Civil War that Federal standards within the military were put into practice on a large scale. Throughout the war, regiments continued to be organized and recruited at local and state levels, but soldiers increasingly were integrated into an army that emphasized Federal military regulation over state militia organization. By the end of the war, the state militia system was discarded in favor of a Federal force. This transformation led to changes in military material culture; many of these changes carry symbolic meaning. Military symbols such as insignia, uniforms, and buttons reflect larger social changes within the country as state governments became secondary to the Federal government.

Defense of the Capital

In April 1861, Washington, D.C., was an unprotected city commanded by an unproven leader. After Fort Sumter fell, Virginians seceded, and Marylanders struggled with their future, the city became more isolated from its political base. The capital was in a war zone and defenseless against attack. Traditionally, unlike many other national capitals, large numbers of Federal troops were not garrisoned in or near the capital. In these early, tense days of the war, fewer than 600 militia and 200 marines manned defensive positions at government buildings and bridge crossings. Resignations within the army's officer corps further weakened preparation for the capital's defense (Cooling 1991:25).

Lincoln's call for 75,000 volunteers to suppress the rebellion quickly resulted in military units reinforcing the vulnerable city. Movement of Federal troops through Baltimore sparked rioting and open rebellion in that city, resulting in the destruction of transportation and communication links between the two cities. Maryland appeared on the brink of secession. Washington, D.C., was surrounded by rebellion. Reinforcing troops soon bypassed Baltimore by way of the Chesapeake Bay. Troops were transported directly to the capital via the Potomac River or by a combined land and water route through Annapolis, Maryland. By the end of April, around 11,000 troops were in the capital (Cooling 1991:31).

Before the war, there was no direct rail link between Richmond and Washington, D.C.; this hindered Confederate operations near the capital. Prewar competition between railroad and steamship companies resulted in combined service between the two cities. The railroad extended from Richmond to Aquia Creek, where passengers and freight were transferred to steamships (Wills 1975:6). An indirect rail service with a transfer at Manassas Junction did exist but was less convenient. Prewar transportation networks, while not totally favorable to the Union, were such that defending troops arrived in sufficient numbers soon enough to stay any Confederate design for a quick assault on the capital.

Many in the military, including general in chief of the army Winfield Scott, believed the capital could not be defended. The city was approachable from all sides. Spread out along the banks of the Potomac and Anacostia Rivers, Washington had only rivers as natural defenses. Along the Virginia side of the Potomac ran Arlington Heights (fig. 7.1). If occupied by the Confederate Army, most Federal buildings could be brought under artillery fire. The Federal government moved quickly to secure the heights as well as the nearby city of Alexandria.

In May 1861, Federal regiments crossed the Potomac River and began constructing a series of fortifications that would, by war's end, transform Washington into one of the most heavily fortified cities in the world. Ini-

Future Site of Fort C. F. Smith

7.1. Washington, D.C., and vicinity, 1862 (Ridgeway 1862).

tially, work consisted of erecting fortifications to guard approaches to Potomac River bridges, the Georgetown aqueduct, and to protect the port city of Alexandria. The "Arlington Lines" protected bridges and guarded the high ground overlooking Washington, D.C. Numerous regimental camps were also established along the Alexandria and Arlington lines. Because participants believed the war would not last long, no thought was given to long-term planning. Further, engineering officers found themselves lacking any knowledge of the military features of the capital (Barnard 1871:8).

In the spring of 1861, the Confederate Army was thinly spread across northern Virginia. Approximately 20,000 troops occupied positions from Leesburg in the north to Aquia Creek in the south. Most of these forces were within 30 miles of Washington, D.C. (Cooling 1991:41). Other than making their presence known through visible demonstrations, a few skirmishes, and raids, these troops did not engage the Union Army. However, their mere presence exerted tremendous pressure on Northern political and military leaders.

In July 1861, Union forces were defeated at the Battle of Manassas, 25 miles from Washington. The Confederates, however, could not exploit their victory. Confederate Gen. J. E. Johnston established his headquarters at Fairfax Courthouse, 15 miles from Washington, D.C. Capital citizens could see Confederate flags flying above the advance positions on Munson's and Miner's Hills (Leech 1986:112; Cooling 1991:66). The Confederate presence in Arlington and northeastern Fairfax counties was restricted to pickets, outposts, and raids (Corbett 1861). These activities kept pressure on the capital and embarrassed the Union leadership. During this time, Washington's only links to the north were the rail line to Baltimore and navigation on the Potomac River.

Before the war, the Potomac River was the main supply route to Washington, D.C. In October 1861, the Confederates finished batteries at Cockpit Point, Freestone Point, Shipping Point, and Evansport on the Potomac and effectively shut down river traffic. These positions were only 20 to 30 miles downstream from the capital. Although manned by inexperienced artillerists, the perceived threat was such that few ships risked running past the batteries (Wills 1975:112). Once again Washington, D.C., felt vulnerable and isolated. For the next five months, the city's only major transportation link to the north was the Baltimore and Ohio Railroad; Maryland still had not committed to the Union. Despite increasing numbers of troops in and around the capital, Federal leadership was either unable or unwilling to mount an attack on the Potomac River batteries. Notwithstanding shortages of some materials, the blockade's actual success was the apprehension and embarrassment it caused Federal leadership (Wills 1975:104). During the winter of 1862, the Confederates withdrew to positions south of the Rappahannock River for tactical and logistical reasons (Wills 1975:155–62).

In the meantime, under the direction of Gen. George B. McClellan, the Union Army was rebuilding and improving the capital's defenses. McClellan placed Col. (later Maj. Gen.) John G. Barnard in charge of building an integrated series of defenses encircling the capital. Initially the city's defense was to include a system of forts, lunettes, redoubts, and batteries mounting nearly 300 guns (Barnard 1871:15). Attention was given to completing defensive positions along the Arlington lines by constructing works to guard major roads and river crossings. Once key strategic locations were protected, the defense network was expanded to strengthen weak or exposed areas. In general, designs for the early works were based on D. H. Mahan's *Complete Treatise on Field Fortification* (1836). By the end of 1861, 48 formal works had been constructed (Barnard 1871:15).

Except for a heavy skirmish at Fort Stevens in 1864, the capital's defenses were never seriously tested by Confederate forces. The defenses acted as a deterrent. After the second battle of Manassas, Confederate forces did not pursue defeated Union troops to Washington, in part because of the formidable defenses surrounding the city and because of Lee's plan for a Maryland invasion.

Improvements to the capital's defensive system continued throughout the war. By war's end, 68 enclosed forts and batteries were arranged in a perimeter defensive line of about 13 miles. Supporting the forts were 93 fortified positions for field artillery, 20 miles of rifle-pits, and 30 miles of military roads (Cooling and Owen 1988:15). The fortifications included 1,400 gun emplacements, but only 807 guns and 98 mortars were ever mounted. The number of troops assigned to the capital's defense shifted throughout the war but on average remained near 20,000 men at all times (Cooling and Owen 1988:16).

The city's vulnerability in 1861 played a large role in forming Federal policy in the eastern theater. During the war, Washington, D.C., became a symbol of Federal control for the nation (Cooling and Owen 1988:1; Cooling 1991). Protecting this symbol was an overriding consideration for Union political and military leaders conducting the war. Further, militarily, the capital became a major troop training and staging area for the eastern war effort. Washington's security dominated all military planning. The capital's safety was ensured before Federal offensive operations were undertaken, and efforts to guarantee the capital's safety continued throughout the war. Fort C.F. Smith reflects the continued effort to strengthen the defenses.

Fort C.F. Smith

After the Battle of Antietam (September 1862), Federal leaders established a commission to reevaluate Washington's defenses (U.S. War Department [O.R.], Series I, vol. IX, pt. 2, 558). As a result of the commission's report, Fort C.F. Smith was built to extend the Arlington line to the Potomac River. The fort's location effectively cut off any enemy advance along the Potomac bluffs, thereby preventing the flanking of several forts and protecting approaches to the Aqueduct Bridge of the Chesapeake and Ohio Canal (fig. 7.2).

Fort C.F. Smith was constructed in 1863 on the site of a farmstead and orchard. The fort's earthworks consisted of two faces and two parallel flanks, in a configuration known as a lunette (W. Owen, personal communication, 1995; fig. 3:1). The fort was unflanked; the earthwork's design was governed by topography and required direction of fire (Barnard 1871:43, 80–81). The fort plans incorporated design improvements developed over two years of war (Benton 1995:3). The perimeter was 368 yards and contained 22 gun emplacements. Once completed, it and Fort Whipple were considered, "the most perfect and beautiful specimens of what may be called 'semi-permanent' field works" (Barnard 1871:32).

Support buildings, located east of the fort, were outside its ramparts and not fortified (fig. 7.3). Sixteen buildings appear on the fort list of May 10, 1865, including three barracks, two mess houses, two cook houses, an ordnance sergeant's house, a guard house, four officers' quarters, and a

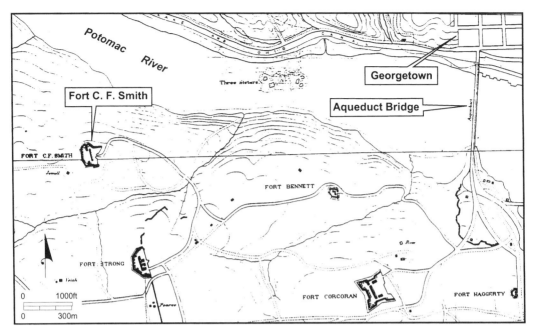

7.2. Detail of topographic map showing the northwest portion of the Arlington Line (Barnard 1871).

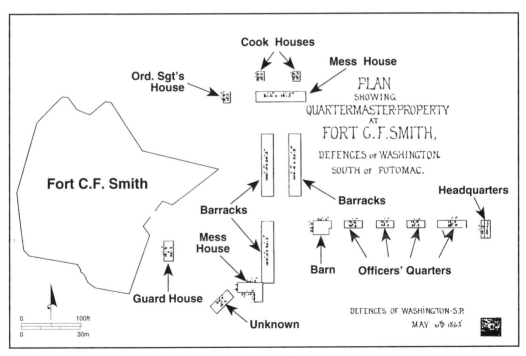

7.3. Quartermaster property map of Fort C.F. Smith, August 1865 (U.S. Quartermaster Department 1865).

headquarters. The guard house was located just east of the main gate. Barracks for the troops, cook and mess houses, and ordnance sergeant's house were aligned perpendicular to the north/south axis of the fort. The officers' quarters extended east, along the top of a ridge. The easternmost building was headquarters. Functions of two other buildings are not identified, although historic photographs show one of the unidentified buildings as a barn or stable. The number and types of buildings probably fluctuated over the course of the war, as the army tended to relocate buildings from one fort to another (W. Owen, personal communication 1995).

Support buildings were not intended to be permanent. Architectural drawings show that building superstructures rested on either brick footers or wood posts. Excavations at Fort Ward in Alexandria, Virginia, uncovered brick piers associated with that fort's barracks (Steve Shepard, personal communication 1998). Considering that buildings were temporary, it is likely that little effort went into their construction. Evidence supporting inferior construction was the destruction of a barracks by a summer storm in 1865.

Soldiers in the Defense of Washington

The soldiers who served in the defenses of Washington and at Fort C.F. Smith saw little, if any, actual fighting during the early war years, and garrison life was considered soft. Once the capital became the hub for the eastern war effort, troops moved in and out of the defenses and camps located around the city. Garrison life continued to be an easy assignment throughout the remainder of the war (fig. 7.4). Enlisted man Stephen Blanding, recalling his duty in the defenses wrote, "With the exception of drilling, guard mounting, and inspection of knapsacks, we had but little to do, and the time passed pleasantly enough, each day shortening our term of service" (Blanding 1889:15). For the most part, garrison life was tedious and boring, a daily repetition of military drill, camp maintenance, and regulations.

Military personnel within the garrison observed a prescribed schedule that coordinated most daily events. Typically, reveille was at 5:40 and taps at 9:00 or 10:00 (Cooling 1991:170). A soldier's official duties included drill, fatigue, guard, orderly, and inspection (fig. 7.5). Within the forts, artillery drill took up four to six hours of a soldier's day. In addition to artillery drill, heavy artillery regiments received infantry and bayonet exercise. General camp and fortification maintenance was undertaken by groups of soldiers organized into fatigue details. The fatigue details gathered firewood, cleared vegetation from the fort's approaches, repaired or constructed structures, and policed the fortifications and camp area. Soldiers were able to relieve the tedium of camp life during off-duty time in

7.4. Photograph of Company K, 2nd New York Heavy Artillery, in front of the Fort C.F. Smith bombproof, August 1865 (courtesy of the U.S. Army Military Institute, Carlisle, Pennsylvania).

7.5. Photograph of Company I, 2nd New York Heavy Artillery, view to the south showing powder magazine and south flank of Fort C.F. Smith, August 1865 (courtesy of the U.S. Army Military Institute, Carlisle, Pennsylvania).

Table 7.1. Regiments and period of occupation at Fort C.F. Smith

Regiment	Date of occupation
5th New York Heavy Artillery, Co. M	May–October 1863
2nd New York Heavy Artillery, Cos. I, K, L	March–May 1864
2nd Pennsylvania Heavy Artillery	May 17–27, 1864
164th Ohio Infantry	May 11–August 1864
1st Battery Maine Light Artillery, "A"	April 21–July 11, 1864
1st Battery Rhode Island Light Artillery, "H"	July 10–October 16, 1864
6th Regimental Massachusetts Militia (100 Days)	July 23–August 21, 1864
1st Massachusetts Heavy Artillery	May 24–July 19, 1865
Battery "D" Maryland Light Artillery	June 1865
2nd New York Heavy Artillery, Cos. I, K, L	August–October 1865

the early evening. Variations to barracks life included sleeping, eating, drinking alcohol, writing, and receiving passes for off-duty excursions to Alexandria, Washington, D.C., or Mount Vernon.

Enlisted men lived in the barracks, while officers had separate quarters, possibly with their families. At Fort C.F. Smith, soldiers lived in three barracks and there were four quarters for officers (fig. 7.3). Meals were prepared in cook houses and eaten in mess houses; officers could choose to eat meals in their quarters.

Few documents detailing the fort's garrison were located. Monthly post returns, showing the number of men present and absent and naming officers assigned to duty, were made for each fort. Unfortunately, returns for Fort C.F. Smith have been lost. However, Owen (Cheek et al. 1995) found that at least 10 different artillery units were garrisoned at the fort (table 7.1).

In May 1864, Brig. Gen., Inspector of Artillery, A. P. Howe inspected Fort C.F. Smith (O. R.: Series I, vol. XXXVI/2:886). At this time, the fort's garrison consisted of 548 men, 1 ordnance sergeant, and 15 commissioned officers of the 2nd New York Heavy Artillery under the direction of Maj. W. A. McKay. Drill in artillery was found to be "very ordinary" and in need of much improvement. Infantry drill was insufficient and in want of "more energy and attention." There was a "great want of improvement" in the garrison's overall discipline. However, the garrison passed inspection and was considered sufficient.

After the war, Fort C.F. Smith was garrisoned for several months. In July 1865, a summer storm leveled several buildings. For a time, tents were erected on the platform foundations of the destroyed barracks. Later these platforms were used for entertainment. Evenings were spent listening to music, with soldiers even sharing a dance with one another. On such nights, the soldiers felt that lights out always came too early (Roe 1899:267–69).

In November 1865, the fort was decommissioned, and the site of Fort C.F. Smith reverted to its prewar owners. Approximately two-thirds of the fort's earthworks survive in excellent condition. However, road construction and residential development destroyed the south section of fortifications. Several buildings were built in the early 20th century just north and northeast of the fort. These buildings destroyed archaeological deposits. Although cultivated for a period of time, the location of the majority of support buildings has not been built upon. In 1995, surviving earthworks and the support buildings' location were purchased by the County of Arlington, Virginia. The county is developing the property into a passive use park, with the goal of preserving the Civil War legacy of Fort C.F. Smith as well as Arlington County's late-19th-century heritage.

Archaeological Investigations

Archaeological testing included systematic shovel tests, a systematic metal-detector survey, and test units (Balicki 1995). No archaeological investigations were undertaken within the fortifications themselves, as they are to be preserved as is and not restored. At the request of Arlington County, artifact distribution maps have not been included, in an effort to discourage looting. Past residents of the property dug for artifacts within and adjacent to the earthworks. Other collectors found only poison ivy in their attempts to collect relics from areas around the fort (Crouch 1978:116).

Archaeological investigations failed to identify any tangible evidence of the fort's support buildings. However, a brick and stone paving may represent a remnant of the fort barn, and a cellar hole roughly conforms to the headquarters location. The cellar hole is more likely associated with a late-19th-century residence at this location. Artifacts from the cellar hole postdate the war, although this does not rule out reuse of the Civil War building.

Artifacts dating from the Civil War to the present were thinly scattered over the location of the support buildings. Test excavation soil profiles indicated that this area had been disturbed by plowing. North of the fort and military encampment, there is a large area containing intact refuse deposits from the military occupation. Several factors, including steep terrain, reforestation, and an absence of post–Civil War activities in this area, contribute to the preservation of these refuse deposits.

Comparative Sites

Comparative collections from Civil War campsites are limited, and artifact information is readily available only from Fort Nelson, Tennessee, and Folly Island, South Carolina. Comparison of these sites with Fort C.F.

Smith provides an opportunity to examine differences in supply, provisioning, armaments, and personal goods between three different camp types. Fort C.F. Smith represents a defensive fort adjacent to a large eastern urban area. Fort Nelson, occupied between 1863 and 1866, was a Union quartermaster's depot and center of military activity located in a western rural setting (McBride 1994). The Folly Island site was an 1863 Union winter camp on a South Carolina barrier island. Fort C.F. Smith more closely resembles Fort Nelson because both were permanent installations dating to a comparable time. However, unlike Fort Nelson, Fort C.F. Smith was primarily manned by regular Federal troops and apparently never had a significant number of nonmilitary occupants or workers. In this respect, Fort C.F. Smith is similar to Folly Island.

Two additional sites are used to aid in the interpretation of spatial artifact distribution at C.F. Smith. Investigations at an 1862–65 Union camp at Gloucester Point, Virginia, provide comparison for camp maintenance (Higgins et al. 1995). This site is notable for the preservation of the structural remains of Sibley tents. The low percentage of non-architectural artifacts recovered from the Gloucester Point encampment precludes the use of this site in most comparative analysis. An archaeological survey at Fort Monroe, Virginia, provided data on refuse disposal and camp maintenance at a military installation occupied from the 1820s to the present (Balicki et al. 1999).

Artifact Distribution, Fort C.F. Smith

Artifacts are not distributed evenly across Fort C.F. Smith. Civil War period artifacts are, for the most part, absent around the fort's support buildings. The majority of Civil War period artifacts were recovered from refuse dumps located away from the fort and habitation area. The observed artifact distribution is interpreted as a reflection of camp maintenance practices and dismantling of the buildings in the fall of 1865.

At the beginning of the war, conditions in the camps near the capital were deplorable. U.S. Sanitary Commission inspections in July 1861 at 20 camps found them unclean, unhealthful, and not well maintained, with soldiers surrounded by "pestilential influences" (Stillé 1997:85–86). The Sanitary Commission worked with the military and civilian government to improve the lives of Union soldiers through distribution of aid and the establishment of hospitals. Partially through the influence of the Sanitary Commission, conditions in permanent camps changed for the better, as the commission called on the military to comply with stated regulations governing camp maintenance (Stillé 1997:87–88).

Maintenance of the landscape around fort living quarters reflects the development of U.S. military regulations and the increasing prominence of the Federal military. The 1861, revised regulations dictated that the officer of the day was to maintain order and cleanliness of the camp, using a fatigue detail or prisoners, if available (U.S. War Department 1980:85). Fatigue was part of everyday military life and included policing camp areas and general maintenance (Cooling 1991:168; Billings 1993:100–101, 177–78). Adoption of Federal regulations by militia troops and development of the Federal military establishment, beginning with McClellan in 1861, led to better discipline and order in camps. This increased discipline was even noted by reenlisting veterans (Griffith 1989:98). Increased military order resulted in increased camp maintenance, a behavior that can be observed in the archaeological record.

Artifact distributions observed at Fort C.F. Smith are believed to reflect policing of habitation areas by fatigue details. The paucity or absence of Civil War period artifacts has been noted at other military sites. The garrison in and around Fort Monroe swelled from a prewar "several hundred" to well over 1,000 soldiers during the war. Numbers increased even more dramatically in April 1862, when nearly 112,000 troops occupied positions in and around the fort (Weinert and Arthur 1989:94–132). While Fort Monroe archaeological investigations indicate that pre–Civil War military artifacts are fairly common, military artifacts from the Civil War period are very rare (Balicki et al. 1999). The presence or absence of military artifacts and the distribution of ceramic ware types lead to the conclusion that through the first half of the 19th century, policing of the fort's landscape increased. Although ironstone is sparsely scattered across the fort, other ceramics with start dates beginning after the 1840s (e.g., yellowware) are rare.

At Gloucester Point, a four-year Union occupation is reflected by only 143 non-architectural artifacts out of 1,248 artifacts (Higgins et al. 1995: 69). When 88 arms-related artifacts are removed, the absence of domestic refuse (55) is even more striking. Further, some artifacts may represent the Confederate occupation of the site prior to the Union encampment (Higgins et al. 1995:82). In all likelihood, the low density of non-architectural artifacts in the camp area is the result of military regulations requiring policing of the camp area.

In summary, policing activities by fatigue details resulted in a spatial distribution of artifacts reflecting camp maintenance practices. The distribution of artifacts in Civil War camps is a reflection of the degree to which the garrison adhered to military regulations governing the policing of camps. Clearly, at Gloucester Point, Fort Monroe, and Fort C.F. Smith, the garrisons policed camp areas, removing much of the refuse from living and work areas. These permanent installations may show more landscape maintenance than field camps. However, evidence for policing the camp landscape was noted at Folly Island, a front-line position (Legg and Smith 1989:72, 86). Clearly, by 1863, camp maintenance was part of the regulated daily routine of military life.

At war's end, most Washington forts were decommissioned and dismantled. Weapons and stores were removed, and the right and title to buildings, fixtures, and timber were turned over to the estimated 1,000 property owners affected by construction of the capital's defenses (Cooling 1991:233–40). Excess materials (lumber, timber, tools) were sold at public auction or stored (Cooling and Owen 1988:16). The Jewell family, prewar owners of the land Fort C.F. Smith was built upon, testified to the Southern Claims Commission that they purchased five or six of the buildings remaining at the fort and "paid $400 for Fort Smith" (Jewell 1877). This expense reflects the purchase rights to salvage. In many cases, salvage rights were given in lieu of later claims for damages by property owners. By paying for salvaged materials, the Jewells retained the right to later sue the government for damages done to their farm during the war. During salvage, much of the fort's structural remains and building superstructures were dismantled.

Artifact Analysis, Fort C.F. Smith

Artifact analysis classified different assemblages into groups proposed by Stanley South (1977:88–139). Artifact pattern analysis is a useful framework for comparing collections. Minor modifications were made to South's system to account for certain artifact types and for variance between the ways different collections were processed. Where useful, some artifact groups were subdivided.

Armaments

Discarded ammunition indicates that soldiers garrisoned at Fort C.F. Smith were equipped with a variety of small arms, including pistols and rifle muskets. Projectiles for the U.S. model 1855/1861 rifle musket and the British model 1853 Enfield rifle musket made up 80 percent of the ammunition found and include the ubiquitous .577/.58-caliber Minié ball and .577/.58-caliber Williams Type III bullets (table 7.2). Miscellaneous ammunition indicated a variety of smoothbore rifles, carbines, and revolvers were also present, but in lower numbers. The majority of the bullets appear to have been discarded, as opposed to being fired. Several Minié balls and Williams bullets carry markings indicating they were extracted. This is interpreted as evidence of guard duty and infantry drill.

Rifle musket projectiles (.577/.58-caliber and Williams Type III) representing 80 percent of projectiles at C.F. Smith is comparable to the 98 percent recovered at Folly Island (Legg and Smith 1989:109–11). However, at Fort Nelson, rifle musket projectiles accounted for only 29 percent of the ammunition found (McBride 1994:151, and this volume). The similarity between Folly Island and C.F. Smith reflects the growth of weapon standardization within the Union Army by 1863, principal occupation by

Table 7.2. Ammunition assemblage from Fort C.F. Smith

Ammunition type	Fort C.F. Smith[a]	Fort Nelson[b]	Folly Island[c]	Gloucester Point[d]
.577/.58 caliber	38	12	104	15
Williams Patent; type III, .57 caliber	11	3		
Army revolver; .44 caliber	1			
Round shot .69 caliber	3			
Round shot .31/.32 caliber	1	2		
Smith's carbine; .50 caliber	1			
Smith & Wesson revolver; .32 caliber	4			
Smith & Wesson revolver; .22 caliber	1	4		
Enfield; .58 caliber; modified (C.S.A.)	1			
.54 caliber, unfired		6	1	4
.69 caliber, carved bullet			1	
.577/.58 caliber, Pritchett (C.S.A.)			2	
.54 caliber, carved		1		
.44 caliber, Henry cartridge		3		
.44 caliber (Watervliet)		1		
.56 caliber, Spencer cartridge		1		
.52 caliber, Smith		1		
.52 caliber, Sharp's		1		
.69 caliber, unfired		2		
.36 caliber, revolver, unfired		3		
.44 caliber, Johnston & Dow bullet		1		
.44 caliber, Colt revolver bullet		1		
Buck shot				5
Percussion caps			29	47
Total	61	42	137	71

a. Balicki 1995:table 5.7.
b. McBride and Sharp 1991:table 7.1.
c. Legg and Smith 1989:table 5.5.
d. Higgins et al. 1995:table 1.

regular Federal troops, and supply to the eastern war effort. In general, eastern theater troops were better armed than those in the western theater (Griffith 1989:41). Further, Fort Nelson was a quartermaster's depot and recruitment station, and these functions presumably account for the larger variety of weapon types (McBride 1994:132–36, 151).

The presence of Williams Type III projectiles at C.F. Smith and the absence of these projectiles at Folly Island is a reflection of troop preference or supply. Williams Type III projectiles were introduced in 1863, and their shorter length readily differentiates them from earlier types of Williams projectiles (Thomas 1981:27; Lewis 1956:125). It is not clear if the Williams bullets, types I–III, carry chronological implications. Thomas (1981:27) suggests that Williams Type III bullets are uncommon on Civil War sites dating prior to 1864. Williams Type III bullets are therefore not unexpected at C.F. Smith, as the fort was built in early 1863 and manned until late in 1865. Further, the lack of earlier Williams versions (types I and II) suggests that these bullets may have been used within specific time spans. Apparently, Williams bullets were not liked by the Union troops, who believed they damaged the gun bore, disregarding ballistic tests that proved the contrary (Lewis 1956:125, 200; Samuel Smith 1994:71–74). In September 1864, orders were given that discontinued inclusion of Williams bullets in packages of cartridges, although those bullets already made into cartridges would be issued (Lewis 1956:200). Older ammunition packages may have been issued to troops in rear positions (C.F. Smith) and not to front-line troops (Folly Island).

Percussion caps were recovered at Folly Island and Gloucester Point (table 7.2). This suggests that at permanent rear camps, such as Forts Nelson and C.F. Smith, percussion caps may not have been issued or weapons were not kept in a ready-to-fire state. In general, rifle drill did not include target practice (Griffith 1989:86–90). Differences in archaeological sampling between the sites may also account for why percussion caps were recovered at only a few sites.

Clothing

Clothing artifacts recovered from Fort C.F. Smith provide a compelling visual link to the Civil War garrison stationed at the fort. Photographs of the fort's garrison in various uniform configurations (figs. 7.4, 7.5) show buttons similar to those found during excavations. Civil War uniforms displayed a wide range of styles, especially at the outset of the war when personal and state militia uniforms were used. However, for most Union enlisted men, the uniform consisted of three main components: a dark blue dress coat, flannel sack coat (fatigue coat), and sky-blue wool trousers (Legg and Smith 1989).

U.S. Army general service buttons were the only type of military button recovered at Fort C.F. Smith. They bear no service branch designation, suggesting that they came from enlisted men's uniforms rather than from officers'. Larger general service buttons were used to fasten the front of a coat, while smaller versions adorned uniform sleeves or forage caps. Two small buttons attached the cap chinstrap to the cap. Recovered general service buttons were standard issue on Federal uniforms from 1851 to circa 1875 (Wyckoff 1984:88–91). Beginning in 1854 and continuing to 1875, general service buttons displaying service branch initials within the shield (A = artillery, I = infantry, C = cavalry, R = riflemen, etc.) were issued only to officers (Albert 1976:38–41).

A variety of nonmilitary buttons were recovered; the majority were porcelain undergarment buttons. These buttons would have been attached to shirts and underwear supplementing the regulation uniform. In addition to buttons, other clothing-related artifacts included suspender clips, grommets from rubber blankets or ponchos, belt-end retainers, forage cap strap buckles, and epaulette fasteners.

Clothing artifacts reflect the incorporation, by 1863, of uniform standardization within the Union Army. The presence of nonmilitary buttons and suspender clips indicates that the regulation uniform was being augmented by non-issue clothing. Types of clothing artifacts from Folly Island are similar to those at C.F. Smith, while clothing artifacts from Fort Nelson display a wider range of nonmilitary buttons. Again, as with arms, the similarity between the C.F. Smith and Folly Island clothing-related artifacts reflects standardization of Union uniforms and the primary occupation at each site by military personnel. At Fort Nelson the large variety of non-issue buttons reflects the presence of a large nonmilitary workforce and soldiers' families (McBride 1994:146–47).

Accoutrements

Accoutrements are items of a soldier's gear which are neither clothing nor weapons (for example, packs, rifle belts, cartridge boxes, etc.). Only a small number of accoutrements, including a sword hanger, several knapsack parts, and two canteen spout fragments were found at C.F. Smith. Likewise, few accoutrements were recovered at Fort Nelson (McBride and Sharp 1991:67 and 110). No accoutrements were recovered at Gloucester Point. In contrast, numerous accoutrements were reportedly found by relic collectors at Folly Island (Legg and Smith 1989:111). The low number of accoutrements from the permanent camps reflects the mundane duties of fort life as opposed to field camps or battle conditions during which the opportunity to lose them was greater.

Kitchen Ceramics and Table Glass

During the Civil War, soldiers were issued standard mess gear consisting of tinned, sheet-iron vessels for both eating and drinking. Consequently, kitchen ceramics and table glass were nonstandard items. However, kitchen ceramics and table glass are recovered from Civil War military sites. At C.F. Smith, a small number (274) of ceramic sherds were found in refuse dumps. The ceramic assemblage contains ironstone, stoneware, whiteware, porcelain, and yellowware (table 7.3). Plain, undecorated ironstone comprises 55 percent of the ceramic assemblage. Only one of the whiteware sherds was decorated. In general, decorated wares were in the minority (14 percent) and included blue-transfer print and annular ware. The minimum number of vessels represented is 12 ironstone, 2 porcelain, 1 stoneware, 1 whiteware, and 1 yellowware. All of the identifiable vessels were plates. However, when ceramic fragments were separated into hollow or flat vessel forms, vessel types were roughly equal (51 percent and 49 percent, respectively) across the assemblage. The fragmentary evidence indicates that the stoneware forms represent utilitarian vessels.

Table 7.3. Ceramic artifacts from Fort C.F. Smith

Ceramic type	Fort C.F. Smith	Fort Nelson	Folly Island	Gloucester Point
Whiteware decorated	1	2	1	1
Whiteware plain	18	291	2	2
Ironstone decorated	27	11		
Ironstone plain	154	136		
Porcelain	10	7		1
Stoneware	59			1
Yellowware	3			
Buff-bodied earthenware	2			
Total	274	447	3	5

Because of increased and more regular contact with civilians and field conditions, permanent military installations should contain more kitchen ceramics and table glass than temporary field camps, where soldiers could not afford the luxury of easily breakable items. This assertion appears to hold true when a comparison is made among the Fort C.F. Smith, Fort Nelson, and Folly Island sites. Ceramics from Fort Nelson showed an almost exclusive use of undecorated whiteware and ironstone (McBride 1994:140–41; McBride and Sharp 1991:57). Tin mess ware recovered at Fort Nelson (McBride and Sharp 1991:54) indicates that the ceramic wares found there complemented issued mess ware. At Fort Nelson, ceramic wares most likely reflect the permanent status of the installation and the large civilian workforce. Only five ceramic sherds were recovered at Gloucester Point, the low number probably reflecting camp maintenance. Although a permanent camp, Gloucester Point was not in close proximity to a large urban area. As expected, kitchen ceramics were virtually absent from the Folly Island assemblage; only three sherds were found there.

Glass tableware artifacts have been interpreted as objects indicating the presence of officers (McBride 1994:145; Legg and Smith 1989:114). At Fort C.F. Smith, glass tableware constitutes a very small portion of the glass assemblage; only three sherds were recovered. In contrast, at Fort Nelson, glass tableware was more common and is interpreted as reflecting the presence of high-ranking officers (McBride 1994:145). Table glass was also recovered at Folly Island and is also attributed to the presence of officers (Legg and Smith 1989:114). The presence of glass tableware in the Fort C.F. Smith assemblage reflects inclusion of trash from officers' quarters in the refuse deposits. Apparently, at Fort C.F. Smith, the garrison drank and ate principally from regulation-issue mess ware supplemented by some ceramics and glassware. The small amount of glass tableware suggests that, at C.F. Smith, officers also drank mainly from regulation mess ware.

Food Procurement

Food procurement was controlled by the company quartermaster but was not yet standardized throughout the U.S. Army. Reconstruction of any general patterns for the Civil War period is difficult. Left to individual quartermasters, food selection reflected government rations, locally available foodstuffs, and regional—as well as, possibly, ethnic—food preferences. Foodstuffs were generally obtained through the Subsistence Department or through commercial sources. Intensive investigations into the provisioning of each regiment stationed at the fort would have to be undertaken in order to gain insight into the fort's provisioning.

The presence of a large quantity of tin can fragments and a metal food jar lid indicate that the Fort C.F. Smith garrison relied partially on canned goods. Metallic food containers have been recovered in large numbers from other Civil War campsites, but these sites were all field camps (Legg and Smith 1989) where supply lines would have extended fairly far from Union-held cities. The army shipped some food rations in metallic food containers, but canned goods were also available from private sources. Glass containers, on the other hand, do not appear to have been used in appreciable numbers by the army to ship rations (Legg and Smith 1989: 116). Presumably any glass containers found in campsites were obtained from sutlers, participation in markets, and packages sent to the troops. The proximity of Fort C.F. Smith to urban markets permitted company quartermasters and soldiers to obtain a larger variety of fresh foodstuffs and items in glass containers, thereby reducing reliance on canned government rations.

At C.F. Smith, glass beverage and food storage container fragments constitute approximately 40 percent of the Civil War artifact assemblage. Food storage containers primarily represent condiments and include cathedral-style pickle jars, sauce bottles, ribbed mustard jars, and nonspecific food containers. These containers reflect widespread use of condiments to enhance rations (Legg and Smith 1989:116; Crouch 1995: 26–27; Switzer 1974). Like ceramics, glass food containers were rare at the front-line Folly Island site, indicating that some nondurable items were selected against. At Folly Island, glass food containers were rare but glass beverage bottles were common (Legg and Smith 1989:114–22). Comparable data from Fort Nelson is not available.

A detailed bottle analysis was not undertaken on the Fort C.F. Smith collection, but beverage container fragments were common and reflect consumption of alcohol, such as beer, brandy, and whiskey. Several factors make examination of alcohol consumption difficult to address, especially considering the likelihood that a good deal of alcohol was consumed off base. At Fort Nelson, alcohol containers were recovered in a lower percentage than at Folly Island, which suggests that there may have been more restrictive policies governing alcohol consumption at permanent installations (McBride 1994:149). Further, unlike at field camps where large numbers of alcohol bottles were often discarded (Legg and Smith 1989:118–25), occupants of Fort C.F. Smith may have returned empties to a bottler, as glass containers were a valuable commodity (Busch 1987). The Crowley and Colemen Bottling Company, Washington, D.C. (1863–66) was the only local bottler identified in the assemblage.

Interpretations

Several conclusions are drawn from this comparative analysis. By 1863, weapons, uniforms, and gear within the Union Army were expected to reflect the rise of military standardization and the transition from an army based on the militia system to an army identified as Federal. As evidenced by the fact that armament and uniform assemblages from C.F. Smith and Folly Island are very similar, these efforts toward standardization were effective. Military symbols had become almost exclusively Federal. At Fort Nelson, the variety of ammunition reflects the function of the fort as a recruitment station and suggests that the western theater may not have been as well supplied. Artifact assemblages from encampments located, as was Fort C.F. Smith, adjacent to urban areas display the variety afforded by increased access to markets and interaction with civilians. Further, permanent encampments with large numbers of non-regular army occupants, such as Fort Nelson, display variety in artifact categories such as clothing. In general, permanent installations, such as Fort C.F. Smith, should contain larger amounts of ceramics and glass tableware, while field camps should display a more limited range of fragile items. The exception may be alcohol containers; the abundance of alcohol containers at Folly Island may reflect consumption and disposal in camp because of front-line isolation. Finally, at both Fort C.F. Smith and Fort Nelson, undecorated wares dominate the ceramic assemblage, although more decorated wares were present at Fort C.F. Smith. The higher percentage of decorated wares at Fort C.F. Smith probably reflects consumer choice afforded by access to larger urban markets.

Nonmilitary-Issue Artifacts Expressing Identity

Within the institution of the military, martial identity was expressed through standardized arms and clothing. Soldiers at C.F. Smith interacted and functioned within a complex hierarchical social context. They engaged in behavior and possessed objects that reinforced or otherwise bonded them within this social fabric. In other social contexts, soldiers would have had a myriad of alternate identities reflecting non-civilian lives and participation in nonmilitary social groupings.

Personal items, kitchen ceramics, some types of clothing, and other artifacts reflect nonmilitary choices made by the soldiers. These artifacts provide a glimpse into an aspect of personal identity not ordained by the dominant social hierarchy. However, these objects must be viewed within the context of the military. The relative abundance or absence, as well as the types, of non-issue objects are important indicators of nonmilitary identity. The non-issue objects recovered at C.F. Smith relate to dietary supplements, augmentation of the uniform, medicine, personal grooming, and alcohol and tobacco use.

Many objects functioned either to supplement or complement standard-issue items. As shown, ceramic wares and table glass complemented the standard mess ware. Although impossible to differentiate from issued container glass, various bottled food items supplemented soldiers' diets. These bottled food items were either received from the quartermaster, from home, or from relief organizations, or they were purchased directly by the soldiers.

To soldiers, the greatest enemy was disease. Within the capital's defenses, measles, dysentery, diphtheria, malaria, typhoid, and pneumonia were common camp diseases (Cooling 1991:176, 179–80). Several proprietary medicine containers provide clues to the afflictions, either actual or perceived, suffered by Fort C.F. Smith's garrison. More serious illnesses were treated by army doctors, while minor ailments were treated by the soldiers themselves.

Fragments of bitters bottles were recovered at C.F. Smith. Bitters, an infusion of alcohol and bitter substances, were marketed basically as cure-alls as well as a substitute for alcohol (Munsey 1970:111–13; Beck 1973:66). In general, the alcohol content of bitters was more or at least equal to whiskeys being sold (Smith 1973:9; Munsey 1970:111–12). When the Revenue Act of 1862 imposed higher taxes on alcohol than on proprietary medicines, bitters were cheaper and gained in popularity (Munsey 1970:111). Further, at least one bitters manufacturer convinced the Army to substitute his product as an invigorant before battle rather than whiskey or quinine (Munsey 1970:112; Smith 1973:9).

At C.F. Smith, proprietary medicine bottle and ceramic ointment jar fragments indicate that soldiers sought cures for numerous ailments or conditions including scrofula, gout, rheumatism, dyspepsia conditions, carminative conditions, and pectoral conditions. Scrofula is a swelling or tuberculosis of the lymph glands. Gout is a metabolic condition marked by painful inflammation of the joints. Rheumatism is inflammation or pain in the muscles. The carminative was taken to aid in the expelling of gas from the alimentary canal (the digestive tract). The pectoral treatment was used to alleviate diseases of the respiratory tract. Finally, dyspepsia is a condition of disturbed digestion.

The medicines provide preliminary insight into the health of Fort C.F. Smith's garrison. Soldiers apparently suffered from muscle soreness and inflammations to the respiratory and digestive systems. They used propri-

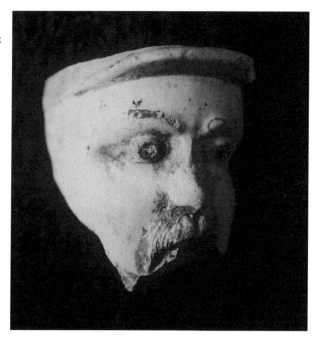

7.6. Tobacco bowl molded to represent a soldier (courtesy John Milner Associates, Inc.).

etary medicines to address their ailments. While some medicines, bitters in particular, were probably a substitute for alcohol, others were used for their reputed curative powers.

The soldiers' primary concern, governing their decision making, was to acquire objects that aided their ability to survive and function within martial society. The garrison at Fort C.F. Smith did not leave behind any lasting expressions of their nonmilitary identities. These other identities, apparently, were less relevant or repressed as the soldiers participated in martial culture. In fact, there is evidence that soldiers chose symbols reinforcing their membership in martial culture. Military identity is clearly manifest in a pipe bowl bearing the likeness of a soldier in a kepi hat (fig. 7.6). For the soldiers at Fort C.F. Smith, during their service, the military institutions had become the social warp onto which the fabric of their daily existence was woven.

Uniforms, buttons, and other gear gave the Federal armies' identity and provided a context. Adoption of Federal military symbols reflects the expanded role of the Federal Army and the lessened dependence on state militias and private organizations. For a soldier, adoption of military symbols meant forgoing civilian identity. At Fort C.F. Smith, one example of a non-issue object displaying an obvious symbolic meaning that acted to reinforce military culture was found. Other non-issue objects complemented or augmented regular-issue items but do not display attributes suggesting social identity. Clearly, by 1863 the Union military had developed into a cohesive social unit where military symbols and regulation functioned to reinforce military identity.

Conclusion

Although the Civil War continues to be the focus of diverse research, an understanding of military garrison life is still emerging. Any understanding is still rudimentary and limited owing to the small amount of comparative material. This chapter has addressed only a few of many potential avenues of research afforded by Civil War camp artifact assemblages. One profound change that resulted from the war was abandonment of the militia system and development of a Federal Army. Basically, this reflects the rise of the Federal government as the dominant political force within the country. The transformation can be seen in uniform and weapon standardization and adherence to military regulation. Over the course of the war, state symbols were replaced by Federal ones.

Examination of artifacts' spatial distribution contributed to a better understanding of camp maintenance, based on regulation. Adherence to regulations demonstrates the expanding role of the Federal Army together with pressures exerted by the military leadership. Examination of the material culture vis-à-vis the different camp types shows that differences exist between camps. These differences are based on several factors including theater of war, type of camp, presence of civilians, and access to markets. Finally, non-army-issue objects show how troops supplemented army materials and provide insight into expressions of identity within the context of the military.

Acknowledgments

The Fort C.F. Smith data used in this chapter are from the 1995 archaeological investigations at the fort (Balicki 1995; Benton 1995; Cheek et al. 1995). The project was sponsored by Arlington County, Virginia. Arlington County Department of Community Planning, Housing and Development, Community Improvement Division staff, particularly Dale Waters, Mary Shoecraft, and Marcia Silberfarb, worked diligently to make the project a reality. Chris Munson, Department of Parks and Recreation and Community Resources, Planning and Design Unit, acted as supervisor for the project.

The success of this project reflects the dedication and individual efforts of the entire John Milner Associates project team. Wally Owen, Civil War historian, generously shared his knowledge and resources on Washington, D.C., defenses. His contributions are greatly appreciated. I am grateful to Charles D. Cheek for his guidance and comments throughout the course of this project. The field team (Charles Goode, Ashley Wyatt, and Caryn DeStefano) did an excellent job under harsh conditions. My family— Mary Jane, Arielle, Jenna and Corinne—provided needed support. Thank you all.

8

The Sheridan Field Hospital, Winchester, Virginia, 1864

Joseph W. A. Whitehorne, Clarence R. Geier, and Warren R. Hofstra

The growing recognition of archaeological sites as important resources for the understanding and preservation of our historical and cultural heritage has spurred many communities to an increased awareness of their belowground history. In the following example, the City of Winchester, Department of Parks and Recreation, initiated an inquiry about newly acquired land that added a significant chapter to the town's already rich Civil War heritage. The inquiry also led to a deeper insight into organizational changes in the U.S. Army imposed by the war's demands. In this process, a simple effort to identify the presence of archaeological sites within the boundaries of a proposed park resulted in the identification of a localized set of Civil War structural features (Geier and Hofstra 1992). The need to manage these remains caused the features to be mapped within their topographic context and investigated using systematic metal detector surveys in an effort to determine the status of preservation of the associated cultural assemblage (Geier, Whitehorne, and Hofstra 1993). Archival research identified the site remains as part of the largest tent hospital constructed during the Civil War; the Sheridan Field Hospital was constructed on the southeast margin of Winchester following the Third Battle of Winchester, or Opequon Creek, in September 1864. The importance of the site to the Civil War heritage of Winchester, and to documenting one application of the Union medical system developed by 1864, led to the study of records of the U.S. Sanitary Commission (U.S.S.C.) at the New York Public Library and to the excavation of one tent platform feature to determine the archaeological integrity of the site (Geier 1994b). Although no major excavation was initiated, the historic research, site survey, and limited feature excavation allowed important, previously unavailable information on the site to be made available. This information included: (a) the historic context in which the hospital was established; (b) the hospital's administration and organization, including the interactions of medical staff with the civilian community and other local hospital sites; (c) the natural and cultural environment of the hospital site; and (d) hospital structure and the site plan for the only remaining segment of the once massive military complex.

The development of a new grand strategy and its implementation on the battlefield during the Civil War are acknowledged by many scholars as presaging the total wars of the 20th century (Hagerman 1988). Rarely is it possible to gain a view of developments in military administration and organization that made execution of such strategy and tactics possible. Civil War commanders reconfigured virtually every logistical system to deal with a large-scale, protracted conflict unparalleled in their experience, thus establishing precedents for many postwar developments. This was especially the case for the Union Army's medical support systems, which began to take forms familiar today. This modernizing trend was revealed in the large temporary hospital built by Union Maj. Gen. Philip H. Sheridan's forces in Winchester.

Sheridan's August 1864 selection to command the recently unified Federal forces in the Shenandoah Valley was reluctantly accepted by President Abraham Lincoln at General-in-Chief Ulysses S. Grant's urging. Despite the tentative start, Sheridan insisted that his command receive the fullest material support possible. Sheridan had long since learned the value and necessity of caring for his soldiers if he expected to get the most from them. He always tried to look after their comfort personally. This was especially the case with the medical care he arranged with Secretary of War Edwin M. Stanton under the auspices of the March 1864 War Department General Order Number 106, which officially created the Ambulance Corps. For the first time during the war, a formally established medical evacuation system effectively linked the battlefield with rear area medical facilities. Ultimately, this plan allowed Sheridan's medical staff to develop the war's largest tent hospital at Shawnee Springs on the southeastern edge of Winchester (Weigley 1968:46; U.S. War Department [O.R.], 1880–1905: Series I, vol. 43:185–87; Adams 1961:99; Sheridan 1888:310).

Sheridan in the Valley, 1864

Every aspect of the Union medical system was available to Sheridan's Middle Military Division when he took command. Surg. James T. Ghiselin was assigned to Sheridan's staff as the medical director. Ghiselin was an experienced field operator, fully familiar with new developments in the Union Army medical system (Gillett 1987:242). As the 1864 Valley Campaign opened, Harpers Ferry or Martinsburg, West Virginia, alternately functioned as the medical supply depot for Sheridan's army. Martinsburg, with its reestablished railhead, also served as a medical evacuation point, 20 miles from enemy-held Winchester.

Throughout August and early September, Sheridan's troops sparred with the Confederate forces commanded by Lt. Gen. Jubal A. Early. The two armies repeatedly maneuvered across the area between Winchester and Harpers Ferry as Sheridan looked for a weakness in Early's deployment. The Union general finally saw an opportunity, and on September 19, he attacked and defeated Early in the Third Battle of Winchester. This engagement compelled the Confederates to withdraw to Fisher's Hill, south of Strasburg. Union forces routed the Confederates there on September 21 and then pressed south to Harrisonburg. Sheridan concluded the combat phase of his operation and brought his men slowly northward to positions along Cedar Creek, imposing maximum economic damage as he withdrew (Heatwole 1998). On October 19, Early assaulted the Federal camps in a surprise attack that Sheridan ultimately converted into a smashing Union success, eliminating Early's force as a significant military factor. These engagements posed a major challenge to Sheridan's medical system.

Casualties generated on both sides by the Third Battle of Winchester, plus the large number of Confederate patients left in town after their army's retreat, led Ghiselin, on Sheridan's order, to implement a contingency plan worked out previously with Secretary Stanton and the surgeon general of the army. When the victorious Federals entered Winchester, virtually every church, public building, and suitable private house was already a Confederate hospital or was taken over for Union casualties. As a result, at 9:00 P.M. on September 19, Ghiselin wired Washington requesting the preplanned assistance. This entailed shipping 400 hospital tents from Harpers Ferry, medical supplies—already loaded in boxcars in Baltimore—for 5,000 patients, and 21 previously alerted medical officers from general hospitals in Washington, Baltimore, and Philadelphia (Brinton 1914:299).

While these personnel and materiel were converging, Ghiselin left medical affairs at Winchester in the temporary control of Surg. Henry A. DuBois while he moved south with Sheridan's combat elements. This arrangement determined the pattern of the campaign's later medical procedures. Patients would be treated by corps field facilities under Ghiselin's general supervision. Thus, all heroic surgery, except after Third Winchester, was performed at field hospitals close to the battlefields. Patients received at the Winchester facilities thereafter were mostly stable. Winchester served as a clearing and evacuation hospital more than as a primary treatment site. Thus, it is unlikely that the Shawnee Springs tent hospital site had extensive surgical facilities or related waste pits (U.S. War Department [O.R.], 1880–1905: Series I, vol. 43: 139–41).

The common practice in the U.S. Army before the Civil War was to requisition buildings for hospitals. However, the isolation of some battle sites and the unprecedented volume of patients compelled the increasing use of tents to house treatment facilities. The tents commonly available were an 1860 modification of the prewar hospital tent and the Sibley model. The former, including poles, pins, and fly, weighed 217 pounds and measured 14 feet long by 14 feet six inches wide by 11 feet six inches high when erected. The tent's wall was 4.5 feet high. Each tent comfortably accommodated eight patients. Although normally pitched about two paces apart, each tent had a flap that allowed it to be connected to other similar tents to make a larger ward (Surgeon General 1870–88, XI: 919).

Three hospital tents, one Sibley tent, and a wedge tent were authorized for each regimental surgeon's use. The Sibley tent, 12 feet high and 18 feet in diameter, was not preferred for patients because its circular layout made it difficult to provide individual treatment. Instead, it generally became an office or storage shelter (Surgeon General 1870–88, XI: 919).

The first full tent hospital was established by Surg. Bernard J. D. Irwin after the Battle of Shiloh in April 1862. The practice soon spread to the Army of the Potomac under the direction of Surg. Jonathan Letterman, who consolidated medical operations at the division level, eliminating brigade and regimental field facilities. This simplified hospital support and reduced duplication of effort. Letterman also set up an evacuation system that allowed more efficient patient withdrawal from the field to hospital. Even though its use would not be officially condoned until March 1864, Letterman's system, with an accompanying ambulance evacuation organization, became the norm throughout the Federal forces (Ginn 1997:16; Adams 1961:76).

The use of tents as treatment shelters was justified because they enabled greater air circulation. This was considered healthier, especially as many physicians believed infection was caused by odors or fetid air. Every effort was made to make the tents as comfortable as possible. Whenever practicable, board floors were placed in the tents, resting on sleepers placed directly on the ground. A trench from 6 to 8 inches deep, dug around the base, with the loose earth thrown around lower edges of the tent wall in cold weather, completed the arrangement (Surgeon General 1870–88, XI: 920). In cold weather, such as that encountered in the Shenandoah Valley during November and December 1864, additional measures were taken to ensure tents stayed warm. Heavy metal wood-burning stoves were not used to any great extent by Sheridan's force because of their bulk and weight. Instead, a common alternative known as the "California plan" was adopted: "A pit was dug about two and a half feet [deep] outside the door of the hospital tent; from this a trench passed longitudinally through the tent, terminating outside its farther or closed extremity. At this point a chimney was formed by barrels one upon the other, or by some other simple plan [such as stones or bricks]. The joints and crevices of this chimney were cemented with clay. The trench in the interior was roofed over with plates of sheet iron or stone. The radiant heat kept the tents comfortable" (Surgeon General 1870–88, XI: 921).

Storehouses, kitchens, and offices were located in spare tents or structures. Frequently, temporary, open-sided wooden structures resembling those found at modern park picnic grounds would be used as shelters. There was no standard design for these wooden structures, and their configuration was determined by the needs and whims of their builders. Latrines, waste pits, and stables were set up as far from patient areas as possible. Personnel were cautioned never to dig pits or latrines near a water source or in a possible drainage area. Ideally, waste pits were dug downhill from camp at least 200 yards away. These pits were to be at least four feet deep and lined with charcoal. If offal could not be burned, it was to be dumped into the pits and lightly covered with charcoal and a few inches of earth on a daily basis. When the hole was filled to within two feet of the top, it was filled in. Latrines and morgues were placed closer because of the need for ready access. Latrines were slit trenches equipped with uprights and poles for balance. They were screened whenever possible. A soldier in the western theater recalled that the latrine in the hospital where he stayed was "18 to 20 rods from my tent and just in front of it was the 'Dead House'" (U.S.S.C. 1861–65, Rpts., 17, 19A, 27; Strong 1961:77).

Casualties were handled by the increasingly effective Ambulance Corps. Well before its March 1864 authorization, locally condoned operations were functioning in the eastern armies, concurrent with Letterman's other innovations. Officers and men trained in emergency care and transport of patients swept the battlefield and moved the injured rearward to field hospitals, using stretchers or assigned vehicles (Surgeon General 1870–88, XI: 948; Adams 1961:83).

Winchester and the Shawnee Springs Locale: The Cultural Environment, September 1864

At the time the Sheridan Field Hospital began taking shape around Shawnee Springs, Winchester, Virginia, was a town of approximately 4,400 people. A market town in one of the most productive agricultural regions in Virginia, it produced prodigious quantities of wheat. In 1860, for example, Frederick County farms alone yielded nearly 225,000 bushels of wheat and supported 8,431 head of cattle (Emory 1964:250, 257). About a third of the cattle were kept for dairying. The remaining cattle were being fattened for urban or military markets. Large numbers of sheep grazed surrounding pastures to supply a local woolen industry. For subsistence, valley farmers depended on corn and hogs.

This prolific agricultural economy and a population of 59 percent farm dwellers supported a hierarchy of urban places in the lower Shenandoah Valley including 28 hamlets, 31 villages, and 17 towns (Mitchell 1995:23, 25). At the apex of the hierarchy stood Winchester, which served as the commercial node for the region. Local farmers came to Winchester to have horses shod, wagon wheels mended, or harnesses repaired much as they could at neighboring villages and hamlets. But many would travel longer distances to this market town to sell produce, buy clothes or tools, and browse in the shops of furniture makers, coach makers, clockmakers, and silversmiths. In addition, at Winchester they could conduct a variety of commercial and legal transactions or board a train and be in Baltimore in a day.

In 1864, the Winchester and Potomac Railroad had been in service for nearly 30 years, linking Winchester with Harpers Ferry and to markets along the Atlantic coast from New York to Alexandria. The Valley Turnpike passed through town like a great spine connecting commercial centers across the broad interior of the Atlantic economy from central Pennsylvania to the upcountry of the Carolinas. Additional turnpikes led west to the Ohio River or east across the Blue Ridge to commercial centers along Virginia's fall line. A market town for its region, Winchester was also a crossroads of interregional commerce and communication.

As much as Winchester was a gateway to the Shenandoah Valley and the upland South, it was also a distinctly Northern-looking town. As one 18th-century traveler put it: "when you see the Shenandoah [Valley] you think you are still in Pennsylvania" (Warville 1964:237). Modern geographers still call the historic valley a "socioeconomic extension of Pennsylvania" (Mitchell 1977:239). The two regions shared the same grain-livestock economy from the late 18th to the 20th century. In the 19th century, a cultural landscape defined by bank barns, I-houses, brick townhouses, and gridded street patterns (fig. 8.1) placed Winchester and its surroundings in the same cultural area as central Pennsylvania (Zelinski 1972:117–28; Glass 1986:22; Ensminger 1992:147–53). Winchester merchants traded in the markets of Baltimore and Philadelphia before turning to wholesalers in the commercial centers of Virginia at Richmond and Norfolk. Not surprisingly, construction of improved roads leading east from town in the 1840s followed establishment of turnpikes and railroads to the north by a full decade (Hofstra and Whitehorne 1996:32–33, 46, 74–75, 95; Hofstra and Mitchell 1993:619–46).

The site Sheridan's staff selected for the largest field hospital erected in the Civil War was distinctly marginal. Extending for three-quarters of a mile north-south along Town Run on the southeast margin of Winchester, the camp lay across floodplains ascending 60 feet and more onto upland ridges enclosing the valley to the east and west. Shawnee Springs, a major water source for the town, lay in the south central camp area, west of Town Run (fig. 8.2). In 1864, the area was almost entirely clear of forest cover except for a few willows and one "large spreading ash" (Frederick County Deed Book [FDB] 26:397). Aside from a few rock outcrops, most of the land in the vicinity of the springs was covered in pasture grass.

The preserved hospital remains lay south of Shawnee Springs about

8.1. Winchester, Virginia, showing location of Sheridan Field Hospital site (abstracted from Winchester, Va., USGS Quadrangle, 1966, photorevised 1987).

200 feet west of Town Creek and on the lower slopes of its valley wall (figs. 8.2, 8.3). In 1864, an angled stone fence divided the site along a north-south axis, and cross fencing defined a series of small house lots. The Millwood Turnpike passed along the base of Camp Hill, westward of the springs, linking this small community to the center of Winchester about one mile to the northwest (FDB 88:83; Geier, Whitehorne, and Hofstra 1993:21).

In 1864, seven lots ranging in size from one-fifth of an acre to nine acres surrounded the springs. Two, enveloping the biggest springs, belonged to Jacob Senseny, who operated a large farm to the east. On the remaining lots stood what deeds describe as huts or small tenements (Frederick County Will Book 22:214), where John Diffenderfer, George Curl, Mary Thompson, William Haymaker, David Fisher, their tenants, or families lived. These lots were among 36 surveyed in the 1750s by a neighboring

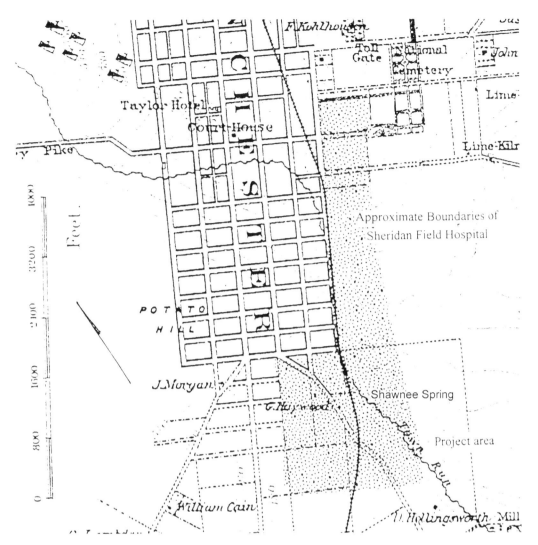

8.2. Town of Winchester, Virginia, 1864, showing location of hospital (abstracted from Gillespie 1873, Map of the Battlefield of Winchester, Va., Sept. 19, 1864; Davis, Perry and Kirkley 1978:pl. XCIX).

landowner who hoped they would serve a growing town population. They sold poorly, however, and many reverted to farm use. The population, displaced or inconvenienced by construction of the field hospital, thus represented a poorer class of tenants and lot holders who benefited from none of the amenities of town life such as public water or paved streets and, at the same time, profited little from the wealth of the surrounding countryside (Geier, Whitehorne, and Hofstra 1993:21–25).

Considering its Northern ties and its position as crossroads of commerce and communication in northwestern Virginia, the lower Shenandoah Valley was deeply divided during the sectional crises of the 1850s and subsequent hostilities between North and South. The little

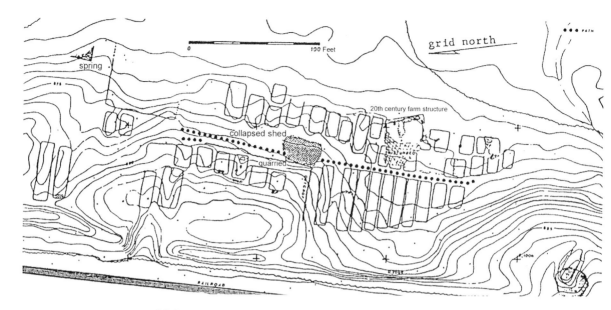

8.3. Sheridan Field Hospital site (courtesy of the Winchester Department of Parks and Recreation).

community surrounding Shawnee Springs also stood adjacent to those Winchester wards where Unionist sentiment was strongest when the Civil War broke out. A native of the region and Civil War diarist, Union Col. David Hunter Strother, described the Shenandoah Valley as "a region which, from its geographical position and mixed population, has always been debatable ground between the contending opinions of the age" (Strother 1866:1). Although Strother called Winchester the "headquarters of treason in the Valley" (Strother 1866:147), he found, on entering the town with Gen. Nathaniel P. Banks in March 1862, that Union forces were "welcomed with many demonstrations of joy by the inhabitants along the route. There seemed to be a great deal of Union sentiment among the middle and lower classes, but no cambric handkerchiefs nor national flags were waved from the better class of mansions" (Strother 1867:182). What route Banks used to approach Winchester is unknown, but the Millwood Turnpike led from Shawnee Springs through a working-class neighborhood commonly known as Potato Hill. Prominent Winchester diarist and ardent secessionist Cornelia McDonald stated that "the mechanics and trades-people were so opposed to secession that it would enrage them if they knew a [Confederate] flag was being made" (McDonald 1934:14–15). So divided was the town that in March 1862, when Confederate commander Thomas "Stonewall" Jackson vacated Winchester, he felt compelled to apprehend and exile 21 prominent Unionists (Phillips 1958: 131–37).

Whether the people clustered in the huts and houses around Shawnee Springs were Unionist or Confederate in sympathy remains unrecorded. A number of Diffenderfer women were among the "Union ladies of Winchester" entrusted to distribute medical supplies from the Sheridan Field Hospital to other military facilities in town (U.S.S.C. Bull., Oct. 1864). Whatever natural features the Shawnee Springs site offered that were conducive to a field hospital, such as cleared land, ample fresh water, or good drainage, the location provided a cultural setting of poorer people least likely to resist the intrusion and most likely to support a sustained Union presence.

Establishing the Sheridan Field Hospital

The officer directing construction of the field hospital was Surg. John H. Brinton, a specialist in such matters from the staff of the surgeon general of the army. Brinton, alerted to move from Washington on the morning of September 20, traveled by special train to Harpers Ferry with medical personnel from other points. The party, with medical equipment and supplies, then moved by wagon train and reached Winchester the night of the 21st. Among others, he was accompanied by Surgs. David McKay and Ferdinand V. Hayden, who would have primary responsibility for establishing the tent hospital (Brinton 1914:291).

On arrival, the doctors found 4,000 Union and 425 Confederate wounded and sick scattered in structures throughout the city. Brinton recalled that by September 25, his patient census was still 4,201 men. He was forced to requisition material from locals, especially cooking utensils such as pots and pans, as little "culinary apparatus" had been placed in the first supply loads. He was surprised at the reluctance of locals to help, as well as at guerrilla attacks made on his medical supply wagons, because so many patients were Confederate. Brinton also turned to the U.S. Sanitary Commission for help. This was a volunteer civilian group established to assist the Army Medical Department in its huge task and to goad it into improving operations (Brinton 1914:293–94; Adams 1961:13).

Col. George A. Muhlech was head of the Eastern Virginia Relief Corps of the U.S.S.C. after May 4, 1864. Commander of the 73rd Pennsylvania Regiment, he resigned in January 1863 and joined the U.S.S.C. This duty brought him into cordial contact with Maj. Gen. Franz Sigel, his former corps commander and senior U.S. commander in the Shenandoah Valley in spring of 1864, thus explaining his selection. Muhlech's headquarters was in Harpers Ferry, but his responsibility extended from Cumberland to Frederick, Maryland; Romney, West Virginia; and anywhere the U.S. Army went in the valley. Harpers Ferry and Frederick were U.S.S.C. supply depots. Muhlech had a large staff of commission agents and local hire personnel (U.S.S.C. 1864–65, Box 165).

As soon as he learned of the problems at Winchester, Muhlech arranged to forward supplies and personnel from Harpers Ferry and to establish a stockpile at Martinsburg, West Virginia. Thirteen four-horse wagons with a substantial cavalry escort shuttled "day and night" from Harpers Ferry to Winchester. Forty relief agents, some from as far away as Philadelphia, were assigned to dispense supplies and provide services. The flow of U.S.S.C. medical supplies began with an express shipment of four pre-loaded boxcars from Baltimore to Harpers Ferry the night of the 21st (U.S.S.C. Bull., Oct. 1, 1864).

The commission also shipped quantities of clothing, bedding, and food from Harpers Ferry to Winchester. On September 22, Agent E. H. Smith was designated Winchester storekeeper to receive, store, and issue this material, most of which began arriving by wagon the same day. On September 26, additional foodstuffs, spirits, mosquito netting and kitchen equipment were rushed to the city. By September 29, the supply emergency was considered over. The Martinsburg railhead was stocked with clothing and bedding under the supervision of Agent S. B. Wescott, who also monitored patient retrograde from there to hospitals farther north. Harpers Ferry depot functioned as the regulating unit for Shenandoah Valley supplies (U.S.S.C. 1864–65, Box 165, Supplies Issued).

On September 22, Ghiselin ordered Dr. Brinton to evacuate as many patients as possible and relieve overcrowding by erecting a tent hospital at Winchester. Ghiselin directed the hospital be placed "in the immediate vicinity of the town, near a fine spring and stream of running water. The hospital was to be of a capacity of four to five thousand beds." The 500 tents ordered by Ghiselin arrived from Harpers Ferry along with as many beds and stoves as could be found. Brinton rode over the ground around Shawnee Springs and developed a layout for the tent city by the evening of September 24. Col. Oliver Edwards, garrison commander, promised the help of 500 men to prepare the ground and to get tents pitched and ditched. His intention was to set up the tents "free, end to end between wooden frameworks" (Brinton 1914:296–97).

A proper camp layout had been prescribed since the days of Valley Forge. Manuals used by the U.S. Army provided sketches and diagrams as guides for establishing camps and stations in a standard manner. Army regulations added further details including information on the width of streets, places for wagon and livestock parks, the proper locations of command posts, troop tents, and latrines, as well as ideal distances between them (Lord 1957, 1: 63, 2: 98).

Brinton made a sketch of his plan for the Winchester hospital and gave it to Surgeon McKay on September 24 to begin construction the next day. Brinton was occupied the morning of the 25th with concerns in the city hospitals, and when he came out to check the progress he was annoyed to discover that the plan had been modified. McKay, a volunteer surgeon, ordered tents to be set up tightly packed with as many as six end to end. With wounded coming in from the Battle of Fisher's Hill, Brinton knew he could not rectify the mess entirely in time. All he could do was order the third and fourth tents struck, leaving pairs of tents along a narrow street. He ordered the remaining tents to be pitched as he had intended originally. The doctors assigned to the facility were billeted in town with Unionist Quaker families, the Millers and the Griffiths, so as to be close to their duties. By September 28, the tent hospital was fully operational and was designated "Sheridan Field Hospital." Having completed his responsibilities, Brinton turned over medical responsibilities to Surg. James V. Z. Blaney and returned to Washington (Brinton 1914:298, 300, 304; Lee 1862–65:696).

Hospital Plan and Layout

Maps and written reports confirm the location of the hospital and associated support encampments across an extensive landscape south and southeast of Winchester around Shawnee Springs (figs. 8.1, 8.2). As noted earlier, the main tent complex lay on the floodplain west of Town Run and on the rolling uplands of Camp Hill, the low ridge extending across the Millwood Pike and west to an extension of Loudoun Street. From Shawnee Springs, facilities associated with the hospital stretched across Town Run, then north along the east side of Kent Street, across the uplands and western slopes of the creek into modern Mount Hebron Cemetery. The streets and turnpikes entering or passing through the hospital joined it to the town and provided ready access to battlefields to the east (Third Battle of Winchester) and south (Fisher's Hill, Cedar Creek).

The postwar development of Winchester removed or covered much of the medical complex. All that remains is a complex of structural features in an area 140 feet east-west by 480 feet north-south, lying on the floodplain and lower valley slopes west of Town Run and south of Shawnee Springs. The site remnant (fig. 8.3) included 48 structural features laid out in a distinct linear pattern. While features vary in size and probable function, all lie within what is interpreted as an encampment or hospital area consisting of two, and possibly three, files of tent structures placed along a central street oriented nine degrees east of magnetic north.

The set of features was landscaped into the mouths of two ravines entering Town Run from the west and across an intervening, descending slope (fig. 8.3). Considerable cutting and filling of the terrain took place to establish the hospital structures. The single exception to this pattern is a structure situated on the apex and end of an upland toe-slope southwest of and above the principal feature complex. Unlike other site structures, this roughly square feature had a well-defined basement. Nails found in association suggest that it may have been a frame structure rather than tent.

Central to the surviving complex of structures is a north-south street which focused movement through the complex and provided the base line for construction of many tent platforms (fig. 8.3). The road extended for 260+ feet, the south end appearing to terminate in the vicinity of the southernmost set of tents. The street was 8 to 10 feet wide in the southern half of the complex between two neighboring tent files. In this area, the road was constructed of limestone rubble fill that elevated its surface and which also was used in constructing flat, tent platforms that extended perpendicular to the road. Excavation of the southernmost tent site west of the road (Geier 1994b; figs. 8.3, 8.4) confirmed that the fill used in the roadway was also used for the tent platform.

The northern half of the street crossed the slopes of the lower valley wall (fig. 8.3). To accommodate this passage, and possibly to generate fill used elsewhere, the bedrock limestone in this area was quarried to a depth of one to two-and-a-half feet to create the road bed. At the north edge of the slope, the road splits. One passage ascends toward a set of large tent platforms, the other extends north along the west side of a large, landscaped structure of uncertain function before descending toward a spring head and a small tent platform complex.

Forty-one rectangular and two nearly square depressions were identified as sub-floor features constructed to serve as platforms for tent structures. With one exception, all are 8 to 15 feet in width. Those with widths of less than 10 feet are typically 10 to 15 feet long or are greater than 30 feet in length, four lying between 40 and 48 feet. These platforms could include individual tents in the smaller range or represent sequences of tents fixed end to end in the larger. Features with widths of 9 to 9.5 feet have lengths of 10 to 15 feet and are probably individual tent structures. Structures 10 to 15 feet wide are most often 16 to 20 feet long. The close proximity of these structures of varied size and shape may reflect modifications to the hospital plan made by Surg. McKay cited earlier.

Despite size variations, all structures are oriented with long axes perpendicular to the street and are placed in clearly defined, parallel sets (fig. 8.3). Typically, features in the files at the south end of the site are separated by one pace or 3 feet. As evidenced in the profile of the single excavated tent platform (fig. 8.4), the soil and rubble fill separating adjoining tent depressions was designed to support the wooden floor stringers for the two neighboring tents (Geier 1994b).

Construction strategies for the feature depressions were similar. While built into irregular terrain, the principal set of tent structures was constructed with adjoining walls landscaped to produce a bounding edge that was leveled. In cases of more widely separated tents placed on the slope central to the site (fig. 8.3), depressions were excavated into what appears to be bedrock limestone. For many structures throughout the complex, the presence of piled, cut limestone and/or handmade brick suggests secondary features such as hearths or chimney bases. For the one excavated tent, a central linear depression excavated along its long axis (fig. 8.4) suggests

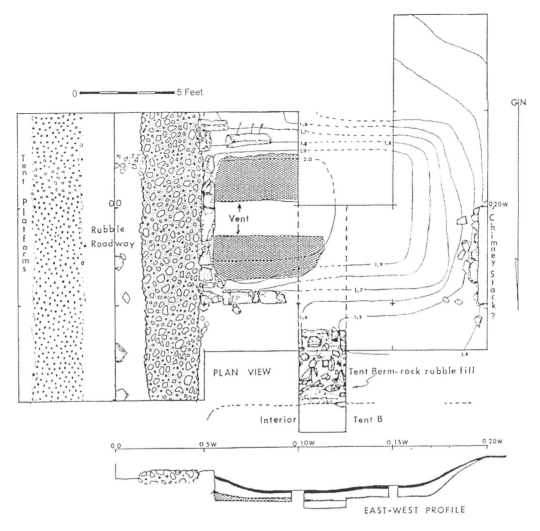

0 ————— 5 Feet

Tent Platforms

Rubble Roadway

Vent

PLAN VIEW

Interior

Tent B

Tent Berm- rock rubble fill

0.20W

Chimney Stack ?

G N

0.0   0.5W   0.10W   0.15W   0.20W

EAST-WEST PROFILE

8.4. Plan of tent feature A (courtesy of the Winchester Department of Parks and Recreation).

the use of a heating process similar to that of the "California plan" discussed earlier.

Community Networking

The Sheridan Field Hospital was a temporary facility established to meet the needs of soldiers wounded in the series of battles fought between September 19 and October 19, 1864. Circumstances in Winchester at the time of its construction caused the initial operation of the facility to extend hospital services to include several homes and hotels throughout the town. Once the hospital was established, the U.S.S.C. increased its support for the medical network. Colonel Muhlech assigned Mrs. W. Fanny Harris, a commission relief agent from Winchester, to operate the diet kitchen at the hospital. Her facilities included a temporary shelter, a storeroom, and two large tents. She fed the entire force of wounded at the field hospital and some of those in the 40 buildings used as hospitals throughout Winchester. By October 1, the hospital had settled into its evacuation role; patients moved through it as rapidly as possible, and only the most critical were retained for any extended period (U.S.S.C. Bull., Oct. 15, 1864). Preparing men for the retrograde in one of the coldest autumns in memory required substantial supplies. William L. Bredell, hospital administrative clerk, worked to straighten out what Colonel Muhlech called "utter confusion." Thomas J. Corbin served as chief of supply and postmaster and was authorized the use of two tents and a wagon. Fresh from battlefield treatment, these men had extensive supply needs. Corbin worked with Asst. Surg. Elisha Harris to assure that the men had clothing and food in preparation for their further retrograde. Additionally, patients at the tent hospital needed blankets, socks, and other clothing as the temperature dropped. By October 16, the tent hospital held about one-third of all patients and one-half of the Union patients in Winchester (U.S.S.C. Bull., Oct. 15, 1864, Nov. 1, 1864).

The proliferation of medical activities in Winchester necessitated a high degree of organization to assure equitable distribution of pharmaceuticals, supplies, and rations. This was in part because of guerrilla activity which impeded the flow of supplies. The situation made for frequent delays, often reducing supplies in Sheridan's army to dangerously low levels and compelling stringent economy measures. At one point, General Sheridan put combat forces on reduced rations to assure adequate food for the patients. Surgeon Brinton and Colonel Muhlech decided the best way to curtail waste was to reduce the number of people authorized to draw items from the Winchester Medical Purveyor, Dr. Patton (Gillett 1987:242–43; U.S.S.C. 1864–65, Box 625, item 6767, NYPL). As a solution, they divided the town into seven districts or wards. Thirty "very devoted" local Union women were designated as a Special Relief Agency, with each ward in the charge of one of the ladies. The other women were divided among the wards as equally as possible to act as assistants. The chiefs of each ward were the only go-betweens for hospitals in their ward and Federal medical supply officials. They alone could draw items and direct their distribution within the ward. Mrs. Mary L. Williams was designated to draw rations for Confederates being treated in private houses and for Confederate physicians living in private houses (U.S.S.C. Bull., Oct. 1, 1864).

The high patient population after the Third Battle of Winchester remained until the end of October. By September 22, more than 4,000 wounded had been moved to the Martinsburg railhead along with nearly 2,000 prisoners of war. An additional 1,000 wounded reached Winchester on September 22 after the Battle of Fisher's Hill, 24 miles to the south.

Only the most serious cases were retained, and the rest were moved by wagon to Martinsburg and then by train to Cumberland or Sandy Hook, Maryland. Additional patients were received as Sheridan continued his advance to Harrisonburg preliminary to his "burning" of the valley (Heatwole 1998). Confederate hospitals were encountered at Mt. Jackson, Woodstock, and Harrisonburg. Federal surgeons considered only the Harrisonburg facility to be adequate and evacuated the wounded who could be moved from Mt. Jackson and Woodstock to Winchester (U.S. War Department [O.R.], 1880–1905: Series I, vol. 43:142; U.S.S.C. Bull., Oct. 1, 1864, Nov. 1, 1864).

After Fisher's Hill, the medical supply base was shifted from Harpers Ferry to Martinsburg. Asst. Surg. Emil Ohlenschlager supervised the issue of supplies and transport of the wounded from there. Wounded were moved daily by wagon from Winchester to Martinsburg, where they normally spent only a few hours before continuing northward. Completion of the rail line in December allowed the collection point to be shifted from Harpers Ferry to Stephensons Depot. Just six miles from Winchester, medical supply was established at the depot, as was the office of the director of medical transport. Surgeon Blaney had at his disposal 50 wagons, 4 hospital railroad cars, and 2 passenger cars to transport the evacuees to Harpers Ferry. The opening of Stephensons Depot also reduced the threat of guerrilla harassment (U.S. War Department [O.R.], 1880–1905: Series I, vol. 43:144; U.S.S.C. Bull., Jan. 1, 1865).

The largest surge of patients into Sheridan Field Hospital occurred after the October 19 Battle of Cedar Creek. Wounded from both sides totaled 4,500, nearly all of whom came under Federal care. Corps field hospitals were established 15 miles south in Stephens City (then called Newtown). Every available ambulance and wagon moved casualties to Winchester. All patients who could travel were shuttled farther north, and by the afternoon of October 21, all but 15 terminal cases had been transported. Before this crisis, no more than 300 patients a day moved through Martinsburg. Thereafter a larger flow was encountered. Between October 23 and October 31, a total of 3,400 men were sent on to Cumberland and Baltimore, some less than an hour after getting off the wagons at Martinsburg (U.S. War Department [O.R.], 1880–1905: Series I, vol. 43:143; U.S.S.C. Bull., Nov. 1, 1864, Jan. 1, 1865).

The Battle of Cedar Creek was the end of major military activity in the valley, with the Union controlling most of it until the end of the war. As Union troops were redeployed and military action was reduced, the need for medical support also diminished. Thus, when winter settled in, as many Winchester facilities as possible were closed, with priority given to the big tent hospital. The patient population, even in these final weeks, remained about 20 percent Confederate. The last exclusively Confederate hospital in the Union Hotel was closed on November 29, and its surgeons began to be sent away for exchange by way of Baltimore and Fort Monroe. The last were gone by early January. By December 13, almost all Union combat injured had been evacuated. Most patients thereafter were suffering from illness or accident. If their condition promised an extensive stay, they were shipped north as quickly as possible. The great tent hospital sent off its last patient on December 28, 1864. The facility was closed formally on January 4, 1865. Medical treatment was provided thereafter by the XIX Corps hospital in town and in buildings around the Taylor Hotel (U.S. War Department [O.R.], 1880–1905: Series I, vol. 23:144; U.S.S.C. Bull., Nov. 1, 1864, Jan. 1, 1865; Parry 1864:26; Lee 1862–65:727; Russell 1912).

The U.S. Sanitary Commission operations remained at a high level until February 1865. Large shipments of foodstuffs, clothing, and toilet articles were received and issued to units leaving the area as the agency gradually shifted operations from Winchester to Stephensons Depot. The last shipment, mostly food, was sent directly to Winchester on April 28. Storekeeper E. H. Smith issued this food to "indigent" civilians. A division hospital continued to operate in the Taylor Hotel until June, with a smaller facility in Berryville, to the west. Significant medical activities terminated in the valley at the end of July 1865 (U.S.S.C. 1864–65, Box 165).

Summary

Archaeological survey, site testing, and historical research at Shawnee Springs in Winchester, Virginia, provided a unique glimpse into one application of Civil War medical systems as they approached their greatest effectiveness in patterns that defined U.S. military medical service until World War I. The Sheridan Field Hospital was the largest temporary hospital of the war (Adams 1961:99–100). Nonetheless, information on its physical character had been lost and very little scholarly effort has been directed toward its organization, its impact on and interaction with the community, or its role in support of Sheridan's 1864 campaign. This chapter begins the process of bringing this significant medical facility into the Civil War heritage of the lower Shenandoah Valley. Preliminary information has been provided on the physical layout and plan of the hospital and the nature of the residential community its construction impacted. In addition, insight has been provided into the manner in which larger medical needs joined the hospital into a network of wards that included as many as 40 private homes and public buildings across Winchester that served as hospital sites after September 19, 1864. The study illustrates how far the Army Medical Department had developed and also reveals the maturity of its traditionally sensitive relations with the U.S. Sanitary Commission, a civilian agency. By 1864, dealings between Muhlech and military doctors show each agency working with the other to assure the best possible patient care. Study of the Sheridan Field Hospital provides a comprehensive example of Civil War medical systems functioning effectively in the context of modern, total warfare, and it allows a different view of the war's effect on a divided Southern community.

Acknowledgments

We wish to recognize the support and funding made available for this study through the Winchester Department of Parks and Recreation. We also wish to thank the archivists and librarians at Handley Library in Winchester, Virginia, the Military History Institute, Carlisle Barracks, Carlisle, Pennsylvania, and the New York City Public Library. Their knowledge and cooperation saved us many long hours of work.

9

Far from the Battlefield

Archaeology at Andersonville Prison

Guy Prentice and Marie C. Prentice

It's hard to imagine the inhuman suffering that ravaged this prison camp over 130 years ago. Like so many Civil War commemorative sites, the prison grounds at Andersonville National Historic Site are now neatly trimmed expanses of grass dotted with stone monuments memorializing the events that transpired here. Until recently, visitors to Andersonville relied primarily on old drawings and old photographs to get a feel of what it must have been like to have been held captive at this most infamous of Civil War prisons. Now, accurate reconstructions of portions of the prison's inner stockade and north gate based on detailed archaeological data help park visitors visualize the size and nature of the prison as well as the oppressive living conditions prisoners faced during their incarceration there.

Archaeological research at Andersonville Prison began shortly after the site was established as a national park. These initial efforts were carried out by Lewis H. Larson, Jr., and Morgan R. Crook, Jr., who conducted excavations in the fall of 1973 and spring of 1974 (Larson and Crook 1975:1). Their investigations included excavations along portions of the outer and middle stockades, the northwest and northeast corners of the inner stockade, and portions of the inner stockade north of the north gate. In 1978, Ellen B. Ehrenhard supervised a series of excavations throughout the prison site including the southwest and northwest corners of the inner stockade, the south gate, portions of the inner stockade near the north gate, and the prison hospital (Ehrenhard 1985). In July 1985, Rochelle A. Marrinan and Kenneth S. Wild, Jr., undertook an electrical resistivity survey of the "shed hospital" grounds located south of the prison enclosure (Marrinan and Wild 1985). Their efforts were largely unrewarded, however, since the survey failed to identify any patterns that could be reliably interpreted as hospital features.

During 1987, 1989, and 1990, archaeological investigations were undertaken by archaeologists from the National Park Service's Southeast

Archeological Center prior to reconstructing three separate portions of the prison in order to enhance the visiting public's understanding. These investigations focused on identifying the northeast corner's location and construction details (Walker 1989), the north gate (Prentice and Mathison 1989), and the southeast corner (Prentice and Prentice 1990) of the prison's inner stockade line. The studies also included examination of posts forming the deadline, a failed prisoner escape tunnel, the original northern inner stockade line, and a portion of the western stockade line added during the building of the prison's northern extension. National Park Service Archeologist Guy Prentice supervised the field excavations during these three seasons of pre-reconstructive investigations, and is now in the process of summarizing (Prentice in prep.) all that is known about the archaeology of Andersonville.

Site Location and Description

Andersonville National Historical Site in Macon and Sumter Counties, in west central Georgia, was formally established as a unit of the National Park Service on July 1, 1971. The total park acreage is 495 acres. The prison portion of the park encompasses about 100 acres.

The prison site is located on the banks of a small, west-flowing tributary of Sweet Water Creek now known as Stockade Branch (fig. 9.1). Several small springs in the vicinity of the prison compound contribute to the creek's flow. Within the prison area, Stockade Branch traverses a small floodplain approximately 115 feet wide at the western end of the compound and 230 feet wide at the eastern end. Most of this floodplain is wet, marshy ground. The ground slopes up steeply (a roughly 12 percent grade) from the floodplain to a fairly level surface approximately 50 feet in elevation above the creek. Mowed grass fields have largely replaced the native pines, loblolly (*Pinus taeda*) and shortleaf (*Pinus echinata*), that once covered most of the prison grounds. Erosion due to rainwater runoff has been, and continues to be, a problem along the slopes bordering Stockade Branch. Conservation efforts have effectively reduced the soil erosion within the park, but in the past, gullies several feet deep were not uncommon.

A Brief History of Andersonville

In November of 1863, Confederate Capt. W. Sidney Winder was sent to Sumter County, Georgia, to assess the potential for building a prison for captured Union soldiers near the village of Andersonville. The deep south location, availability of fresh water, and proximity to the Southwestern Railroad made Andersonville a favorable prison location. In addition, Andersonville had a population of fewer than 20 persons and was, there-

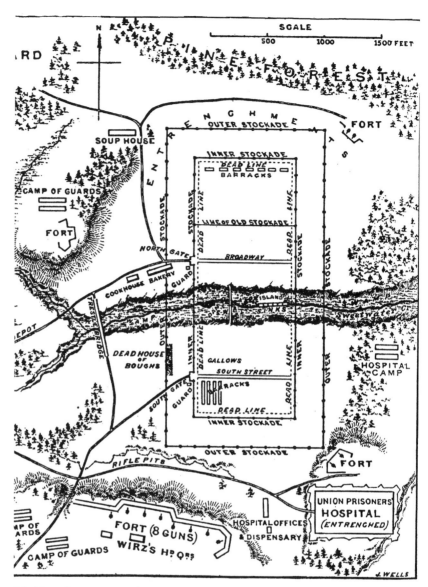

9.1. Map of prison grounds and surrounding area at Andersonville (J. Wells, *Century Magazine*, vol. 18, Mann 1890; courtesy of the National Park Service–Southeast Archeological Center).

fore, politically unable to resist construction of such an unpopular facility. When Andersonville was chosen as the prison site, the necessary lands were rented from two property owners, Benjamin B. Dykes and Westley W. Turner, at a sum of $30.50 per month, respectively.

After the prison site was selected, Capt. Richard B. Winder (Sidney Winder's cousin) was sent to Andersonville to construct a prison capable of holding 6,000 prisoners. Arriving in late December of 1863, he adopted a design that encompassed roughly 16.5 acres, 4.5 acres of which were marsh, which he believed was large enough to hold 10,000 prisoners. The prison was to be rectangular in shape with Stockade Branch of Sweet Water Creek flowing roughly through the center of the compound (fig. 9.2). The prison was designated Camp Sumter but became better known as Andersonville.

Construction at Andersonville began in January 1864, when slaves were impressed to fell trees and dig ditches for the prison stockade. The original stockade was approximately 1,010 feet long and 780 feet wide. The walls were constructed of locally obtained pine logs approximately 22 feet in length, hewn square, and set vertically in a wall trench dug roughly 5 feet deep. According to historical accounts, the poles were hewn to a thickness of 8 to 12 inches and "matched so well on the inner line of the

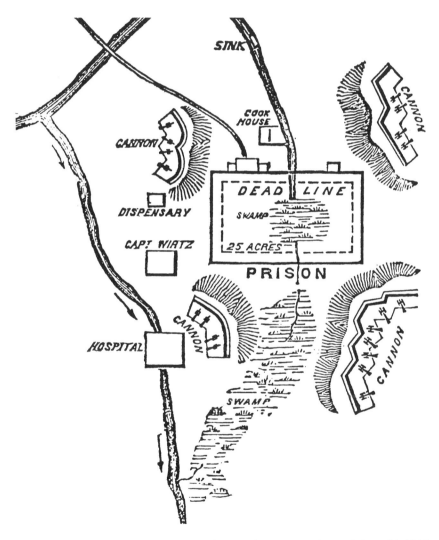

9.2. Portion of a map appearing in *U.S. Sanitary Commission Bulletin*, vol. 1, no. 21, 1864 (courtesy of the National Park Service–Southeast Archeological Center).

9.3. View from outside the South Gate (R. K. Sneden, Topographical Engineer Corps, 1864, on file at the National Park Service–Southeast Archeological Center; reproduced courtesy of same).

palisades as to give no glimpse of the outer world across the space of the deadline" (Hamlin 1866:48–49).

Two gates were positioned along the west stockade line (fig. 9.3). The gates were described in historic accounts as "small stockade pens, about 30 feet square, built of massive timbers, with heavy doors, opening into the prison on one side and the outside on the other" (Bearss 1970:25). Each gate contained wickets or door-sized entryways. Outside the walls, the gates were flanked by sentry boxes.

Prisoners began arriving in late February of 1864 and were held under guard until completion of the stockade on March 21, 1864. Soon after, construction began on the deadline (figs. 9.4, 9.5). It consisted of a light fence or "frail scantling . . . nailed to stakes driven at intervals of from six to ten feet into the ground" (Bearss 1970:26). The deadline delineated a no-man's land roughly 15 to 25 feet wide inside the stockade wall and served to prevent possible escapes by keeping prisoners away from the stockade wall. Anyone who crossed the deadline was immediately shot by prison guards who manned small observation platforms dubbed "pigeon roosts" at 30-yard intervals along the top of the inner stockade wall. The deadline was removed for a few weeks in September after thousands of prisoners were transferred from Andersonville to other prisons. During this time, restrictions were lightened and prisoners were allowed to dismantle the deadline and use its scraps for fuel and other purposes. Captain Wirz, commandant of the prison, had the deadline rebuilt in mid-October,

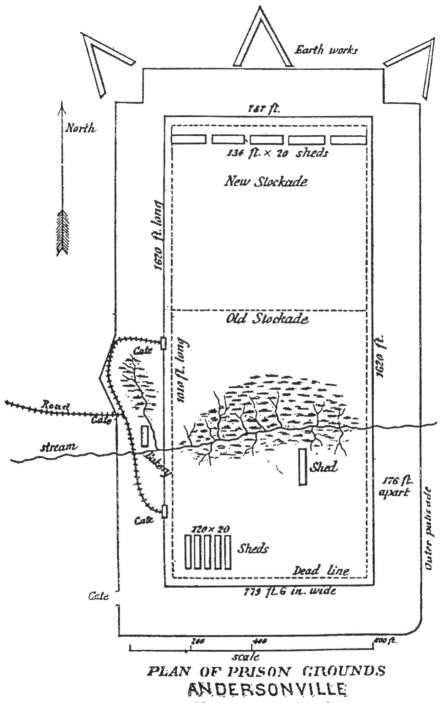

9.4. Map of Andersonville Prison, summer 1865 (Hamlin 1866; courtesy of the National Park Service–Southeast Archeological Center).

9.5. Photograph of prison taken from a pigeon roost overlooking the swamp, dated August 1864, with deadline in foreground (courtesy of the National Park Service–Southeast Archeological Center).

however, when he felt fraternization between prisoners and guards had gone too far.

Between May 8 and June 8, 1864, the prison population climbed from just under 13,000 to over 23,000. Consequently, it was decided that a larger prison was necessary, and by mid-June work was begun to enlarge the prison. The prison's walls were extended 610 feet to the north, adding roughly 10 more acres and bringing the total area enclosed to 26.5 acres. The extension was built by Union prisoners, consisting of 100 whites and 30 blacks, in about 14 days. On July 1, the northern extension was opened to the prisoners who subsequently tore down the original north stockade wall for use as fuel and building materials. The addition could not have occurred at a better time. By July 25, there were a reported 29,400 prisoners at the camp, and by August 8 the prison population expanded to well over 33,000.

Stockade Branch, the stream that was originally intended to provide the main source of water for the prisoners, quickly became a cesspool of human excrement and offal. To obtain better sources of water, numerous wells were dug by prisoners. In the midst of this suffering, a spring of fresh water suddenly gushed forth just inside the west wall of the inner stockade. Viewed as the result of divine intervention and credited with saving numerous lives, it was dubbed Providence Spring (Bearss 1970:47).

The digging of wells, in addition to furnishing prisoners with much-needed drinkable water, also provided them another benefit: opportunities for digging escape tunnels. Under the ploy of digging wells, some prisoners dug tunnels beneath the stockade and under the cover of night tried to reach the safety of Union lines. More than 80 escape tunnels were discovered and backfilled by the prison guards, but of all the attempts made by tunneling, only one successful escape was reported. All other successful escapes occurred while prisoner work details were outside the prison. The escapees simply slipped off while the guards weren't watching (Bearss 1970:50).

Overcrowded conditions, insufficient supplies of food and medicines, lack of adequate fresh water, and little more than blankets for shelter led to deplorable living conditions. Malnutrition and disease ran rampant, and the mortality rate soared, soon reaching more than 100 deaths a day. Carted off to a nearby cemetery, the corpses were buried shoulder to shoulder in seemingly endless trenches with consecutively numbered headboards used to mark each grave. Each number corresponded with a name entered on a list of the dead that was principally maintained by prison hospital clerk Dorance Atwater. By the end of the war, the number of marked graves totaled 12,920 (Bearss 1970:147).

Threatened by Union raids (Sherman's troops were marching on Atlanta), Brig. Gen. John H. Winder, Commissary General for Confederate prisons and post commander at Andersonville, ordered defensive earthworks and a middle and outer stockade built around the prison. Construction of the earthworks began July 20th and consisted of a star fort located southwest of the prison, a redoubt northwest of the north gate, and six redans. One redan was located at the northwest corner of the prison, one at the northeast corner, two at the southeast corner, one midway along the north wall, and one midway along the east wall.

The middle and outer stockades were hastily constructed of unhewn pine logs set vertically in wall trenches about four feet deep. The middle stockade posts (fig. 9.6) projected roughly 12 feet above the ground surface and encircled the inner prison stockade as well as the four corner redans. It had one gate located midway between the north and south gates of the original prison stockade. Construction of the middle stockade was completed on September 1. The outer stockade, which was never completed, was meant to encompass the entire prison complex, including the earthworks located outside the middle stockade. The posts of the outer stockade extended about five feet above the ground surface.

While trying to prepare for any possible enemy action, the Confederates also had to contend with the forces of nature. On August 9, the prison was inundated by a torrential rainstorm. The rising waters of the rain-swollen Stockade Branch "undercut the stockade, and about 100 feet of the west wall, where it crossed the bottom, was swept away" (Bearss 1970:31). Fearing a mass breakout, Captain Winder ordered every available guard to assist in repairing the stockade. Additional rains hampered

9.6. Photograph of middle stockade (*foreground*) and inner stockade, western side looking south (from Stereopticon Slides, 1867; courtesy of the National Park Service–Southeast Archeological Center).

efforts, but by August 12, stockade repairs were finally completed. Erosional damage was apparently extensive over the whole site; a map of the prison drawn in the second week of August shows gullies five to six feet deep paralleling the east and west walls just inside the prison stockade walls.

By early September, Sherman's troops occupied Atlanta and the threat of Union raids on Andersonville prompted the transfer of most prisoners to other camps in Georgia and South Carolina. By mid-November, all but about 1,500 prisoners had been shipped from Andersonville, and only a few guards remained to police them. Transfers to Andersonville in late December 1864 increased the numbers of prisoners once again, but even then the population totaled only about 5,000 prisoners.

In mid-March 1865, prisoner exchanges were once again resumed between the opposing armies. Andersonville's prisoners were promptly made available for parole by Captain Wirz, who began shipping his charges by rail and boat to Big Black Bridge in Mississippi. When it was suggested that Jacksonville, Florida, would be an easier site of exchange, arrangements were made to transfer prisoners there. By April 1865, all but 20 sick prisoners had been shipped out with hopes of being paroled at Jacksonville, but all were returned to the prison when the exchange was canceled by U.S. Maj. Gen. Quincy A. Gillmore. They remained there until early May when all prisoners were paroled at Baldwyn, Florida, thus ending the prisoner occupation of Andersonville.

In the 14 months during which Andersonville operated, at least 12,920 of the roughly 45,000 prisoners who entered its gates died as a result of malnutrition, exposure, dysentery, smallpox, scurvy, and various other diseases, and sheer brutality. Andersonville, with the ignominious distinction of having the highest mortality rate of all Confederate prisons (about 29 percent), was by no means unique with regard to the horrid conditions prisoners of war suffered in both North and South. Elmira, New York, where roughly one of every four Confederate prisoners died, was the North's grim cognate. Other prisoners held at camps such as Camp Douglas and Point Lookout in the North and Libby and Salisbury in the South fared little better. In all, approximately 50,000 Union and Confederate soldiers died while held in military prisons, and thousands more died soon after their release. In the aftermath of the Civil War, the Confederate prison at Andersonville was singled out for atrocities that had occurred in military prisons on both sides. Seeking retribution for the inhuman conditions that plagued Andersonville, Capt. Henry A. Wirz, the commandant of the prison, was arrested, tried, and later hanged for his complicity in what had transpired at Andersonville. Wirz holds the ignominy of being the only person executed for war crimes following the Civil War.

Andersonville Prison after the War

Soon after the war ended, Andersonville gained the attention of Clara Barton, founder of the American Red Cross. Using the burial rolls compiled by Dorance Atwater and Confederate records, Barton, accompanied by Capt. James M. Moore and 34 men, arrived at Andersonville on July 25, 1865, to identify the graves of the individuals buried there. Completing her mission by mid-August, Barton and her party were able to place names on all but 460 of the 12,920 marked graves by matching numbers on the burial records with numbers on the wooden headboards placed with each burial. The remainder of the dead (that is, 460 graves), who were listed in the original burial rolls as "unknown," received the inscription "Unknown Union Soldier" on their headboards. Afterward, when she returned to Washington, Barton lobbied for establishing Andersonville as a national cemetery.

During the late 19th century, the prison site was revisited by a number of people who recorded the prison at various stages of disintegration. Mary Shearman visited the site in May of 1867 and discovered deep erosional gullies inside the inner stockade wall. She also noted that portions of the deadline were still standing and that a black man had planted a corn patch in the northeast corner of the prison (Bearss 1970:164). A year later, a correspondent for the *Boston Spectator and Weekly Advertiser* visited the prison site to find that locals were tearing down the stockade for fuel. Plans were also being made to mark the corners of the inner stockade with posts (Bearss 1970:166). In 1869, an inspecting army officer commented that "the Stockade is rotting, and has fallen in a couple of places" (Strong 1869, cited in Bearss 1970:161). In 1873, Albert Webster and his wife visited the prison and found many posts rotted and fallen. They also noted that the north gate was still standing (Webster 1873:323).

Other visitors to the prison included J. L. Ball, who stopped at the site in 1881 and learned that the south slope had been planted in corn in 1879 and in cotton in 1880. It was also noted that most of the stockade had fallen by then (Ball 1881). Jerus Bryant arrived at the site in 1883 to assume his post as cemetery superintendent. When he arrived, he met George Kennedy, a black man who was renting the prison property. Bryant noted that only a few stockade posts remained standing and that Kennedy was apparently felling them for use as fence rails and cane souvenirs (Bearss 1970:170). In 1884, Benjamin Gue similarly noted that posts from the stockade were being made into split rails. He stated, too, that most of the posts, with the exception of the eastern inner stockade line, were lying on the ground, decaying, although the stockade line was still traceable (Bearss 1970:170). A former prisoner, S. Creelman, visited the prison in 1889 and found that the land had been purchased by George Kennedy and another black man, and that they had planted the fields in cotton. Creelman was still able to trace the outline of the prison, however, by the remaining post stumps (Bearss 1970:171).

On January 28, 1891, George Kennedy sold his portion of the prison to the Grand Army of the Republic of Georgia (G.A.R.). The G.A.R. then cleared the grounds of undergrowth and planted ornamental hedges. They also graded roadways around the property, through the central area of the prison, and from the central road to Providence Spring. In 1896, the property was deeded to the National Women's Relief Corps (W.R.C.) by the G.A.R.

The W.R.C. continued to improve the prison grounds. They erected a wire fence, built a caretaker's residence and stable, and planted Bermuda grass (Bearss 1970:173). In 1902, they erected a granite building over Providence Spring. In 1910, the W.R.C. transferred ownership to the U.S. Army, which maintained the site until it was designated a national park in 1970.

During the 1930s, members of the Civilian Conservation Corps (C.C.C.) constructed a series of culverts to reduce soil erosion and filled in existing gullies. Stone markers were erected at significant reference points, including the inner stockade's four corners and the north and south gates. Concrete pillars were placed between the stone markers delineating the inner stockade and the deadline.

Archaeological Investigations, 1987–1990

In the spring of 1987, John W. Walker undertook the first phase of pre-reconstruction work by excavating 216 feet of stockade line at the northeast corner of the prison (Walker 1989). As Walker's crew chief, Guy Prentice supervised the excavations during the 1987 investigations. He also directed the second and third phases of pre-reconstruction work, which included excavation of the north gate in 1989 (Prentice and Mathison 1989) and 229 feet of stockade line at the southeast corner of the prison in 1990 (Prentice and Prentice 1990). The primary method of investigation during all three field seasons consisted of first exposing the stockade wall trenches and other features by stripping away the plow zone. Cross-section trenches were then placed at several locations along and across the exposed wall trenches to reveal details in wall trench construction and pole placement.

The Prison's Inner Stockade Extension

The 1987 SEAC field investigations at the prison's northeast corner (fig. 9.7) uncovered roughly 216 linear feet of stockade wall that was part of the 10-acre northern extension added in late June 1864. The addition was built by Union prisoners held at Andersonville and was constructed by digging a trench roughly 5 feet deep and 2 feet wide, then setting the posts in the center of the trench and backfilling around the posts. Longitudinal cross-section trenches excavated along the stockade wall revealed the remains of the original posts and diagonal bands of fill running west to east in the northern wall and north to south in the eastern wall. The diagonal fill zones indicated that when the prisoners set the posts, they proceeded from the west, backfilling as they went along, working their way to the northeast corner, then turning and continuing in the same manner toward the south.

Preservation of the stockade posts in this portion of the site was very good, so it was possible to determine the placement and sizes of posts exposed in the trench. The good preservation also revealed that construction of the stockade extension differed significantly from the original prison construction. The prisoners had used unhewn pine logs rather than the hand-hewn, squared posts used by the earlier slave gangs. Further, unlike the slave gangs, the prisoners had piled the excavated earth on either side of the trench in a less systematic manner, so that when they backfilled around the posts, a patchwork of soil colors resulted. The more methodical construction methods employed by the slave gangs were examined while investigating the north gate in 1989 and the southeast stockade corner in 1990.

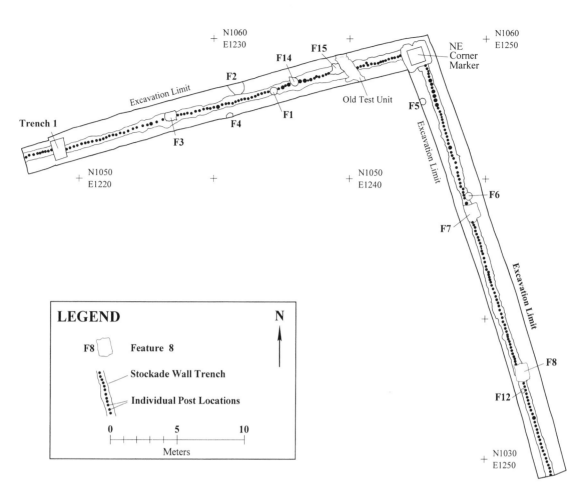

9.7. Map of features and post locations identified in northeast corner excavations (courtesy of the National Park Service–Southeast Archeological Center).

The Original Stockade Construction and the North Gate

The search for the north gate was initiated in the spring of 1989 near two stone monuments erected in the 1930s to mark its putative location. As the western stockade wall trench was initially exposed with the box blade, a consistent pattern of stockade trench fill soon became apparent (fig. 9.8). This pattern consisted of a band of orange soil running along the western half of the trench and a band of dark red soil along the eastern half. The two bands were often separated by a band of gray soil and the remains of wooden posts running down the center of the trench.

The soil banding observed in the west stockade wall trench in plan view was duplicated in the cross-section trench profiles. These profiles made it apparent that the banding observed in the main excavation unit was the result of the methodical manner in which soils were dug to form the wall trench and later backfilled around the posts. Soils in this portion of the site naturally grade from an orange color at the ground surface to a dark red

9.8. Photograph of west inner stockade wall trench showing color banding in the area immediately north of the North Gate (courtesy of the National Park Service–Southeast Archeological Center).

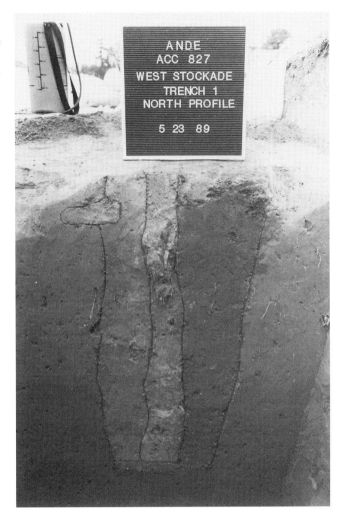

color at a depth of five feet. The banding of soils evident in the wall trenches thus indicates that when slave gangs excavated the trench, the uppermost orange soils were consistently thrown toward the exterior of the prison, while the deeper red soils were thrown toward the interior of the prison. When these soils were backfilled into the wall trench, posts placed in the center of the trench prevented the two soil colors from mixing, thereby creating the banding effect.

The well-preserved posts encountered during the 1989 investigations (fig. 9.9) substantiated historical accounts describing the original stockade construction as using squared pine posts set close together in a wall trench roughly five feet deep. Materials recovered during these investigations (fig. 9.10) included an iron ax head, an ax head fragment, 1 brass and 1 iron buckle, 19 cut nails, a brass fiddle-shaped padlock cover stamped with a crown symbol and the letters GR (probably for King George III, who reigned in England from 1820 to 1830), an alkaline

9.9. Sequence of preserved posts encountered in 1989 excavations (courtesy of the National Park Service–Southeast Archeological Center).

glazed stoneware sherd, pig and cow bones, and 202 wood post samples. The ax heads were probably the remains of tools used by slaves to construct the original stockade. The cut nails were also probably used in construction of the prison. The numerous pig and cow bones recovered from the stockade wall trenches were probably the remains of meals consumed by slaves who built the original prison.

A portion of the original north wall of the prison (fig. 9.11) was also uncovered during the 1989 investigations, at a point roughly 180 feet

9.10. Artifacts recovered during the North Gate excavations (courtesy of the National Park Service–Southeast Archeological Center).

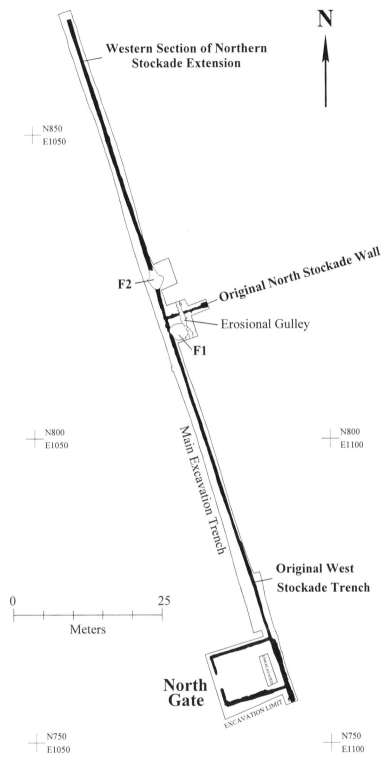

N

N850
E1050

Western Section of Northern
Stockade Extension

Original North Stockade Wall

F2

Erosional Gulley

F1

N800
E1050

N800
E1100

Main Excavation Trench

Original West
Stockade Trench

0   25

Meters

North
Gate

UNEXCAVATED

EXCAVATION LIMIT

N750
E1050

N750
E1100

9.11. Map showing location of some of the features and posts encountered during the 1989 North Gate excavations (courtesy of the National Park Service–Southeast Archeological Center).

from the north gate. The original north wall had been torn down by the Union prisoners following the building of the northern prison extension in July 1864. Trench 3 was excavated to examine the original north wall. The west profile of Trench 3 exhibited the same wall trench shape and form as the western stockade trench, having a flat bottom with slightly inwardly sloping sides. No posts were found in the trench, and the sides of the wall trench showed no signs of distortion or collapse. This suggests that when the prisoners pulled the posts from this section of the original stockade wall they pulled to the east, thereby preserving the original trench shape. This is in contrast to the opposite or east profile in Trench 3 where the northern side of the wall trench flares outward near the ground surface. The flaring at this point in the trench suggests that when the posts were removed by the prisoners they were pulled toward the north. The flaring was probably the result of digging along the north side of the wall to loosen the poles so that they could be tipped or pulled out.

The profiles in Trench 3 also provided enough evidence to conclude that the methods used to dig and backfill the original west stockade were the same as those used for the original north stockade. In other words, during the digging of the wall trench, the uppermost orange-colored soils were piled toward the exterior of the prison and the deeper red soils were piled toward the interior of the prison. When the soils were backfilled around the posts, the posts prevented the two soils from mixing, thereby creating a banding effect. Although the original northern stockade wall trench fills were disturbed when the prisoners pulled out the posts on July 1, 1864, portions of the original fill zones were preserved at the bottom of the trench.

The North Gate

The north gate was located roughly 794 feet south of the northwest corner of the prison and consisted of a box-like enclosure projecting westward from the main stockade (fig. 9.12). The gate walls were constructed in the same manner as the original stockade with squared posts set in a wall trench roughly 5 feet deep. The gateways into and out of the gate were centered on the east and west walls of the enclosure. The dimensions of the north gate were actually 27.6 feet by 34.8 feet and not the 30 by 30 feet reported in historical accounts. The doorways of the gate were also roughly 9.5 feet wide rather than the reported 12 feet.

The Southeast Corner Investigations

The 1990 field investigations were successful in locating the southeast corner of the inner stockade line and determining the nature of its construction. Approximately 229 feet of stockade line were excavated in the process (fig. 9.13). Although post preservation was typically poor, the walls of the southeast corner were apparently constructed with squared

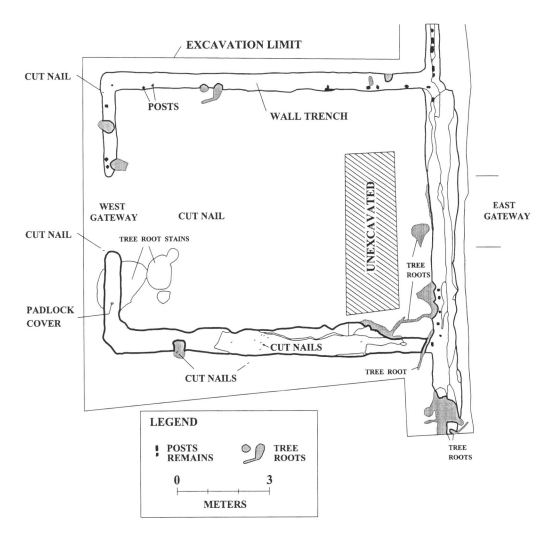

9.12. Distribution of features in North Gate area (courtesy of the National Park Service–Southeast Archeological Center).

posts set in a wall trench roughly 5 feet deep in a manner similar to that found for the inner stockade line in the north gate area. The banded soil effect encountered during the previous year's excavations was replicated at the southeast corner. This time the banding pattern consisted of a yellowish brown sand strip running along one side of the stockade wall trench and a band of whitish sand along the other side. The two bands were often separated by a band of grayish brown soil resulting from the decomposed posts located in the center of the trench.

The banded pattern of wall trench fills found at the southeast corner and the north gate reflects the uniformity with which the stockade wall was constructed by the slave gangs. While digging the wall trench, the uppermost soils were consistently thrown to the outside of what would be

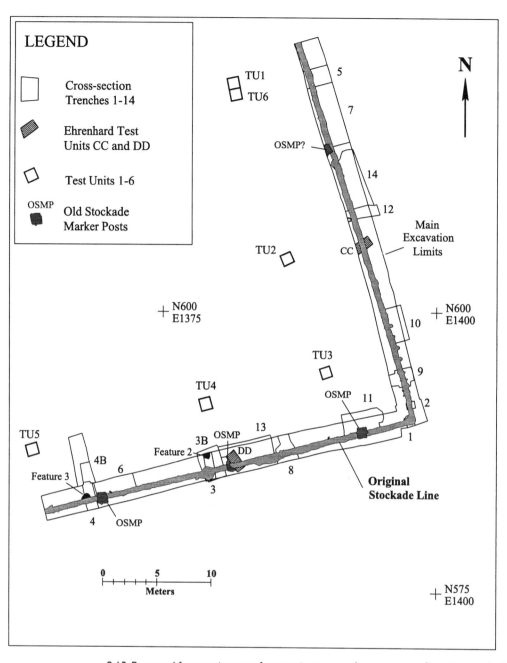

9.13. Posts and features in area of excavations at southeast corner of interior stockade (courtesy of the National Park Service–Southeast Archeological Center).

the prison enclosure, while the deeper subsoils were thrown to the inside. The posts were then set in the middle of the trench and the fill on both sides of the trench was packed around them. At the southeast corner, where the deeper soils are naturally whiter than the light-brown soils nearer the ground surface, this resulted in a white band on the interior side of the stockade posts and a light-brown band of soil bordering the exterior of the posts. In the northwest gate area where the natural soil colors grade from orange to red, this resulted in an inner red band and an outer orange band of soil separated by posts.

Prisoner Escape Tunnel

During the 1990 excavations, a failed prisoner escape tunnel was also discovered along the southern stockade wall (fig. 9.14). These excavations currently provide the only archaeological data collected to date regarding prisoner escape tunnel construction at Andersonville. Within the excavated units, the widest section of the escape tunnel was about 3 feet. Based

9.14. Photograph of profile wall of cross section Trench #3b showing collapsed prisoner escape tunnel (courtesy of the National Park Service–Southeast Archeological Center).

on profile map reconstructions, the tunnel was approximately 20 inches high, just big enough for a man to crawl through.

This corner of the prison was apparently chosen as a tunnel location because of the soft, easily dug, sandy soils. Unfortunately for the attempted escapees, the soft soils also caused the downfall of the escape attempt. Dug just deep enough to pass beneath the stockade, the sandy soil and several stockade posts collapsed into the tunnel before it could be extended more than 1 meter past the stockade line.

Recovered Artifacts

A total of 497 artifacts were collected during the 1990 investigations. Among these are numerous items which provide glimpses of the prisoners' lives, including what they ate and wore during their confinement. The food remains include carbonized beans, as well as pig, cow, and rabbit bones. Clothing items include pieces of cloth, iron and brass buckles, military insignias, and glass and metal buttons. A recovered silver filigreed band with intact eraser was all that remained of a pencil probably used to write letters home or perhaps to make entries in a diary.

The Deadline

During the 1987 and 1990 excavations at the northeast corner and southeast corner, respectively, isolated postmolds were encountered on the interior side of the stockade wall that are currently interpreted as the remains of the deadline rail that was erected to keep the prisoners a safe distance from the stockade wall. In each case, lumps of white colored soil originally interpreted as white kaolin clay were found in the postmold fill. The reason for the presence of the white clay was unknown, and Walker (1989:55) suggested that it may have been used as a dietary supplement. It is now believed that the whitish clay was actually the result of attempts to retard the deterioration of the deadline posts by the application of lime. A description of this wood preservation treatment is described in an article dated November 1837:

> Accident in some instances, has led to the discovery that lime applied to wood, preserves it from decay. The white-washing of fences is practiced, more as a substitute for paint, and for appearances sake than to prevent decay. Even this superficial mode of applying lime is of some use in preserving wood. Having full confidence in the efficacy of lime, as a preservation of wood, to make fence posts less subject to rot, I have this season, for the first time, used it as follows:—I provided a number of narrow boards, about three feet long, of various breadths, and one inch thick, with a hole in the end of each. When the hole in the ground was ready for the reception of the post, some lime was put into it; on this lime the post was placed and some of the narrow boards were then selected, and placed to and around the post in the hole. The ground was then rammed into the hole after the

usual manner, and when filled, the boards were drawn out. This is done with greater facility, by putting a stick into the hole in the upper end of the board, by which it may be raised by a lever or prise, if too fast to draw out otherwise. The boards being all removed, fill the space they occupied with quick lime: if but partially, it is better than if totally slaked, because as it slakes it will expand and makes the post quite secure. From three to five posts with hewn or uniform butts, will require one bushel of lime. Boards to surround the post half an inch thick, (and perhaps this thickness of lime may be sufficient) would not take half that quantity. The lime is all the additional expense, except the extra labor (which is very trifling) to be incurred by setting a fence, with that part of the posts in the ground enveloped in lime. (*Southern Agriculturalist* 1845:592)

As far as we are aware, this is the only archaeologically documented use of this 19th-century wood preservation technique.

Conclusion

Although the archaeological work conducted at Andersonville has contributed greatly to our current knowledge of how various parts of the prison camp were built and has aided accurate reconstructions of the northeast corner, southeast corner, and north gate for the visitors who come to Andersonville National Historic Site, it still remains difficult to imagine the horribly crowded and squalid conditions that resulted in so much suffering and death here. With a mortality rate of about 29 percent, nearly one out of every three prisoners who entered the gates at Andersonville never walked out, and many of those who survived carried the scars of their imprisonment for the rest of their lives. Today, those who take time to walk around the site and contemplate the events that happened on these hallowed grounds cannot help but walk away with a deep sense of compassion and reverence for those who suffered and died here. Clearly, Andersonville National Historic Site acts as a visual reminder, if nothing else, to those who visit that the brutality of war does not end with the last shot on the battlefield.

10

Antietam

The Cultural Impact of Battle on an Agrarian Landscape

Elise Manning-Sterling

Antietam Farmstead Survey

Archaeological testing conducted at two farmsteads on the Antietam National Battlefield, in Sharpsburg, Maryland, contributes to a better understanding of the physical and cultural landscape during the Civil War. Two yards associated with thriving Civil War era farms, the Samuel Mumma homestead and the Locher/Poffenberger tenant cabin, were the focus of the research. The Mumma farmstead was burned by Confederate troops on the morning of the battle to prevent use by Federal sharpshooters. The Locher/Poffenberger log cabin was the home of Alfred Poffenberger, a tenant farmer, and his family.

Archaeology is best understood when placed within larger historical, political, and social contexts, with express emphasis on underlying cultural and symbolic views of the physical landscape. Archaeology viewed within this larger context revealed that at two times in the 19th century, the landscape became a symbolic manifestation of this farming community's identity and values. Local farmers' participation in the agricultural reform movement beginning after 1830 showed their willingness to commit to new and popular ideas that altered long-established domestic practices. This was demonstrated through changing patterns in trash disposal and farmyard use. In order to study how the Battle of Antietam affected the local community, a cultural model of stress response was adopted, based on the work of Rowntree and Conkey (1980). This model delves into "how human needs and wants are manifest symbolically in the landscape" (Rowntree and Conkey 1980:459) and allows insight into the battle's cultural impact. The study of the Sharpsburg landscape revealed that, in a number of ways, local residents reestablished the war-torn countryside in order to provide a sense of constancy and order.

The Agricultural Movement

The period between 1820 and 1850 was one of radical social change, a major aspect of which was agrarian reform. "The farm became the symbol of Americanism" (Bullion 1986:74), which meant that the agrarian landscape had to reflect the nation's prosperity and importance. There was intense pressure from agricultural societies and reformers, as well as an increasingly influential agricultural press, for "improvement" of farmsteads and the rural landscape (Bullion 1986; Larkin 1994). Proponents of a transformed landscape articulated their ideas in the agricultural almanacs, newspapers, and catalogs that were widely circulated among farmers throughout the country.

The importance of improving the landscape was fervently proclaimed by the agricultural press, which had become the "collective spirit of the American agrarian conscience" (Bullion 1986:74). Transformation was to be accomplished by affirmation of positive images and the ridicule of negative characteristics through symbolic imagery. To improve the farmer's self-image, the press presented a "model farmer" (Herman 1994) who was compared to his antithesis, the slovenly farmer. The model farmer's goal was to "conclude the transformation of untamed landscape into cultured countryside," by using the implements of husbandry (Herman 1994:36). The different ends of the spectrum were concisely presented as Farmer Snug and Farmer Slack (Grettler 1991). Farmer Snug's farm had well-fed livestock which "serenely grazed over equally stylish farmhouses, gardens, and yards. Trash was neatly deposited in excavated pits and not suffered to clutter the yard. Wood-efficient paling and post-and-rail fences replaced wasteful worm fences" (Grettler 1991:5). His antithesis, Farmer Slack, had a dilapidated shack which sat in the midst of a trash-littered, unfenced yard, trampled by underfed and uncontained livestock, and surrounded by untended fields (Grettler 1991:5).

The conquest of the untamed landscape was to be accomplished through the construction of fences, large barns, and neat farmhouses. Farmers were encouraged to adopt practices that resulted in more efficient use of time, labor, and money, including better stock selection, increased crop variety, and modern agricultural tools (Larkin 1994; Herman 1994). Only a select few could call themselves "farmer," but the definition did not exclude tenant farmers who upheld the ideals of agricultural improvement so that they too could be considered as elite model farmers (Herman 1994).

The vision of a transformed agrarian world extended to seemingly insignificant aspects of everyday life. The way a farm family threw away trash came under scrutiny, and the appearance of the farmyard came to be a critical factor which determined whether a farmer was improved or slovenly. The old ways of trash disposal, where "housewives tossed broken vessels and trash out the most convenient door or window and threw bones and food scraps into the yard to be picked over by the domestic animals" (Larkin 1994:177), were no longer acceptable. Soon the actual character of a farmer was equated to, and judged by, the state of his fields and yard. By the 1830s, imagery that in the early part of the century portrayed an unkempt farm run by a bad farmer evolved into the "dwelling places of the drunken and vicious" (Larkin 1994:190).

Sharpsburg Landscape

The 1862 Sharpsburg landscape was described as "winding, fertile valleys of clear streams, rich in broad corn-fields; and white vine-covered farmhouses, half hidden in old apple-orchards," and a patchwork of wood lots and fields of corn and clover surrounded by miles of post-and-rail fences (Richardson 1865). The farmsteads were dispersed across the landscape, neighbors frequently being separated by a quarter mile or more. Most farmhouses and barns stood at the end of a long drive leading from a thoroughfare. In this isolated setting, prosperous farms were visible to the community, while owners maintained their privacy in daily activities.

The Hagerstown Valley, Washington County, Maryland, was settled before 1740 by immigrants from England, Scotland, Switzerland, France, and, most notably, Germany, along with second-generation German Americans who migrated from eastern Pennsylvania (Scharf 1968:981). Settlers brought ancestral farming practices and ingrained concepts of settlement and architecture with them. The domestic architecture present on the Maryland landscape reflects the people who settled the area. Largely a product of the movement of German and Scots-Irish families into Maryland, simple architecture of log dwellings and buildings became prevalent in the 18th and 19th centuries, primarily in the central and western parts of the state, including Washington County (Westlager 1969: 144). In contrast to the prevalence of simple domestic architecture was a decided preference for large utilitarian barns. It was easy for passersby to know the ancestry of many farmers because it "appeared to some Anglo-American observers that German farmers were more intent on erecting spacious barns for their cows and horses than in enlarging the dwelling houses for their families" (Westlager 1969:217).

Both Alfred Poffenberger and Samuel Mumma were from well-established families; their parents or grandparents came from Pennsylvania to settle in Washington County. The Mummas and Poffenbergers were prolific and maintained prosperous farms (Williams 1968). One major difference between the two families was their relationship to the land; Alfred Poffenberger leased his land, while Samuel Mumma owned his farm. Study of these two sites allows for social and economic comparative analysis between tenants and landowners. The combined use of historic and archaeological resources, including details of farm production and land use, architecture, and artifact assemblages, provides insight into the lives of these two farming families, the larger neighboring community, and how all three were affected by the battle.

Locher/Poffenberger Site History

The Locher/Poffenberger Site is located on a 2,617-acre tract of land first registered in 1750 (Joseph 1994:24). From the earliest recorded sale, wealthy absentee landlords kept this parcel as an investment while residing in large houses elsewhere in Sharpsburg or in other states. The 1814 deed of sale to Philip Grove indicated that there were buildings on the tract (Joseph 1994:3–4). In 1840, Grove divided the land between his son Joseph and married daughter Mary Grove Locher, who leased out her tract to tenant farmers (Joseph 1994:3–4). The Locher/Poffenberger site name, used in this article, represents the names of both the owner and the tenant at the time of the 1862 battle.

There is no indication in the historic documents who occupied the Locher cabin or farmed the land in the first half of the 19th century. Though the title is clearly documented, the history of occupation and the sequence of construction of the various buildings on the property are more obscure. Pre–Civil War archaeological deposits are all that remain to impart information about tenants who resided earlier in the century. The first reference to a tenant was in the 1860 census; Alfred Poffenberger was listed as the resident. He was one of 14 children of John Poffenberger and Nancy Miller (Williams 1968:856). In 1860, Alfred, age 26, lived in the cabin with his wife, Harriett, a young son and a daughter, a male farmhand, and a 12-year-old male slave. His personal estate was worth $500.

Farmstead Layout and Architecture

Located on a small limestone knoll, the log tenant house overlooked a farm lane and a stone-lined well. There was a small orchard to the east. The house, yard, and orchard were encompassed by a post-and-rail fence. An unmortared stone cold cellar with an arched stone roof was built into the hillside south of the cabin. The cellar was covered with earth and sod and contained two doors which made it accessible to both the cabin and the public lane.

The Locher/Poffenberger farmhouse, modified several times during the 19th century, today is a two-room cabin, one and a half stories high (fig. 10.1). At its largest, the building consisted of three rooms, each representing a unique construction episode. The original one-room log structure was built around 1811. A log addition, since razed, was built onto the south cabin wall sometime early in the 19th century. The rooms were similar in size and construction techniques. The new front entryway was

10.1. Photograph of Locher/Poffenberger farmhouse, 1934 (courtesy of the Antietam National Battlefield).

located on the eastern wall of the addition. Sometime after the Civil War, a frame addition was built onto the north end of the structure.

Mumma Farmstead Site History

A patent for the 324-acre tract of land on which the Mumma farmstead is situated was first granted in 1791 by George Orendorff. Orendorff and his family built a house, barn, stables, and spring house. They may actually have begun building before the 1791 patent date (Wilshin 1970:11). Jacob Mumma moved from his home near Lancaster County, Pennsylvania, late in the 18th century. In 1796, he purchased a three-tract farm totaling 324 1/4 acres from Orendorff for £5,500. In order to buy this property, he borrowed £500 from a Pennsylvania neighbor, which he paid back by 1802. Over the next 12 years, Mumma bought several other properties in the area (Wilshin 1970:11).

Jacob Mumma, along with his wife, Elizabeth Hertzler, and their 6 children, set up their home on the Mumma farmstead. In 1831, he turned the farm over to his youngest son, Samuel. Samuel Mumma, Sr. (born 1801), married Barbara Hertzler, who bore 5 children. His later marriage to Elizabeth Miller in 1834 produced 11 children. The actual number of children, step-children, grandchildren, and farmhands who lived at the Mumma homestead in 1862 is unknown. The large number of residents is suggested by 12 beds itemized as lost during the battle (table 10.1).

Table 10.1. Claim No. 334 Congressional Case, filed May 29, 1885 by Samuel Mumma, Jr., Executor of Samuel Mumma *Deceased* vs. The United States

One House Destroyed by Fire		2,000.00
One Barn		1,250.00
One Spring House & Hog Pen		100.00
Stock Taken		460.00
Grain of Different Kinds		537.25
Household Furniture Clothing & c		1,422.43
Farming Implements Wagon_____?		457.50
Fence distroyed [*sic*]		590.00
Hay		480.00
Land damaged by traveling & Buriel [*sic*]		150.00
Fifteen Cords Wood		37.00
		$7,472.18 [*sic*]
Panels P. Fence		360.00
Panels Worm Fence		477.90
Corn	16 Acres @ 13.20	355.00
Fodder	16 Acres @ 5.00	88.00
Irish Potatoes	100 Bushels @ 1.00	100.00
Sweet Potatoes	10 Bushels @ 1.50	15.00
Apples	75 Bushels @ .50	37.00 [*sic*]
Steers	6 @ 20.00	150.00 [*sic*]
Calves	2 @ 6.00	12.00
Colts	2 @ 30.00	60.00
Horse	1 @ 100.00	100.00
Shoats	9 @ 3.00	27.00
Hogs	9 @ 10.00	90.00
Sheep	8 @ 5.00	40.00
Chickens	200 @ 0.15	30.00
Turkeys	12 @ 0.50	6.00
Ducks	2 @ .25	0.50
Gardens	2 @ 10.00	20.00
House		2,000.00
Bedsteads	12 @ 4.00	48.00
Beds	12 @ 16.70	240.00
Quilts	10 @ 10.00	100.00
Sheets	12 @ 1.75	21.00
Pr. Slips	20 @ 0.50	10.00
Towels	36 @ 12 1/2	4.50
Three Ply Carpet	80 yards @ 1.14	91.20
Carpet	164 yards @ 0.40	65.60
Oilcloth	17 yards @ 1.12 1/2	19.12
Bureaus	3 @ 12.00	36.00
Secretary	1 @ 15.00	15.00
Wardrobe		14.00
Chests	2 @ 3.00	6.00
Corner Cupbords	2 @ 12.00	24.00
Safes	3 @ 15.00	15.00
Winged Tables	3 @ 5.00	15.00

(continued)

Table 10.1—*Continued*

Stands	2 @ 1.25	2.50
Washstands & Pitchers	3 @ 1.25	3.75
Washstands	3 @ 1.50	4.50
Parlor Stand	1 @ 6.00	6.00
Eight Day Clock		12.00
Looking Glasses	7 @ 1.50	10.50
Cane Bottom Chairs	6 @ 2.00	12.00
Rocking Chair		7.00
Chairs	30 @ .50	15.00
Lounge		2.00
Lot of Books		10.00
Pair Blinds		5.00
Oilcloth Blind	4@ 1.00	4.00
Tinplate Stoves	3 @ 10.00	30.00
Drum		4.00
Parlor & Cook Stove		20.00
Set China Dishes		12.00
Tea Set<n>China Ware		15.00
Set Common Dishes		7.00
Goblets	1 Dozen	3.00
Tumblers	2 1/2 Dozen @ 0.10	3.00
Stem Glasses	1 Dozen @ 0.05	0.60
Knives & Forks	3 Dozen @ 3.00	9.00
Silver T. Spoons	10 @ 1.00	10.00
Plated Table Spoons		2.40
Glass Dishes	8	-
Common Spoons	3 Dozen @ 0.50	1.50
B. Butter Knives	2 @ 0.50	1.00
B. Salt Spoons	1 @ 1.00	1.00
Salt & Pepper Boxes	4 Sets @ 0.31 1/4	1.25
Kitchen Furniture		25.00
Sugar	100 # @ 0.10	10.00
Coffee	12 # @ 0.15	1.80
Stone Jars	19 @ 0.12 1/2	2.37
Glass Jars	10 @ 0.15	1.50
Large Crocks	1 Dozen @ 0.25	3.00
Large Crocks	6 1/2 @ 0.25	6.24
Crocks Preserves	12 @ 1.00	12.00
Crocks Marmalade	12 @ 1.00	12.00
Crocks Applebutter	8 @ 0.75	6.00
Firkins Lard	200 # @ 0.7	21.00
Bacon	225 # @ 0.10	22.50
Bbls. Vinegar	4 @ 5.00	20.00
Wine	16 Gallons @ 1.50	24.00
Empty Barrels	8 @ 0.50	4.00
Vinegar Hhd.	1 @ 2.00	2.00
Pickels	1/2 Barrel	4.00
Washtubs	7 @ 0.50	3.50
Washing Machine		3.00

Churn		1.50
Copper Kettles	2 @ 5.00	10.00
Salt	5 Sacks @ 2.00	10.00
Pepper	5 # @ 0.25	1.25
Sausage Grinder & Stuffer		3.00
Lard Press		0.75
Side Saddle	2 @ 10.00	20.00
Riding Bridles	5 @ 1.00	5.00
Bags	60 @ 12 1/2	7.50
Tar	1/2 Bbl.	2.00
Tallow	60 # @ 0.10	6.00
Hard Soap	150 #	10.50
Dried Corn	1 Bushel	2.00
Dried Apples	1 Bushel	1.00
Dried Peas	1/2 Bushel	1.50
Dried Beans	1/2 Bushel	0.75
Dried Cherries	1 3/4 Bushel	4.00
Muslin	108 Yards @ 0.20	21.60
Calico	100 Yards @ 0.15	15.00
Cottonades	12 Yards @ 0.25	3.00
Casinett	12 Yards @ 62 1/2	7.50
S. Yarn	4 # @ 1.00	4.00
Shawls	3 @ 5.00	15.00
Crape Shawl	1 @ 15.00	15.00
Square Shawl	10 @ 3.00	30.00
Cloaks	5 @ 10.00	50.00
Made Clothing for the Family		500.00
Matirs	1 Set @ 3.00	3.00
Barn Destroyed		1,250.00
McCormick R.		50.00
Wheat Drill		35.00
Grain Rakes	2 @ 10.00	20.00
Wheat Fan		20.00
Threshing Machine		10.00
Wheat Screen		6.00
Forks	1 Lot @ 6.00	6.00
Plows	6 @ 2.00	12.00
Wagon Gear	6 Sets @ 10.00	60.00
Plow Gear	5 Sets @ 2.40	12.00
Halters	7 @ 1.00	7.00
C. Gear	1 Set @ 2.00	2.00
Wagons	2 @ 72.50	145.00
Shop Tools		20.00
Cutting Box		3.00
Harness	2 Sets @ 10.00	20.00
Buggy Harness		25.00
Wheat in Barn	80 Bushels	100.00
Rye	20 Bushels @ 0.75	15.00
Corn	25 Bushels @ 0.65	16.25
Hay Burned	35 Tons @ 12.00	420.00
Hay	11 Tons @ 8.00	88.00

(continued)

Table 10.1—*Continued*

R. Straw	75 Bundles @ 0.70	5.25
Hog Pen		50.00
Springhouse		100.00
Wheat Taken from Stack 75 Bushels		93.75
49 Acres of Ground Encumbered		
so that it cannot be seeded		490.00
		7,820.63
Sleigh Blankets	5 @ 4.40	22.00
Buffalo Robe		3.50
Baskets	3 Bushels @ 0.40	1.20
Market Baskets	4 @ 0.50	2.00
Wool Wheel		0.50
Real		1.00
Ottomans	2 @ 5.00	10.00
Straw	15 Tons @ .650	97.50
Pasturing on Farm		50.00
For Road Through Farm		15.00
Wood	15 Cords @ 3.00	45.00
Hogs	4 @ 10.00	40.00
Injury done to Carriage		10.00
Large Map U.S.		7.00
Flutes	2 @ 5.00	10.00
Music Box		5.00
Wheel Barrow		3.25
Carriage Whips	2 @ 1.50	3.00
Riding Whips	3 @ 0.50	1.50
Glass Lamps	2 @ 1.75	3.75
		330.95

After addition of five hundred Dolls. allowed for Made Clothing &c.
(Witnesses)
Henry F. Neikirk
Henry Piper
William Rubeth

Source: Mumma 1885.

Farmstead Layout and Architecture

The Mumma farmstead revolved around a two-and-one-half story brick and frame house behind which stood several small wood and stone out-buildings, including a spring house, all encircled by a picket fence. A large barn sat across the farm lane from the house; beyond it was an apple orchard. The first house on the lot was a frame structure erected on a limestone foundation with a full basement (Walker and Bedell 1993:5). The original basement, stone foundation, and frame house were probably built by the Orendorffs. Sometime later, probably after the property was sold to Jacob Mumma, a three-walled brick addition was built abutting the frame section. Like the earlier frame structure, the brick addition was built on a limestone foundation (Walker and Bedell 1993).

During the battle, the frame section burned to the ground, but the three brick walls remained. According to Samuel Mumma, Jr., "In the spring of 1863 we rebuilt our house and had just moved in a few weeks before the army went to Gettysburg" (Mumma 1906). It is possible that a temporary, frame room was also built immediately after the war. The extant frame section was built sometime later, as evidenced by alterations in the brick walls to accommodate its construction (Walker and Bedell 1993:6–7).

Battle of Antietam

The overwhelming loss of life and destruction incurred during the Battle of Antietam caused Sharpsburg and the surrounding countryside to be placed under severe national scrutiny. The battle and its aftermath were well documented by soldiers, civilians, news correspondents, and other visitors. Letters, diaries, and other accounts detail the landscape and cultural environment in 1862.

After the Battle of South Mountain on September 14, residents watched in dismay as the armies descended on Sharpsburg. With a battle imminent, townspeople were forced to make critical decisions: either leave for safety or stay and protect their homes and possessions. One farm wife wrote, "During the battle, the occupants had to leave their homes, and when they returned, they found that everything eatable or movable taken, not even a dish or spoon left" (Davis n.d.:52). The Mumma, Poffenberger, and Piper families, whose farms sat prominently on the battlefield, took their children and horses and stayed with relatives.

Alfred Poffenberger

Prior to the battle, Poffenberger and his family abandoned their home in the West Woods. Confederate forces occupied these woods the night before and throughout the day of battle. A letter written by artillerist William P. Poague states that on the evening of the 16th, "Raines battery must have bivouacked near mine—at a straw stack near Alf. Poffenbergers" (Poague 1895 in Carman 1895–1902).

The farm was used during and after the battle as a field hospital. Sgt. Edward Moore of Poague's Battery indicated that the Confederates moved their damaged artillery past "Jackson's field hospital" on the Poffenberger farm in the aftermath of the West Woods engagement (Priest 1989:176). The farm's position and resources would have made it a prime hospital site. The cabin provided shelter for the wounded, and there was fresh water in the well. The farm lay behind Confederate lines, and the road leading from the West Woods, past the cabin, toward the Potomac, was an effective evacuation route for wounded Southerners. After Lee and his army retreated across the Potomac, Union forces occupied the farm for four weeks.

Samuel Mumma

The Mumma family left their home on the afternoon of September 15th. Samuel Mumma, Jr., described the scene: "Father and mother and the younger children left in the two-horse carry-all (the older children walking as there's a large family) going about 4 miles and then we camped in a large church." The family "took nothing as they were cannonading . . . and were afraid that there would be a battle at once. Some clothing was gotten together and the silverware was packed in a basket ready to take, but in our haste to get away, all was left behind" (Mumma 1906). On the night of the 16th, Samuel Mumma and a friend went back to the house to get some clothing but found that "everything of value had been taken" (Mumma 1906).

The assignment to burn the Mumma house fell on volunteers of the 3rd North Carolina Infantry (fig. 10.2): "Before the sun rose, perceiving that the Mumma House . . . was well adapted to the protection of sharpshoot-ers. . . . I ordered its destruction and called upon volunteers . . . selecting two of them they immediately carried out my orders by setting fire to the house, which was soon destroyed" (De Rossett 1896 in Carman 1895–1902). Apparently the fire was set by throwing a piece of wood from a Confederate cook fire through an open window (Mumma 1906).

Battle Aftermath

When the battle subsided, local residents returned to find a landscape of death and devastation. The scenery which two days prior had been de-scribed as a valley "varied into squares of the light green of nearly ripened corn, the deeper green of clover, and the dull brown of newly ploughed fields" (*Daily Dispatch* 1862:Sept. 23) was now fields "plowed with shot, watered with blood, and sown thick with dead" (Richardson 1865). The landscape was almost unrecognizable:

> The sultry air was laden with the smoke of gunpowder and of the smoulder-ing ruins of burnt houses and barns and straw piles. The fields were ploughed by cannon balls and strewed thick with all manner of debris. Fences were demolished, and rails in splinters; the green corn blades were in shreds, and trampled into the dust. The trees of the woods looked as if they had been threshed by a giant's flail. (Williams 1968:335)

10.2. Burning of Mr. Mumma's house and barns (courtesy of the Antietam National Battlefield).

Fields were littered with the accoutrements of war—caissons, knapsacks, cartridge boxes, muskets, shot and shell, and strewn with bloated horse carcasses. One woman visiting the battlefield noted that "there were 60 or 70 dead horses lying in the fields, which made the atmosphere anything but agreeable" (Davis n.d.:52). The military contracted local farmers to collect and burn the horse carcasses; Samuel Mumma removed and burned a total of 55 horses which died on his land (Stotelmyer 1992:10, Reilly in Ernst 1993:116).

The greatest problem faced by the military and civilian population was the multitude of human corpses. One soldier reported that, "Ride where one might for a space of perhaps a mile and a half in width in places, and four or five miles in length, the dead were on every side" (Scharf 1968: 251). "The next day the hideousness of the sight was greatly increased. And when the soldiers were buried, many of them simply by having a little earth thrown over them, their projecting feet, faces, an arm here and there a head, formed a spectacle too horrible" (Williams 1968:336). A Pennsylvania soldier on burial detail wrote:

> The weather was phenomenally hot, and the stench from the hundreds of black bloated, decomposed magotty bodies, exposed to a torrid heat for three days after the battle, was a sight truly horrid. . . . Over head floated large numbers of those harpies of the air, buzzards, awaiting an opportu-

nity to descend to earth to partake of the cadaverous feast. (Whistler 1906, in Stotelmyer 1992:10)

The smell of the battlefield extended several miles, forcing local residents to close their windows and doors against the offensive odor (Stotelmyer 1992:12). Corpses were buried in shallow graves or trenches where they had fallen. Samuel Michael wrote:

Shericks land joining ours is as common for graves as the cornstalks are on a forty acre field. . . . they are taking them away very fast // taking them off to the north // they have removed and taken away about six thousand // and if they take ten times that many more away then they will not have them all. (Michael 1862)

Some corpses had only "dirt thrown over them, and the hogs had rooted the shoes off with the feet in them and it was a common thing to see human bones lying loose in gutters and fence corners for several years, and frequently hogs would be seen with limbs in their mouths" (Riley, in Stotelmyer 1992:16).

The remains of many Northern soldiers were taken away soon after the battle, but overlooked Southern and Northern burials remained for years. The bones of these abandoned burials continued to haunt local townspeople and farmers such as D. R. Miller, who looked to his pasture where more than 300 Confederate soldiers were buried, many with their "bones exposed" (Maryland 1869). Farmers on the battlefield continued to plow up bones throughout the 1860s and well beyond, even after all identified graves had been disinterred and given proper burial (Stotelmyer 1992:21–22, 28, 34–38).

A total of 96 Confederate soldiers were buried on the land of "Mrs. Lucker." According to an 1869 survey of Confederate burial places, 8 soldiers from the 15th Virginia and the 53rd Georgia were "buried in Mrs. Lucker's barn field near an old well; have been plowed over" (Maryland 1869:21, 23–29, 32–33, 39). More than 100 unknown soldiers in numerous trenches were buried on the Mumma property including crop fields and near the family graveyard (Maryland 1869:36–37). In his claim to the U.S. government, Mumma estimated the damage done by travel and burial on his property to be $150 (Table 10.1).

While the fields and orchards were turned into graveyards, houses, barns, and churches were transformed into makeshift hospitals. A reporter from the *New York Tribune* reported that in one barn alone there were 1,120 wounded and:

within the distance of two miles, are three more hospitals, each having from six hundred to seven hundred in them and long trains of ambulances standing in the road waiting to discharge their bloody loads. . . . Every private dwelling is filled with the wounded. Carpets are torn up, costly furniture removed, and comfortable mattresses spread upon the floor. (Scharf 1968:252)

Requisitioning houses for hospitals was often not done with the owner's blessing. Samuel Michael related:

Elizabeth took sick and died from the typhoid fever. The doctors say she . . . was doing very well on Sunday. . . . On Monday they forced a hospital in our house // Kate and Mother fought them hard. . . . it frightened her and she . . . was taken with severe hemorrages at the nose and bowls and died on the 24th of October. The Hospital was continued in our Parlor for several weeks. I do not recall how many has died in it // they have left it now // it looks like a hog pen. (Michael 1862)

The death brought by the battle was also extended to the local population in the form of typhoid fever, dysentery, and diarrhea contracted from the soldiers and hospitals. Samuel Michael continued, "the worst of all, the disease of the hospital has afflicted three of our family. . . . Mother died with this disease and the 20th of November was buried /// She was a beautiful corps" [*sic*] (Michael 1862).

Jacob Miller wrote a letter to his daughter informing her of the local deaths:

Your Unkle Daniel Miller is no more. . . . He was not well when he left home the day before the big battle // he was taken with a diarear which was a very common complaint with the troops and Citizens. . . . Mrs. Adam Michael is no more // she took her flite this day a weak // her oldest daughter had just gon before her about eight or ten days // the other daughter and Kalille wore both down and verry ill at the same time but are geting better,—Hellen and Janet have had a severe attack of tayfoy fevour but are both geting better. . . . Jacob and Annmarys children nearly all or perhaps all had Scarlet fevour but are all geting well-// Henry Mummas wife is no more, she departed this life about two weaks since // she had the same fevour // nearly all or quite all of John Smith famly wore down but are geting better. . . . many other citizens and hundreds of soldiers have been taken with the same, and many died, it is an army disease thus ads an addition to the Horrers of war. (Miller 1862)

Tombstones in the Mumma family cemetery attest to the deaths of young Sharpsburg residents after the battle. One tombstone stands "in Memory of Ann Mary wife of . . . died Nov. 25, 1862 Aged 27 yr 4 mo & 3 days" who was buried with "Emma Kate died Nov. 26 1862 Aged 2 yr & 7 days."

When people returned to their farmhouses and log cabins, the destruction of their personal property was startling. Samuel Miller's daughter wrote, "It was distressing enough to those pore people when they returned from the cave to see their homes in ashes" (Miller 2/8/63). One soldier described the scene: "Not a building about us which was not deserted by its occupants and rent and torn by shot and shell; not a field which has not witnessed the fierce and bloody encounter" (Noyes in Scharf 1968:250). A wounded Confederate soldier wrote that he was hospitalized in a church in the village of Sharpsburg from which "the top had been knocked off by a shell." Samuel Michael wrote, "our house and barn that we live in is very much injured by the shells" (Michael 1862).

To a large degree, the loss of property and food occurred during Union occupation in the battle's aftermath. A week after the battle, the local newspaper proclaimed, "The region of county between Sharpsburg and Boonsboro has been eaten out of food of every description. The two armies of from 80 to 100 thousand each, have swept over it and devoured everything within reach" (*Herald and Torchlight,* Hagerstown, Maryland, September 24, 1862). Samuel Michael lamented that:

> the Yankeys took all of our corn about seven hundred bushel about three hundred bushels of potatoes, 27 loads of hay destroyed. . . . They stole 6 head of horses // Killed nearly all our Hog's and sheep and 1 stear and 1 cow // stole all of our beef and took all of the apples // hardly left the trees stand // our loss is upwards of 2 thousand dollars. (Michael 1862)

The farmers' tales of loss were many: horses taken by the cavalry; cows, sheep, and pigs slaughtered to feed the troops; corn and wheat confiscated; and miles of fencing burned for campfires. Mr. Mumma, engaged in conversation with a soldier during the Gettysburg Campaign, said he "hoped the next time they fought, they would get out of his cornfields, as he gathered no corn or crops that year" (Mumma 1906).

Samuel Miller described the inundation of troops who commandeered farms and stripped the remaining fences and crops from the fields:

> I think by Spring I will not have any fence left, except an outside fence around my home farm and one field fenced off. . . . We have nine acres wheat down on all of our land and if the army had not been hear I would have had upward of a hundred. Many of the farmers have not sown a handfull.—if the soldiers all go away we will have a fine chance for a large crop of corn next summer if we can get the fenses made. (Miller 12/7/62:28–30)

The monumental loss incurred by many of the farmers, augmented in many cases by denial of claims for reimbursement, was the source of discouragement and distrust of the Federal government. Mumma received little remuneration for the damage to his farmstead. Attempting to get compensation 26 years after the battle, Samuel Mumma, Jr., testified that Generals Meade and Sumner promised him payment for requisitioned supplies, but the quartermaster refused to give him receipts for the crops and livestock. Samuel said his father "had made little effort to get receipts, as he was an old man and very much discouraged by the loss of his house and barn" (Mumma 1888). The war years were long and full of hardships. Three years after the battle, Samuel Michael wrote: "We have not built up our fences yet. . . . Things are very gloomy here to what they once were" (Michael 1865).

Agricultural Setting, 1862

The 1860 agricultural census of Washington County portrays prewar Sharpsburg as a district of prime land, crops, and animal husbandry. Typically, wheat, Indian corn, and hay, along with rye, oats, and Irish potatoes were the crops raised. Individual farmers produced hundreds of pounds of butter, as well as some wool and honey. Many farms maintained wood lots which were considered as income in reserve; the wood lots provided lumber, cord wood, and fence posts. Apple orchards, some with a few pear or cherry trees, were common, and the fruit, wine, and jams produced were used by the farm household or sold locally. The crop fields, orchards, lanes, and farmyards were delineated by rail or post-and-rail fences. The large wooden barns sheltered horses, milk cows, swine, and sheep.

The Alfred Poffenberger and Samuel Mumma farms were typical of the local agricultural profile in types of crops and livestock and in the level of farm production. Alfred Poffenberger farmed the primary crops plus clover on 72 acres. He also had 20 acres of unimproved land, including a wood lot. He cultivated a small apple orchard and kept horses, cows, and swine. The farm, valued at $5,000, indicated a worth of about $54 an acre. The majority of farms in the Sharpsburg area were valued at between $40 to $64 an acre. Samuel Mumma, Sr., owned 150 acres of land, comprised of 120 improved and 30 unimproved acres. Mumma's land, valued at $11,000, or approximately $73 an acre, was one of the six most valuable farms. He also closely followed the local trend in crops grown and livestock kept and slaughtered.

Both Alfred Poffenberger and Samuel Mumma, Sr., were considered to be good men by their neighbors. According to interviews made during compensation investigations, Alfred was said to be a "good farmer" working "good land," growing a "variety of farming staples of all kinds" (Office of the Quartermaster General, Record Group 92, Entry 812, File M917). Mumma was described as "a gentleman of good character and standing in the neighborhood . . . whose reputation for honesty was high" (Mumma 1888:46, 48).

The majority of the Poffenberger crops were either damaged by artillery and small arms fire or lost through impressment by Federal troops. Poffenberger's claim for crop loss was denied because investigators could not identify which losses were due to Confederate or Union forces. Alfred appears to have eventually made out well: between 1867 and 1869, he was paid more than $800 for crop damage earlier estimated at $645. Poffenberger's situation was unique in that he was overcompensated while many neighbors received no remuneration at all. Several relatives did not fare well either; Joseph Poffenberger received no money on a claim of $2,277.55, and Samuel Poffenberger received $7.50 on a claim of $731.75 (Stach 1996:11).

Undisputedly, the civilian who lost the most was Samuel Mumma, Sr.; his damages were estimated at more than $10,000 (Table 10.1). All the family's personal possessions, including furniture, clothing, china, glassware, crocks, foodstuffs, silverware, as well as real estate (house, barn, outbuildings) and agricultural equipment, were stolen or destroyed. Much of the damage to buildings and land was attributed to Confederate forces, but the majority of Mumma's crops, stores, livestock, and miles of fencing were taken by Union forces. The Federal government accepted no responsibility for damage incurred by the Confederates and never compensated him for damage attributed to the Union Army. Despite his losses, Mumma acquired the capital he needed to rebuild his house by the spring of 1863.

Farmers and other residents of Washington County emerged from the Civil War poorer both in spirit and material wealth. In order to get enough money to replace lost crops, livestock, and equipment, many farmers had to sell timber off of their wood lots. Many "were compelled to mortgage their lands to pay for horses and cattle which they had to buy in place of those taken by the soldiers, and upon these mortgages the interest charged was at the rate of from 8 to 10 per cent" (Williams 1968:367).

Farmers sank into financial straits from which they never recovered; the depreciated currency resulted in higher land and grain prices. Because banks required collateral to secure loans, farmers often asked their better-off neighbors to endorse notes. "One failure frequently involved a half dozen farmers in a neighborhood" (Williams 1968:367). Smaller landholders, who could not survive in this economic climate, sold their lands, resulting in the consolidation of farms into fewer hands. Between 1860 and 1870, agricultural censuses indicated that the number of individuals listed as farmers declined by 13 percent. After the battle, Sharpsburg farmers faced many difficulties. They could choose to rebuild their farms and weather the financial troubles or seek new opportunities in midwestern states such as Iowa and Illinois. In many cases, the move west was delayed a few years until after the war. In November 1863, Jacob Miller wrote, "Jacob Mumma is about to Start for Ilenoise [sic] next Monday and Says if he is pleased with that Country he will buy land and Settle down he could not get a farm hear to rent to Suit him" (Miller 11/16/1863).

In the decade following the war, Alfred Poffenberger prospered. Although he was still a tenant farmer, he greatly increased acreage under cultivation to 199 acres; the land had an estimated value of $13,000, or

$65 per acre. Poffenberger was as well off as about half the Washington County farmers between 1860 to 1870. He doubled his crop output, almost doubled the amount of livestock he owned, and added sheep to his farm. Even with these changes, the Poffenberger farmstead would have looked much like it did at the time of the battle. The layout of fields remained the same, although they had new rail fences. He continued to farm in Sharpsburg until the mid-1870s, when he too moved to Iowa.

During the same time period, Samuel Mumma, Sr., increased his acreage by only 29 acres. Estimated at $101 per acre, his land was still considered very valuable. However, Samuel had a less productive farm than eight years earlier; there was a drastic decrease in almost all produce and a reduction in stock. In fact, the value of Mumma's farm production was just over $2,000, while Poffenberger's value was almost $3,000. The explanation for the Mumma decline is simple: by 1870, two sons were working their own farms. In 1876, Samuel Mumma died at the age of 75, leaving his farm to his son and daughter-in-law.

Archaeological Excavations

The Mumma and Locher/Poffenberger farmsteads had great archaeological research potential for several reasons. First, historic documents detail the occupants of the farmsteads. Today, both farmsteads contain a standing domicile. One section of the Poffenberger cabin has stood since the first quarter of the 19th century. The house on the Mumma farm was constructed in the spring of 1863 over the foundation of the original structure. Archaeological excavations provided artifact and distribution data which denote changing yard use.

Excavations at the Mumma and Locher/Poffenberger sites produced stratigraphically mixed 19th-century yard deposits. The Locher/Poffenberger yard deposit was distinguished by a concentration of artifacts dating between 1810 and 1900. The Mumma deposit was characterized as a less dense scatter of domestic debris dating from the late 18th through the 19th centuries. There was a substantial overall difference in the size of the domestic deposits, with more than 8,600 artifacts at Locher/Poffenberger and approximately 4,000 at Mumma. Although artifacts dating throughout the century were mixed vertically and the two assemblages varied in density, they can still be employed effectively by identifying artifacts by date, by employing general temporal groupings, and by using spatial distributions for inter- and intra-site comparisons.

Locher/Poffenberger Farmstead

The 1995 archaeological survey of the Locher/Poffenberger farmstead involved the excavation of shovel test pits on the knoll where the cabin is situated, including the north and east yards, the lower bedrock benches to the west, and down slope near the old farm lane and well to the south (fig. 10.3). During the second phase of testing, 50 cm (1.6 ft.) square units were excavated on a 10-meter grid. Larger 1-m (3.3 ft.) units were then excavated, their location based on artifact concentrations and features. The assemblage as a whole contains small sherds and artifacts consistent with sheet refuse and material thrown into the yard and subsequently trampled by the cabin's occupants.

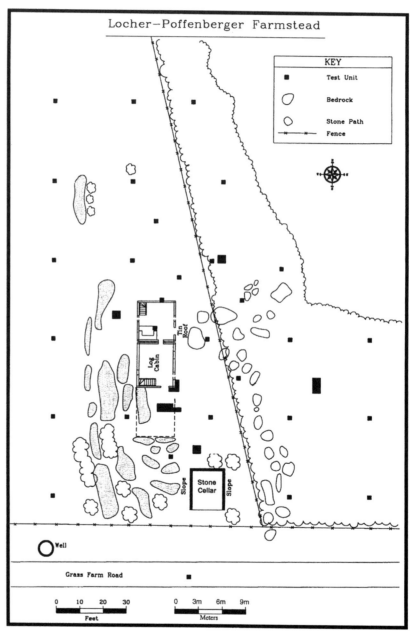

10.3. Excavations at Locher-Poffenberger farmstead (courtesy of the National Park Service, National Capital Region, and URS Greiner Woodward Clyde).

Mumma Farmstead

In 1993, contract archaeological excavations were conducted within the Mumma house (Walker and Biddell 1993). The resulting archaeological assemblage did not readily indicate the physical trauma inflicted on the site during the battle. The archaeologists noted that:

> Surprisingly, other than these burnt ceramics (Redware = 47 and refined earthenware = 20) and the melted glass (n = 29), there was little evidence of the burning of the original structure. One would expect a thick layer of charcoal and construction debris to remain after such an event. This was not, however, encountered. It is probable that the debris was removed during the rebuilding of the house, leaving only a scatter of artifacts. (Walker and Bedell 1993:34)

These observations are similar to those resulting from the 1997 excavations. The density of architectural remains was not unusually high for a domestic site dating to this period. The 1997 archaeological excavations in the Mumma yard identified features dating from the late 18th century through the Civil War era (fig. 10.4). In general, a thin scatter of domestic refuse, including 18th- and 19th-century ceramics and glass, and architectural remains, such as nails and window and brick fragments, were recovered from the house yard.

Locher/Poffenberger Artifact Distribution Analysis

The archaeological evidence suggests that the people living at the Locher/Poffenberger farm threw at least some of the trash out the doors of the farmhouse. When rooms were added to the house, the disposal pattern shifted and reflects new door locations. However, disposal of some domestic debris at the site was not as simple or expedient as tossing food remains out an open door. Another element of discard in certain portions of the yard changed from the early years of the site's use.

Early in the 19th century, the Locher/Poffenberger tenant farmhouse consisted of a one-room log cabin with two doors that opened onto the north and south yards. The distribution of artifacts dating from 1780 to 1830 (fig. 10.5) shows that trash was commonly tossed out the southern door. A less dense concentration of early-19th-century artifacts occurred outside the north door. The disposal of trash at this time was concentrated in, but not restricted to, areas adjacent to doorways. This has been identified as the Brunswick Pattern of refuse disposal by South (1977). In addition, sherds of early 19th-century refined earthenwares were encountered in smaller numbers throughout the entire yard area.

When the log addition was built around the first quarter of the 19th century, it covered the old south yard area. As a result, and not surprisingly, there was a drastic change in the trash disposal patterns. As indi-

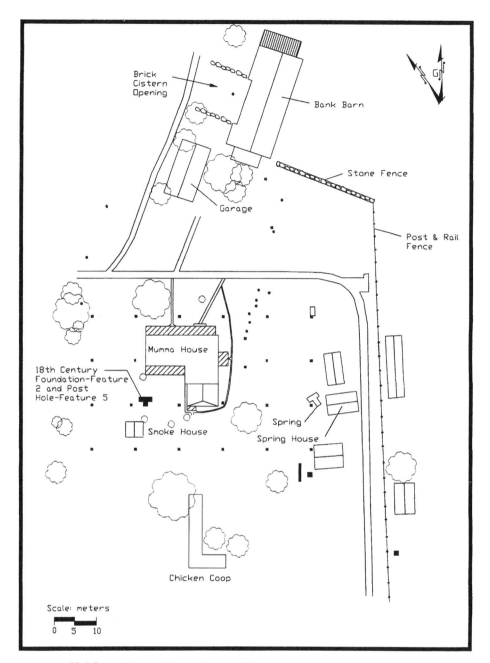

Brick
Cistern
Opening

Bank Barn

Stone Fence

Garage

Post & Rail
Fence

Mumma House

18th Century
Foundation-Feature
2 and Post
Hole-Feature 5

Spring

Spring House

Smoke House

Chicken Coop

Scale: meters

0   5   10

10.4. Excavations at Mumma farmstead (courtesy of the National Park Service, National Capital Region, and URS Greiner Woodward Clyde).

cated by the distribution of post-1830s ceramics (fig. 10.6), tenants still dumped trash relatively close to the cabin, but in the northern yard rather than the southern. A less dense but discernible concentration at the end of the stone walk in the east yard suggests that there was also a trend toward removing trash further from the cabin. The northern and eastern sections of the yard share an important trait: they are not visible to the public. The

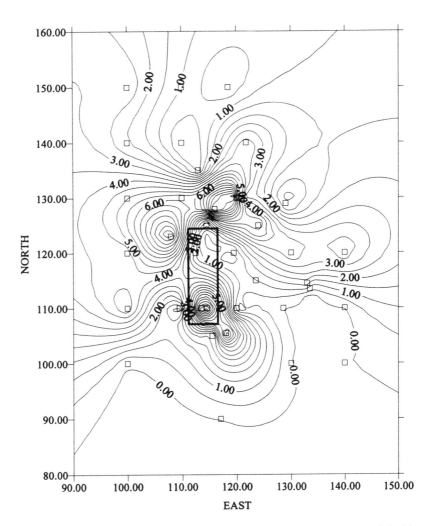

10.5. Pre-1830 ceramic distribution at Locher/Poffenberger Farm (courtesy of the National Park Service, National Capital Region, and URS Greiner Woodward Clyde).

use of the southern yard as a trash dump appears to have been all but abandoned by this time. The disposal of trash in the northern more "private" part of the site continued through the postbellum period, as indicated by the distribution of white granite wares (fig. 10.7).

The change in trash disposal patterns beginning about 1830 is a result of several factors. Construction of the new log room may have resulted in an immediate change in disposal patterns. However, it does not explain why, in the long run, tenants did not throw items out the eastern door of this new room. Perhaps there was a change in tenancy and the new occupants established their own habits of yard maintenance and trash disposal patterns. In any case, household trash was removed from public view, a pattern that continued throughout the rest of the century, even with changes in tenancy.

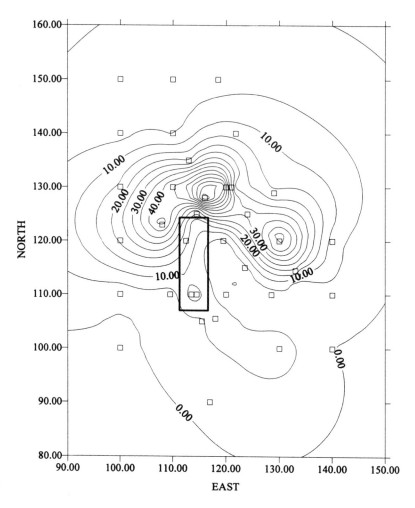

10.6. Post-1830 ceramic distribution at Locher/Poffenberger Farm (courtesy of the National Park Service, National Capital Region, and URS Greiner Woodward Clyde).

Mumma Artifact Distribution Analysis

The Mumma ceramic analysis also indicates an alteration in the density of trash and disposal patterns through time. Ceramics associated with earlier occupations, circa 1780–1830, are primarily dispersed around the house (fig. 10.8). The ceramic concentrations indicate that discard focused in two areas: southwest of the house and directly north in the front yard. The distribution map of post-1830 ceramics (fig. 10.9) indicates that later refuse was primarily deposited west and southwest of the house. The front yard was no longer favored for trash disposal. Around 1830, there was an obvious decline in domestic material deposited in the yard. This period corresponds to a change in the Mumma farm ownership when, in 1831, Jacob Mumma handed the farm over to his youngest son, Samuel. The

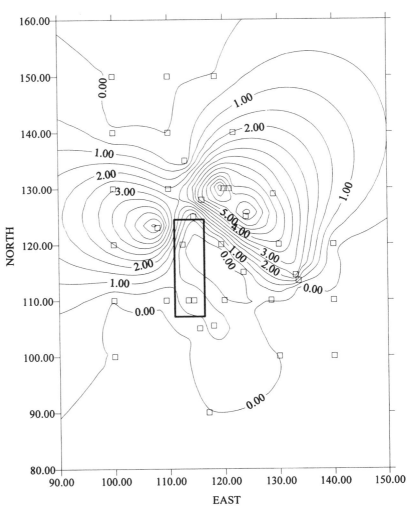

Right: 10.7. White granite distribution at Locher/Poffenberger Farm (courtesy of the National Park Service, National Capital Region, and URS Greiner Woodward Clyde).

Below: 10.8. Pre-1830 ceramic distribution at Mumma Farm (courtesy of the National Park Service, National Capital Region, and URS Greiner Woodward Clyde).

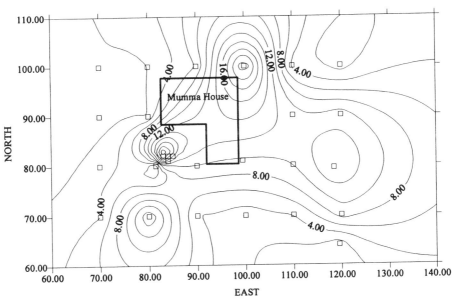

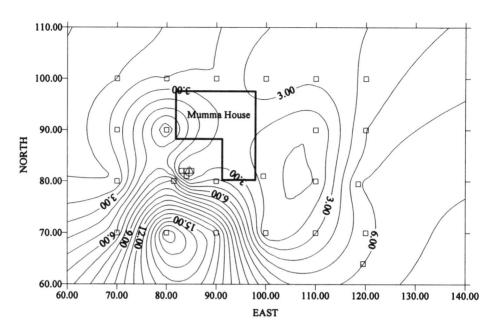

10.9. Post-1830 ceramic distribution at Mumma Farm (courtesy of the National Park Service, National Capital Region, and URS Greiner Woodward Clyde).

shift in yard trash disposal may well be associated with new ideas that were part of the agricultural reform movement.

Alterations in the Landscape

A major focus of research centered on the use of the landscape, the layout of farms in western Maryland, and how both were affected by social and economic influences. Events and forces that influenced this rural community during the 19th century included: the Battle of Antietam and its aftermath; improvements in production and technology; advancements in transportation, including construction of the nearby Chesapeake and Ohio Canal; and alterations in the composition and structure of farm households. Among these, archaeological and historical research concluded that discernible changes in the use of the landscape at the two farmsteads were related to two motivating forces that originated at the national level. Both shaped Sharpsburg's physical and symbolic landscape during the 19th century. The forces were the agricultural reform movement of the second quarter of the 19th century and the devastating 1862 Battle of Antietam. The agricultural movement advanced a new perspective for the agrarian world that changed the manner in which farmers viewed themselves, their neighbors, their farms, and their community. Through the use of symbolic imagery, reformers were able to persuade a largely agrarian nation to alter the landscape by cleaning it up. The result of this campaign is visible archaeologically in changing patterns of trash disposal and yard maintenance through time.

While changes in trash disposal were real but subtle, the Battle of Antietam and its aftermath had a much greater impact on the social fabric of the community through death and loss of property and livelihood. The battle placed social, economic, and emotional stress on Sharpsburg residents who were forced to reevaluate their lives within a changed environment. The farms and rural setting, which were the physical manifestation of people's hard work and devotion to the land, as well as symbols of prosperity and permanence, had been devastated. However, the archaeological evidence for the battle is not proportional to the extensive damage inflicted on the civilian countryside. Houses and barns were rebuilt, crops replanted, and new fences erected. Restoration of the landscape demonstrated a commitment to reestablish the way of life that existed before the battle.

Differential Use of the Farmyard

Archaeological evidence indicates that both Samuel Mumma and the Locher/Poffenberger tenants accepted to some degree the tenets professed by the agricultural movement. The occupants of the two farmsteads, however, demonstrated differences in interpreting the strict behavioral guidelines set by the reformers. What factors account for the different treatment of yard areas by two locally respected farmers? Two of the most obvious explanations for observed differences at the Mumma and Locher/Poffenberger farmsteads include visibility to the public and differences between land ownership and tenancy. The different patterns in yard use at the two farms could reflect a combination of these factors.

As a modern farmer, young Samuel Mumma seems to have adopted the progressive ideas of agricultural reform. When he inherited the thriving farmstead from his father, he lost no time in making improvements; the household trash was no longer thrown directly out the front door, and the farmyard was cleaned and encircled with a picket fence. His commitment to modern farm implements was apparent in the list of items lost during the battle, including a McCormick reaper, one wheat drill, two grain rakes, a wheat fan, a threshing machine, a wheat screen, and six plows. He continued to invest in modern tools after the battle, as evidenced by the 1870 Washington County Agricultural Census, where he is listed owning more than $4,000 worth of agricultural equipment.

At the Locher/Poffenberger farm, the presence of diachronically distinct trash disposal patterns suggests that at some point, the tenants in residence also began to participate in the agricultural movement. In the earliest occupation, trash was primarily thrown out doorways into the yard. Throughout the century, debris continued to be thrown into the yard, but after circa 1830, trash went out the north door or was brought down the stone path and tossed into the east yard. Despite a lack of commitment to a pristine yard, Alfred Poffenberger was not Farmer Slack. The Poffenberger fields had paling fences, which, though not as efficient as post and rail, were still effective at controlling livestock. The crops he cultivated were prolific and his livestock was well kept, as evidenced by the value of his farm products. And unlike Farmer Slack, "good farmer" Poffenberger was well thought of by his neighbors. Poffenberger might well have settled for a good reputation rather than a meticulously clean yard.

Visibility

The dissimilar disposal patterns exhibited at Mumma and Locher/Poffenberger farms could be a consequence of differences in visibility. The Poffenberger cabin was visible only from a small farm lane. Because the house is situated on a knoll, the yard area and any domestic trash, especially behind the house, was concealed from passersby. Only family or close friends would have been aware of its somewhat unkempt appearance. The Mumma farm, on the other hand, stood in the open among hundreds of acres of agricultural fields; it was visible for miles. The Mummas were perhaps subtly pressured into improvements by this greater visibility, while their less evident and less prominent neighbors were more relaxed about the appearance of their secluded farmstead.

Land Ownership versus Tenancy

The disparity in farmyard upkeep may indicate a distinction in focus between tenant farmer and landowner. Ownership of a home and land not only demands an investment of time and money but also the demonstration of a strong commitment to the community. The landowner's house is a symbol reflecting prosperity to neighbors and permanence on the landscape. The Mummas' decision to rebuild their house and outbuildings soon after the battle demonstrates permanence on the land and their desire to reestablish and reinforce their place in the community.

The tenant is tied to the land only insofar as the effort expended on cultivation will be repaid in profit. According to Herman (1994:48), "It was to the tenant's advantage to invest labor and capital in the cultivation of crops but not to improve land, buildings, and fences beyond the barest passable minimum." Alfred Poffenberger appears to have surpassed the bare minimum of upkeep in his rented domain, but he did not go overboard in this endeavor. He turned his compensation back into crops and livestock. This strategy allowed him to buy his own land in Illinois.

Battle-Related Stress and the Symbolization of the Landscape

The Battle of Antietam was followed by Federal occupation. Both caused total devastation to the agrarian landscape around Sharpsburg. The trauma was not apparent archaeologically. Instead, archaeology indicated little difference between the time prior to the battle and the time afterward. It is proposed that this lack of evidence of trauma is a manifestation of a continuum, indicative of larger cultural processes. How can the battle's cultural impact be determined when there is negligible archaeological evidence? The case is presented here that in a cultural response to stress, a form of symbolization occurs in which the landscape takes on more complex meanings. By studying the altered landscape, it is possible to elicit insight into the changing worldview of the Sharpsburg community.

In a study of the historic preservation movement in Salzburg, Austria, Rowntree and Conkey (1980) adopted an ecological model of stress response which could be applied to the cultural domain. They proposed that, "The process through which symbols are created, elaborated upon, and modified (and hence the process whereby the cultural landscape is created and transformed) is rooted in—and a part of—societal processes" (Rowntree and Conkey 1980:459).

This model is relevant to this research as it looks at the phenomenon of cultural stress, in this case the Battle of Antietam, which causes deviation from the norm and results in a lack of control and predictability. The use of environmental symbols is a strategy through which a group can enhance predictability which will reduce cultural stress.

> Symbols in the landscape also convey information about position in time. Historic buildings, monuments, and statues all signify social continuity by evoking not just specific memories of what has gone before, but also that there was existence and life before. Environmental symbols have strong potential to create and communicate temporal depth. Such symbols have a traditionalizing effect. . . . Some of the attributes that contribute to traditionalizing are rigidities of style, recognizable order and pattern . . . conformance to physical features, and the actual permanence, visibility, and formal aspects of architecture, raw materials, and the use of space. (Rowntree and Conkey 1980:462)

The Sharpsburg landscape prior to the battle, with its well-maintained farms and clearly delineated fields and orchards, already symbolized order, prosperity, permanence, and community cohesion. After the battle, the devastated landscape reflected death, destruction, and chaos. Apparently Sharpsburg farmers were quick to rebuild the landscape to provide a bridge between their way of life and values prior to the battle and that left as their legacy for future generations. In the study of Salzburg's historic preservation process, it was noted that local residents had selected forms associated with specific time periods and events and transformed them into "timeless symbolic forms that are significant in the present and are guaranteed a future as well" (Rowntree and Conkey 1980:474). The intention of Sharpsburg residents to provide a sense of constancy between pre- and post-battle periods is evidenced in a number of ways. Archaeological excavations at the two farmsteads indicate a continuation of deposition patterns and yard use. A resumption in the types of crops and produce grown, agricultural use of fields and orchards, and the reconstruction of fences and houses are all indicated in the historic documents and maps.

The archaeological and historical study reveals that the farmers of Sharpsburg, Maryland, viewed the agrarian landscape as more than just good cropland. At two times in the 19th century, the landscape became the symbolic manifestation of this farming community's identity and values. Participation in the agricultural reform movement beginning about 1830 demonstrates that many local farmers were willing to commit to new and popular ideas that altered long-established agricultural methods and domestic practices.

On the other hand, while the rural landscape was significantly changed by the Battle of Antietam, this altered world was not acceptable or tenable to the people of Sharpsburg, who strived to return it to its previous condition. When their houses were ransacked and their crops and possessions were stolen and destroyed, the citizens rebuilt fences, replanted crops of wheat and Indian corn, constructed houses on old foundations, and raised new livestock. Their continuity of land use reveals their desire to return to their prewar way of life by rejecting the chaotic forces which intruded into their world.

11

"Four Years of Hell"

Domestic Life in Harpers Ferry during the Civil War

Paul A. Shackel

Public memory of Civil War events provides an interesting commentary of the social and political environment of our nation. Often one memory is chosen over another memory to represent the dominant culture. The following case study on Harpers Ferry is about one aspect that is often neglected in Civil War memory—the effects of the war on everyday civilian life. An overview of wartime domestic life in Harpers Ferry provides some insight into this forgotten and tragic aspect of the war. Further, it will be shown how the National Park Service's creation of "great men" histories helped to foster a sense of national unity and patriotism.

While the John Brown story is often portrayed as an event leading to the Civil War, the official National Park Service Civil War history at Harpers Ferry is mostly concerned with commemorating Stonewall Jackson's siege and capture of the town (see, for instance, Frye 1987). This phenomenon, honoring the achievements of a general, is not unique to Harpers Ferry. It is present in many other nationally significant sites that commemorate the various American wars.

Although the deification of great men became part of the collective memory immediately after the Civil War (Blight 1989), until recently little emphasis was placed on the war's impact on civilian life (see Geier and Winter 1994). Even though they were sometimes far from the everyday conflict of the war, many civilians were affected by it. Why the stories of civilian lives have been excluded from the official histories at many battlefield parks, in favor of the in-depth study of troop movements, battlefield strategies, and generals, is a very interesting phenomenon. These current park interpretations dictate the importance of great men and emphasize an implicit social hierarchy and an obedience to a larger social structure. The social structure is made to appear eternal and inevitable. Therefore, while the official Civil War history of Harpers Ferry is about Stonewall Jackson's siege and capture of the town, we can create another important history of the war by developing a context for much of the archaeological material from this era. This "other" history includes the stories of everyday citizens, such as Mrs. Stipes and her boardinghouse, and Doctor Marmion, a civilian who stayed in town to care for the wounded.

Early Confederate Occupation and the Dismantling of Harpers Ferry

When the Confederate forces bombarded Fort Sumter on April 12, 1861, Harpers Ferry soon felt the repercussions. Five days later, Virginia seceded from the Union and the following day, Virginia militia was ordered to take Harpers Ferry (Murfin 1989). Lt. Roger Jones, stationed at Harpers Ferry with 42 men of the U.S. Mounted Rifles, did not receive aid from the local militia. Only 12 armory employees, fearing loss of their livelihoods, agreed to help the lieutenant defend Harpers Ferry and the U.S. Armory (Hern 1996:52–53). Outnumbered by 360 advancing Confederates, Jones set fire to the Federal factory buildings and abandoned the town (Mauzy 1861). The townspeople, in an attempt to salvage their livelihood, saved most of the armory's machinery (*Spirit of Jefferson,* May 4, 1861:2).

The arsenal burned, but the fire caused minimal damage to the musket factory on the Potomac River. The rifle factory, the former Hall's Rifle Works, was untouched. More than 4,000 guns survived in useable condition. During the next two months under Confederate occupation, armorers loyal to the secessionist cause worked at the armory until funds ran out (Shewbridge 1861).

When Col. Thomas Jackson became the garrison's overall commander, he seized buildings and arms manufacturing machinery. Union sympathizers had their property destroyed or carried off by troops (Henderson 1955:93). Families who rented armory buildings were ordered to vacate their homes, forcing them to obtain shelter elsewhere. Citizens were "dragged from their homes and confined in filthy guard houses, a prey to vermin and objects of insult to the [Confederate] rabble that guarded them" (Barry quoted in Snell 1960a:9). The Confederates used their homes and at least one church as barracks.

Robert E. Lee replaced Jackson with Gen. Joseph E. Johnston on May 23, 1861. Lee considered Jackson "too pugnacious, too secretive, and too unpredictable" (Hern 1996:71). Johnston established his headquarters on Camp Hill, immediately declared Harpers Ferry "untenable," and began to withdraw troops to Winchester (U.S. War Department 1880–1905, O.R. 2 1880:471). The Confederates dismantled the gun factory and moved more than 300 operable machines to Richmond, Virginia, and Fayetteville, North Carolina (Hern 1996:56). On June 13, when word came that 2,000 Federal troops were nearby, Johnston ordered the immediate evacuation of the town. The following day, they set fire to the armory buildings and destroyed the railroad bridge over the Potomac River (Murfin 1989). Harpers Ferry lay abandoned (fig. 11.1).

11.1. Abandoned U.S. rifle works on Halls Island, Harpers Ferry (courtesy of Harpers Ferry National Historical Park).

The town was "a ghost of its former life" (U.S. War Department 1880–1905, O.R. 2 1880:471). After the Confederate withdrawal, many displaced families returned to town with wagon-loads of furniture. The armory superintendent's house stood open, locks broken, furniture removed, papers and letters strewn across the surrounding grounds. People scavenged whatever they could from the building (Strother 1861:11). Even women and children could be encountered at all hours of the day and night loaded with booty or trundling wheelbarrows freighted with all imaginable kinds of portable goods and household furniture (Barry 1988:109).

The Federals Take the Heights and Later Create a "No Man's Land"

On July 21, 1861, Gen. Robert Patterson, commander of the Union forces opposing Johnston's Confederates, saw an opportunity to occupy Harpers Ferry and fortify Maryland Heights. The Union troops did not leave a favorable impression among the inhabitants. A local historian, Joseph Barry, reported that troops continued to loot and rob the town, much as the Confederates did previously. They "helped themselves to most of what was left by the rebels" (Barry 1988: 109). By the end of August, many Federal troops had left Harpers Ferry. While stationed on the surrounding heights, the soldiers continued to shoot at targets in town (Barry 1988:112).

The Federals abandoned Maryland Heights at the end of October 1861, and between August 1861 and February 1862, the town was largely unoccupied by Union and Confederate troops. Barry noted that the Confederate scouts kept the town in a state of terror (Barry 1988:116), and General Banks wrote that the town "is a picture of desolation" (U.S. War Department 1880–1905, O.R. 5 1880:676). Annie Marmion, a resident, also noted that "most people know the meaning of blockade. To the Village of Harpers Ferry as to other places it meant threatened starvation, but it also meant desolation inconceivable" (Marmion 1959:6). Generally, "all that winter—'61–'62—Harpers Ferry presented a scene of the utmost desolation. All the inhabitants had fled, except a few old people, who ventured to remain and protect their homes, or who were unable or unwilling to leave the place and seek new associations" (Barry 1988:121).

Federal Reoccupation and Jackson's Siege

Union troops moved into Harpers Ferry during night of February 22, 1862. The Federals occupied Loudoun, Bolivar, and Maryland Heights, and officers arrived with their families (Snell 1960a:50). Most of the Federal troops in Harpers Ferry were new and undisciplined, and Colonel Miles, commander of Harpers Ferry, often complained about the lack of battle-ready soldiers in his command. In fact, one week before the Confederate invasion of Harpers Ferry in September 1862, four new regiments were stationed at Harpers Ferry.

The Confederates captured the heights amid Union confusion and lack of leadership. Without any alternative, Miles surrendered. The Confederates captured 73 pieces of artillery and 10,000 small arms, 200 wagons, and 12,500 prisoners. A military investigation of the surrender found Miles's actions "amounting to almost imbecility, led to the shameful surrender of this important post" (quoted in Hern 1996:190). The next day the Confederates withdrew from Harpers Ferry to join Lee and Jackson at Sharpsburg, Maryland.

After the Battle of Antietam, Lee retreated into Virginia and Union troops reoccupied Harpers Ferry. The Federal XII Corps, Army of the Potomac, reoccupied Maryland Heights on the 20th of September. On the 22nd, the 2nd Division of the XII Corps encamped on Loudoun Heights (Hern 1996:192).

Union occupation of Harpers Ferry in the fall of 1862 was not pleasant. After Chaplain John H. Strickland of the 145th Pennsylvania arrived in Harpers Ferry in October, he described the town's water and food as contaminated with "living creatures . . . pork alive with skippers" (quoted in Hern 1996:196). Soldiers lay about the town with diarrhea, dysentery, rheumatism, measles, and colds. They continually came to the chaplain looking for a discharge (Hern 1996:196). A soldier from the 5th New York Heavy Artillery wrote: "There is nothing here but desolation and magnificent scenery. . . . [T]he smells are not very agreeable as there are a number of dead horses still remaining unburied" (Frederickson 1863).

Gen. George Meade ordered Harpers Ferry evacuated on June 28, 1863, and most of the equipment and artillery were removed to Washington, D.C., via the Chesapeake and Ohio Canal. Federal troops marched to Gettysburg for one of the war's major confrontations. The Confederates had uncontested control of Harpers Ferry into the first few days of July. They found large quantities of abandoned commissary, quartermaster, and ordnance supplies (Hern 1996:222). After Lee's retreat from Gettysburg, the Federals reoccupied Harpers Ferry.

Federals Reoccupy Harpers Ferry after the Battle of Gettysburg

Federal troops made their way into town on July 13, 1863. One soldier described it as desolate and in ruins: "[W]ar has had its effect and laid every thing waste and barren and the entire place is not worth $10" (Moulton in Drickamer and Drickamer 1987:124). Martial law prevailed in the town, guards were stationed at every street corner, and no one could proceed without showing a pass. Children needed passes to school, and after dark no one could roam the street without a pass. If they did not have one, they could be placed in the guardhouse overnight. Charles Moulton noted that he saw the guardhouse filled every morning (Moulton in Drickamer and Drickamer 1987:166).

Lower Town Harpers Ferry became a major depot and supply center. A government bakery that supplied bread to the troops stood in the arsenal yard. The army slaughtered cattle in either the Arsenal Square or the musket factory yard. A post office and an express office were established along with a hospital. Harpers Ferry seemed secure, and citizens and merchants slowly reinhabited the town to provide services to the occupying army. Boardinghouses were established to cater to soldiers and other visitors, such as wartime correspondents (Snell 1959:60; Moulton in Drickamer and Drickamer 1987:130). A soldier, Joseph Ward, wrote in August: "You have never seen a place grow as this has since we came in. Now the streets about sunset are full of ladies, but when we came there was none to be seen" (Ward 1985:70).

Rules limited merchants' activities, as prices, weights, and measurements were strictly regulated. If merchants did not obey these standards, soldiers confiscated their goods (Moulton in Drickamer and Drickamer 1987:146). Products were scarce, and many consumers purchased whatever was available, since quality products were few and far between. Moulton noted: "If you purchase a piece of cheese at the Sutler's and it is full of grubs, big, fat, and enough for fish bait, and you choose to mumble about it, that kind of vendor will console you with the fact that maggots will not get into bad or poor cheese" (Moulton in Drickamer and Drickamer 1987:127).

During February 1864 a smallpox epidemic spread through town. The influx of people, including prisoners, newly freed slaves, and Union troops, contributed to the outbreak. The army immediately established hospitals to quarantine the disease (Moulton in Drickamer and Drickamer 1987:166).

Revitalization of Occupied Harpers Ferry

Merchants slowly reoccupied the town until Sheridan refortified it in 1864. The army secured Bolivar Heights to create a park for wagon trains (O.R. 1880 43(1):745). An immense supply depot developed there. The Ordnance Department established a place to issue and repair weapons and ammunition. The army also established a large medical depot (Snell 1960b:39–40; see Whitehorne, Geier, and Hofstra, this volume).

By the middle of August, merchants and citizens flocked back to town and it again became a bustling center. Moulton described this new energy: "The street is blockaded from morning till night with army wagons" (Moulton in Drickamer and Drickamer 1987:204). Many journalists came to Harpers Ferry to report on the Union reoccupation and the following campaign. Artist James Taylor, sent by Frank Leslie to cover the 1864 Shenandoah Campaign, described the dire situation of one of the town's people: "Mrs. Stipes catered to sojourners at the Ferry to the extent of table board and lodging, not from choice but necessity caused by her husband's business reverses owing to the War, and his inability to catch on again, when it fell to the lot of Madam to entertain transients to keep the wolf from the door" (Taylor 1989:30).

In Harpers Ferry, most archaeological materials from the Civil War era date from this revitalization era, 1864 through 1865. The best documented archaeological materials are from the backyard of Mrs. Stipes's boardinghouse, which Edward Taylor sarcastically called "Hotel de Stipe." Historical records show that Mrs. Stipes operated the boardinghouse as early as October 1862 (Young 1863). Archaeology provides a microcosm of material life of boardinghouse occupants in an occupied town.

Pollen and phytolith analyses reveal a picture of the landscape and everyday life in an occupied Union town. The landscape is dramatically different from the earlier armory era when it contained well-manicured grass lawns (see Shackel 1996:94–97). The Civil War deposits are void of phytolith and pollen grasses, and they were replaced with weeds. Weed pollens include pigweed, goosefoot, nut-grass, carpetweed, purslane, chickweed, wire-grass, tomatillo/ground cherry, and buffalo bur (Cummings 1993a:7.25, 1993b; Rovner 1993:6.8).

Mrs. Stipes's establishment provides an abundance of information on foodways. The analysis by Brett Burk (1993) provides some clues to the daily diet of the boardinghouse residents. For instance, turtles are common in the area's riverine environment, and their presence in the archaeological record hints that Mrs. Stipes used turtle for her boardinghouse soups (Burk 1993:10.8). The presence of eastern cottontail also suggests that she used other wild foods to supplement her family's or their tenants' diets (Burk 1993:10.9).

A variety of domestic birds are included in the faunal assemblage, including goose, turkey, and chicken (Burk 1993:10.9). Both the goose and turkey assemblages are small. The foods are not the average boardinghouse fare, and they may be the remains of a holiday meal. There is also the possibility that Mrs. Stipes's husband hunted these birds to supplement meals and stretch the income from boarders (Burk 1993). Chicken is the largest assemblage of fowl, and most parts were found at the site. This fact implies that the boardinghouse keeper raised chickens in her yard and butchered some of them for food (Burk 1993:10.9).

Domesticated mammals, such as pig, cow, sheep, and goat, comprise most of the boardinghouse diet, consisting of more than 49 percent of the biomass of the entire assemblage. Cow (35.9 percent) is far greater then the other mammals, and pig comprises the second largest biomass percentage (11.4 percent). Sheep/goat biomass is small (Burk 1993:10.9–10.11). The presence of teeth and skull elements from pig, cow, and sheep suggests menu items such as calf-head soups. A search through contemporary cookbooks confirms that these meals were common (see, for instance, Hall 1855:66; Tyree 1879:77).

Twice as many pig bones (25 percent, n=27) as cow bones (13.8 percent, n=9) were butchered with a cleaver and/or axe. The greater use of an axe or cleaver on pigs is attributed to home or local processing (Burk 1993). Therefore, the boardinghouse keeper supported local markets rather than solely relying on mass-butchered meats from eastern centers.

The overwhelming majority of the remaining cow bones have saw marks (86.2 percent), which suggests that beef, in contrast to pork, apparently came from larger distribution centers. From the Civil War era animals were mass butchered and processed to supply large armies. Sawing facilitated mass butchering at a central processing point, and then the meats were transported to central localities, such as Harpers Ferry, for distribution. The presence of sawed cuts of meat in the boardinghouse assemblage shows that the boardinghouse keeper probably bartered with the army's commissary, or that she acquired it by some open trade with the east. Therefore, Harpers Ferry residents were not restricted to local markets during the later part of the war.

During the period of Sheridan's Valley Campaign, entrepreneurs erected a set of "shanty kitchens" that lined the Winchester and Potomac

11.2. Sketch of Lower Town, Harpers Ferry, with shanty kitchens (courtesy of Harpers Ferry National Historical Park).

Railroad bed, about 100 feet from Mrs. Stipes's boardinghouse (fig. 11.2). Evidence of open trade and access to larger regional markets is evident in the shanty kitchens' assemblage. Local entrepreneurs took advantage of the poor quality of market and military foods and catered to civilians' and soldiers' palates by operating these facilities. A large quantity of oyster shells found in the archaeological record, transported from the Baltimore markets, is another indication of the foods that Harpers Ferry residents received from larger markets in an attempt to diversify their foodways and to make a profit (Shackel 1993).

Trash found in Mrs. Stipes's boardinghouse yard provides additional information on the boarders' diet. Materials include peanut shell, walnut shell, cherry pit, peach pit, pumpkin seeds, watermelon seeds, egg shell, clam shell, and a very large quantity of oyster shell. Other foods, identified by pollen, include fig and raspberry (Cummings 1993a:7.25).

The assemblage of containers from Mrs. Stipes's boardinghouse includes many wares and types. The assemblage includes American gray salt-glazed stoneware jars, tin cans, and glass jars (Lucas 1993). Included are a variety of ceramic platters for serving large suppers. Matched plates were almost nonexistent. Plates include ironstones and edge-decorated whitewares, undecorated whitewares, and a variety of whiteware transfer prints, including green, red, and brown prints. Some flow blue decoration on plates is also present. Transfer-printed and hand-painted pearlwares (monochrome and polychrome) make up a small portion of the assemblage (Shackel et al. 1993). The large variety of dinnerware indicates that Mrs. Stipes's boardinghouse was far from the high style to which many Washington correspondents were accustomed.

Martial law forbade the sale and consumption of alcohol, and the provost marshal was responsible for enforcing these rules (Moore 1962:122–23). The military sometimes raided households suspected of bootlegging liquor. Those found with liquor in their houses or caught selling liquor within the boundaries of Harpers Ferry were forcefully removed outside the military district (Drickamer and Drickamer 1987; Lincoln 1879:135). Apparently, the provost marshal had limited control, since bootlegging prevailed throughout town. Archaeological materials from the backyard of Mrs. Stipes's boardinghouse reveal an abundance of wine/champagne bottles, though her establishment was next door to the provost marshal's office (Shackel et al. 1993).

Medicinal bottles are also present in the boardinghouse context. While some have concluded that people may have consumed patent medicines for their alcohol content (Bond 1989) or for their medicinal content (Larsen 1993), it is possible that the rate of disease and the pain and suffering caused by the war contributed to the consumption of these goods. There are many letters that document the poor health conditions in town. Since medical facilities may not have been readily available to soldiers with minor maladies, they depended upon self-medication.

Artifacts often considered part of a domestic assemblage are of interest. Twenty-seven straight pins, one safety pin, and one brass thimble—all items associated with clothing production or repair—are present in Mrs. Stipes's boardinghouse assemblage. These items are not unusual for military sites. The "housewife" was a sewing kit used by soldiers for the mending of their garments. It became an especially important kit, because issued clothing was sometimes of poor quality (Wiley 1971:64; Stern 1961:53–54; Beverly 1992).

The boardinghouse assemblage also contains military artifacts, suggesting some form of mixed use or cohabitation of military and civilians. Buckles, including a knapsack buckle, are present in the assemblage. Other militaria include a .22-caliber cartridge case, a musket ball, a percussion cap, and Minié balls ranging from .42 to .57 caliber. Also included were more than 20 tobacco pipes.

Sheridan's Shenandoah Campaign

On August 28th, 1864, Sheridan began his historic campaign down the Shenandoah Valley, and Taylor, a resident of Mrs. Stipes's boardinghouse,

11.3. Union troops occupying Camp Hill, Harpers Ferry (courtesy of Harpers Ferry National Historical Park).

documented the event (fig. 11.3). As many as a thousand wagons, escorted by thousands of Union soldiers, supplied Sheridan's efforts. The wagon trains returned to Harpers Ferry, usually filled with wounded soldiers, from both sides, and prisoners. In the late summer and early fall, the Federals processed an average of 100 prisoners a day through Harpers Ferry (Drickamer and Drickamer 1987:206). After Sheridan soundly defeated Early at Winchester on September 19 and again three days later at Fisher's Hill, the Confederate hold on the valley weakened. By the end of September, the Baltimore and Ohio Railroad repaired and opened the line to Martinsburg, facilitating supply of the Union Army. After a victorious campaign down the valley to Staunton, Sheridan withdrew to Martinsburg for the winter, and the supply depot was shifted back to Harpers Ferry (Snell 1960b:47–49; Moulton in Drickamer and Drickamer 1987: 218).

Harpers Ferry once again became a bustling town as many military support activities increased. For instance, there is evidence that surgery was performed in nonmilitary areas, such as Dr. Marmion's office. Today, the doctor's office no longer exists. Its foundations are buried under about one foot of topsoil, and the grounds are incorporated into a terraced landscape. Previous archaeology was designed to locate landscape features (Cotter 1959) and for stabilization needs (Inashima 1981). Recent archaeology (Parsons 1995) located the foundations of Marmion's office, and some work was done in the building's yard (fig. 11.1). The Civil War era assemblage contains both domestic artifacts and military objects. The latter includes buckles, a canteen, and uniform pieces. Most notable is the large quantity of Union uniform buttons found in and around the building. One can imagine Dr. Marmion, or some other military doctor, cutting a uniform open, buttons flying, in preparation for surgery or amputation. This type of assemblage is noted at other Civil War medical sites (Geier et al. 1989:124–25; Geier 1994a:204–8).

At the end of the war, Harpers Ferry existed in a deteriorated state. Union troops occupied the town for more than a year after Lee's surrender at Appomattox. One resident wrote that every day you could hear "the ear-piercing notes of the fife and the boom of the drum . . . on the streets" (Barry 1988:140). Many Confederate sympathizers returned to Harpers Ferry only to find their dwellings ransacked, rented by the U.S. government, or occupied by squatters.

"What a God forsaken place!" wrote Annie Marmion, describing the condition of Harpers Ferry. A New Englander visiting the town wrote about the destruction and general decay of the town: "Freshets tear down the centre of the streets, and the hill-sides present only ragged growths of weeds. The town itself lies half in ruins. . . . Of the bridge across the Shenandoah only the ruined piers are left; still less remains of the old bridge over the Potomac. And all about the town are rubbish, filth and stench" (from Murfin 1989:23). A Maryland resident commented, "Churches have become hospitals; gardens and pleasure grounds, graveyards; private residences, barracks and stables. Most of the inhabitants have fled. . . . Only nature is as calm and magnificent as ever" (from Murfin 1989:23). "By all accounts it had been [four] years of hell" (Hern 1996:292).

Rewriting a Civil War History

At most national parks and in most Civil War histories, why is the focus almost exclusively on interpreting the great men at the expense of the civilians? Why are the stories about Mrs. Stipes's boardinghouse and Dr. Marmion's medical practice absent from park interpretations? Archaeology has a unique role in telling the story of people who have been traditionally excluded from history, and these histories continue to be ignored at national parks.

David Glassberg writes about creating historical consciousness. He notes that "public historical imagery is both a reflection of the larger culture, and its prevailing ways of looking at the world, and a major element in the shaping of that culture. Since every way of seeing the world—past and present—excludes hundreds of alternatives from view, the power to define what particular version of history becomes the public history is an awesome power indeed" (1990:2).

Public memory is about how an institution, group, or formal organization selects and interprets a memory to serve their needs. People search for common memories to meet their needs (Thelen 1989:1123–24). As historian David Blight (1989:1169) writes: "Historical memory is . . . a matter of choice, a question of will. As a culture, we chose which footprints from the past will best help us walk in the present."

The official expression by the National Park Service at Harpers Ferry is concerned with promoting and preserving the ideals of cultural leaders and authorities. It is interested in social unity and maintaining the status quo. The National Park Service interprets the past by presenting a reality that helps to reduce competing interests. It presents the past as abstract and timeless and sacred. The deification of Stonewall Jackson at Harpers Ferry is about his leadership abilities and his men's unquestioned commitment to him and their cause. The interpretation emphasizes an implicit social hierarchy and an obedience to a larger social structure. The social structure is made to appear eternal and inevitable.

If we challenge the interpretation of the "great man" myth of the Civil War, we find that the histories are not really sacred. More importantly, the archaeology of the lives of working-class and middle-class people contributes to creating a counter-memory of the Civil War era. If historians and archaeologists work diligently to support this counter-memory, it will become part of the official memory of the Civil War.

Acknowledgments

I am grateful to Clarence Geier and Stephen Potter for inviting me to participate in their session at the 1998 Society for Historical Archaeology Conference on Underwater and Historical Archaeology. I also appreciate their willingness to allow me to take part in this volume. I thank Barbara Little for her comments and suggestions during the writing of this manuscript. The review comments provided by Doug Scott and Larry Babits are also appreciated. They have all helped to make this chapter stronger and more coherent.

12

"The Colored Laborers Work as Well as When Slaves"

African Americans in the Breadbasket
of the Confederacy, 1850–1880

Kenneth E. Koons

Historically the Valley of Virginia has been renowned for its high levels of agricultural production. The earliest farmers of the region—Scots-Irish and German migrants from Pennsylvania who arrived beginning in the 1730s as well as settlers of English extraction from east of the Blue Ridge—typically practiced unspecialized subsistence agriculture at first but quickly established a commercially oriented, mixed, grain-livestock economy. Farmers raised a broad range of crops and livestock, emphasizing products for which extra-regional markets had developed. By the late 18th century, although diversity of enterprise continued to characterize valley farming, wheat emerged as the crop of main commercial importance in the region (Mitchell 1977). Increasingly during the first half of the 19th century, commentators acclaimed the valley as a prime agricultural district and "the great wheat-growing section of the State" (*Southern Planter* 1856:237). By the antebellum period, farmers in the Valley of Virginia—defined for this chapter as comprising the nine counties of (from north to south) Frederick, Clarke, Warren, Shenandoah, Page, Rockingham, Augusta, Rockbridge, and Botetourt (fig. 12.1)—produced a disproportionate share of Virginia's wheat crop. At midcentury, for example, valley farmers produced 22 percent of Virginia's wheat harvest on only 9 percent of the improved acreage (Koons 2000:6). On the eve of the Civil War, the Valley of Virginia formed a major wheat-growing center of the upper South (Gray 1941:876). High levels of agricultural production continued during subsequent decades so that during the Civil War, the degree to which the South relied on the valley as a source of foodstuffs and forage for its armies led to the idealization of the region as "the breadbasket of the Confederacy."

In accounting for the unsurpassed agricultural productivity of the valley, historians and other commentators point to the natural endowments

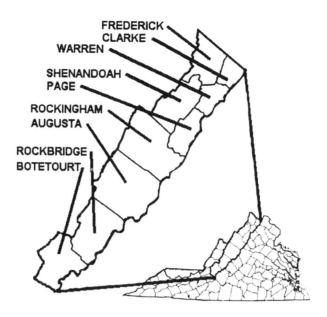

12.1. The Valley of Virginia (courtesy of the author).

of the region, such as its temperate climate and the high fertility of its limestone-based soils. They further note the industry and farming methods of yeoman farmers who inhabited the valley in large numbers. Conspicuously absent from many accounts, however, is any extended discussion of the role African American slaves played in the economic growth and development of the region. Indeed, most narratives that mention slaves tend to underestimate their numerical presence in the valley and, with a few pages devoted to discussion of "the Negro Element," are generally dismissive of their cultural influence on the region as well (Morton 1980:141–46). Conventionally, the small farmers who dominated rural valley society practiced a mixed agriculture and relied principally on the labor of family members; by avoiding staple crops, they could forgo slave labor (Kellar 1928:355–56). Also, historians have pointed to the large number of Germans whose religious convictions "as a rule" led them to abjure ownership of slaves (Wayland 1907:179–86). Given that the valley held far fewer slaves than did tobacco-growing regions east of the Blue Ridge, many historians assumed slavery in the valley to have been attenuated, moribund, not well entrenched, and therefore insignificant to an understanding of the region's social and economic past.

Historians of slavery in the United States have focused mainly on the institution as it developed on plantations where labor-intensive staple crops such as tobacco, cotton, or rice were produced on a large scale. With few exceptions, they accorded scant attention to the significance and functioning of slavery as it was practiced in the Valley of Virginia and similar agrarian settings. In these areas, the agricultural cycle of a mixed farming economy and the unevenness of its rhythms of labor contrasted markedly with monocultural staple-crop plantations. Only recently have some historians begun to examine more carefully the institution of slavery as it was practiced in the valley and to expose as myth some of its conventional generalizations (Simmons 1997; Simmons and Sorrells 2000; Dew 1994; Brundage 1983). Further, if the significance of slavery and the cultural influence of slaves in the Valley of Virginia and similar regions have been underappreciated by historians, the economic lives and social experiences of resident African Americans during the period after the Civil War is terra incognita.

Prompted by the lack of attention to this subject, this essay sketches the broad outlines of slavery and its aftermath in the Valley of Virginia, focusing on the economic and sociocultural experiences of African Americans during the period from circa 1850 to 1880. Statistical data and interpretations set forth here may prove useful for contextualizing and interpreting the fragmentary qualitative information relating to slavery and the experiences of freed black laborers after the Civil War that sometimes arises in the study of a particular community of the valley or an investigation of other aspects of the region's past. Published county-level federal census data are used throughout to show trends pertaining to the Valley of Virginia as a whole. To examine developments in one locale of the valley and to particularize regional trends, the analytical focus is set, at times, directly upon Shenandoah County in order to exploit individual-level data from the federal censuses. These data document basic facts of life for members of 19th-century populations in ways not possible with data aggregated at the level of the county.

Shenandoah County makes an especially attractive choice for the microlevel analysis of valleywide trends. Aside from its central location within the nine-county region (figs. 12.1, 12.2), throughout the period this county was home to fewer blacks than any other county in the valley. The relatively small number of African Americans who lived there during the period improves possibilities for the successful linkage of manuscript census data—from one census schedule to another and from one census year to another—upon which depends some analyses presented here.

Slaves and Free Blacks in the Antebellum Valley of Virginia

One historian described slavery in the Valley of Virginia as "a sprinkling of slaves who gave sluggish assistance to their owners" (Phillips 1946: 344), a view unsupported by facts readily available to anyone willing to examine the federal censuses. Indeed, data on the numerical presence of slaves, alone, are sufficient to refute this assessment. At midcentury (table 12.1), almost 25,000 slaves (20 percent of the total population) resided in the valley, and for 1860 the corresponding figure stands at nearly 24,000

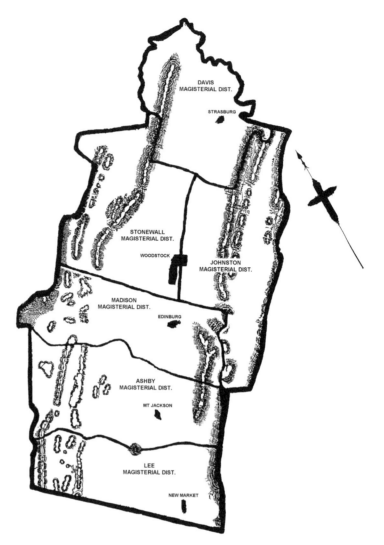

12.2. Shenandoah County, Virginia, adapted from "Outline Plan of Shenandoah and Page Counties, Virginia," in Lathrop and Griffing 1991, 8–9 (courtesy of G. P. Hammond Publishing).

(18 percent). Throughout the late antebellum period, then, nearly one in five members of the total valley population was held in bondage. Overall, the number of slaves as a proportion of the white population declined slightly during the 1850s, a shift consistent with the assertion of one historian that "in 1860, the imminence of Civil War depreciated slave values and gave a stimulus to a more active selling of them in the cotton states" (Morton 1980:145). The total number of slaves declined by nearly 1,300. But in two contiguous counties of the upper valley, Rockingham and Augusta, the absolute number of slaves rose during the period. One of the most striking features of data showing slave numbers during the antebellum period is the unevenness of slaves' spatial distribution through the

Table 12.1. Whites, free blacks, and slaves in the Valley of Virginia, by county, 1850 and 1860 (first line = 1850, second line = 1860)

County	No. free whites	%	No. free blacks	%	No. slaves	%	Total	%
Augusta	18,983	77.1	574	2.3	5,053	20.5	24,610	99.9
	21,547	77.6	586	2.1	5,616	20.2	27,749	99.9
Botetourt	10,746	72.1	426	2.9	3,736	25.1	14,908	100.1
	8,441	73.3	306	2.7	2,769	24.0	11,516	100.0
Clarke	3,614	49.2	124	1.7	3,614	49.2	7,352	100.1
	3,707	51.9	64	0.9	3,375	47.2	7,146	100.0
Frederick	12,769	79.9	912	5.7	2,294	14.4	15,975	100.0
	13,079	79.0	1,208	7.3	2,259	13.7	16,546	100.0
Page	6,332	83.3	311	4.1	957	12.6	7,600	100.0
	6,875	84.8	384	4.7	850	10.5	8,109	100.0
Rockbridge	11,484	71.6	364	2.3	4,197	26.2	16,045	100.1
	12,841	74.4	422	2.4	3,985	23.1	17,248	99.9
Rockingham	17,496	86.2	467	2.3	2,331	11.5	20,294	100.0
	20,489	87.5	532	2.3	2,387	10.2	23,408	100.0
Shenandoah	12,565	91.3	292	2.1	911	6.6	13,768	100.0
	12,827	92.3	316	2.3	753	5.4	13,896	100.0
Warren	4,493	68.0	366	5.5	1,748	26.5	6,607	100.0
	4,583	71.1	284	4.4	1,575	24.4	6,442	99.9
Valley	98,482	77.4	3,836	3.1	24,841	19.5	127,159	100.1
	104,389	79.0	4,102	3.1	23,569	17.8	132,060	99.9

Sources: U.S. Census Office 1854, 1864.

valley (table 12.1). In Clarke County, in the northern valley, for example, at midcentury slaves composed nearly 50 percent of the population, while in nearby Shenandoah County slaves accounted for only 7 percent. In the three counties immediately south of Shenandoah—Rockingham, Augusta, and Rockbridge—slaves constituted approximately 12, 21, and 26 percent, respectively, of each county population.

The greater number of slaves relative to the white population in Clarke County is attributable to the county's early settlement by Tidewater and Piedmont planters seeking fresh lands for the large-scale production of tobacco. Once settled, even though they turned increasingly to wheat as a cash crop, they retained the large numbers of slaves typical of the older society east of the Blue Ridge (Hofstra 1986:1–12; Wayland 1957:81). Elsewhere in the valley, varying densities of slave populations are more difficult to explain. Some explanations posit a negative correlation between slavery and slave ownership on one hand, and the proportion of Germans on the other. Thus, Shenandoah and Rockingham Counties, settled heavily by Germans, and where large numbers of their descendants resided during the 19th century, contained comparatively few slaves. In contrast, the upper-valley counties of Augusta, Rockbridge, and Botetourt, where Scots-Irish rather than Germans dominated numerically in

Table 12.2. Slaveholding in Shenandoah County by occupation, 1850

Occupation	No. slave owners	%	No. slaves	%	Average slaves per master
Farmer[a]	79	49.4	494	63.3	6.3
Merchant	17	10.6	62	7.9	3.6
Physician	8	5.0	30	3.8	3.8
Keeper of ordinary	5	3.1	30	3.8	6.0
Attorney	4	2.5	16	2.0	4.0
Tanner	4	2.5	16	2.0	4.0
Tailor	3	1.9	7	0.9	2.3
Teacher	3	1.9	23	2.9	7.6
Ironmonger	2	1.3	10	1.3	5.0
Joiner	2	1.3	2	0.3	1.0
Clerk	2	1.3	6	0.8	3.0
Miller	2	1.3	2	0.3	1.0
Millwright	2	1.3	2	0.3	1.0
Blacksmith	1	0.6	1	0.1	1.0
Cabinetmaker	1	0.6	1	0.1	1.0
Clergy	1	0.6	7	0.9	7.0
Clerk of the Senate	1	0.6	7	0.9	7.0
Commissioner of the Revenue	1	0.6	1	0.1	1.0
Coppersmith	1	0.6	1	0.1	1.0
Deputy sheriff	1	0.6	7	0.9	7.0
Shoemaker	1	0.6	2	0.3	2.0
Toll gatherer	1	0.6	1	0.1	1.0
No occupation listed	18	11.3	53	6.8	2.9

Sources: Shenandoah County, Virginia, U.S. Census Returns (SCMCR) 1850b, 1850c.
a. The largest slaveholder in the county, who owned 92 slaves, was listed as a "farmer" in the population (and agricultural schedules) but, in the manufacturing schedules, is identified as the proprietor of an iron manufacturing establishment.

the settlement process and during the 19th century as well, slaves were held in larger numbers (Wayland 1907:180–86). Also, some historians have explained the greater prevalence of slaves in the upper valley by noting the many iron manufacturing establishments and suggesting that slave labor was exploited heavily for iron production and other manufacturing activities, as well as for agriculture (Brundage 1983:12; Kellar 1928:356).

While large numbers of valley slaves did work at iron production (Brundage 1983; Dew 1994; Lewis 1979; Starobin 1970), a preponderance of slaves labored on farms. In Shenandoah County, for example, where at midcentury the population comprised 12,565 whites (91.3 percent), 292 free blacks (2.1 percent), and 911 slaves (6.6 percent) (U.S. Census Office 1854), about 2 out of every 3 slaves belonged to a farmer. The 1850 Shenandoah County slave schedules identify 197 slaveholders; of these, 160 (81.2 percent) could be linked to the 1850 population schedule. Seventy-nine slaveholders (49.4 percent) were farmers (including one "merchant and farmer") who, collectively, owned 494 (63.3 percent) of the slaves (table 12.2). To summarize, at midcentury approximately one-half of all Shenandoah County slaveholders were farmers, and collectively they owned nearly two-thirds the slaves.

Elsewhere in Shenandoah County, masters from a variety of occupations owned slaves. Leaving aside the 18 (11.3 percent) slaveholders with no occupation listed in the population schedules, non-farm slaveholders included a broad cross-section of professionals, artisans, and storekeepers, with merchants, physicians, keepers of ordinaries, attorneys, tailors, tanners, and teachers as the most frequent occupational designations. Together, 44 members of these occupations accounted for ownership of 184 (23.6 percent) slaves whose owners' occupations could be discerned. One or two members each of a host of other occupational groups owned the remaining slaves (Shenandoah County, Virginia, Manuscript U.S. Census Returns—hereafter SCMCR—1850a, 1850b, 1850c).

Frequency distributions of sizes of slaveholdings in Shenandoah County in 1850 and 1860 show remarkable similarity from one decade to the next (tables 12.3, 12.4). Slave holdings tended to be small; more than

Table 12.3. Slaveholding in Shenandoah County, 1850

Size of slaveholding	No. slaveholders	% of total owners	No. slaves	% of total slaves
1	67	34.4	67	7.4
2	26	13.3	52	5.7
3	21	10.8	63	6.9
4	11	5.6	44	4.8
5	19	9.7	95	10.4
6	13	6.7	78	8.5
7	10	5.1	70	7.7
8	5	2.6	40	4.4
9	6	3.1	54	5.9
10	2	1.0	20	2.2
11	2	1.0	22	2.4
12	2	1.0	24	2.6
13	3	1.0	39	4.3
14	1	0.5	14	1.5
15	1	0.5	15	1.6
16	1	0.5	16	1.8
17	1	0.5	17	1.9
22	1	0.5	22	2.4
29	1	0.5	29	3.2
38	1	0.5	38	4.2
92	1	0.5	92	10.1
	195	99.8	911	99.9
1–2	93	47.7	119	13.1
3–5	51	26.2	202	22.2
6–8	28	14.4	188	20.6
9–13	15	7.7	159	17.5
14–92	8	4.1	243	26.7
	195	100.1	911	100.1

Source: SCMCR 1850c.

Table 12.4. Slaveholding in Shenandoah County, 1860

Size of slaveholding	No. slaveholders	% of total owners	No. slaves	% of total slaves
1	58	34.5	58	7.7
2	24	14.3	48	6.4
3	16	9.5	48	6.4
4	14	8.3	56	7.4
5	11	6.5	55	7.3
6	6	3.6	36	4.8
7	11	6.5	77	10.2
8	8	4.8	64	8.5
9	3	1.8	27	3.6
10	4	2.4	40	5.3
12	2	1.2	24	3.2
13	3	1.8	39	5.2
14	1	0.6	14	1.9
17	1	0.6	17	2.3
19	1	0.6	19	2.5
20	1	0.6	20	2.6
21	1	0.6	21	2.8
24	1	0.6	22	3.2
30	1	0.6	29	4.0
36	1	0.6	92	4.8
	168	100.0	753	100.0
1–2	82	48.8	106	14.1
3–5	41	24.4	159	21.1
6–8	25	14.9	177	23.5
9–13	12	7.1	130	17.3
14–36	8	4.8	181	24.0
	168	100.0	753	100.0

Source: SCMCR 1860b.

one-third of all slave owners—the modal group—owned only one slave and nearly one-half of all slave owners owned only one or two slaves. This evidence is consistent with imagery sometimes invoked in the literature on slaveholding in the valley, of yeoman farmers laboring alongside the one slave, or perhaps two, they owned (Simmons 1997:164). Given that close to 50 percent of all slave owners owned only one or two slaves, and nearly 75 percent of all slave owners owned fewer than six, such imagery might reflect well the situation for a majority of farmers who owned slaves.

From the perspective of slaves rather than owners, however, membership in a group of one to five slaves belonging to one owner would not have been the dominant experience. In both 1850 and 1860, the local structure of slaveholding was such that nearly two-thirds of all slaves (64.8 percent) were owned in groups of six or more, and about one-fourth of them were owned in groups of fourteen or more (SCMCR 1860b). Thus, for a majority of slaves in Shenandoah County, work experiences, leisure activities, and the ordinary activities of everyday life would have been carried out with other slaves and family members rather than as solitary individuals in the company of whites and in isolation from other slaves. Some slaves, perhaps many, among those owned as the sole work-force of an individual slave owner, lived as solitaries in an outbuilding, a kitchen ell, or perhaps an upstairs garret. It should not be imagined, how-ever, that this was the normative experience for a majority of slaves.

Some slaves owned by non-farmers in Shenandoah County probably would have been hired out to local farmers needing supplemental or sea-sonal labor. Slave hiring was widely practiced in nearby Augusta County (Simmons and Sorrells 2000), and scattered evidence indicates it prevailed elsewhere in the valley as well (Brundage 1983:11–12). As was the case everywhere it was practiced (Barton 1997), in the Valley of Virginia slave hiring added a degree of flexibility to the system by providing a mecha-nism by which excess slave labor could be distributed to those with de-mand for additional labor. Annually, in the first week of January, owners arranged for the hire of their slaves. In Clarke County, one diarist ob-served in early 1855 that "hiring the servants is all the talk now. people went out & hire from other men at about $100. 110. 120 or so . . . youth 20. 10 or board and clothes" (Hibbard 1854–55:20, 55). In Rockbridge County, in 1854, farmer Henry B. Jones hired out a slave of his, 26 years of age, for $150, and two female slaves for $40 each. In earlier years, he routinely hired out the labor of two or three of his slaves. In 1855, he recorded in his diary that three of his "twelve servants . . . are hired out" (Turner 1979:6, 14, 21, 31, 51, 59, 63).

Evidence in the 1860 slave schedules of Shenandoah County confirms and illuminates this anecdotal evidence. In the column entitled "Name of Slave Owners," the census enumerator listed the names of all persons who utilized slave labor, whether or not they owned them. In instances of slaves who were rented instead of owned, the enumerator listed information about both the slaves and their actual owners. These entries reveal that 25 individual masters hired to others the labor of no fewer than 60 (7.9 per-cent) of the 753 slaves in Shenandoah County. A total of 37 (4.9 percent) individuals listed as slave owners rented some or all of the slaves whose labor they utilized. Many slaves who were hired out appear to have be-longed to unsettled estates or to widows whose husbands had owned slaves (SCMCR 1860b).

Bondsmen and women were not the only African Americans who dwelled in the Valley of Virginia and helped work its farms. Free blacks, too, resided there. Numbering more than 3,800 persons in 1850 and more than 4,100 in 1860, free blacks composed 3.1 percent of the total popula-tion of the valley (table 12.1). In antebellum Shenandoah County, free blacks numbered about 300 persons—292 (2.1 percent) in 1850 and 316 (2.3 percent) in 1860 (U.S. Census Office 1854, 1864)—and they worked

Table 12.5. Occupations of free blacks residing in households headed by whites, Shenandoah County, 1860

Occupation	Number
Farmhand	15
House servant	1
Day laborer	1
Hostler	1
Nurse	1
Shoemaker	1
No occupation listed	55

Source: SCMCR 1860a.

mainly as domestic servants or farmhands. In 1860, among free blacks who lived in the households of their white employers, and for whom occupations are known, more than half of them labored as farmhands, and most of the others worked as domestic servants (table 12.5). Also, many of the 55 free blacks living in white households, and for whom no occupation was listed, probably engaged in farmwork or domestic service as well. Consistent with other evidence of free blacks serving as an important source of labor on farms is that farmers dominated numerically among white heads of households whose members included free blacks (table 12.6). Thus, for example, Levi Funkhauser, a northern Shenandoah County farmer who owned one slave, had a free black carrying the occupational designation of "farmhand" living in his household. Similarly, Reuben Moore, a farmer of southern Shenandoah County who owned one slave, included ten free blacks among members of his household: two women, each with three children, a 21-year-old male designated as a "farmhand," and a 23-year-old female. Manassa Blackburn, an iron manufacturer who owned three slaves, counted two free blacks among his household (SCMCR 1850b, 1850c). In these cases and others like them, free blacks and slaves might live in the same household settings, and certainly they worked, socialized, and perhaps even established families together.

In 1860, 57 independent households headed by free blacks existed within Shenandoah County (table 12.7). The establishment and continuing maintenance of independent households required ownership of assets or access to financial wherewithal. This is reflected in the value of assets owned by free blacks who lived in such households; 42 of 57 free black heads of household owned personal effects of some value, and 9 owned real estate. In all cases, however, the value of these assets was small indeed. As with free blacks who lived in the households of whites, farm labor and domestic work dominated the occupations held by members of these households. Free blacks living in independent households achieved more occupational diversity—as a blacksmith, boot and shoemaker, farmer,

Table 12.6. Occupations of white heads of households with free blacks living within, Shenandoah County, 1860

Occupation	Number
Farmer	29
Physician	5
Blacksmith	3
Merchant	2
Potter	2
Artist	1
Attorney	1
Butcher	1
Carpenter	1
Carriage maker	1
Collector of claims	1
Conductor on railroad	1
Cooper	1
Farmhand	1
Iron manufacturer	1
Mason	1
Milliner	1
Postmaster	1
Shoemaker	1
Tanner	1
Tanner and farmer	1
Teacher	1
Tinner	1
No occupation listed	7

Source: SCMCR 1860b.

forgeman, or wagoner—than those living in white households. However, in contradiction to the assertion of one historian that "almost all of the free Negroes in the three counties [of Warren, Frederick, and Shenandoah] worked at some craft such as blacksmith, cooper, teamster, and the like" (Schlebecker 1971:463), both the number and proportion of Shenandoah County free blacks engaged in such occupations was small.

Thus, in the late antebellum Valley of Virginia, free blacks and slaves lived in similar socioeconomic circumstances. Free blacks, especially those who lived in the households of whites but also including most living independently, seem to have formed an impoverished, permanent source of domestic or farm laborers for hire by whites. For the great preponderance of free blacks, most markedly those living in the households of whites, free status translated to economic or material circumstances little different from those of slaves.

Slaves and free blacks formed a significant labor force in the antebellum Valley of Virginia. Together, through their labor, free and enslaved African

Table 12.7. Occupational structure and property holding among free blacks living in free black households, Shenandoah County, 1860

Occupation	Number	Among property owners, dollar value of	
		Real estate	Personal estate
No occupation listed	19	100; 150; 200	10 (x4); 20 (x2); 25 (x4); 50 (x2); 75; 80; 100 (x2); 270 [average = 53]
Farmhand	15	300; 400	25 (x5); 40; 100 (x3); 200; 300 [average = 88]
Day laborer	6	400	20 (x2); 180 [average = 73]
Washerwoman	6	400	20; 25 (x2); 50; 75 [average = 39]
Barber	1	320	
Blacksmith		11,000	175
Boot/shoemaker	1		300
Cook	1		10
Farmer	1		600
Forgeman	1		
Railroad hand	1		
Seamstress	1		
Wagoner	1		
Wagon maker	1		25
Well digger	1		50

Source: SCMCR 1860b.

Americans contributed to the rise and continuing development of the Valley of Virginia as a highly productive agricultural region that a few years later would gain renown as "the breadbasket of the Confederacy."

Civil War and Freedom

It is well known that during the Civil War farmers in the valley sustained enormous losses of agricultural resources because of Confederate impressment and Union foraging and depredations. The worst destruction came in the autumn of 1864 when the region became a particular target of Federal armies seeking to destroy the Southern capacity to provision its armies (Taylor 1989; McPherson 1982; Eby 1961; Hildebrand 1996; Horst 1967). After the autumn campaign, Gen. Philip Sheridan reported to his superiors that "the whole country from the Blue Ridge to the North Mountain has been made untenable for a rebel army. I have destroyed over two thousand barns filled with wheat, hay, and farming implements, and over seventy mills filled with flour and wheat, have driven in front of this army over four thousand head of stock, and have killed and issued to the troops over three thousand sheep" (quoted in Horst 1967).

Destruction was so great that by 1870, five years after Appomattox, almost without exception, numbers of livestock on hand and production of major field crops remained far below prewar levels. Production of corn sagged 52 percent below the level of 1860, rye 35 percent, and hay 11 percent. The number of horses dropped 15 percent, milk cows 6 percent, beef cattle 24 percent, sheep 30 percent, and swine 46 percent. Although destruction of agricultural produce and infrastructure was severe, its consequences were not sustained. If, for working purposes, the word "recovery" is understood to mean simply that prewar production levels of most agricultural products are achieved or surpassed, then, contrary to widespread popular imaginings as well as scholarly assertion, recovery can be said to have occurred by 1880. By then, nearly all agricultural production indices had risen higher than antebellum levels. Also, the Valley of Virginia remained a center of wheat production within the state. Wheat production increased 10 percent during the 1860s and 14 percent during the 1870s. In 1880, valley farmers cultivated 14 percent of the improved acres in Virginia but produced 31 percent of the total wheat crop (Koons 2000:8–10).

The agricultural economy of the valley thus rebounded during the 1870s, and by the end of the decade, valley farmers essentially had achieved recovery. But how did former slaves and free blacks fare during this tumultuous period of war and rebuilding? In particular, how did African Americans reorganize and reintegrate into postbellum agricultural labor markets? Documentary sources offer few details about the transition. In an oblique reference to the emancipation of slaves, one valley inhabitant, describing in late 1865 the difficulties of rebuilding that lay ahead, made reference to the "disorganized" labor of farmers (Sangston 1865:15). Toward the end of the period, in 1878, a Shenandoah County observer wrote that "the colored laborers work as well as when slaves, improving every year and more easily controlled than after the war; they are very well contented when well managed" (Pollard 1878:50). This enigmatic observation is of little help in discerning how African Americans in the Valley of Virginia pursued economic opportunities newly available to them in freedom. Did former slaves become wage laborers for white farmers? Did they farm as sharecroppers rather than wage laborers or rent land from white farmers in order to farm for themselves? Did they reject agricultural labor altogether by seeking economic opportunity in the region's service towns? Did many prefer to leave the region altogether? Data in the various schedules of the 1870 and 1880 federal censuses help address these questions and illuminate related issues as well.

The Aftermath of War

In the spring of 1870, Carrie Bushong, a young farm girl who lived in southern Shenandoah County, near New Market, described the stream of migrants leaving the valley: "Sam and Will Harshbarger started to Tennes-

Table 12.8. Total population of the Valley of Virginia by county, 1860–1880, and percent rates of growth, 1860–1870 and 1870–1880

	1860	1870	1880	% rate of growth 1860–70	% rate of growth 1870–80
Augusta	27,749	28,763	35,703	3.7	24.1
Botetourt	11,516	11,329	14,089	-1.6	30.8
Clarke	7,146	6,670	7,682	-6.7	15.2
Frederick	16,546	16,596	17,553	0.3	5.8
Page	8,109	8,462	9,965	4.4	17.8
Rockbridge	17,248	16,052	20,003	-6.9	24.6
Rockingham	23,408	23,688	29,566	1.2	24.8
Shenandoah	13,896	14,936	18,204	7.5	21.9
Warren	6,442	5,716	7,399	-11.3	29.4
Valley	132,060	132,192	160,884	0.1	21.7

Sources: U.S. Census Office, 1864, 1872, 1885.

see week before last and Ant Belle Boles started for Ind[iana]. Jim went there last August. A great menee young men are going west from this and Page counties. Seven ware here one night from Page on the way to difrent parts of the west and the Negroes are going south. Elias Good went to Ind[iana] last summer" (Bushong 1870).

To Carrie Bushong, at least, it appeared that the Valley of Virginia was emptying. Given the enormity of destruction produced by the Civil War, it is not surprising that some valley inhabitants chose to abandon the region. Nonetheless, most evidence bearing on the issue of population growth during the postwar years belies Carrie Bushong's impressions. The valley population remained stable from 1860 to 1870, with modest population growth in some counties counterbalancing mild population decrease in others (table 12.8). During the subsequent decade, every valley county experienced demographic growth, implying expansion of economic opportunity. Everywhere during the 1870s, growth rates exceeded 5 percent, and in some counties the growth rate stood at about 30 percent. As with the valley as a whole and many of its constituent counties, Shenandoah County experienced uninterrupted population growth from 1860 to 1880, with the 1860 population of almost 14,000 increasing by more than 4,000 by 1880. Shenandoah County achieved the highest growth rate of any county in the valley during the 1860s (7.5 percent). In the subsequent decade, at a growth rate of 22 percent, it matched the valley as a whole and formed one county in a group of four contiguous ones—Rockbridge, Augusta, and Rockingham were the other three—with growth rates between 20 and 25 percent. Thus, the populations of some counties declined during the 1860s, but the populations of most valley counties increased throughout the period, with especially rapid growth during the 1870s.

Table 12.9. White and African American population of the Valley of Virginia by county, 1860–1880, and percent rates of growth, 1860–1870 and 1870–1880 (first line = whites, second line = African Americans)

	1860	1870	1880	% rate of growth 1860–70	% rate of growth 1870–80
Augusta[a]	21,547	22,026	26,393	2.2	19.8
	6,202	6,737	9,310	8.6	38.2
Botetourt[a]	8,441	8,166	10,159	-3.3	24.4
	3,075	3,163	4,650	2.9	47.0
Clarke	3,707	4,511	5,145	21.7	14.1
	3,439	2,159	2,537	-37.2	17.5
Frederick	13,079	13,863	14,997	6.0	8.2
	3,467	2,733	2,556	-21.2	-6.5
Page	6,875	7,476	8,846	8.7	18.3
	1,234	986	1,119	-20.1	13.5
Rockbridge	12,841	12,162	14,660	-5.3	20.5
	4,407	3,890	5,343	-11.73	7.4
Rockingham	20,489	21,152	26,133	3.2	23.5
	2,919	2,516	3,433	-13.8	36.4
Shenandoah	12,827	14,260	17,198	11.2	20.6
	1,069	676	1,006	-36.8	48.8
Warren	4,583	4,611	5,958	0.6	29.2
	1,839	1,105	1,411	-40.6	27.7
Valley	104,389	108,227	129,489	3.7	19.6
	27,671	23,965	31,395	-13.4	31.0

Sources: U.S. Census Office, 1864, 1872, 1885.
a. Patterns of population growth in two contiguous upper Valley counties—Augusta and Botetourt—present intriguing anomalies. In both counties, during the 1860s and the 1870s, the African-American population increased much more rapidly than the white population. In Botetourt County during the 1860s, the white population declined at the rate of about 3 percent while the black population rose 3 percent.

The pattern of population growth among African Americans differed dramatically from that of whites (table 12.9), confirming Carrie Bushong's impression that many blacks were leaving the valley. In 1870, some 3,700 fewer African Americans resided in the valley than were present a decade earlier, representing a decline of more than 13 percent. This is not surprising in light of the exodus throughout the South of large numbers of slaves during the late months of the war and immediately afterward (Gates 1965:356–57). Whereas the white population decreased in only two valley counties during the 1860s, and then at relatively modest levels (3 to 5 percent), the black populations of seven counties declined between 10 percent and 40 percent. With only the exception of Frederick County, in the 1870s the pattern reversed itself; the black population of every other county grew rapidly, with growth rates from a low of 14 to a high of 49 percent. The valley's black population increased 31 percent during the 1870s, while the white population increased at a rate of 20 percent. In Shenandoah County, population growth conformed generally to that of the valley as a whole. Whereas the white population increased steadily during the period, the county's African American population fell precipitously during the 1860s—by almost 37 percent—and then soared—by nearly 49 percent—during the 1870s. Thus, the approximately 1,100 African Americans present in Shenandoah County in 1860 (nearly one-third of whom were free blacks) fell to 676 by 1870 but then increased to more than 1,000 by 1880.

A short-lived political experiment helps view this process in more detail. Virginia's so-called Underwood Constitution, promulgated in 1869, divided each county of the state into townships and made provisions for the residents of each township to elect local government officials. Although this system was abandoned in 1875, the resulting administrative units were carried forward as magisterial districts that still exist today (Dabney 1971:373). Officials divided Shenandoah County into six magisterial districts and also recognized five towns whose populations they enumerated separately. Woodstock, the county seat, sits astride the border separating the magisterial districts of Stonewall and Johnston, while each of the remaining four magisterial districts features an independent town within its borders (fig. 12.2). In both 1870 and 1880, federal census officials working in Shenandoah County employed these civil divisions as census enumeration districts. Consequently, county-level census data may be disaggregated, and individual-level census data may be compiled, into magisterial districts as well as towns enumerated separately. This in turn permits observation of differential rates of population growth within the county and of the spatial distribution of African Americans within the county.

In 1870, the population of each magisterial district stood at between 1,500 and 2,550 persons, and each of the five towns ranged between 270 and 860 persons. In the ensuing decade, towns as well as magisterial districts experienced population growth. Each district grew more rapidly than the town situated in its midst, with one exception: in Mount Jackson, the population increased 83 percent during the decade. In both 1870 and 1880, characteristic of a thoroughly agrarian society, four of every five members of the total population lived in the rural magisterial districts rather than in towns (table 12.10).

Patterns in the growth and distribution of the African American population differed markedly from the general population. A disproportionately large share of Shenandoah County's African American population resided in the southern third of the county—Ashby and Lee districts and the towns of Mount Jackson and New Market (table 12.10). In 1870, 50 percent of all African Americans in the county inhabited one of these four civil divisions; the corresponding figure for 1880 is 60 percent. Woodstock formed another center of African American presence in the

Table 12.10. Total population and black population of each magisterial district and town of Shenandoah County, 1870 and 1880, and percent rate of growth, 1870–1880

	Total population			Black Population		
	1870	1880	% rate of growth 1870–80	1870	1880	% rate of growth 1870–80
Magisterial districts						
Davis	1,713	1,988	16.1	78	76	-2.6
Stonewall	1,933	2,625	35.8	13	20	53.8
Johnston	1,507	1,993	35.2	28	20	-28.6
Madison	2,549	2,763	8.4	34	32	-5.8
Ashby	2,375	2,980	25.5	143	180	25.9
Lee	2,098	2,574	22.7	70	175	150.0
Rural subtotal	12,175 (81.5%)	14,923 (82.0%)	22.6	366 (54.4%)	503 (51.1%)	37.4
Towns						
Strasburg	580	647	11.6	54	58	7.4
Woodstock	859	100	16.4	128	186	45.3
Edinburg	452	478	5.8	14	6	-57.1
Mount Jackson	270	494	83.0	50	114	128.0
New Market	600	662	10.3	61	118	93.4
Town subtotal	2,761 (18.5%)	3,281 (18.0%)	18.8	307 (45.6%)	482 (48.9%)	57.0
Shenandoah County	14,936 (100.0%)	18,204 (100.0%)	21.9	673 (100.0%)	985 (100.0%)	46.4

Sources: SCMCR 1870, 1880a, 1880b; U.S. Census Office 1885.
Note: Members of the black population in each magisterial district and town were hand-counted from the 1870 and 1880 manuscript population schedules of Shenandoah County. Problems with legibility resulted in minor discrepancies between the totals for the black population listed here, and those listed in tables 12.9 and 12.11.

county. In the remainder of the county, by contrast, growth was negligible (such as in Stonewall district) or the African American population actually declined.

In describing the consequences of the Civil War in the Valley of Virginia, one writer asserted that "in their freedom," black men and women "could not be expected to stay on the farms where they had been slaves. They crowded into the towns 'as if they could not be free in the country'" (Davis 1945:280). Evidence from Shenandoah County supports this assertion; in both 1870 and 1880, almost 50 percent of Shenandoah's African American population resided in county towns rather than rural districts. The figure is 46 percent in 1870 and 49 percent in 1880 (table 12.10). Woodstock alone held fully 20 percent of the county's African American population in 1870 and 19 percent in 1880. Interestingly, however, throughout the period very few African Americans resided in the two magisterial districts adjacent to Woodstock. This is in contrast to the situation in the southern tier of the county where the African American popu-

Table 12.11. Whites and blacks in the Valley of Virginia by county, 1870 and 1880 (first line = 1870, second line = 1880)

	No. whites	%	No. blacks	%	Total	%
Augusta	22,026	76.6	6,737	23.4	28,763	100.0
	26,393	73.9	9,310	26.1	35,703	100.0
Botetourt	8,166	72.1	3,163	27.9	11,329	100.0
	10,159	68.6	4,650	31.4	14,809	100.0
Clarke	4,511	67.6	2,159	32.4	6,670	100.0
	5,145	67.0	2,537	33.0	7,682	100.0
Frederick	13,863	83.5	2,733	16.5	16,596	100.0
	14,997	85.4	2,556	14.6	17,553	100.0
Page	7,476	88.3	986	11.7	8,462	100.0
	8,846	88.8	1,119	11.2	9,965	100.0
Rockbridge	12,162	75.8	3,890	24.2	16,052	100.0
	14,660	73.3	5,343	26.7	20,003	100.0
Rockingham	21,152	89.4	2,516	10.6	23,668	100.0
	26,133	88.4	3,433	11.6	29,566	100.0
Shenandoah	14,260	95.5	676	4.5	14,936	100.0
	17,198	94.5	1,006	5.5	18,204	100.0
Warren	4,611	80.7	1,105	19.3	5,716	100.0
	5,958	80.5	1,441	19.5	7,399	100.0
Valley	108,227	81.9	23,965	18.1	132,192	100.0
	129,489	80.5	31,395	19.5	160,884	100.0

Sources: U.S. Census Office 1872, 1885.

lation in Mount Jackson and New Market, and their adjacent rural districts, grew quite rapidly. Lee magisterial district manifested by far the highest growth rate of any minor civil division in the county.

In 1870, almost 24,000 African Americans dwelled in the valley and composed 18.1 percent of the total population (132,192). During the subsequent decade, African Americans in the valley increased to more than 31,000, or 19.5 percent of the total population of 160,884 (table 12.11). In 1880, African Americans still formed about one-fifth of the total valley population. After a precipitous decline during the 1860s, a decade of rapid demographic expansion ensued so that by 1880 the absolute number of African Americans living in the valley exceeded the number present there at midcentury by nearly 3,000 persons (tables 12.1, 12.11).

What kinds of employment were available to African Americans who lived in the valley after the Civil War, particularly after 1870 when their numerical presence there increased so dramatically? Data in the 1870 and 1880 population schedules permit observation of household living arrangements among African Americans, as well as their occupations, during the postwar period (tables 12.12, 12.13). The most striking aspect of these data is the continuing homogeneity of the African American occupational structure and the degree to which African Americans remained rela-

Table 12.12. Occupations of African Americans living in households headed by African Americans and in households headed by whites in the magisterial districts and towns of Shenandoah County, 1870

Occupation	Magisterial districts Households headed by		Towns Households headed by	
	Blacks	Whites	Blacks	Whites
Laborer	51	18	43	8
Domestic servant	20	31	17	39
Works on farm	8	13		2
Cook		2		
Seamstress		2		
Blacksmith	1		1	
Shoemaker	1		1	
Farmer	1		1	
Works on road	2			
Barber				
Carpenter			1	
Tanner			1	
Preacher			1	
Illegible			1	

Source: SCMCR 1880b.

tively propertyless. The postbellum African American socioeconomic profile of Shenandoah County is remarkably similar to that indicated by the occupational structure among free blacks during the antebellum period (table 12.7). As before the Civil War, most African Americans worked on farms or in domestic service, whether they lived in independent households or as members of white households. Also, about two out of every three heads of white households with African Americans living within were farmers (table 12.14). Whites, too, engaged in domestic service and farm labor, but a full range of occupational diversity prevailed among them, and no whites lived in black households serving as farm or domestic laborers. In 1870, a handful of blacks worked in skilled artisan trades, just as a few free blacks had on the eve of the Civil War, but by 1880 virtually no African Americans were employed as artisans. Thus, from midcentury to at least 1880, continuity prevailed in the occupational structure among African Americans except that, to the degree that occupational diversity among blacks existed at all, it appears to have narrowed during the 1870s.

In Shenandoah County's 1880 population schedules, only five African Americans carry the occupational designation of "farmer" (SCMCR 1880b). In light of the "disorganization" of rural labor prevailing in the immediate aftermath of the Civil War, one might reasonably expect greater representation of African Americans among farmers. Given the

Table 12.13. Occupations of African Americans living in households headed by African Americans and in households headed by whites in the Ashby and Lee magisterial districts and the towns of New Market and Mount Jackson, 1880

Occupation	Ashby and Lee magisterial districts		New Market and Mount Jackson towns	
	Households headed by		Households headed by	
	Blacks	Whites	Blacks	Whites
Farm laborer	72	18	20	6
Servant	5	19	14	19
Day laborer	1	4	11	
Cook	5	3	3	9
Nurse	5	1	1	1
Porter		2	1	
Waiter		1		3
Washerwoman	5			
Works where work can be found				
Errand boy		1	5	
Barber			3	
Barber and servant				1
Farmer	2		1	
Gardener		2		
Hostler				1
Wood chopper			1	
Works in brickyard				1
Works in quarry			1	

Source: SCMCR 1880b.

capital requirements of farming (Shifflett 1982:11–13, 16–24), it should not be surprising that few, if any, African Americans engaged in agriculture as owner-operators. However, one might expect that white farmers, having lost a servile labor force but continuing to own land needing to be worked, would have arranged for African Americans to farm their land as tenants. In 1868, for example, James J. Martin of Augusta County, entered into such an arrangement with George Carter, whom he had bought as a slave in 1855 (Sheffer 1855). By a "memorandom of an agreement . . . George Carter (coloured)" obligated himself to "farm or crop Airy-Mount farm in connection with Mr. Jacob Wiseman for a term of three years," with Carter binding himself

> [t]o furnish or be at the expense of half the labour of preparing ground for crops, putting on fertilizers etc. and cultivating, harvesting, thrashing and delivering to market. He also to furnish half the labour to repair and keep in good repair the fences on said farm, and cut and haul fuel for said Martins house and kitchen. That is half the labor—Wiseman furnishing the

other half of the labour. And said Carter binds himself to cut and prepare at the house or wood-yard fuel for Martin's kitchen fires, also to feed and attend said Martin's stock as heretofore on Sabbath. And in consideration of the foregoing the said Martin binds himself to give said Carter one sixth of the crops thus raised, also to furnish him with a house and garden and fuel for said house and team to haul said wood, tops or dead wood to be used, and pasture one cow. (Martin 1868)

Any similar agreement between white farmers and African Americans in Shenandoah County has not yet come to light, but once again the census data provide details where the documentary record is silent. The 1880 agricultural schedules distinguished for the first time among farmers who owned their land, those who rented for shares, and those who rented for cash. Linking the African Americans shown as "farmers" in the population schedules of 1880 (SCMCR 1880b) to the information about them listed in the agricultural schedules of that year reveals one to have been an owner and at least three to have been tenant farmers. Of the tenant farmers, two farmed for shares of products raised and one farmed for a "fixed money rental." One black farmer in the population schedules could not be found in the agricultural schedules (SCMCR 1880a).

By 1880, only a handful of African Americans farmed in Shenandoah County, as owner-operators or as tenants. With only one exception, those who did farm independently did so on a smaller scale, not consistent with the commercial agriculture as practiced by white farmers during the era. Robert Smith of Davis magisterial district owned the 17 acres he farmed and on which he raised 2 acres of corn and 10 of wheat, with 1 acre utilized for apple trees. His livestock included one horse, two cows, and three hogs (SCMCR 1880a). One black renter, Harrison Fadeley of Ashby

Table 12.14. Occupations of white heads of households with African Americans living within in Ashby and Lee magisterial districts and the towns of Mount Jackson and New Market, 1880

Ashby and Lee magisterial districts		Mount Jackson and New Market	
Farmer	18	Brickmaker and layer	1
Herdsman	1	Carriage maker	1
Manufacturer of woolen goods	1	Dry goods merchant	1
Physician	2	Farmer	5
Works on farm	1	General merchant	2
		Hotel proprietor	4
		Livery man	1
		Minister	2
		Physician	4
		Works in carriage factory	1
		No occupation listed	1

Source: SCMCR 1880b.

magisterial district, used four horses to work 165 acres of improved land for a share of the produce. He grew 28 acres of corn and 32 of wheat and owned 30 hogs and 12 head of cattle (SCMCR 1880a). Given that in 1880 the average number of improved acres per farm in Shenandoah County was 73 (U.S. Department of the Interior 1885), the farm worked by Fadeley formed a comparatively sizeable holding. This cannot be said of the holdings worked by the other three black farmers. Emmett A. Strather of Ashby district farmed 20 acres for shares, 12 of which he planted in corn and 8 in oats, most likely to feed his two horses, two hogs, and eight barnyard fowl. Similarly, John Johnson of Stonewall magisterial district rented, in this case for a fixed amount, a farm comprising 25 improved acres of tillable land and 26 of permanent grasses or pasture. He planted 15 acres of corn and sowed 10 of wheat, and he owned one horse, four cows, and four hogs.

After the Civil War, the continuing importance of African Americans to the valley's rural economy was as agricultural laborers rather than as semi-independent tenants or fully independent owner-operators. That the over-whelming preponderance of African Americans who participated in farm-ing in the postbellum Valley of Virginia did so as laborers rather than as tenant farmers is consistent with the views white farmers held about Afri-can Americans. A so-called Crop, Stock, and Labor Report, prepared by the Virginia commissioner of agriculture in 1878, published responses to a host of questions about matters relating to agriculture, including labor, which formed part of a circular distributed in various Virginia counties. Among the questions asked were: "How do the negroes work as tenants?" "Is the tenant system increasing or decreasing?" "How do you like white, as compared with negro labor?" Correspondents were to respond on the basis of their own experiences but also were asked explicitly to represent opinion in their counties generally (Pollard 1878:9).

In response, one Rockingham County farmer reported that "[there are] few negro tenants [and the tenant system is] decreasing." Similarly, a cor-respondent from Augusta County asserted that, "As tenants, the negroes are not good, they lack management." And from Botetourt County: "Ne-groes do not make very good tenants" (Pollard 1878:15, 17, 49). Given that in 1880 only 7 to 9 percent of farms in Shenandoah County were operated by tenant farmers (table 12.15), it appears that valley farmers did not prefer tenancy as a way of organizing and exploiting capital and hu-man resources to produce agricultural commodities. But on the practice of African Americans serving as tenant farmers, white farmers of the valley were unequivocal: because of perceived shortcomings of African Ameri-cans as farm tenants they should be avoided.

Tenancy was not widespread in the postbellum valley countryside, es-pecially when compared with its prevalence in regions east of the Blue Ridge (Shifflett 1982:39–47). When white farm owners did let out some

Table 12.15. Types of land tenure in Shenandoah County, 1880, by magisterial district

District	Owner		Rents for cash		Rents for shares		No information		Total	
	No.	%	No.	%	No.	%	No.	%	No.	%
Davis	245	87.8	5	1.8	17	6.1	12	4.3	279	100.0
Stonewall	337	92.3	2	0.5	14	3.8	12	3.3	365	100.0
Johnston	251	91.3	6	2.2	18	6.5	0	-	275	100.0
Madison	193	95.6	2	1.0	4	2.0	3	1.5	202	100.1
Ashby	258	89.0	1	0.3	27	9.3	4	1.4	290	100.0
Lee	258	89.6	7	2.4	19	6.6	4	1.4	288	100.0
Total	1,542	90.8	23	1.4	99	5.8	35	2.1	1,577	100.1

Source: SCMCR 1880a.

or all of their land, they rented to whites. To fulfill their needs for labor, however, farmers preferred black laborers. As a Shenandoah County farm correspondent reported: "[as laborers] Negroes . . . are preferred [over] white men when well overlooked." Similarly, a farmer of Rockingham County noted that "negro labor is preferred," and a Botetourt County farmer agreed: "colored [laborers] are preferred." Given these attitudes, it is easy to see why so few black farm tenants, and so many black farm laborers, appear in Shenandoah County. Only in Augusta County did a correspondent perceive "very little difference" between black and white laborers (Pollard 1878:15, 17, 49, 50).

Correspondents from all counties agreed that older black laborers worked better than younger ones, apparently because of their greater tractability as workers. A correspondent from Rockingham County reported that "the old negroes work well. Young negroes [are] but of little account, generally idle and dissolute." A writer from Augusta County echoed these sentiments when he asserted that "the old negroes work well, but the younger generation is worthless." A correspondent from Botetourt County observed: "the freedmen who were grown when made free work very well, but those who have grown up since then are worthless" (Pollard 1878:15, 17, 49).

The "Crop, Stock, and Labor Report" repeatedly indicates that the trait white farmers valued most in agricultural laborers was their tractability. In the postwar period, older African Americans who were former slaves were favored as farm laborers over younger African Americans who lacked the discipline and deference of slavery. If younger black workers were perceived as less compliant and submissive than their elders, white laborers would have been even less desirable as laborers when judged by this standard. The claim of one modern writer that farmers of the postwar valley "preferred white workers who would take more initiative, work more steadily, and need less watching" (Davis 1945:311) thus does not stand up to close scrutiny.

Conclusion

In the antebellum Valley of Virginia, free blacks and slaves formed a significant element of the agricultural labor force. Their contribution to a mixed farm economy helped the valley emerge as a prosperous agricultural region. With the demise of slavery, large numbers of African Americans left the valley, but by 1880 their numerical presence exceeded that of midcentury. During the postwar era, a disproportionately large share of the African American population lived in towns rather than in the countryside, but prewar patterns of labor endured. Despite the profound transformations produced by the Civil War for all valley inhabitants, fundamental continuity prevailed in the economic opportunities available to blacks. The great preponderance of African Americans continued to serve whites as farmhands and domestic servants, much as they had before the war. Thus, in the postbellum period, African Americans living in what had been the breadbasket of the Confederacy were free of bondage but not of servile status.

Acknowledgments

For reading earlier drafts of this chapter and providing helpful comments and suggestions, the author wishes to thank Ellen Eslinger, Megan Haley, Warren R. Hofstra, and Turk McCleskey. Also, special thanks to Jean Martin Glasgow for providing access to family papers and manuscripts, and to David Hess for technical assistance with maps and tabular materials.

13

"Free within Ourselves"

African American Landscapes
at Manassas National Battlefield Park

Laura J. Galke

> Forward we went across a green meadow, where the children had
> played and the sheep gamboled in the peaceful past, into the dark and
> dreadful woods, reeking with blood and sickly with the scent of death.
> —**Lt. Eneas N. Lamont, 101st New York Infantry,**
> **Birney's Brigade, Battle of Second Manassas**

> We build our temples for tomorrow, strong as we know how, and we
> stand on top of the mountain, free within ourselves.
> —**Langston Hughes (Huggins 1995:309)**

Manassas National Battlefield Park (Manassas Battlefield) is the well-known location of two major Civil War engagements. Created in 1940, this national park preserves within it the landscape of a typical, Northern Virginia Piedmont community. This chapter focuses on the nature of the mid-19th-century community and specifically on three sites occupied by black Americans.

Manassas is located approximately 25 miles southwest of Washington D.C. (fig. 13.1). The park was formed to preserve the sites of the First and Second Battles of Manassas, thanks to a generous donation by the Robinson family. Although military activities inspired preservation of this landscape, the social history of this community has been equally well preserved, if only incidentally. In fact, while the nature and importance of battles commands our attention, they represent only a small portion of the landscape's human history. Middling plantations, small farms, tenant farms, and a vibrant community composed of European Americans, enslaved African Americans, and free African Americans existed here during the mid-19th century. The social history is no less worth preserving than the brief but significant military events.

The current boundaries of Manassas Battlefield preserve several examples of 19th-century domestic Piedmont community. These include middling plantations: Brownsville/Folly Castle, Pittsylvania, Rosefield,

13.1. Location of Manassas National Battlefield Park.

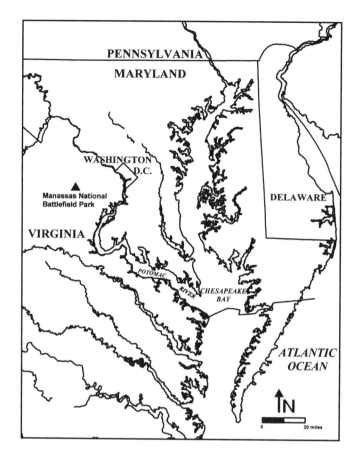

Pohoke and Portici, Spring Hill, Hazel Plain, and Peach Grove. Free black residents are represented by the Robinson house, the Mahala Dan house, the Nash house, and the Maggie Lewis cabin. White middling farmers resided at Avon, Christian Hill, and Meadowville. White tenancy is represented by the Brawner family at Bachelor's Hall. Examples of 19th-century transportation, commerce, and education are represented by the Stone Bridge, Stone House, Sudley Post Office, the Alexandria–Warrenton Turnpike, Ball's Ford, Lewis Ford, Poplar Ford, Sudley Ford, Groveton School House, and the village of Groveton. Manassas Battlefield preserves a significant cultural landscape offering a variety of resources.

The purpose of this chapter is to consider some ways in which African American ethnicity was reflected in the 19th-century landscape of Manassas. The information was obtained from three archaeological sites, part of two separate archaeological investigations performed under the direction of Stephen R. Potter. These were at Portici (Parker and Hernigle 1990) and the Stuart's Hill Tract (Galke 1992a). The goal is simple: to provide material evidence that African Americans living in the Virginia Piedmont during the Civil War era possessed a subculture that, in some cases, and with attentive consideration, can be recognized in the archaeological remains. The fact that this subculture is poorly represented in written documents does not render it intangible. Though this culture was often private and repressed, its origins and nature have not been forever lost to us.

The author wants to make it clear that there is no monolithic African American culture. Rather, it is hoped that by describing assemblages recovered from sites inhabited by black Americans, patterns can be seen which are clearly influenced by traditions that appear to ultimately derive from, or are influenced by, African customs. These patterns, once defined and recognized at a number of sites, can be used to determine ethnicity at sites where documentary sources may be unavailable, ambiguous, or silent.

Material expressions of ethnicity were not unique to black Americans. Examples of artifact patterning that reflect particular economic or ethnic groups have been documented archaeologically for some time. This chapter focuses on African American patterning discovered at archaeological sites within Manassas Battlefield in an attempt to enhance current documentation and definitions concerning the ways in which these people expressed their ethnicity throughout the 19th century.

This chapter explores the variety of material expressions of African-inspired traditions that both enslaved and free black Americans implemented between 1830 and 1880. These material expressions include the mundane as well as the ritual. Three archaeological case studies illustrate the mid-19th-century material expression of African American culture. Two of the cases represent slave occupations at middling but prosperous plantations known as Portici and Brownsville (fig. 13.2). The third case study is from the site of a small frame house dating to the last quarter of the 19th century known as the Nash house site, home to a free African American family (fig. 13.2).

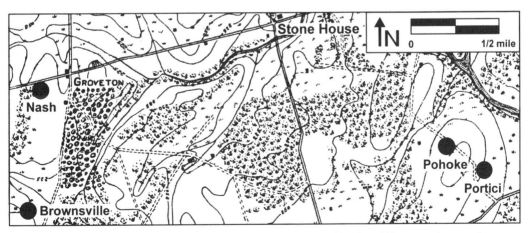

13.2. Maneuver grounds of the first and second battles of Manassas, showing placement of Portici, Brownsville, and Nash sites (courtesy of the National Park Service, National Capital Region).

The Portici plantation is the first case study. It evolved from an early 18th-century tenant farm known as Pohoke. Profits from tobacco cultivation allowed the modest farm to grow to a middling plantation by the early 19th century. The plantation was renamed Portici, after an ancient Roman village at the base of Vesuvius, which was prone to frequent fires (Parker and Hernigle 1990:16). Thirteen African Americans worked at Portici on the eve of the Civil War. Artifacts recovered from a field quarter habitation and from a domestic occupation within the main house demonstrate the ethnicity of their African American inhabitants.

Brownsville was a thriving middling plantation throughout the 19th century. It was home to 22 enslaved black laborers on the eve of the Civil War (McCartney 1992a:52). Distinct remains of African American material culture were discovered within the cellar of a structure used, and likely occupied, by enslaved workers.

The third case study was the Nash site, which consisted of the remains of a mid-19th-century frame building with a stone chimney. The Nash site was a postbellum domestic structure of an African American family. While the occupation was rather brief (ca. 1865 to ca. 1900), a distinctive ritual deposit was recovered archaeologically which appears to derive from West African traditions (Galke 1992b; 1992d:137).

The potential for such middling plantations and small rural sites to provide information about 19th-century lifeways has not yet been fully realized. The results of these archaeological investigations allow tentative interpretations of the artifact assemblage that appear to characterize an evolving, dynamic African American culture. These interpretations and examples are offered to help create a better understanding of the origins of modern black American culture (Franklin 1997:41).

The case studies demonstrate the presence of African artifacts and African-inspired material culture, as well as adaptation of European-American manufactured goods into black American contexts. The method by which most Africans came to the New World precludes the direct importation of much material culture (Walsh 1997:97). It comes as no surprise then that they would have used available items, both natural and European/American, and renegotiated their meaning to fit their own worldview and practices (Mintz and Price 1976:51, 55). Archaeological discoveries from Manassas Battlefield demonstrate that African American culture was dynamic and that participants used material items available to them in conjunction with their African ideological elements. Their heritage helped black Americans create a viable sense of identity, history, and pride. Colonoware, blue glass beads, finger rings, gaming pieces, and a unique cache of quartz crystals were found in association with African American habitations at archaeological sites on the Manassas Battlefield and at other black American sites as well (Brown and Cooper 1990; Brown and Brown 1998; Ferguson 1992; Galke 1992b, c, d; Garcia-

Herreros 1998; Harris 1998; Jones 1995; Logan 1995; Logan et al. 1992; Parker and Hernigle 1990; Patten 1992; Stine et al. 1996).

A Brief History of the Northern Virginia Piedmont

Throughout the Chesapeake region during the 17th and 18th centuries, settlement favored the tidewater area, where the many waterways that dissected the coastline provided excellent transportation and trade routes (Isaac 1982:16). At that time, the Virginia Piedmont, where Manassas is located, represented the frontier. Expansion and development in the Piedmont was vigorous by the end of the first quarter of the 19th century.

Mid-19th-century Manassas was a seemingly unremarkable place characterized by middling plantations, small farms, and tenant farmsteads. It was a community struggling to cope with the major changes in agricultural practices occurring throughout Virginia and Maryland. Tobacco cultivation, which drove the region's settlement initially, resulted in a dispersed settlement pattern. Exhausted soils, inexpensive land, and the preeminence of water travel in the 17th and 18th centuries encouraged settlement of pristine territory. Throughout the opening decades of colonial European settlement, land transportation routes either did not exist or could not keep up with settlement, so riverine travel continued as the preferred method of transport. Reliance on tobacco came with a price, as depressions and severe market fluctuations made the sole cultivation of tobacco too risky financially, and by the 19th century, only the largest, most wealthy, and agriculturally diversified plantations could survive. At that time, many Virginians sought to revitalize their farm income by raising cereal grain crops. The transition from tobacco to cereal grains had a considerable impact on land use. Grain crops required mills for processing, and surplus could be sold to bakeries, all of which encouraged the development of towns and a system of roads, unlike tobacco cultivation. Diversification in production also provided farmers with greater insurance against price fluctuations in any single crop.

African American Material Culture Studies

Patricia Samford identified two major approaches to the study of African American sites (1994). The first approach seeks to identify patterns of material culture that can be reliably attributed to black Americans by the excavation of sites historically tied to blacks. Known patterns of artifact association can then be used to assess and interpret archaeological assemblages at sites of unknown ethnicity. The second major approach seeks to discover West African cultural influences or remnants reflected in the archaeological record. This is accomplished through favorable comparison of African site assemblages and black American site assemblages (Brown and Cooper 1990; Brown and Brown 1998; Galke 1992 b, c, d; Garcia-Herreros 1998; Harris 1998; Logan 1995; Jones 1995). These approaches are not necessarily mutually exclusive.

In a paper concerning African religious artifacts in the New World, Charles Orser (1994:39) identified two types of material culture which most clearly demonstrate an African-inspired origin: Colonoware and brass-alloy amulets known as figas. A much broader definition of African American material culture is pursued by Archaeology in Annapolis, a research program sponsored jointly by the Historic Annapolis Foundation and the University of Maryland, College Park. Several caches of material were recovered from special contexts at the Slayton house that were interpreted as derivative of African American traditions and rituals. Figure 13.3 shows an amalgam of these materials which are generally composed of everyday European-American goods. The features from which these caches were derived date to the late 19th and early 20th centuries. Interpreting these assemblages as derivative of African American culture is ambitious, but not without supporting documentation (T. H. Smith 1994; Wall 1995).

The influence of African American population size upon the retention and development of black American culture is a matter of some debate among social historians and archaeologists. The amount and intensity of interaction with European-American culture is also considered a factor in

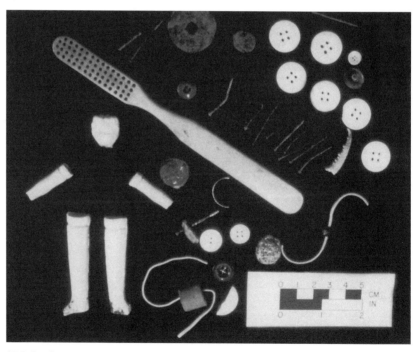

13.3. Artifacts recovered from the Slayton House in Annapolis, Maryland (courtesy of Dr. Mark P. Leone, Archaeology in Annapolis).

the ability of enslaved populations to develop and maintain a distinct culture. Much of our current knowledge derives from large plantation contexts. However, assemblages indicative of African American traditions are not limited to large plantations. An increasing urban database (Logan 1995; Logan et al. 1992; Jones 1995) and middling plantations such as those at Manassas (Parker and Hernigle 1990; Galke 1992a, b) indicate that African American material culture and ethnic markers are just as likely to be found in these contexts. The degree of expressed ethnicity *does not necessarily* increase as one proceeds south (Fitts 1996). In addition, many scholars assert that the size of a plantation's slave population (Orser 1994), the social standing of African Americans within the community, or the location of enslavement (that is, urban vs. rural) (Fitts 1996) may play a role in determining whether and how slaves expressed their ethnicity (Friedlander 1985; Wheaton and Garrow 1985). Although the author is not prepared to refute these arguments, experience with urban and rural sites in Maryland and Virginia suggests that the material expression of African American culture is perhaps more common than currently recognized and is not necessarily related to the size of the enslaved plantation population or the degree of urbanization. Greater concentrations of African-derived traditions and rituals are not necessarily a product of a rural environment characterized by large populations of enslaved labor.

Case Studies

Portici Plantation

The Portici mansion house was built by the Ball family during the early 19th century, probably in 1822, judging from the date on the chimney (fig. 13.4). This middling plantation developed from a modest, 18th-century tenant-occupied farm originally known as Pohoke (Parker and Hernigle 1990:31). Following the latest trends in agricultural management, Portici was a successful, multiple-grain-producing plantation in the early 19th century. On the eve of the Civil War, Portici was occupied by Fannie and Frank Lewis, who managed the 769-acre property with the aid of 1 free black and an average of 12 enslaved African Americans (Parker and Hernigle 1990:20). The Lewises abandoned Portici by July 21, 1861, the day of the Battle of First Manassas (Parker and Hernigle 1990:20–21). The house stood abandoned much of the war but was occupied sporadically by troops passing through the area (Parker and Hernigle 1990:24). Portici burned to the ground, probably in 1864 (Parker and Hernigle 1990:25). The remains were completely exposed during archaeological investigations conducted there in 1986 through 1988 (fig. 13.5).

In discussing the archaeological investigations, there is a need to distinguish between two distinct but related contexts. Excavations at the Portici site were conducted at the mansion house and at one of the field slave

13.4. Portici, photo taken during the Civil War (courtesy of the National Park Service, National Capital Region).

13.5. Portici foundation as revealed by archaeology (courtesy of the National Park Service, National Capital Region).

quarters. Field servants were housed approximately 750 feet northwest of the mansion house (Parker and Hernigle 1990:58) (fig. 13.2). Investigations revealed that field slaves used the nearby abandoned cellar depression of the 18th-century tenant house, Pohoke, for trash disposal (Parker and Hernigle 1990:37). Pohoke was located about 30 feet to the south of the field slave quarters. The mansion's domestic slaves appear to have been housed in the Portici basement, in a cellar that extended beneath the entire house. Sealed below the 1864 fire episode of ash, burned ceramics, and molten glass, an eight-inch-deep occupation layer was found. It contained an accumulation of domestic refuse that included fragments of Colonoware. The presence of a small hearth further supported the interpretation that the domestic slaves inhabited the cellar (Parker and Hernigle 1990:53). Colonoware, a low-fired earthenware likely made by enslaved African Americans from local clays, formed 50 percent (no less than 24 vessels) of the utilitarian earthenware assemblage recovered from the cellar of the mansion house (Parker and Hernigle 1990:101, 230).

Three ceramic gaming pieces were found in and around the Portici mansion, including one from the cellar debris (Parker and Hernigle 1990:209). Two finger rings, one of ebony wood and the other of carved horn, were recovered within the remains of Portici (Parker and Hernigle 1990:218). Ebony derives from Africa and Asia, so this particular ring, discovered within the mansion's kitchen wing, was carefully preserved by a slave despite the harsh conditions of transport to the New World. Unworked ebony reached the United States through normal trade, to be worked into objects for many uses. However, no evidence for other manufactured items from ebony were found at this site, nor at any other sites at Manassas. It seems more plausible that this ring belonged to an enslaved domestic servant. Accounts from witnesses indicate that although slaves arrived in the New World with little clothing and no material goods to speak of, small items of adornment were often incidentally transported (Walsh 1997:97–99). This ebony ring may serve as an example of this type of curation.

Enslaved artisans occupied the Portici field slave cabin, as evidenced by the presence of carpentry and blacksmithing tools as well as several items used for sewing (Parker and Hernigle 1990:161–65, 214, 265). The frame cabin measured approximately 12 feet square and had a stone end chimney. The structure rested on four stone piers (Parker and Hernigle 1990:47–48). A Colonoware bowl, dating from the mid-19th century (fig. 13.6), was one of at least eight such vessels found at the site. Portions of at least eight Colonoware reed-stem tobacco pipes were also found in contexts related to enslaved field workers (Parker and Hernigle 1990:117–18). Three gaming pieces were found at the field slave quarters, including a notched and polished bone fragment (fig. 13.7; Parker and Hernigle 1990:208). Five additional gaming pieces were recovered from the refuse

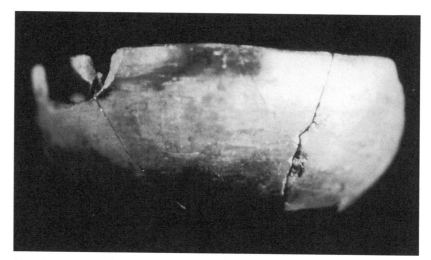

13.6. Colonoware bowl recovered from enslaved African Americans' midden at Portici (courtesy of the National Park Service, National Capital Region).

pit/cellar hole of the nearby Pohoke structure. A blue glass bead with ground facets was also recovered (Parker and Hernigle 1990:217).

Brownsville Plantation

Brownsville (fig. 13.2) was another prosperous, middling plantation. The diversity of the cereal crops raised and the animals present demonstrate that owners William and Anne Lewis embraced the latest farming techniques popularized during the 1850s (McCartney 1992a). The Lewis fam-

13.7. Gaming pieces from sites at Manassas associated with African Americans (courtesy of the National Park Service, National Capital Region).

ily owned 1,000 acres, of which 700 were improved fields (McCartney 1992a:53). A number of horses, oxen, cattle, sheep, and pigs were reported in the agricultural census. While corn was the largest crop raised, oats, potatoes, sweet potatoes, and hay were also grown (McCartney 1992a:52).

The number of enslaved people residing at Brownsville increased steadily during the 19th century, from 8 in 1835 to 14 in 1853. At the time of the Civil War, a maximum slave population of 22 was present (McCartney 1992a:52). According to the census, these enslaved African Americans lived in four separate dwellings (McCartney 1992a:52).

Archaeological investigations revealed the remains of three mid-19th-century outbuildings (Galke 1992c:64). All three structures were oriented in the same manner, indicating that they were likely contemporaneous. At least two of these structures were used and perhaps occupied by slaves. Interestingly, all three structures were in direct association with the house, unlike Portici, where field slaves were located some distance from the main house. Structures 2 and 3 were mapped, but for the most part, their 19th-century contexts were left undisturbed. Nineteenth-century strata were sampled from structure 1.

Structure 1 (fig. 13.8) measured 16 feet by 26 feet and stood only about 30 feet northeast of the main house (Galke 1992c:68). Excavation revealed a cellar hole, approximately 6 feet deep, which ran the full length of

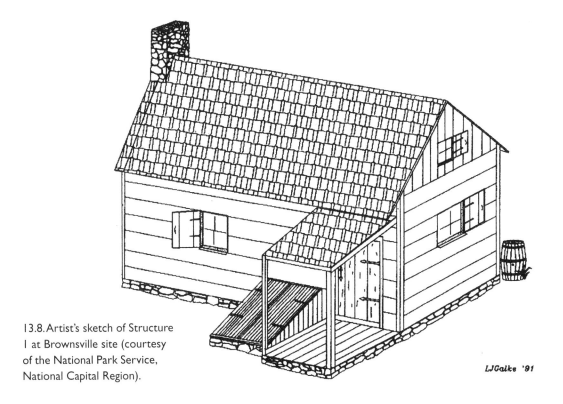

13.8. Artist's sketch of Structure 1 at Brownsville site (courtesy of the National Park Service, National Capital Region).

LJGalke '91

the structure (Galke 1992c:67). Diagnostic evidence recovered from the cellar indicates that the structure dated to at least the late 18th century and stood until at least the mid-19th century (Galke 1992c:68). Items representative of African American material culture were recovered from the structure remains. These included Colonoware bowl fragments and reed-stem tobacco pipes. No evidence of any decoration was present on these vessels, nor was there evidence for ritual incising, such as that noted by Leland Ferguson (Ferguson 1992:26, 110–16). Ferguson goes on to state that Colonoware sherds with ritual incising were most often recovered from rivers adjacent to large plantations and not within inland contexts (Ferguson 1992:114).

Six ceramic gaming pieces were discovered at Brownsville. All but one exhibited the characteristic waterworn edges and geometric shape that distinguish these items from typical ceramic sherds. One unfinished, circular gaming piece was found which is believed to represent an early stage in the production process (Galke 1992c:79). A blue bead was also found within structure 1 (Galke 1992c:79).

Two quartz crystal conglomerations were found at Brownsville. The larger conglomeration was found in association with the slave quarters, but in a disturbed context. A one-inch-diameter quartz crystal was found within the cellar fill of structure 1.

The Nash Site

Few historic records exist for the Nash site. A structure shown on a circa 1878 sketch map created for the Fitz John Porter trial corresponds to the site location and is labeled "Nash." Next to the dwelling, also in script, are the words "School H[ouse], built since the war, occupied by colored people" (anonymous ca. 1878). The Nash site is located near the town of Groveton, about two-thirds of a mile north of Brownsville (fig. 13.2).

The site was apparently the home of a post–Civil War African American family (McCartney 1992b:126–27). Census records from Groveton, Virginia, indicate that in 1880, the Nash household was composed of Philip, his wife, Sarah, and their five children, ranging in age from 2 to 12 (McCartney 1992b:123). The Nash house was situated on the Brownsville tract, owned by the Leachman family in postwar Manassas, so the Nash family may have rented the dwelling. Philip Nash, a farmer, may have worked for the Leachman family, given the proximity of their home to Brownsville. Leachman is reported to have paid $490 in wages, including board, to his farm workers (McCartney 1992b:59).

Archaeological evidence indicates that the Nash house was a frame or log structure that measured approximately 16 by 20 feet and rested on stone piers (fig. 13.9). A fieldstone chimney was located on the structure's south side. Artifacts indicate that the structure was destroyed by fire, evidenced by the presence of burned and annealed cut nails, incinerated mud dauber nests, and the remains of large, charred wooden beams.

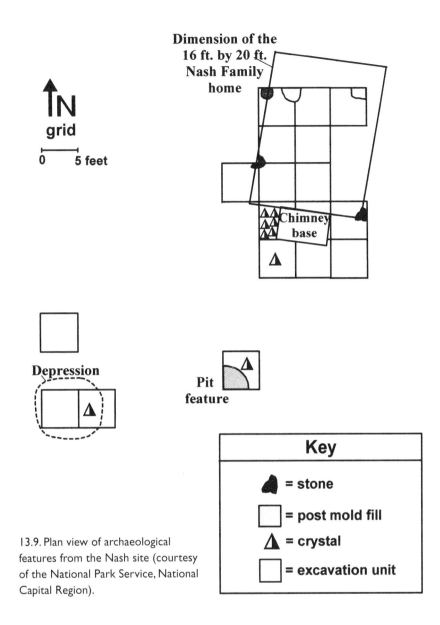

13.9. Plan view of archaeological features from the Nash site (courtesy of the National Park Service, National Capital Region).

A number of artifacts recovered during archaeological investigations are believed to derive from African traditions. Three geometrically shaped, stone gaming pieces were found in three different excavation units surrounding the house; two of these are depicted in figure 13.7. A blue glass bead was also recovered. A cache of six quartz crystals, a piece of galena, and a Native American quartz arrowhead were found in an apparent ritualized context, buried alongside the exterior, western side of the stone chimney (fig. 13.10). Quartz crystals do not occur naturally in this portion of Virginia. Such crystals have been found within a number of African American contexts, especially where enslaved black laborers lived (Jones 1995; Logan 1995; Logan et al. 1992). Based upon its position in the structural remains, the cache is believed to date to the construction

13.10. Ritual cache buried next to chimney at the Nash House (courtesy of the National Park Service, National Capital Region).

phase of the structure, sometime after 1865. There were three additional quartz crystals found at the Nash site, each one near a feature: one near the hearth, one in a borrow pit, and one near an unidentified circular feature located south of the structure (fig. 13.9). A quartz crystal cache analogous to that found at the Nash site was discovered at the Charles Carroll house site (Jones 1995; Logan 1995; Logan et al. 1992).

Items similar to those found in such archaeologically recovered caches occur in African *minkisi* (sing. *nkisi*), or spirit bundles (Brown and Cooper 1990; Jones 1995; Logan 1995; MacGaffey 1991; Thompson 1983). The composition, meaning, and use of such bundles varied greatly. The components were placed in various containers and could include "leaves, shells, ceramic vessels, [and] cloth bundles," to name a few (Thompson 1983:117). Robert Farris Thompson (1983:128–29) has found evidence that the *nkisi*-making tradition continues in the United States today.

Items of African American culture are likely not limited to the above-defined classes. In *Conjuring Culture*, Theophus Smith (1994) demonstrated that African American culture is fluid and that it readily adapts and reinterprets materials from other cultures. The work of Zora Neale Hurston revealed the adaptive reuse and redefinition of everyday objects into objects of profound ritual significance (Wall 1995). Close reading of her ethnographies of early 20th-century Southern black American culture indicated that thresholds (of both households and yards), corners of rooms and homes, and hearths were sensitive areas in the culture of conjuring.

One could argue that there is little more to a structure than corners, thresholds, and hearths. These features define what a structure is, and it would be hard to have an excavation unit within a structure that could not be considered a part of, or in close proximity to, a hearth, corner, or threshold. However, the work of Kenneth Brown and his associates at the Levi Jordan plantation confirms the pattern of ritual caches discovered at corners, thresholds, hearths, and other areas of significance (Brown and Cooper 1990; Brown and Brown 1998; Garcia-Herreros 1998; Harris 1998).

Discoveries at the Nash site at Manassas Battlefield in Virginia (Galke 1992b, d), the Carroll house in Annapolis, Maryland (Jones 1995; Logan 1995; Logan et al. 1992), and the Slayton house in Annapolis, Maryland, confirm the importance of corners, hearths, and/or thresholds. The materials which compose these ritual caches include natural objects such as stones and crystals, as well as items of European-American manufacture. It is important to note that no two caches contain the same items; location and context are as important to these traditions as the items in them.

In 1988, Archaeology in Annapolis discovered several *minkisi* within several first-floor rooms of the extant 18th-century Charles Carroll house in Annapolis, Maryland. One of the *nkisi* is depicted in figure 13.11. Charles Carroll, one of the signers of the Declaration of Independence, owned a number of enslaved laborers. The quartz crystal caches discovered at the house date to the early 19th century. Numerous sources on African folklore and traditions detail the importance of circular items, kaolin clay, and white-colored objects such as those found within the Carroll house assemblage (fig. 13.11; Jackson 1997; MacGaffey 1991; Parker and Hernigle 1990; Raboteau 1978; Stuckey 1987; Thompson 1983; Wall 1995). While the meanings of individual *nkisi* are complex and

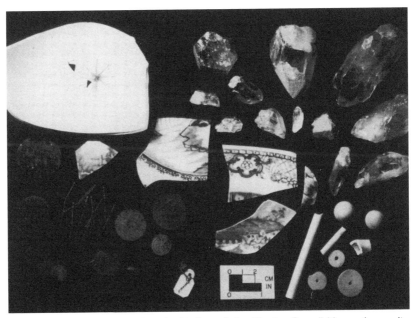

13.11. Cache of items buried in the kitchen of the Charles Carroll House, Annapolis, Maryland (with permission of Archaeology in Annapolis)

varied, and we will likely never fully understand all levels of meaning in a particular specimen, their West African derivation seems clear.

Summary

Archaeological investigations and documentary research from three Manassas Battlefield domestic sites show that black Americans lived and labored at each. Artifact types were recovered which occur with some frequency within known black American contexts elsewhere, including Colonoware, blue glass beads, quartz crystals, and gaming pieces. In addition, the Nash family site contained a special ritual cache which incorporated materials of European-American, African American, and Native American manufacture, as well as natural objects.

Most items used and made by 19th-century black Americans could not exhibit explicitly African characteristics. Items of direct African origin were not readily available in the 19th-century landscape. The ebony ring recovered from Portici provided one exception, which may owe its successful transport to the New World to its small size. It is clear that the entire assemblage of materials found within African American contexts requires sensitive analysis in order to recognize and identify ritual caches, adaptive reuse of items, and so-called ethnic markers.

Colonoware was recovered from both plantation sites. Typical Colonoware vessel forms consisted of bowls and reed-stem tobacco pipes. While refined tablewares formed the majority of *total* ceramic assemblage used by enslaved laborers at both Portici and Brownsville, Colonoware formed about 50 percent of the *utilitarian earthenware* subassemblages at each of these sites. However, there is an apparent rejection of Colonoware by the postwar Nash family, as none was discovered at this free African American family site. Did the Nash family reject Colonoware because it represented a painful reminder of enslavement? To date, Colonoware fragments have not been recovered from post–Civil War contexts at Manassas Battlefield, and the meaning and geographical extent of this pattern provides an avenue for future study.

The Nash family created a ritual cache that appears to reflect an African heritage. The Nash site's assemblage of crystals, a Native American quartz projectile point, and a piece of galena provides explicit evidence for a continued preservation and evolution of African-inspired traditions after emancipation. The Nash family African heritage survived geographical displacement and physical enslavement to be incorporated into the very fabric of their home.

Other items suggestive of black American ethnicity found at Manassas Battlefield included blue glass beads and ceramic or stone gaming pieces, which were found at all three sites. A notched bone discovered at the Portici field slave quarter may also represent a gaming piece. The use of these items for games is conjectural, as is the assignation of an African American cultural identity. However, these items consistently appear associated with African American contexts at Manassas (Parker and Hernigle 1990; Galke 1992c, d; Patten 1992).

There is no monolithic New World African culture. Enslaved laborers and free Africans came from a variety of different African subcultures and traditions. In the New World, they encountered a variety of social and economic situations that sometimes placed limitations on the expression and development of black American culture. What is significant is that a connection between Old World African traditions and New World African American traditions is continuous and unbroken by the middle passage. This is important, as it allows these traditions to be identified in the material record found at archaeological sites, whether from large or middling plantations, from enslaved workers, or from free African American family homes.

Current research suggests that assemblages reflecting African traditions may be more prevalent than we currently realize. Today, archaeologists recognize African American ethnicity at urban sites (in both pre- and post-emancipation contexts), middling plantations, and small domestic homes. They are redefining and expanding black American artifact classes. Unlike the Carroll house *minkisi* from Annapolis, which date to the early 19th century, the Nash collection dates after the Civil War, about 70 years later. Black Americans had, and have, a strong sense of identity, and they have expressed and maintained that culture throughout the middle passage, slavery, emancipation, and into the present (Hall 1990; Smith 1994; Wall 1995). Evidence for black American ethnicity is present in a variety of contexts but may be subtle; interpretations without supporting historical documentation are risky. Increasingly, archaeologists are looking to sources from the fields of folklore, religion, and art (Fulop and Raboteau 1997; T. H. Smith 1994; Wall 1995) to support their theories.

Whether urban or rural, on large plantation or tenant farm, 19th-century black Americans created and maintained their own culture, which was not written about but was performed privately, leaving precious little material evidence in the archaeological record. Interpreting these assemblages requires sensitivity, an appreciation of the complexity and variety of African culture, and contextual research. Historical archaeology can contribute greatly to the recognition and preservation of this culture by being aware of its private nature and its diverse material manifestations.

14

Battling beyond First and Second Manassas

Perseverance on a Free African American Farm Site

Erika K. Martin Seibert and Mia T. Parsons

> The Robinson house is used as a Yankee hospital. In a visit there this morning, I found 100 of them [Yankees] packed in the rooms and yard as thick as sardines. Several of them are officers, and one of the corpses was that of a brigadier general. I did not learn his name. The wounds of the majority were undressed, the blood had dried upon their persons and garments, and altogether there the most horrible set of beings it has been my lot to encounter.
> *Charleston Daily Courier,* September 11, 1862

This description of the Robinson house, written by Confederate reporter Felix Gregory de Fontaine, appeared in a South Carolina newspaper as a firsthand account of the aftermath of the Second Battle of Manassas that took place from August 28 through August 30, 1862.

The Robinson house site was a prominent feature on the battlefield landscape, and it continues to be an important landmark at Manassas National Battlefield Park (fig. 14.1). Research into historical records, such as tax and court records, census data, civil war journals, and oral history interviews, enabled researchers to compile a social history of the Robinson family. Archaeological data gathered at the Robinson house site during National Park Service excavations performed in 1995 and 1996 supports Civil War accounts and information gleaned from the historic record. This study also confirms the Robinson family's continuity and perseverance through the antebellum and postbellum eras.

In this chapter, we explore various aspects of research performed at the Robinson house site. Researchers considered the property in regard to its position during the Civil War but also regarded the Robinson family as part of a diverse African American community in Manassas during the antebellum and postbellum periods. An examination of the cultural landscape of the Robinson house site explores the family's use and perceptions of space as a cultural marker, as well as their adaptation to social change. We argue that the Robinsons may have perceived space differently than

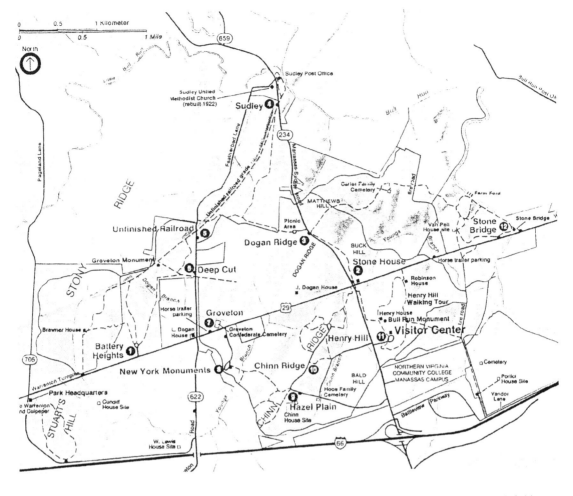

14.1. Manassas National Battlefield Park (courtesy of Manassas National Battlefield Park).

their white counterparts, based on adaptations of African cultural traditions. In addition, by using comparative architectural data we examine issues of racial tension within the larger community.

Artifacts from the excavations represent nearly 100 years of the family's presence and persistence in the Manassas area. Examination and interpretation of this material culture provides an opportunity to include concepts of race as an integral part of the context. The recovered material culture illustrates technological growth of the antebellum and postbellum periods, as well as the family's ability to retain their cultural identity. A minimum vessel analysis of glass and ceramic artifacts dating from the 1860s through 1936 supports interpretations which incorporate W. E. B. Du Bois's concept of "two-ness" for African Americans. We assert that this notion of two-ness is reflected in consumer goods found at the Robinson house site as the family struggled to claim an American identity by buying into a national consumer culture, as well as retaining their African identity through various methods of using that material culture, including playing the traditional African game *mankala*.

From the postbellum era through the Civil War, Reconstruction, and segregation, also known as the Jim Crow era, the ideological implications of being an African American changed on national, regional, local, and individual levels. Documentary and archaeological evidence from the Robinson house site provides a unique opportunity to explore changing meanings for this community and family. In addition, by viewing race as part of the context for comprehending particular social situations, this alternative interpretation may produce a more comprehensive understanding of life for this historic community.

Social Context of the Robinson House

Tax records for the Robinson tract began in 1842 when James Robinson was listed as the property owner who paid taxes on 171 acres with no added buildings. An entry in the deed book (Prince William County Virginia Court Deed Book 16, 1840:223), dated August 5, 1840, confirms that Robinson purchased the acreage from John Lee, a prominent local landowner. These statistics remain the same through 1848. In 1849, the deed record for Robinson changed with $100 listed in the *Added/Bldgs.* column, implying that the first Robinson house was built sometime between 1848 and 1849.

The historical record indicates that James Robinson was a free African American born in 1799 (Turner 1993). No documentation has been found to identify his parents. Oral tradition contends that James Robinson's father, a wealthy white landowner and slave owner, was a member of the Carter family descended from Robert "King" Carter of Westmoreland County, Virginia, and that his mother was one of Carter's slaves (Lillian Robinson, personal communication 1993). Oswald Robinson, a great-grandson of James Robinson, lived near Manassas National Battlefield Park and participated in many interviews and articles over the years, passing along memories of his family's history. In a 1987 newspaper interview, Oswald Robinson traces his lineage from Landon Carter, grandson of Robert "King" Carter, who took as his mistress a slave on his plantation, Pittsylvania, located near Manassas (Friedman 1987:1). A son named James was born in 1799, later known as "Gentleman Jim." James was born free (Sweig 1977:22). Although Robinson was born free, he apparently was "bound out" for a period as a young man. The expression "bound out" refers to a system of indentured servitude. During an 1872 court case in which James Robinson charged the U.S. government for property stolen or destroyed during the Civil War, Robinson's status was addressed. When questioned by counsel, Robinson explained that he was born free but was later bound out to learn a trade. He went on to testify that he was never taught that trade and instead worked as a farm laborer (Robinson 1872 claim, on file, Manassas National Battlefield Park [hereafter MNBP]).

There is documentation that during Robinson's early life, he worked in a tavern for Thomas Hampton in Brentsville (Burgess 1994). In 1842, Robinson acquired 171 acres of land from John Lee. This land was worked by the Robinson family and eventually became a prosperous farm. James and a slave named Susan Gaskins had six children, all born into slavery. Susan and four of the children were property of John Lee. Eventually, Robinson was able to free two of his sons by purchasing them from Lee. The remainder of his family was freed upon Lee's death in 1847.

The first Robinson house was built as a small cabin. This house went through a series of structural additions in the 1870s and 1880s. The 1840s section was completely removed in 1926 when the house was rebuilt again. The 1926-era Robinson house stood until 1993 when arson damaged 60 percent of the structure. Today the foundation walls are all that remain.

The Civil War Era and the Robinson House

The original Robinson house was utilized during both battles of Manassas. With the onslaught of the Civil War in 1861, the first major land battle occurred near Manassas Junction, Virginia, on July 21, 1861. Confederate forces concentrated at Manassas to protect the railroad junction and made their stand along the west bank of Bull Run (fig. 14.2).

At dawn on July 21st, Union troops began a diversionary attack at the Stone Bridge. Later that morning, Union forces crossed Bull Run at Sudley Ford and attempted to turn the Confederate left flank. Col. Nathan Evans rushed troops to Matthews Hill and delayed this Union advance until reinforcements could arrive. To support Evans's line, Capt. George Davidson deployed a 6-pounder gun north of and, later, in the turnpike in front of Robinson's lane (U.S. War Department 1880–1905, O.R. I-2 1880, 1885:563).

About noon, 600 South Carolinians of Hampton's Legion took possession of the ground around the Robinson house (U.S. War Department 1880–1905, O.R. I-2 1880, 1885:566). Finding these locations too exposed to Union artillery fire, they formed a new line in the Warrenton Turnpike in front of and to the east of Robinson's gate (Warder and Catlett 1862:42, 47, 48). After a futile attempt to stem the Union advance, the Confederates were pushed back to and beyond the Robinsons' yard (U.S. War Department 1880–1905, O.R. I-2 1880, 1885:349). The battle raged throughout the afternoon, but the Confederates were ultimately victorious and drove the Union Army back to Washington.

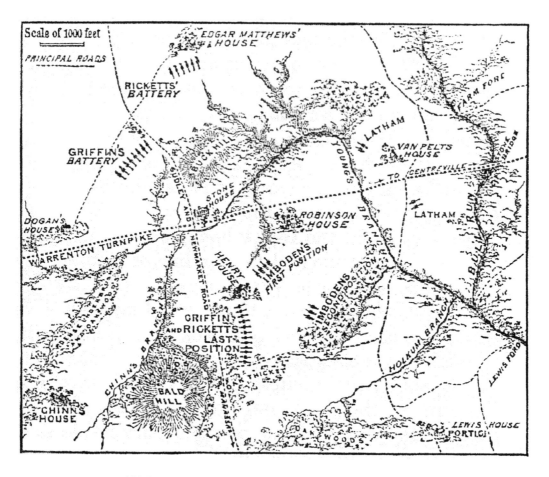

14.2. Plan of Bull Run battlefield during First Manassas (*Battles and Leaders of the Civil War*, 1956, vol. 1: 233; courtesy of Manassas National Battlefield Park).

Despite its location amidst the fighting, the Robinson house escaped major damage. As the battle raged, James Robinson sent his family to the Van Pelt house, where they took refuge in the cellar. Unable to join them, Robinson himself hid under the turnpike bridge over Young's Branch (Eyles 1862). After the battle, Robinson reportedly found 13 dead rebels in his yard (*Irish-American*, August 1, 1863:2).

The following year, the two armies met again on the battlefield of Manassas. Fighting began at the Brawner farm (see Chapter 1) and continued the following day along an unfinished railroad northwest of Henry Hill. On August 30, Longstreet struck the weak Union left flank, but darkness ended the battle and allowed the Union's shattered army to withdraw to Centreville (U.S. War Department 1880–1905, O.R. I-2 1880, 1885).

The Robinson farm remained safely behind Union lines through most of the second battle. Gen. Franz Sigel, commanding the 1st (I) Corps of Pope's Army, established his headquarters on the Robinson farm (U.S. War Department 1880–1905, O.R. I-12 1880, 1885:32, Atlas Plate 22–

4). During this battle, the Robinson house was used as a field hospital (U.S. War Department 1880–1905, O.R. I-12 1880, 1885:302; *Irish American*, August 1, 1863; Lyon 1882, Hennessy 1985). In 1993, Oswald Robinson reported that as a young boy he saw his great-aunts smoking long clay pipes in front of the hearth of the family home. Oswald went on to say "it [smoking] was a habit they started after the Second Battle of Manassas to smother the stench of bodies" (Gould 1993:A1).

Following Second Manassas, many local farms and houses behind Union lines, including the Robinson farm, were subject to pillaging by the soldiers. Fences were burned, and forage and other supplies were often taken. An article in the *Rebellion Record* in 1862 describes the landscape as witnessed after the battles: "Most of the fences have been demolished. The race of fences, in this part of Virginia, seems to have expired. . . . The timbers were shattered, broken, and scarred with powder. The stream is deep, rapid and impetuous. On the opposite bank a high bluff arises, covered with scanty foliage, and overhung in some places with trees and shrubbery. . . . We can see traces of the conflict in shattered trees and broken trunks, limbs and boughs" (Moore 1862:289 in Joseph 1994:22).

The Manassas community suffered greatly during the Civil War, losing houses, crops, woodland, livestock, fences, and, most importantly, the lives of soldiers and civilians. To recover financial losses incurred during the battles, some owners submitted war claims to the government. On February 2, 1872, James Robinson appeared before the Commissioners of Claims appointed under the Act of March 3rd, 1871. His case was based on the claim that Union troops raided James Robinson's farm during Second Manassas. Robinson (1872) claimed that $2,608 worth of personal property was either taken or destroyed by Union men under the direction of General Sigel. The claim included the loss of 25 tons of hay, 60 bushels of wheat, 20 bushels of corn, 2 horses, 7 hogs, 3 barrels of fish, 800 pounds of bacon, 2 fat cattle, 12 acres of corn, groceries and provisions, beds and furniture, garden house and services, fence rails, and 25 acres of oats. Of the lost material, Robinson was reimbursed for $1,249, less than half of what he claimed.

We also learn through the claim that James Robinson (1872), a loyal Union sympathizer, remained on his farm through both battles, while his son, Tasco, whom we believe Robinson bought out of slavery, was employed by the Union Army. Robinson family oral tradition contends that Bladen Robinson was the son who "hired himself as a personal valet to Confederate Captain Hill, and followed him through many battles, including Vicksburg. When the war was over, Captain Hill paid him a small annual pension in $1, $10, and $20 gold coins. The coins were carefully preserved and have been handed down to several members of the family" (Oswald Robinson, oral communication, 1995). The Robinson family remained on their farm until 1936, when they sold their land to the federal government as an addition to Manassas National Battlefield Park. The Robinson house has remained unoccupied since the National Park Service acquired the property. Archaeological investigations of the Robinson farmstead provide an opportunity to study almost 100 years of occupation, accumulation, and discarded material culture by one family.

African American Landscapes

Persistence of certain African traditions may be seen in the landscape of the Robinson house site during the pre– and post–Civil War eras. The various phases of building and rebuilding may reflect the family's retention of regional and/or African traditions, as well as their changing view of the landscape (Martin et al. 1997). While tradition reflected in the landscape may be perceived as regional, this analysis explores the possibility that the Robinsons' African heritage may have influenced their perception of both their material world and the space around them.

James Robinson seemed to be a well-respected member of the rural, Virginian society in which he lived. The Robinson papers, which include accounts, ledgers, letters, bills, and invoices, lend insight into James Robinson's business transactions. Many transactions took place between Robinson and prominent landowners in the Manassas area. In fact, Robinson was the third wealthiest African American in Prince William County by the mid-19th century (Hernigle 1991:6) and was engaged in transactions with some of the wealthiest families in the community.

A recent study of free African American landscapes in Virginia by Robin Ryder "provides additional insights and comparative architectural data" (Martin et al. 1997:169). Ryder's study focuses on the Gilliams, a free African American family living on a Virginia farmstead from the early 1800s to the early 1900s. Like the Robinson family, the Gilliams were free and did considerably well. This "was a direct contradiction of the ideology which supported the power relations in effect under the system of racial slavery" (Ryder 1991:2). The Gilliam house was approximately 2,000 square feet and constructed of logs with a wooden chimney (Ryder 1991:7). Scholars suggest that dwellings of this type (log houses with wooden chimneys) imply a lower economic status, yet Ryder indicates that during the antebellum period the family's resources were impressive and were larger "than two-thirds of the taxable population of Prince George County" (Ryder 1991:6). Ryder explains that the Gilliam family put an unfashionable wooden chimney on their rather large house as a way of "lessening the possibility of being viewed as a threat to the existing social order by increasing social distance" (Ryder 1991:9). If the Gilliam house had a brick or stone chimney rather than a wooden one, it would lessen the "otherness," which posed a threat to whites who wanted to define themselves as a superior group (Ryder 1991:9). Ryder's paper suggests that as with antebellum slaves, free blacks were conscious of their surrounding landscapes. Free African Americans probably felt constantly scrutinized by their white counterparts.

The first Robinson house was a one-and-a-half-story log structure with approximately 400 square feet (fig. 14.3). It had a stone chimney, a wood shingled roof, horizontal wood siding, and a wooden porch on the back, as well as gardens and outbuildings. This structure stood for approximately 30 years, from circa 1848 until sometime in the 1870s. At that time, a two-story addition with another stone chimney was added to the east side. During these modifications, the porch, which served as a connection between the house interior, the yard, and outbuildings, remained on the back. In the 1880s, a shed was attached to the west side of the 1840s house. This shed may have been used as a kitchen extension or storage area. In 1926, the 1840s structure and the shed were dismantled, and a new two-story addition was built on to the remaining 1870s extension (fig. 14.4). At this time, the porch was moved to the "front" of the house. In 1993, 60 percent of the 1870/1926 dwelling was destroyed as a result of arson. It was deemed unsafe, and the remaining exterior walls were dismantled.

Space around the house was utilized throughout the occupation period, and a number of outbuildings and gardens were utilized for almost a century. Compared to the landscapes in Ryder's study, the Robinson landscape shows some different approaches to negotiating tolerance during the same period. For instance, the first Robinson dwelling consisted of

14.3. Civil War–era view of the Robinson House (courtesy of Manassas National Battlefield Park).

14.4. View of the 1936-era Robinson House (courtesy of Manassas National Battlefield Park).

approximately 400 square feet of living space—much smaller than Gilliam's approximate 2,000 square feet. The Gilliam house had a wooden chimney that represented a lower economic class during the early 19th century, while the Robinson house (ca. 1847) had a stone chimney. Ryder's theory that the Gilliams did not want to seem ostentatious to their neighbors, and in turn compensated for their large house by building a wooden chimney, was possibly taken one step further in the Robinsons' case. Robinson lived in a comparatively small dwelling for almost 40 years, even when he was the third wealthiest African American in the county. At one point during this period, as many as six to eight people lived in the dwelling, yet Robinson did not build an addition. Perhaps Robinson, not wanting to appear socially equal to his white neighbors, chose not to put an addition on his house until later. This could have been the family's strategy to reduce conflict in a dominant white society. Robinson's house was in clear view of the Henry house (figs. 14.1, 14.2). The Henrys, Robinson's closest neighbors, were not only part of dominant society but also descendants of Robert "King" Carter. It is possible that James Robinson did not want to appear wealthier than the Henry family, who had a relatively small house up until shortly after the Civil War, at which time a substantially larger dwelling was built (Hernigle 1991:9). The Robinsons waited until the 1870s to build an addition to their home, well after the Henry house was enlarged. The Robinsons may have maintained a smaller house until the 1870s for several reasons. Robinson may not have been able to afford a larger house until the postbellum era; another possibility is that the Robinsons' African heritage influenced their use and perception of space.

The Robinson landscape provides an interesting study of a free African American homestead portraying certain African traditions in the style of building and use of space. African Americans typically built small homes by choice, guided by specific survival strategies. Both slaves and freemen have been known to follow an African tradition of using the dwelling mainly for storage and sleeping and using the yard as an extension of the house (Ferguson 1992:69–71, 77–82). The Robinsons used the back porch as a connection between two spaces—outside and inside—and, in turn, the backyard was an extension of the house, where much activity took place. The family probably used outdoor space for activities such as cooking, socializing, and entertaining. In the backyard, they had easy access to their outbuildings and gardens, and so it is likely that they spent a great deal of time there. However, during excavations at the Robinson house site, very few artifacts were found close to the house, while most material culture was uncovered in excavation units around the perimeter of the immediate yard. One explanation for this may be that the Robinson family practiced yard sweeping. This African, as well as Southern, tradition continues even today and is supported by the archaeological and ethnographic record.

In the 1870s, about 20 years after the Henry house was enlarged, Robinson built the first addition to his home. In the 1880s, a side shed or kitchen extension was added. These additions may reflect the changing times. A larger living space could accommodate more relatives, and, possibly, activities moved inside. The shed and extra chimney provided more space for indoor cooking, especially when the weather would not permit such activities outdoors. Although the times changed, the Robinsons did not give up or lose their ethnic identity, but rather they integrated their own ideas about building and lifestyles. The porch remained on the back of the house and provided access to gardens and outbuildings until 1926. At that time, a new porch was built on the front when the 1840s structure was replaced by a new two-story addition. Relocation of the porch suggests that the Robinsons may have spent a considerable amount of time outside, but perceptions and use of the outdoor space changed significantly. The porch was no longer a transition area to outdoor workspace. Rather, it became part of an area to greet outsiders arriving from the turnpike, as well as to maintain access to the outside world. The addition and rebuilding in later periods is also reflective of Robinson's ability to fully recover from the devastation of the Civil War. Evidence of the family's recovery is also supported by material culture recovered during excavations. A minimum vessel analysis and research into the traditional African game *mankala* show that the family was buying into a uniquely "American" national consumer culture, while still retaining part of their African identity.

Material Culture

Artifacts recovered during excavation reflect technological growth during pre– and post–Civil War eras, as well as the family's ability to recover from the emotional and physical destruction of the war. Innovations in technology are reflected in the farming implements identified on site. Early deposits contained evidence of animal-drawn plows and carts, while later deposits indicate tractors and other modern farming implements. A more modern form replaced an earlier type of butter churn. The sheer quantity of artifacts recovered from one trash pit reflects the family's ability to recover financially from their substantial losses during the war.

The trash pit, identified as Feature 34, is located south of the house foundation between several outbuilding features discovered during excavations (fig. 14.5). Archaeological excavation took place in this area be-

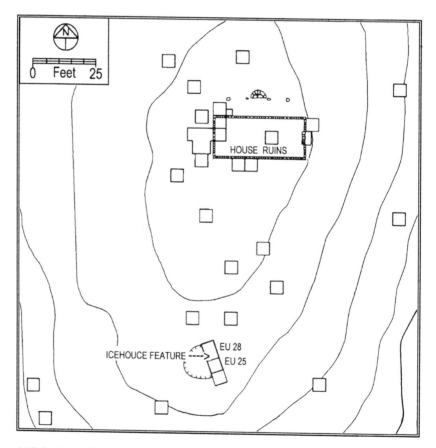

14.5. Robinson House archaeological site showing icehouse feature (courtesy of Harpers Ferry National Historical Park).

cause a large depression was observed on the ground surface, and because Robinson family recollections placed an icehouse/trash pit here. Excavation Units 25 and 28 covered 60 square feet. The feature was a deep unlined pit excavated to approximately 6.5 feet below current ground surface. Upper deposits yielded artifacts dating from the 20th-century Robinson occupation to the early National Park Service era. Lower deposits produced artifacts dating from the mid to late 19th century. The feature's nature and size, along with information from the historic and archaeological records, support identification of this pit as an icehouse during the early occupation and as a trash pit during later years (Parsons 1996:75). Because the feature was used as a trash pit over several generations, a large number of artifacts were recovered. In order to interpret this material culture and study the family's consumer behavior, a minimum vessel analysis was conducted.

A minimum vessel analysis, or vessel count, is the identification of the minimum number of glass and ceramic vessels in an assemblage. In the Robinson house analysis, "vessels [were] identified through the process of sorting, mending, and comparison of sherds with existing vessels" (Lucas 1990:1). A vessel analysis produces a greater understanding of consumer and social behavior and insight into the complexity of group behavior. This type of analysis uncovers how different individuals or groups, such as the Robinson family, placed meaning on material culture. Studying this material culture in its context shows that the Robinson family used different methods for negotiating racism and overcoming changing racial ideologies in postwar Virginia. Aspirations of the Robinson family, reflected in the goods they consumed, show their understanding of contemporary patterns of consumption, while their position as a "farming" family provided the Robinsons with the ability to negotiate the need to operate within the mass consumer marketplace.

Ceramics from the icehouse/trash-pit feature include refined tableware comprising 75 percent of the ceramic minimum vessel count. Some of the oldest tablewares in the collection are identified as pearlwares. Among the pearlwares are two sherds of green shell-edged flatware and an example of engine-turned, color-glazed hollowware. The shell-edged wares include a "bud" pattern decoration of a type commonly produced from 1800 to 1840 (Hunter and Miller 1990). Many pieces of tableware appear to have been manufactured around the turn of the 20th century. For example, a green transfer-printed sherd with the "wild rose" pattern, manufactured by Adams/Tunstall, dates from 1896 to 1914 (Godden 1964). Whiteware with simple gilded annular banding and gilded and molded motifs also produced in this era were included (Lucas 1991). While some tablewares are identified as older, turn-of-the-20th-century forms, newer patterns are also present. Since the Robinsons did not sell their farm to the National Park Service until 1936, ceramics dating to the 1920s and 1930s are present and were probably considered the latest fashion when purchased. A teacup and saucer of Japanese porcelain with the "Geisha Girl" pattern has a post-1921 date (Schiffer 1986), and sets of American shell-edge ware from East Liverpool, Ohio, potteries also date to the 1920s (Hunter and Miller 1990). There are a number of different patterns associated with these American shell-edged wares. This suggests the Robinson family may have followed dominant Victorian material dining standards in which consumers assembled sets of matching or similar wares in lieu of large set purchases (Garrow and Klein 1984:221). The vessel count also contains refined wares that were probably considered decorative pieces. Porcelain that may have been acquired for decorative purposes is represented by two Japanese plates with orange/tan gilded borders and painted landscape scenes and a Japanese vase with a floral pattern.

The Robinson family's desire to operate within set standards of the time and to have ceramic decorative items in their home may be evidence of their social awareness and aspiration. Some researchers suggest that the rights of citizenship were symbolically associated with position in society (Mullins 1996). Consumer behavior may be interpreted as one method the Robinsons, as African Americans, used to negotiate their position in society and, more directly, in their immediate community.

Container glass artifacts reflect the Robinsons' knowledge of the mass consumer marketplace and strategies for survival. Because the Robinsons were farmers, it is not surprising that canning and other food storage containers make up a large percentage of the glass. Glass jars indicate the family was living a relatively self-sufficient and resourceful lifestyle. Container glass deposited by the Robinsons also reflects the family's participation in the consumption of mass-produced goods and brand-name items. Examples of mass-produced goods include Chesebrough Vaseline, Listerine, Noxema, Frey's Vermifuge, two types of perfume bottles, Hoyts ten-cent cologne, Sloan's Liniment, Vick's Vaporrub, Rawleigh's tonic and alternative, Smith Brothers cough syrup, Lysol, Pepsi Cola and other sodas, Dill's Flavoring Extracts, McCormick and Co. Extract and Spices, and Carter's ink bottles. During the late 19th and early 20th centuries, mass-produced goods such as glass and ceramic items became less expensive and easier to obtain.

Etiquette books were extremely popular because they set the rules for "genteel" society; for example, they set rules dictating the right place settings for the dining table and choices of other material objects necessary for position in an ideal Victorian society. Out of social position came the rights of citizenship, and these things embodied the American dream—owning land, living in your own home, and possessing the proper material objects. At a time when goods were becoming less expensive and more readily available, African Americans gained access to these things and pursued their American dream and, with that dream, certain rights. In addition, during the segregation era following Reconstruction, racist sentiments toward African Americans grew. These two phenomena—owning the American dream and increased racist ideology—occurred simultaneously, developing an inverse relationship between consumer desire and race relations. In other words, as consumer desires became more similar between whites and African Americans, race relations between groups degenerated (Kathleen Rand Reed, personal communication, June 1997).

During the latter half of the 19th century and the early 20th century, material objects such as table settings and brand-name goods came to symbolically define position in society. Along with this position came the rights to citizenship and the label "American." At the turn of the century, W. E. B. Du Bois noted the "two-ness" with which many African Americans struggled. He referred to the ability of African Americans to be both "African" and "American" as "double consciousness." He wrote, "One ever feels his two-ness,—an American, a Negro; two souls, two thoughts, two unreconciled strivings; two warring ideals in one dark body, whose dogged strength alone keeps it from being torn asunder" (Du Bois 1903: 362, 365). This idea of double consciousness may have been a way in which the Robinson family survived during times of social injustice and racism in the late 19th and early 20th centuries. Displayed by their material possessions, the Robinsons symbolically linked themselves with the rights of citizenship. Aspirations for citizenship and position are reflected by the ceramic and glass assemblage from the minimum vessel count. The ceramic assemblage reflects the family's ability to operate within the mass consumer marketplace. The ceramics exhibit a variety of designs and decorative techniques, as well as individual matched sets. These refined tablewares, as well as the decorative ceramic items the family had in their home, indicate knowledge about Victorian standards of dining and decoration, which may be reflective of their social aspirations. Glass items recovered from the feature are also indicative of the family's participation in mass consumer culture, particularly the large quantities of brand-name items. Other glass materials found in the vessel count exhibit methods for providing the family with the *option* of entering a mass marketplace that may have been racially exclusive under some circumstances. Both the glass and ceramic assemblages contained a number of food-storage and preservation vessels. Practicing home food preservation may have been part of this farming family's lifestyle but may also have made them feel self-sufficient and diligent, in contrast to racial stereotypes of the time which depicted African Americans as poor, inferior, and even lazy. Studying the consumer behavior of the Robinson family provides insight into the relationships among race, class, and material culture in this local community. These relationships may provide a means for a more comprehensive understanding of African American life and methods for combating racism, in both the past and present.

While ceramic and glass artifacts from the icehouse feature reflect the Robinson family's desire to be a part of American culture, other items of material culture at the site suggest retention of a portion of their African identity. Since Robinson's wife and children were all slaves at one time, the presence of artifacts traditionally associated with slave sites was not surprising at this site. Archaeological investigations at the Robinson house site yielded artifacts that may have once been overlooked or unrecognized as traditional African cultural markers. Along with Colonoware, quartz crystals, buttons, beads, and Native American projectile points, a large quantity of gaming pieces possibly associated with the ancient African/ Asian game *mankala* were recovered. Although it has recently been debated whether or not these artifacts are gaming pieces or gizzard stones from domestic fowl, we believe that the interpretation should remain open, considering these objects were found in association with other cultural markers from sites on the battlefield. These objects were fashioned into specific geometric shapes with worn edges from sherds of glass and European ceramics (fig. 14.6). These artifacts could be associated with several other games, such as checkers, but the repeated occurrence of the specific geometric-shaped unglazed ceramics on African American sites throughout the Chesapeake, Virginia, and Caribbean regions supports interpretations that these artifacts are associated with the traditional African game *mankala*.

Mankala, derived from the Arabic word *manqala* meaning "to move," is the generic name for a large family of games documented as one of the most widely distributed board games in the world (Townshend 1979:794). Examples of the game *mankala* are recorded in all parts of sub-Saharan Africa and in numerous regions of the Middle East, Arabia, and Central, South, and Southeast Asia (Townshend 1979:794). Also, archaeologists recognize the transmission of *mankala* to America, with gaming pieces identified at a number of slave and slave-related sites. *Mankala* gaming pieces have been identified at several other sites within Manassas National Battlefield Park (Portici and Brownsville; see Chapter 13), as well as on other plantation sites such as Jefferson's Poplar Forest and at Drax Hall in Jamaica (Armstrong 1990 in Patten 1992).

There are hundreds of variations, as well as names for the game, recorded from region to region. Example of other names include *sunka* (Indonesia), *pallanguli* (India and Sri Lanka), *tamilnadi* (India), *olinda keliya* (Sri Lanka), *abala'e* (Ethiopia), *baré* (Ethiopia), and *wari* (Ghana) (Bell 1988). The object of the game is to move tokens—consisting of stones, beans, seeds, nuts, shells, or any other type of small objects—across a series of holes that are in rows either on a gaming board or dug into the ground. There is no distinction between the tokens; the object of the game is to redistribute the tokens according to established rules and capture as many pieces as possible.

One anthropological study of the game designates the skills required for being a good *mankala* player as cunning, vigilance, foresight, resilience, perseverance, discretion, memory, and self-control (Townshend 1979:795). Townshend contends that "African mankala can be viewed as a highly efficient enculturating device, with reference to both moral-intellectual and social values, and as a training mechanism in elementary survival techniques" (Townshend 1979:795). These characteristics may have been embedded in a belief system that enabled a free African American family to persist and prevail under adversity in antebellum and postbellum Virginia.

During the 1996 excavations at the Robinson house site, approximately two dozen possible gaming pieces were found in areas around the house foundation ruins and in the backyard (Parsons 1996:56). Examples of these objects found at the Robinson house site and several other sites in Virginia are typically small, reworked, irregularly shaped sherds of glass and pottery. The majority of ceramic pieces appear to be either porcelain or unidentified white-paste ceramics. In several excavation areas, two to four pieces were deposited together. The use of broken bits of glass and historic ceramic to play a traditional African game may exemplify a form of cultural concealment. Broken sherds of glass and ceramic would have been common at any 18th- or 19th-century household and would not have been detected in association with an African tradition or custom. Further research into the origin and interpretation of these objects is warranted.

Discussion

Material culture collected at the site combined with an examination of the landscape and the Robinson family's social history demonstrate this remarkable family's methods for enduring times of destruction and social injustice. The family countered antebellum racist attitudes and endured the physical and emotional devastation caused by the Civil War. They also overcame changing racial ideologies in post–Civil War Virginia. Studying artifacts, architectural evidence, and the use of space at the Robinson house site reveals that within this local community, race, material culture, and the use of space are connected and provide a means for a more comprehensive understanding of African American life and methods for combating racism. Despite the years of adversity, the Robinsons survived and remain a strong voice in the Manassas community. Members of the family participated in excavations, assisted in the research, and volunteered in an oral history project. Information contributed by the Robinson family provides a link between past histories and present interpretations. The insights of the family aid professionals in presenting a history which is conscious of a past that has been constructed through discourses which have often excluded groups according to race, class, gender, and power relations. These groups have a relationship to each other and to certain events, periods, and places in time. Together with other studies, this information about African American life presents an exceptional research opportunity at Manassas National Battlefield Park to investigate different aspects and issues within the African American community. In turn, a more comprehensive picture may be produced which will provide insight into future research, museum exhibits, and interpretations.

III

New Methods and Techniques

The four chapters in this section illustrate how new strategies of archaeological investigation can contribute to the interpretation of military, and in particular, battlefield, events. Three chapters are a product of the same study. Chapter 16 introduces a program of systematic metal detecting recently carried out in four different historically significant sections of Antietam Battlefield. In this chapter, the historical context of the study areas are introduced and the manner in which the study was conducted is presented. The projects indicate the importance of systematic metal detecting to the investigation of battlefield sites but also illustrate how archaeologically significant remains can still exist in landscapes that have been extensively collected.

Building on this introduction, chapters 17 and 18 analyze significant categories of militaria recovered from the sites. Chapter 17, presented by Bruce Sterling, includes a review of musketry and bullets available to the combatants. The nature and spatial distribution of different types of bullets are used to consider the military events that took place locally. In chapter 18, Jeffrey Harbison analyzes the artillery artifacts from the same data set. Following a presentation of the characteristics of the artillery available to both sides in the battle, distributions of artillery-related artifacts are interpreted with respect to the historical record of the engagement.

In chapter 15, John Cornelison again considers the value of systematic metal detector surveys to the analysis of military sites. In this study, attention is drawn to events associated with the Battle of Chickamauga in Georgia. Areas of the battlefield threatened by planned road construction required archaeological study of potential impact. Metal detecting was one technique of evaluation used. Through its application, Civil War artifacts were obtained, which, when placed in historical context, served to aid in the identification of certain corridors used in the Union withdrawal from the battlefield.

15

The Archaeology of Retreat

Systematic Metal Detector Survey and Information System
Analysis at the Battlefield of Chickamauga, September 1863

John E. Cornelison, Jr.

In preparation for planned construction of Highway 27 along the west
side of Chickamauga and Chattanooga National Military Park, archaeological surveys of the highway project corridor were conducted. The goal
of these projects was to determine the extent of impact, if any, that
planned construction would have on cultural resources associated with
the battlefield. In 1992, staff at Chickamauga and Chattanooga National
Military Park requested assistance from the National Park Service's
Southeast Archeological Center (SEAC) for a metal detector survey of the
U.S. Highway 27 corridor (fig. 15.1). Archaeological compliance for this
project had been previously conducted by the Georgia Department of
Transportation (GA DOT) (Bowen 1990; Brown 1977; Brown and Evans
1977; Honerkamp, Evans, and Will 1982). While available records indicated that most of the Battle of Chickamauga took place east of the construction corridor, retreating Federals withdrew across the study area. It
was not known prior to the survey if such short-duration activities would
leave an archaeological signature or whether, if they did, meaningful interpretations could be constructed from the data.

Archaeologists from SEAC conducted the survey and limited testing
with the aid of local volunteers and park staff. In preparation for the
project, all available historic maps of the park area were digitally assembled and compared to the modern landscape. To interpret battle dynamics and delimit site boundaries, the corridor was systematically surveyed by metal detectors using the same methodology as that applied at
Little Bighorn National Battlefield (Scott and Fox 1987:19; Hacker and
Mauck 1997:10).

The project consisted of five short-duration metal detector surveys conducted over a period of 18 months. These surveys covered the construction corridor from Lytle Road to McFarland Lane. Four surveys were
supervised by the author, during which artifacts located during systematic

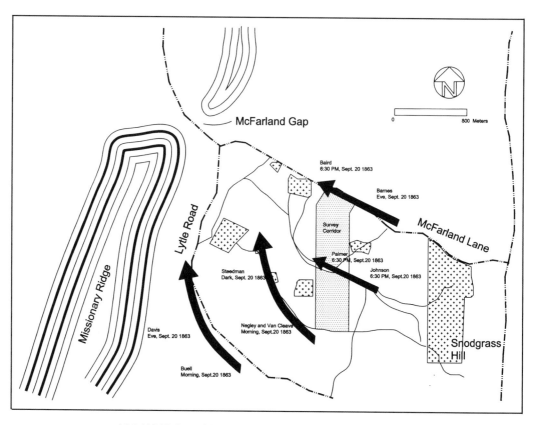

15.1. U.S. Highway 27 project corridor relative to Civil War–era military positions (courtesy of the National Park Service–Southeast Archeological Center).

metal detector sweeps were mapped using a Sokkia Set 5A electronic total station, Global Positioning System (GPS), and a Brunton compass with tape. The fifth survey was directed by a GA DOT archaeologist. During this last survey, artifact locations were vaguely mapped without the benefit of degree readings. On a subsequent visit, however, the author was able to map the GA DOT flags and tie artifact locations into the previous surveys. Artifacts were retrieved and added to the Automated National Cataloging System (ANCS) used to document the entire artifact sample.

As a result of the five surveys, 586 artifacts were recovered and mapped. Of these, 268 date to the Civil War era and another 94 to the Spanish-American War era. The dispersal pattern of the Civil War artifacts was shown to follow lines of retreat used by routed Union forces and an ensuing bombardment by Confederate artillery. Artifacts identified as having been disposed of reveal the tactical instability that beset the Union troops as they began their headlong flight to Chattanooga following the Battle of Chickamauga on September 20, 1863.

The Battle of Chickamauga

Following the capture of Chattanooga, Tennessee, on September 6, 1863, Gen. William S. Rosecrans, commander of the Army of the Cumberland, began an advance toward Atlanta, Georgia. He slowly moved his army southward until they were met by Gen. Braxton Bragg's Army of Tennessee near Chickamauga Creek. On the morning of September 19, 1863, the two armies were aligned for approximately six miles along the creek banks. Through the first day, the battle drifted westward. Although casualties were high on both sides, neither side established an advantage and the battle came to a standstill.

Fighting resumed on the morning of September 20. The Confederates launched a determined but unsuccessful attack on the Union left flank commanded by Maj. Gen. George Henry Thomas. When failed efforts to redeploy troops caused a gap to open on the Union right flank, Lieut. Gen. James Longstreet's troops charged into the gap dividing the Union line. With the line divided, Longstreet wheeled his forces to the right, outflanking the Union Corps of Maj. Gen. Thomas L. Crittenden and Maj. Gen. Alexander McCook. Both of these corps fled the field along with the Union commander, Rosecrans (fig. 15.2).

Maj. Gen. George Henry Thomas's Corps continued to hold the Union right, fighting from behind prepared breastworks on Snodgrass Hill as they were pressed by elements of D. Harvey Hill's Confederates. The reorganized Union soldiers, many armed with repeating rifles, doggedly clung to their position. Through the day, the Confederates slowly pushed the Union forces back into a wedge-shaped defensive position. At about 3 P.M., when Thomas was nearly out of ammunition and was threatened from the rear, he was reinforced by the troops of Maj. Gen. Gordon Granger. With Granger's support, Thomas held his position on Snodgrass Hill until dark, when he withdrew in orderly fashion toward Chattanooga.

The Union Army retreated toward Chattanooga in both ordered and disordered formations. The retrograde movements of several units (figs. 15.1, 15.2) are of importance to interpreting the results of the highway corridor survey. These include: (1) Maj. Gen. Don Carlos Buell's withdrawal down Lytle Road; (2) the movements of elements of Brig. Gen. Horatio P. Van Cleave's and Brig. Gen. James S. Negley's Divisions along an intermittent stream on September 20th; (3) the movements of the troops of Brig. Gens. John M. Palmer, Richard W. Johnson, and James B. Steedman near the center of the survey corridor; and (4) the movements of Brig. Gen. Absalom Baird and Col. Sidney Barnes along McFarland Lane. In the weeks following the Battle of Chickamauga, the Confederate Army laid siege to Chattanooga. It was not long until the siege was broken and the stage was set for Sherman to begin his march to the sea.

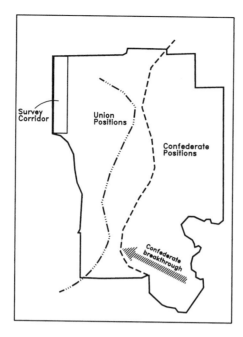

Battle Lines
Sept. 20th 1863 AM

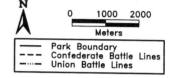

Battle Lines
Sept. 20th 1863 PM

15.2. Battle of Chickamauga showing general troop movements relative to project survey corridor (courtesy of the National Park Service–Southeast Archeological Center).

Research Methodology

In 1972, Dean R. Snow demonstrated the data potential of battlefield archaeology (Snow 1981). In his work for the National Park Service at the Saratoga Battlefield, he discarded traditional archaeological techniques and chose instead to use aerial photographs, magnetometers, and soil probes to locate battlefield positions. His work showed that there was enormous historical and cultural data potential in the preserved battle-fields of the National Park Service.

Fifteen years later, Douglas Scott and Richard Fox showed the effectiveness of using metal detectors and volunteers to obtain information about battlefields at Little Bighorn Battlefield (Scott and Fox 1987:21). Based on the results of their testing (Fox and Scott 1991), these researchers later described a post–Civil War battlefield pattern. The identification of a pattern begins with the determination of individual actions based on the distribution of artifacts with unique signatures or characteristics (for example, rifling patterns on bullets, ejector marks, or firing pin marks). These individual patterns are aggregated into unit patterns, which in turn form the battlefield pattern. In describing the essence of battlefield archaeology, Fox and Scott (1991:97) write that "tactics prescribe combat behavior. All cultures have combat tactics, some more rigidly defined than others. In the absence of unit tactical disorganization, signature patterning may reflect prescribed deployment."

The individual weapons used by the majority of Civil War soldiers, however, did not produce artifacts with unique signatures. This makes determination of individual movements extremely difficult, if not impossible, on most Civil War and earlier battlefields. Therefore, individual actions must be deduced from artifact patterns understood as unit actions.

One method used to compensate for the lack of unique bullet signatures was illustrated by William B. Lees (1992:1; 1994:52). His study of the Mine Creek Battlefield led him to conclude that "unfired" or "dropped" bullets provide the best basis for reconstructing troop positions because they mark the precise location of individuals. Concentrations of fired bullets falling behind unit positions, on the other hand, are most likely indirect indicators of lines, and thus these represent a "ghost" of those positions (Lees 1992:8). Similar logic underlies the present study of troop movements associated with the Battle of Chickamauga.

Following testing at several other Civil War and Revolutionary War battlefields (Cornelison 1995a, 1995b, 1995c; Cornelison and Hageseth 1995; Cornelison and Leslie 1996), it was determined that the retreat data from Chickamauga was not dense enough to be aggregated into meaningful patterns. For displaying the Chickamauga data, a Geographic Information System (GIS) software, ArcView, and its built-in database utilities were used. Once the artifacts were entered into a database, selected categories of artifacts were superimposed upon terrain graphics, thus permitting interpretations of the artifact distributions.

Volunteer metal detector operators were asked to walk in straight lines along a predetermined path and were initially aligned abreast at roughly 10-foot intervals. Spacing changed as a result of electronic interference between machines and because of the uneven and heavily vegetated nature of the corridor. Every attempt was made to keep the volunteers moving in the proper direction with the correct spacing.

When an artifact was encountered, it was recovered, and a determination of age was made. If the artifact was modern, it was placed in a general collection bag. However, if it was determined to be from the Civil War era, the artifact was flagged, bagged, assigned a field specimen number (FS), and later recorded using a GPS unit, an electronic total station, or a Brunton compass and tape.

The planned Highway 27 corridor underwent metal detector survey along its entire 1.5-mile length bordering the western edge of the Chickamauga battlefield area. The width of the survey varied, but it was generally confined to the 120-meter width of the construction corridor. The entire corridor survey constituted approximately 17 acres (6.9 hectares) of land. The survey project was conducted in five survey areas (fig. 15.3). These are described and discussed separately below.

Survey Area 1

Survey area 1 covered an area 650 feet by 400 feet, beginning at Lytle Road and running north along the centerline of the proposed Highway 27 corridor. Six volunteers, the park historian, and two archaeologists were present. The surveyors began on the west side of the centerline and headed north. The volunteers were spaced approximately 10 to 15 feet apart to prevent electronic interference between their metal detectors. Controlling the spacing was extremely difficult because of the uneven wooded terrain. Once the survey crew reached the 225-centerline marker, the survey was continued on the east side of the centerline, heading south. In all, four passes were made on the east side of the centerline (two north and two south). The initial survey produced 109 artifacts. Evidence of the cannonade that the fleeing Union troops received was recovered in the form of polygonal shell fragments, iron shot, and shell fragments with Borman fuse threads.

A monument base was also located during the initial survey. The base measures 54.5 by 54.5 inches and is presumed to mark the location occupied by the 9th Michigan during the battle. The location is described as follows:

> The monument was [to be] located in the extreme southwest corner of the park, three-fourths of a mile from the Videto House on an eminence about 200 feet above the road leading through McFarland's Gap and overlooking the Dry Valley Road, and the scenes of the disaster to the right wing of the army on Sunday, the 20th of September, and near the position where it checked the routed troops that Sunday afternoon. (Robert Smith Printing 1899)

Because of logistical problems, the monument was never mounted on its base: "The monument to this regiment was first located, and the foun-

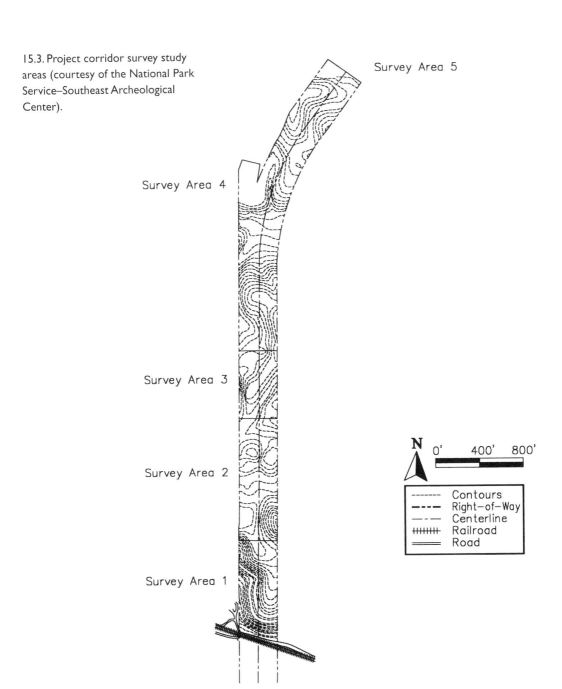

15.3. Project corridor survey study areas (courtesy of the National Park Service–Southeast Archeological Center).

Survey Area 5

Survey Area 4

Survey Area 3

Survey Area 2

Survey Area 1

N

0'   400'   800'

```
-------  Contours
----  Right-of-Way
-- -  Centerline
HHHHH  Railroad
====  Road
```

dation placed, on the crest of the ridge overlooking McFarland Gap, the scene of the regiments greatest triumph, but owing to lack of transportation and appliances the location had to be changed to the base of the ridge, where it now stands, a sentinel at the gateway of the park" (Robert Smith Printing 1899). The marker stood at the second location from 1895 until it was removed during the construction of the new Highway 27 in 1996.

Survey Area 2

Survey area 2 began on the east side of the centerline where survey area 1 ended. Since there were sufficient volunteers, the east side was completed in one pass. Sixteen volunteers, the park historian, one student volunteer, and three SEAC archaeologists participated in the survey. The volunteers began locating .45–.70-caliber bullets from the Spanish-American War era. These bullets were confined to one hill location. Initially, these objects were collected and mapped, but the sheer number precluded mapping each non–Civil War object. All subsequent .45–.70-caliber bullets were placed in a general collection bag.

Just north of the .45–.70-caliber firing range, the surveyors encountered a World War II firing range saturated with .45-caliber bullets. This area was passed over as the .45-caliber bullets made additional survey impractical. The area was mapped with a Brunton compass and tape.

The survey was stopped several hundred yards short of what was presumed to be the main Civil War retreat route, based on the 1896 Betts map, where Johnson and Palmer's units presumably passed. This documented retreat route was a road regularly crossed by an intermittent stream. The stream is currently bordered by an extremely thick privet hedge. The survey crew attempted to cross the stream on the centerline cut, but the depth of the stream and the thick privet hedge prevented the area from being surveyed. The surveyors, therefore, turned and continued south along the west side of the centerline. Very few artifacts were recovered from this section.

Three concentrations of artifacts warranted further investigations in survey area 2. The first of these was located slightly north of the survey area 1 boundary. A cluster of 34 "dropped" Minié balls was located. To assess the significance of this find, a one-meter square (Excavation Unit 1) was excavated in 10 centimeter levels. From the number of Minié balls present in the area, it appeared that a full or nearly full cartridge box had been dropped. The square was excavated to determine if any other artifacts were dropped at the same location. No additional artifacts were recovered from the unit.

The second concentration consisted of 15 "dropped" Minié balls. A second one-meter square (Excavation Unit 2) was excavated to determine the nature of this concentration. Five unfired percussion caps were recovered in the excavation unit.

The third concentration of artifacts consisted of one "J" hook, one triangle-shaped ring, and four small knapsack buckles. A one-meter square (Excavation Unit 3) was placed in an area where the Civil War era knapsack parts were recovered. It was hoped that nonmetallic personal items would be recovered from the dropped knapsack, but no other Civil War artifacts were recovered.

In the course of the survey, efforts were also directed toward locating a house site which historic maps (Betts 1892) placed on the south side of the privet hedge. The house site, which contained a large amount of agricultural material, was easily located, though no Civil War era artifacts were identified there.

An east/west survey was conducted in the survey area 2 gully where the previously mentioned 15 "dropped" bullets and 5 percussion caps had been located. A few additional Civil War era artifacts were recovered, including an Enfield ramrod. The ramrod was probably dropped, since the artifact pattern in the narrow gully indicates that it was probably used as an impromptu retreat route.

Survey Area 3

This survey area is located in the north end of the right-of-way. Sixteen volunteers and three SEAC archaeologists surveyed this area. Artifact concentrations were generally light. However, along one ridge, a widespread scatter of caltrops (anti-cavalry pointed objects) was identified. Upon reaching the privet hedge, the survey was continued to the north, on the west side of the centerline. In the survey corridor from the 34 Minié ball-drop south to the .45–.70-caliber concentration, only three Civil War artifacts were recovered.

Survey Area 4

The post-battle map (Betts 1896) and historic record indicate that part of the Union retreat took place through the intermittent stream area. This area was not surveyed during previous trips because of the density of the privet hedge. It was decided that another survey attempt would be made after the vegetation was removed. Bulldozers were used to remove most of the topsoil to clear the area. The survey area was extremely wet and had been scraped to subsoil in many places. The survey was conducted, and a few .45-caliber slugs and other modern debris were recovered. There was no evidence of a retreat route in this area.

Survey Area 5

This survey area is located at the north end of the project corridor where the alignment turns north toward McFarland Lane. McFarland Lane is important because historic records indicate that the Union forces of Brigadier Generals Baird and Barnes retreated along this route. The survey recovered several potentially significant artifacts and revealed several artifact patterns along McFarland Lane. Artifacts recovered include a U.S. belt buckle and five unfired, solid base, two-ring, .58-caliber bullets. Unfortunately, the project archaeologists failed to record artifact locations at the same accuracy levels as the previous surveys. The shortcomings of the survey methods were resolved by accurately mapping the artifact flags left behind.

Material Culture

Civil War artifacts believed attributable to the events at Chickamauga include a diverse array of weaponry and accoutrements of the sort one would expect from a battlefield setting. Twelve percussion caps were recovered from the corridor survey. All are brass and have skirts. The caps range in diameter from .2255 inches to .2630 inches. The number and placement of the percussion caps suggests that some Union soldiers in their haste to leave the battlefield were dropping anything that might impede their progress.

One hundred thirty-four Minié balls were recovered during the corridor survey. Approximately 84 percent (n = 113) of these were of the unfired, or "dropped," three-ring types. Of this total, 104 were .58-caliber (92 percent), 2 were .54-caliber, and 5 were .69-caliber.

Two British-made Enfield-Pritchett-type Minié balls were recovered. Both sides imported large quantities of Enfield weapons and bullets during the war (Coates and Thomas 1990:19). The Confederates also produced their own Enfield-type bullets (Coates and Thomas 1990:19) because of supply difficulties imposed by the Union blockade. Both of the recovered specimens were unfired. One was a .54-caliber, and the other was a .577-caliber Minié ball.

The remaining 15.5 percent (n = 21) of recovered Minié balls were fired and consisted of a .69-caliber Minié ball and 20 Minié balls that were too badly damaged to obtain a proper caliber measurement. Of these 20, 13 fall within one standard deviation of the mean weight of the unfired .58-caliber Minié balls in this collection, and all but one fall within two standard deviations of the mean .58-caliber weight. It is therefore reasonable to assume that 19 of the 20 (95 percent) fired bullets are .58-caliber. This percentage is similar to the proportion of .58-caliber Minié balls in the dropped group (104 of 113 or 92 percent). The unfired to fired ratio is 84.3 to 15.7 percent, or approximately 5 to 1.

Five unfired, solid base, two-ring, .58-caliber bullets were also recovered. They appear to have been made for the Spencer carbine. The Spencer carbine was introduced in the spring of 1863 for use by the Union cavalry (Scott and Hunt 1997:84). Many Union guard units purchased these weapons with personal funds (Fred Prouty, personal communication 1996).

Twenty-three lead pistol balls were recovered during the project. Seventeen (74 percent) were .36-caliber and six (26 percent) were .44-caliber. Thirty-seven pieces of spherical shot were recovered during the survey. Shot of this type was fired as part of an artillery projectile. Coggins

(1990:67) states that "spherical case (shrapnel) was used against troops, usually at ranges of 500 to 1500 yards." These shells had a fuse and a small bursting charge. If the fuse was set properly, the charge would explode over the enemy soldiers, raining the shot down similar to a giant shotgun blast. The typical 12-pound shell contained 78 lead shot, while the 6-pound shell contained 38 lead shot (Coggins 1990:67).

Artillery shot can be divided into two types based on the material: iron (n = 22) and lead (n = 15). Since the bombarded area was under Union control, it can be reasonably assumed that the shot came from a Confederate polygonal shell that will be discussed later. Ten of the lead shot were determined to be .69-caliber, while 21 of the iron shots were .75-caliber.

All of the identifiable artillery projectiles were found to be Confederate polygonal types (n = 14). These spherical shells, produced with a central cavity packed with gunpowder, would break into 12 or 18 parts when the powder exploded (Dickey and George 1993:30). With the exception of one shell fragment located along McFarland Lane, all of the artillery shell fragments and lead shot were recovered in association at the corridor's southern end.

One polygonal fragment had threads to allow a Borman-type fuse to be inserted. Borman fuses were circular discs threaded so they could be screwed into a shell. The top of the fuse was graduated in seconds and quarters. A special cutter was used to make a hole in the fuse corresponding to the length of time desired before the shell exploded. When the shell was fired, flames from the explosion lit the powder in the fuse, which hopefully burned for the appropriate amount of time (Coggins 1990:82; Dickey and George 1993:441).

One hundred six caltrops (fig. 15.4) were clustered together in the northern extent of the project corridor. This type of item was thrown in roads and in front of defensive positions as a deterrent to cavalry attacks. The caltrops would catch the hooves of the horses, hobbling them. They were made of iron and were about two inches from point to point.

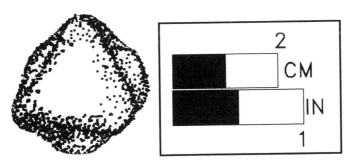

15.4. Sample of conserved caltrops (courtesy of the National Park Service–Southeast Archeological Center).

Six brass and iron knapsack components were also recovered in the corridor. These consisted of one "J" hook, one triangular-shaped ring, and four small buckles. These six items represent most of the metal located on a Civil War era knapsack (James Ogden, personal communication).

Two iron rifle-band spring clips were recovered. The spring clips are used to hold the barrel bands in position. The barrel bands in turn keep the barrel securely fastened to the stock. As previously mentioned, an Enfield-type ramrod was also recovered.

Six lead gaming pieces were recovered at the top of a hill. All six were Minié balls that had been hammered flat to produce a disc shape. Civil War soldiers commonly worked bullets into a multitude of objects, such as pipes, statues, and gambling objects, such as poker chips (Harris 1987:56) and dice. Civil War soldiers often created these artifacts during long periods of inactivity. The hill on which the gaming pieces were located was near the spot where the 9th Michigan was assigned provost duty during the battle. It is possible that a Michigan soldier lost the gaming pieces or that they were dropped during the retreat.

One bayonet scabbard tip was recovered. This metal object was sewn to the scabbard and kept the tip of the bayonet both from wounding and being damaged while in the scabbard. In addition, 14 buckles were recovered during the survey. Two were parts of a knapsack. One standard-issue U.S. Army belt buckle was located along McFarland Lane. The remaining 11 buckles were either agricultural or could not be assigned to a temporal period.

Interpretation

Artifact distribution maps were created using the GIS ArcView program. This powerful program allows the operator to query tabular data, in this case the artifact inventories, and display spatial data graphically. Contour maps created in AutoCAD were overlaid with the GIS data to provide a visual representation of artifact distributions relative to local terrain conditions and historic features.

Historic accounts report that some of the Union units left the field in a tactically stable manner. Other Union units left the field in wild flight, with no sense of order. Several significant concentrations of artifacts were noted in the survey corridor. These areas were labeled A to E from north to south, to avoid confusion with survey areas 1–5. Areas A to E appear to illustrate this stability/instability dichotomy of the Union retreat from the Chickamauga Battlefield. Although no direct documentary evidence discussing the retreat area has been located, several historic references can be used to show the state of the soldiers during the retreat.

Area A is located at the northern end of the corridor where it begins to turn east toward McFarland Lane. The distribution of anti-cavalry cal-

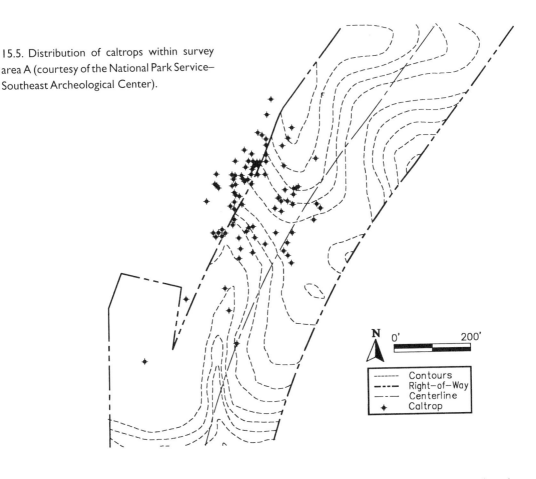

15.5. Distribution of caltrops within survey area A (courtesy of the National Park Service–Southeast Archeological Center).

N

0'   200'

--------- Contours
— — — Right-of-Way
— ∙ — Centerline
✦   Caltrop

trops on the northern end of the project corridor (fig. 15.5) shows that the units passing through this area were under pressure, or believed they would be under pressure, from Confederate cavalry. The caltrops are distributed within a north/south topographic saddle. The east/west corridor created by the saddle was completely covered with caltrops, ensuring that any cavalry pursuit by the victorious Confederates would meet with disaster as numerous horses were lamed. The distribution of these artifacts indicates that the Union units in this area were tactically stable as they retreated. The systematic and tactical placement of these objects demonstrates that the military command structure was still functioning. If the command structure were broken down, the units would have deteriorated into an every-man-for-himself situation and it would be unlikely the caltrops would have been so thoughtfully positioned. Another indicator of the tactical stability of the units passing through is the lack of other military equipment. Units suffering from tactical instability tend to discard military equipment that might impede their flight, even if such equipment is potentially lifesaving. There is ample evidence of this from Little Big Horn Battlefield (Fox 1993:68) and other Civil War battlefields, such as the defeated Union troops throwing away equipment following First

Manassas (Foote 1958:81). There is also ample evidence, from this survey, of Union troops discarding essential equipment as their units became unstable at Chickamauga. Since Palmer and Johnson's units retreated along this route prior to the final collapse of the Union Army, they are likely candidates for the placing of the caltrops. However, supporting documentary evidence has not been located.

Areas B, C, and D are located in the middle of the project corridor. Two of these areas contain large concentrations of dropped Minié balls—15 in area B and 34 in area C. In addition, 9 percussion caps were located with the Minié balls. Customarily, dropped bullets are indicative of where a military unit was positioned when they were receiving enemy fire. Recovered artifacts around area B show no evidence of enemy rifled-musket or artillery fire. Similarly, there is very little evidence of rifled-musket fire and no artillery fire in area C. Both of these Minié ball concentrations were probably created when individual soldiers dropped their cartridge boxes in an attempt to move away from the enemy with great speed. The standard issue of ammunition consisted of 10-round packs (Coates and Thomas 1990:27) that included 12 percussion caps (Todd 1980). Four packs of 10 rounds were usually carried in an individual soldier's cartridge box (Todd 1980:187).

Area E, at the south end of the corridor, is the only location that shows evidence of a Union military unit retreating under direct attack. Approximately 200 feet from Lytle Road, there is a large hill oriented northwest to southeast. From historic accounts and archaeological evidence, it is known that units retreated through this area under Confederate bombardment. In this area, polygonal artillery shell fragments were found in association with lead shot (fig. 15.6). Several of the iron fragments were mendable, leading to the conclusion that these artifacts, in association with lead shot, were the result of a single shell air burst. The totality of these artifacts along with their locations suggest that they are part of a burst pattern created when a single Confederate artillery shell exploded, sending its deadly cargo earthward in a pattern similar to that of a shotgun burst. The presumed Confederate battery locations involved are recorded on the 1896 Betts map. The relative trajectory of the artillery shells can be determined from the artifacts' spatial distribution. If the mean range of 1,300 yards for a 12-pounder Napoleon cannon (McKee and Mason 1980) is used to buffer the artifacts' location, the approximate line that the cannon were firing along can be established. However, the exact position cannot be determined because the cannon may have been firing from a location much closer than their maximum range. When the trajectory is projected back from the artifacts, it becomes apparent that the mapped location of the Confederate cannon is very accurate.

A number of unfired Minié balls were also recovered on the southwest slope of the hill. By 3:00 P.M. on September 20, 1863, the Confederate left,

15.6. Distribution of artillery and shot within survey area E (courtesy of the National Park Service–Southeast Archeological Center).

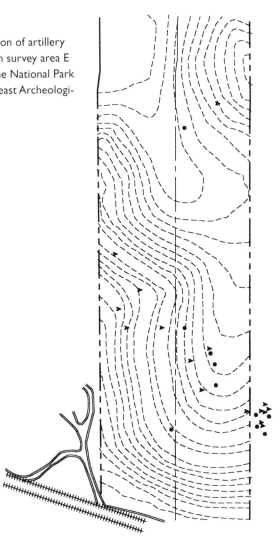

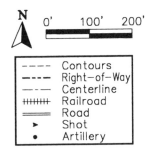

under the command of Major General Hindman, was located approximately 450 yards from this area. Hindman's men had engaged Thomas on the southwest portion of Snodgrass Hill. It is possible, therefore, that the dropped bullets in this area are reflective of Union defensive fire. This could indicate that the Federal units in area E maintained some degree of tactical stability even though they were under an artillery barrage.

Except for two Minié balls, all fired bullets are in the southern half of the corridor. It is interesting that in the central part of the corridor, where there is very little evidence of Confederate pursuit, the Union units appear to be tactically unstable. In contrast, on the southern half of the corridor, Union forces were under artillery bombardment, yet the military units show evidence of being tactically stable.

Conclusion

The retreat of the Union forces from Chickamauga is a very poorly understood part of the battle. Several types of patterns are present including group activity such as the placing of caltrops and individual activities such as the discarding of bullets and equipment. Understanding these patterns will aid in the interpretation of poorly understood battlefield activities. The artifact patterns recovered in the survey corridor cannot be specifically tied to individual military units. They can, however, be used to reconstruct probable behavior based on the state of soldiers entering the area and known military behavior.

Results of this and other battlefield surveys clearly indicate that behaviorally meaningful artifact patterns can be obtained. Fox and Scott (1991:93) have shown that soldiers behave in tactically prescribed manners as long as unit stability is maintained, and this may be reflected in the archaeological record. Similar to the models expounded by Fox (1993: 337–39), the data from this survey shows the results of tactically stable and unstable military retreats. The artifact patterns presented here show that military order, or its absence, can be examined archaeologically. Thus, scientific, historically relevant determinations can be made regarding the actions of individuals and groups in a battlefield setting.

In summary, this project provided valuable information concerning the tactical condition of the Union troops as they passed through the corridor area. The archaeological results show evidence of tactically stable units passing through the corridor and continuing to function as military units. Other archaeological data from this project indicates that other individuals or units passed through the area in tactically unstable conditions with little to no semblance of military order.

16

Surveying the Civil War

Methodological Approaches at Antietam Battlefield

Bruce B. Sterling and Bernard W. Slaughter

In 1994, the National Park Service and URS Greiner, Inc., launched a four-year archaeological survey of portions of the Antietam National Battlefield, the site of one of the hardest-fought battles of the Civil War, in an effort to identify and inventory military and other cultural resources (fig. 16.1). Since the days of battle, the Civil War has captured the imagination of not only Civil War buffs and scholars but people from all walks of life. Today, battlefield park shops are full of books on the history of the Civil War, its battles, its soldiers and generals, and descriptions of ordnance and tactics. The Battle of Antietam is no exception, with numerous battle narratives available that describe all aspects of the conflict. Of key interest to battle historians and Civil War enthusiasts are detailed descriptions of the battle that outline specific troop movements and military tactics. However, these battle descriptions are based on eyewitness accounts from soldiers, reporters, and local citizens, often written many years after the war. As at all battlefields, the events at Antietam were chaotic and turbulent. Because of the inherent confusion, participant recollections of the battle and its gruesome aftermath may only tell part of the story. As Bruce Catton noted:

> It all looks very simple and orderly on the map. . . . But in reality there was nothing simple or orderly about any part of it. Instead there was an appalling confusion of shattering sound, an unending chaos of violence and heat and intense combat, with fields and thickets wrapped in shifting layers of blinding smoke so that no man could know and understand any more of what was happening than the part he could see immediately around him . . . battle lines swaying haphazardly in an infernal choking fog . . . attack and counter attack taking place in every conceivable direction and in no recognizable time sequence. (Catton 1962:269)

Just as researchers and historians turned to original documentary sources to help understand the events that unfolded at Antietam, so too

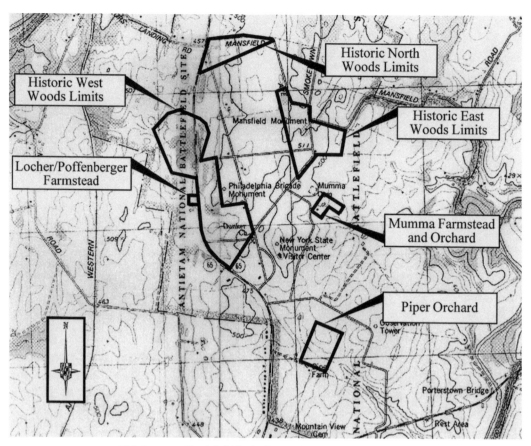

16.1. Antietam Battlefield Park showing survey project areas (courtesy of the National Park Service, National Capital Region, and URS Greiner Woodward Clyde).

are archaeologists looking to Civil War battlefields, camps, and forts. Like military history, archaeology attempts to make relevant contributions to the knowledge and interpretation of battles—to impose order on chaos. Unlike military history, battlefield archaeology is in its infancy. In the opening chapter of *Look to the Earth: Historical Archaeology and the American Civil War* (Geier and Winter 1994), Steven Smith argues that historical archaeologists can and must make relevant contributions to the understanding of the Civil War. The combined use of archaeological data and historic documentation will provide "a more complete picture of the past" than can be achieved from a single perspective (Steven Smith 1994:8). Smith believes that archaeologists who investigate Civil War sites can gather new information with which to address focused research questions. The work conducted at Antietam Battlefield is part of a growing trend among historical archaeologists contributing to an expanding database from which more encompassing statements about the war may be made in the future.

What archaeological evidence still remains in the ground at historic battlefields? A question commonly asked by visitors during the Antietam archaeological survey was "Is there really anything left after all these years?" This question goes to the heart of one problem facing historical archaeologists. It is an unavoidable fact that relic hunting has taken place on Civil War battlefields. Such collecting often began on the day of the conflict, first by soldiers, then by civilians. After the Battle of Gettysburg, a reporter for the *New York Herald* wrote, "The air, the trees, the graves are silent. Even the relic hunters are gone now, and the soldiers here never awake to the sound of reveille" (Angle 1947:449). Relic hunting, long illegal on federal property, was once commonplace on public lands and private holdings later incorporated into the parks.

With such an inherent bias in the archaeological record, what methods can be used to gather reliable and significant archaeological information from a large Civil War battlefield? A principal goal at Antietam was to determine effective survey methods for gathering such data. Several surveys and excavations employing metal detectors on battlefield sites have met with notable success, including studies conducted by Lees (1994, 1996) in Oklahoma and Kansas; Clay (1990) in Kentucky; Pratt (1995) in Ohio; Scott (1989) at the Little Big Horn; Legg and Smith (1989) on Folly Island in South Carolina; and a Revolutionary War site by Sivilich in New Jersey (1996).

Metal detectors as an archaeological field tool were slow to catch on, possibly because of a reluctance among archaeologists to use an instrument often associated with amateur and avocational collectors. Despite problems and biases, there has been a marked rise in the use of metal detectors by archaeologists since the mid-1980s. The shift toward using metal detectors in archaeology has been primarily on military sites, where metal objects are the most numerous remnant of the military presence.

The primary task of the Antietam Battlefield survey was to determine whether military cultural remains were still present and whether they constituted a significant archaeological resource. To achieve this goal, archaeological research was designed to demonstrate the effectiveness of systematic metal detector survey on Civil War battlefields and to show how archaeological analysis can contribute new insights into the battle through different avenues of research and interpretation.

The Battle of Antietam

Today, almost 135 years after the end of the Civil War, the landscape at Antietam still possesses much of the pristine rural character encountered by battle participants. George Stevens of the Union VI Corps described a view of the landscape as it appeared before the battle:

> Among the delightful and fertile valleys which beautify the State of Maryland, none is more charming than the one through which the Antietam winds its tortuous course. . . . Its yellow harvests, glowing and ripening in

the September sun; its undulating meadows and richly laden orchards; its comfortable farm houses . . . the ranges of hills, rising on either side of the stream, diversified by vales or deep gullies . . . the whole scene is one of surpassing beauty. (Schildt 1997:136)

However, for Union and Confederate soldiers and the innocent citizens of Sharpsburg, this pastoral scene soon changed.

By the fall of 1862, after more than a year of fighting, the Union had not attained the swift victory it expected. Confederate forces, emboldened by their successes, felt the time was right to bring the war north into Maryland, where they hoped to gain support and fresh troops. The Confederates anticipated that success on Northern soil would help to gain England and France as allies, influence a growing Northern peace movement, and force the Union to the bargaining table. The Union Army, well equipped and with superior numbers, was poised to deliver a crushing defeat to the Southern forces. Encouraged by intercepted intelligence of Confederate movements, the notoriously cautious General George B. McClellan was prompted into action when he realized that he now had the means "with which if I cannot whip Bobby Lee, I will be willing to go home" (Sears 1983:115).

On September 17, 1862, the Army of the Potomac, numbering 87,000 under the command of General McClellan, and Gen. Robert E. Lee's Army of Northern Virginia, numbering 35,000, met in battle near Antietam Creek outside Sharpsburg, Maryland. The battle raged for a single day, leaving more than 23,000 Confederate and Union soldiers lying on the field or in makeshift hospitals dead, dying, or wounded. The scene of carnage was described by Confederate General James Longstreet:

one hundred thousand men, with five hundred pieces of artillery, had engaged in titanic combat. As the pall of battle smoke rose and cleared away, the scene presented was one to make the stoutest heart shudder. There lay upon the ground, scattered for three miles over the valleys and the hills or in improvised hospitals, more than twenty thousand men. Horace Greeley was probably right in pronouncing this the bloodiest day in American history. (Longstreet 1896)

While the Union claimed victory, having successfully stopped the first Confederate invasion of the North, tactically the battle was a draw. McClellan's army suffered significant damage, and Lee's forces were allowed a virtually unchallenged retreat across the Potomac River. The "victory" at Antietam was interpreted by President Lincoln as divine providence, fortifying his decision to enact the Emancipation Proclamation. This controversial political move served to shift the focus of the war, successfully preventing the Confederacy from gaining its much needed European allies.

The Archaeological Assessment of the Battlefield

As part of its Systemwide Archeological Inventory Program, the National Park Service developed a plan for recording and evaluating archaeological resources within Antietam National Battlefield. The plan was proposed because of concerns that archaeological sites could be adversely affected by park operations, development, visitor use, and other activities. The Park Service's present plan includes the ambitious proposal to restore much of the landscape to its condition on the day of the battle. Throughout the 19th and 20th centuries, woodlots were logged, fences torn down or rebuilt, and orchards and pasturage transformed. Restoration of woodlots and orchards, once battle landmarks, are included in plans for future public interpretation.

The archaeological survey encompassed all cultural resources within the park, including prehistoric, military, and historic domestic sites. During the survey, five historic farmsteads were investigated, including the Locher/Poffenberger tenant cabin and the Mumma farmhouse (Chapter 10). Four prehistoric sites were also identified during the investigations. This chapter concentrates on the methods and results of the systematic metal detector survey which focused on battle-related resources from areas slated for reforestation, including the West, North, and East Woods and the Mumma and Piper orchards (fig.16.1).

The West Woods Survey

The initial phase of the Antietam survey was conducted within a 75-acre parcel of primarily plowed fields which were once the West Woods. The woods, a stronghold and staging area on the Confederate left and center under Maj. Gen. "Stonewall" Jackson, acted as a screen, concealing the strength and movements of Confederate forces. The Confederates controlled the woods throughout the battle by holding off a few significant but brief incursions by Union forces. The most notable was the ill-fated advance by Maj. Gen. Edwin Sumner's II Corps. Sumner, unaware of the dangers, led his men directly into the West Woods, where they were quickly surrounded on three sides. Surprised and unable to maneuver, his forces were decimated by the ensuing fire. More than 2,000 men were shot down within 15 minutes. Only a remnant of Sumner's men reemerged from the woods to join other battered Union elements in the East Woods.

The importance of the West Woods survey was that it provided important information on the efficacy of sampling strategies that directed future work. Approximately half of the West Woods survey area was covered with a 100 percent metal detector survey, from which 1,608 metal anomalies were identified and flagged. Because of the size of the survey area and the number of metal anomalies identified, only a small sample could be excavated in the time allotted for the survey.

Two sampling strategies for recovering metal detector anomalies were tested across the survey area. The first involved excavating a percentage of the flagged hits, varying from 10–20 percent, along narrow transects. The second involved excavating all metal detector anomalies within block areas. Instead of the anticipated substantial artifact density, both block and transect sampling yielded only a light density of military items across the survey area. At this early stage, it was unclear whether the low recovery rate was attributable to testing methodology, earlier collecting activities, or a combination of both.

Comparison of these two sampling methods demonstrated that systematic excavations along transects provided greater distributional data on battle-related artifacts across larger expanses of landscape. Excavations in block areas provided limited, discrete data on particular battlefield locations. Because the survey involved testing expansive areas across which fighting occurred, it was determined that more complete data concerning battle activities as a whole could be gathered by using linear transects rather than blocks. The block excavations used alone left large gaps in distributional data over the wider battlefield survey areas. Further, it was determined that, because artifact data was diffuse across the landscape, an increase in the sample size during testing would enhance the effectiveness of a metal detector survey.

In order to compare the systematic metal detector survey results with more traditional archaeological approaches and to identify nonmilitary components such as prehistoric and historic domestic sites, shovel test and surface inspection survey was also conducted. In the West Woods, 292 systematic shovel tests were excavated, which resulted in the recovery of two military artifacts, no prehistoric material, and a variety of historic material associated with domestic sites. The surface inspection achieved similar poor results, with only two military items recovered. The ratio of military artifacts to the number of shovel tests excavated represents a dismal 0.7 percent recovery rate. In comparison, metal detecting during the entire survey involved excavating approximately 4,555 hits that produced 1,679 military and possible military artifacts, or a recovery rate of 37 percent. The results were indisputable; metal detector survey is the only viable method for data recovery on a large battlefield site. Systematic shovel testing and surface inspection, indispensable on most archaeological surveys, were shown conclusively to be ineffective when doing battlefield archaeology.

Based on the results of work conducted in the West Woods, it was determined that significant military-related archaeological resources were still present. Recovery of this material convinced archaeologists and the Park Service that more work was necessary to refine survey methods. The most significant accomplishment of the West Woods survey was adoption of a more comprehensive strategy for retrieval and analysis of military remains for other survey areas.

Revised Methodology

In each survey area, a grid was established with linear transects aligned at eight-meter intervals. A metal detector sweep, two meters wide, along each transect resulted in a 25 percent sample for each survey area. To maintain accuracy and consistency, each metal detector transect was delineated by a string line. An experienced metal detector operator, using a sophisticated metal detector (in this case, the White's 6000 Di-Pro with headphones), walked and detected along each transect. Every hit or metal anomaly was marked in place with a pin flag for later excavation. Most sophisticated metal detectors have readouts that indicate the type of metal and can be set at different levels of discrimination to ignore iron objects. However, for battlefield surveys that involve all types of military items, including many made of iron such as artillery fragments, all metal hits should be flagged.

A team of two archaeologists subsequently excavated every flagged anomaly in each transect. Using a metal detector, they would relocate the anomaly. It was not necessary to use a sophisticated metal detector, as the machine was required only for pinpointing and quick retrieval. An inexpensive detector with a small coil was adequate. Smaller coils are more efficient for pinpointing anomalies, while larger coils are better suited for the initial broad detection sweeps. The topsoil was excavated and placed on a tarp. The detector was utilized to quickly determine if the anomaly remained in the ground or was on the tarp. Excavation would continue until the metal detector indicated that the metal artifact was no longer in the ground. The object was then expeditiously retrieved by dividing the soil on the tarp into increasingly smaller portions, with the detector applied as a check each time, until the object was recovered. These methods facilitated efficient and prompt retrieval of the metal artifacts.

All identified military or possible military items recovered were collected and designated with a unique artifact number designated by transect. Its location was re-flagged with its new number designation. Each flagged location was then surveyed with a laser transit. In this way, artifact distribution maps were produced that aided in discerning significant concentrations and spatial relationships for interpreting the military presence across the battlefield.

An important lesson learned during the metal detector survey was gaining an understanding of the limitations of metal detectors. It is simply impossible to recover all metal items from the coverage area. Although a 25 percent sample was attempted, this sample reflected the area covered, not necessarily artifact recovery. Within the two-meter-wide metal-detected transects, there were certainly still metal objects left in the ground undetected. If a second operator with a detector passed over the same transect area, additional metal anomalies would likely be identified. Further, additional material would be identified if a survey area was replowed and artifacts were reoriented or moved closer to the surface, offering a better target for the machine. As one experienced operator stated, "you can never get it all."

Many factors influence the effectiveness of metal detectors; one of the most important is the surface condition. For best results, the detection coil at the base of the machine must be kept level, immediately above the ground surface. This is easily accomplished on ground with low vegetation such as in a plowed field or an active pasture with low grass. Other factors affecting the efficiency of detectors are depth, size, and orientation of the metal object. Soil conditions, including variations in moisture, compactness, mineral content, and the presence of bedrock outcrops, also affect efficiency. Weather and other subtle environmental conditions such as windy or stormy days and even nearby power lines or electric fences disrupt accuracy. (For a more detailed discussion of the uses of metal detectors in archaeology, see Connor and Scott 1998:76–85.)

The North Woods Survey

The first opportunity to implement the revised testing strategy came during investigations in the North Woods. The North Woods was an important staging area and zone of retreat for Union troops, primarily General Hooker's I Corps. Union troops passed through the woods under a rain of Confederate artillery shells and small arms fire, on their way to the fighting at the Miller Cornfield and West and East Woods:

> Things along the Federal line turned terribly sour. As Hartsuff's men started to pass through the North Woods, the Pennsylvania Reserves took a fearful drubbing. Minies whizzed through the air thick as bees. . . . When the line halted in the clearing just on the northern fringe of the plowed field [southern edge of North Woods] . . . the soldiers grew more listless as the seconds wore into minutes. Some rested on one foot, then on the other, like children waiting for a pass to the outhouse. Some prayed quietly. . . . The occasional sickening thud of a round striking home punctuated the nerve-wracking silence along the line. (Priest 1989:53)

The systematic metal detector sampling of the 19-acre North Woods recovered 311 military artifacts and 39 artifacts potentially associated with the battle. The military assemblage is composed primarily of small arms projectiles and fragments of artillery ordnance. The historic record, supported by archaeological evidence, indicates that no Confederate troops occupied or passed through the North Woods. Because of this unique battle situation, it was surmised that all unfired or dropped bullets recovered from the survey area would be associated with Union forces, and all fired bullets and artillery attributed to Confederates. The large North Woods assemblage became a useful analytical tool relevant to studying the military supply and use of small arms and artillery by both armies engaged at Antietam. Also, the unexpected recovery of short-range, fired round ball and pistol shot raised questions concerning the reported location of Confederate forces near the North Woods. Analysis of the North Woods military ordnance collection provided a foundation on which subsequent research and analysis of all the material from the project would be based. Results of the analysis and interpretations of the small arms and artillery from Antietam are presented in Chapters 17 and 18 respectively.

The North Woods assemblage represents a density of 18 artifacts per acre. This is quite impressive when compared to the results of the West Woods survey, which recovered only 2 artifacts per acre. The variation in collection strategies and sample size, in part, explains some of the differences in artifact density between the two areas. More importantly, the factor of differential land use in the North Woods was determined to greatly affect military artifact densities.

Today, the North Woods terrain can be roughly divided into two areas delineated by a plowed field to the east and a cow pasture to the west. A comparison of archaeological data from the two areas illustrates the impact of uncontrolled collecting on battle-related resources. The pasture area in the North Woods yielded significantly higher numbers of artifacts than did the plowed field to the east (fig. 16.2). Confirmation of relic hunting in the North Woods was provided by the former landowner, Lynn Culler. His family owned the property from 1952 to 1992 and allowed metal detecting in the plowed fields. In order to protect grazing livestock, permission was never granted for relic hunting in the pasture (Lynn Culler, personal communication, 1996). The contrast between military artifact density recovered from the pasture and the plowed portions of the North Woods indicates that pasture areas potentially serve as protected portions of battlefields, yielding significantly greater artifact densities.

The West Woods survey area was under private ownership until its recent acquisition by the NPS and was also heavily farmed and plowed. These conditions suggest that the area was most likely subjected to heavy collecting. In fact, a weathered sign on a broken-down stand located at the edge of the West Woods read "Artifacts for Sale." Because of heavy fighting in the West Woods, it was reasonable to assume that a large number of artifacts would be recovered during the survey. However, this was not the case, further illustrating the impact collecting has on archaeological deposits. Though original artifact densities no doubt varied across the park

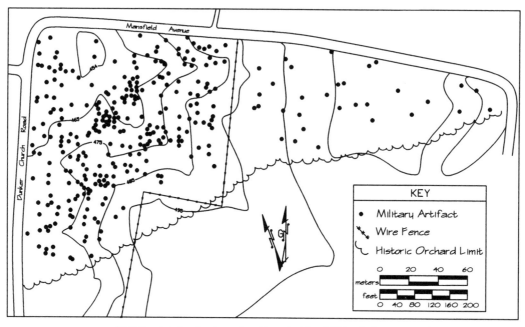

16.2. Spatial distribution of artifacts in North Woods (courtesy of the National Park Service, National Capital Region, and URS Greiner Woodward Clyde).

according to battle intensity in each area, this alone cannot account for discrepancies between the pasture area in the North Woods and the plowed portions of the North and West Woods. Throughout the Antietam survey, differences in artifact densities were often associated with differential land use. The East Woods survey area was predominantly plowed and produced a lower military artifact density. Conversely, the Mumma Orchard survey area, which produced a large number of military artifacts, was pastureland.

An exception to this trend occurred in Piper Orchard, presently equally divided between pasture and plowed fields, where the greatest percentage of artifacts came from plowed fields. This high density can be attributed to a number of factors, including topography, intensity of battle zone, and duration under Park Service stewardship. The historic Piper Orchard has been under Park Service stewardship the longest of all the survey areas. Artifact densities in the orchard provide important comparative data for examining how both land use and ownership can differently influence artifact recovery. To improve results on battlefield surveys, preliminary assessments should be made concerning the accessibility to collectors, amount of time under protective ownership, and history of agricultural use. Such an assessment can provide pertinent information to help establish appropriate field methodologies and intensity of coverage. Artifact densities identified at Antietam in protected pastures illustrate that meaningful numbers of military artifacts can still be identified at battlefield sites.

The Mumma Orchard Survey

The Mumma Orchard, less than 5 acres, is located in the central battle-field, south of the East Woods and the Miller Cornfield. This area, under Confederate control early in the battle, passed into Union hands as troops moved to the fighting at the Sunken Road. The orchard is located just north of the Mumma farmhouse and barn which were burned by Confederate forces to prevent their use by Union snipers. Although both Union and Confederate forces passed through the area, little attention was paid to the orchard in battle accounts.

Artifacts encountered during the orchard survey chiefly consisted of fired small arms and artillery ordnance attributable to either side. However, an interesting military feature was encountered in the northern third of the survey area, as evidenced by a linear concentration of dropped Union small arms ordnance and various military accoutrements indicating the location of Union troops (fig. 16.3). The identification of this feature appears to support the use of a linear transect strategy for metal detector survey on large battlefields. In this instance, the positioning of the test transects in the Mumma Orchard appear to closely parallel the troops' alignment. Identifying this artifact concentration and military feature provided an opportunity to test the effectiveness of the field methods developed for the Antietam survey. Would this linear military feature be evident if test transects were originally aligned perpendicular to it? To test this proposition, a series of supplemental transects were placed perpendicular to the test transects. The results were startling. The concentration went

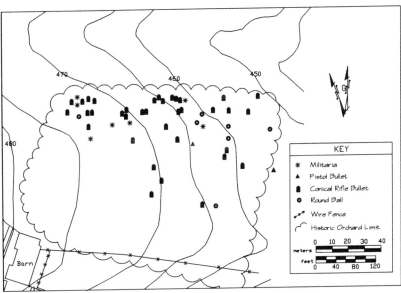

16.3. Artifact distribution in Mumma Orchard area (courtesy of the National Park Service, National Capital Region, and URS Greiner Woodward Clyde).

virtually undetected in the perpendicular transects alone. Because the narrow linear feature was composed of a loosely scattered arrangement of dropped ordnance, artifact recovery was more effective along the feature's long axis. The transects placed perpendicular to the narrow feature uncovered fewer artifacts. The nature of specific military features representing troops in formation is difficult to detect with test transects that cross perpendicular to a feature's long axis. This suggests that a survey strategy designed with transects placed perpendicular to one another would provide a more effective means of detecting linear military features. Alternatively, the most effectual methodology for battlefield survey would entail 100 percent metal detector coverage. Unfortunately, full coverage may not be the most practical method, given time and cost constraints.

The Mumma Orchard linear concentration indicates the probable location of elements of Kimball's Brigade (14th Indiana, 8th Ohio, and 7th West Virginia Regiments) on the afternoon of the battle (Antietam Battlefield Board 1904:1–5 P.M.). The archaeological imprint places Kimball's Brigade at the northern edge of the orchard, in a low wide gully with a view of the East Woods to the north and the Roulette farm to the east, both of which were Union controlled.

The orchard was the fall-back position for Kimball's Brigade, which, low on ammunition, disengaged from the struggle against Confederates in the Sunken Road. Kimball's Brigade on battle maps is on the orchard's southern edge on high ground, within view of Confederate terrain near the Sunken Road and Dunker Church (Antietam Battlefield Board 1904). Based on archaeology, the placement of Kimball's Brigade is nearly a hundred yards further north, in a low drainage area below the hillcrest. Although this is a minor spatial difference, it is a crucial tactical distinction. This position would have been a far safer location for troops shielding themselves from enemy fire. Just prior to their engagement at the Sunken Road, Kimball's Brigade stopped in a similar low spot, possibly on the nearby Roulette farm: "We passed through the yard into an orchard, where we halted and were ordered to lie down; we were now close to the line of battle engaged but owing to the formation of the land, the balls were mostly going overhead" (Rownsdale n.d.:2). Their position in the Mumma Orchard, based on the archaeological record, was chosen for the same reason, offering a respite from bullets and shells. An account from Captain Brevert of the 8th Ohio Regiment describes their position in the afternoon: "The fighting seems to rage with unabated fury. Though we are comparatively safe in our present position, every minute someone is struck" (Galway 1961). Here, even though they are still taking casualties, the position on the Mumma farm would certainly have been more secure in this low area, rather than on the hilltop shown on the battle maps.

The sometimes ambiguous and often contradictory battle accounts illustrate the difficulty in adequately tracing movements and positions of individual regiments and companies. It is necessary for researchers and

Civil War historians to take into account all available information, including archaeology, to gain an understanding of troop movements and position.

The East Woods Survey

The East Woods survey area encompassed approximately 12 acres, a small portion of the original woodlot. Located near the center of the battlefield, the woods offered cover for Union troops advancing west toward the Dunker Church and "Stonewall" Jackson's forces in the West Woods. This Union advance was composed mainly of the XII Corps under Maj. Gen. Joseph Mansfield, who was mortally wounded on the edge of the woods. The ensuing clash of Union forces against numerous Confederates including Brigadier General Hood's Texans helped transform these once peaceful woods into a raging battle zone. The cornfield and the western border of the woods may well have experienced "the most savage and consuming fighting American soldiers ever engaged in" (Catton 1962:270). The tree cover offered by the woods also served as a refuge for wounded and dying soldiers and for troops making their way to the rear to re-form under their colors, where "dead and living bodies [were] everywhere, little groups of men trying to help wounded comrades to the rear, shattered limbs of trees lying on the ground in a tangle, wreckage of artillery equipment strewn about, . . . the air alive with bullets, and streaky sheets of acrid smoke lying in the air" (Catton 1962:277). In the cornfield on the edge of the East Woods, Confederate General Hood related that "on no other field in the whole war was he so constantly troubled by the fear that his horse would step on some helpless wounded man" (Catton 1962:276).

Unlike other surveyed areas, the East Woods was subjected to heavy Confederate artillery fire (see Chapter 18) and was traversed and held by numerous units of both armies. This confusing and intense battle situation hinders analysis of the East Woods archaeological military assemblage. In addition, the mainly plowed survey area produced a relatively low artifact density, although the battle was intense. However, the variety of military material was surprisingly diverse with numerous artifacts related to clothing and accoutrements. For example, the recovery of military buttons was twice that of any other survey area. Other personal items recovered included shoulder scale fasteners, a canteen hook, a "U.S." belt buckle, gun parts, and numerous percussion caps. The concentration of personal items and accoutrements may be a battle signature associated with the carnage in this area. One veteran wrote that it was "the most terrible fire that they ever had to endure. Rifles were splintered and broken in men's hands, canteens and haversacks were riddled, platoons and companies seemed to dissolve" (Catton 1962:270). Other survey areas, though under heavy fire, did not constantly change hands and experience the intensity associated with the East Woods.

Another indication of battle intensity in the East Woods was identified during the survey. Amorphous melted lead fragments were common in the East Woods but rare in any of the other survey areas. These most likely originated from bullets or case shot balls that had been fired during the battle and had become imbedded in fences, branches, and timber. A British observer described the scene ten days after the battle: "in about 7 or 8 acres of wood there is not a tree which is not full of bullets and bits of shell. It is impossible to understand how anyone could live in such a fire as there must have been here" (McPherson 1988:331; from Luvaas 1959:18–19). The dead and useless wood left in the forest would have been eventually burned during clearing activities. Any lead ordnance embedded in this wood would melt, forming these amorphous drops.

Differentiation of Military versus Nonmilitary Artifacts

The battlefield of Antietam consists primarily of agricultural fields farmed before and after the conflict. Consequently, an inordinate number of non-military metal objects, such as nails, fence staples, fence wire, nuts, bolts, and plow parts, were recovered. Attempts were made to develop viable expeditious methods to discriminate between these metal items and military artifacts. To determine to what degree the metal detector operator and sophisticated metal detectors were able to discriminate between non-military and military artifacts, experiments were conducted using color-coded flags to distinguish different hits. For instance, the White's machines were able to locate to some degree of accuracy non-iron metal anomalies. Readings of lead, brass, copper, and zinc were often found to be military items. These anomalies were marked with orange flags. Large and dense iron objects often registered with a strong audible reading. These audible readings often denoted iron military artifacts, such as shell fragments, and were also marked with orange flags. Weak or fragmented readings—denoting probable "junk" metal anomalies, such as iron wire, nails, staples, and so forth—were designated with white flags. All flagged hits were excavated, and records were kept of the resulting items recovered for each color-coded flag. The results of these attempts at setting a viable standard for discriminating out some "junk" metal were not promising.

The recovery of military and possible military material from hits designated with orange flags was generally around 50 percent. The majority (generally over 85 percent) of the white-flagged hits proved to be "junk" metal. The recovery rate of military items from white flag designated hits ranged from 15 to 33 percent. This suggests that even experienced operators will miss a significant portion of military artifacts if operator discrimination is allowed. Because it was not possible to reliably predict whether an item was military simply by using a metal detector, it was determined that all hits should be excavated for an accurate survey.

During the Antietam survey, there were areas, often near farmsteads, which produced a large amount of metal detector background noise, indicating the probable locations of farm dumps, old wire fences, and trash concentrations along roadways. Even with a machine set at full discrimination, under these conditions, the audible signal from the machine may be more reminiscent of a Geiger counter. Such conditions were encountered at the previously unidentified Miller tenant house in the North Woods, at a 20th-century trash dump in the East Woods, and near the Mumma barn. In these areas and in the Mumma yard, attempts were made to metal detect on full discrimination with only non-iron hits flagged and recovered. The results in these instances were complete failures—no military material was recovered. Apparently, a large density of "junk" iron can mask the detector signal, effectively shielding military items.

The Piper Orchard Survey

On the day of the battle, the Piper farmhouse was the headquarters of Confederate General James Longstreet. To the north, the 18-acre Piper Orchard was situated within the Confederate center between Union forces and the Confederate-held town of Sharpsburg. The northern half of the orchard on a hilltop offered a view of the Piper cornfield and the well-worn farm lane known as the Sunken Road. Throughout the day, the Piper Orchard was under the sole control of the Confederates and functioned as a staging area for the unfortunate participants and reserves during the contest at the Sunken Road.

The first troops to engage the entrenched Confederate troops in the road were Brigadier General French's Division of the 2nd (II) Corps. They were later joined by reinforcements including General Meagher's Irish Brigade. After hours of fighting, Union forces ultimately overran the Confederate line and charged through the cornfield to the edge of the orchard. A desperate counterattack was orchestrated by Gen. D. H. Hill with musket in hand and General Longstreet directing artillery fire. The Union thrust was repelled, and the tattered Confederate center reformed around the Piper farm. General Longstreet later recounted that a final assault on his position at this time might have defeated General Lee (Catton 1962:298). In the aftermath, Union General Richardson recounts: "In [the Sunken] road there lay so many dead rebels that they formed a line which one might have walked upon as far as the eye could see" (Sears 1983:247). The earthen road was said to be stained so red with blood it was to become forever remembered as "Bloody Lane."

The systematic metal detector survey implemented in the Piper Orchard produced the largest assemblage of military artifacts recovered during the project. The majority of artifacts consisted of bullets and artillery ordnance fragments associated with the battle for Bloody Lane. Analysis of this assemblage was enhanced by the unique battle situation at the orchard. The majority of dropped bullets were attributable to Confederates, while fired bullets and artillery were associated with Union forces. This assemblage could then be compared with the artifacts recovered from the North Woods. (These analyses are presented in Chapters 17 and 18.)

Civil War Reenactments and Artifact Reproductions

During the Piper Orchard survey, a concentration of used cannon friction primers and well-preserved military buttons was recovered near the reported location of Confederate artillery batteries. However, upon closer examination these artifacts were determined to be modern reproductions. The proprietor of the Piper House, Lou Clark, confirmed that a cannon firing had been filmed for a battle documentary at this location a month prior to our survey. The implication is that reenactments, often a great educational tool, can have a negative impact on the battlefield resource. The distinction between reproductions and originals can be problematic for researchers (Clay 1990:3), and the likelihood of their presence should be taken into account during analysis.

Participation of Volunteers during the Piper Orchard Survey

An important part of the archaeological work at Antietam was incorporating non-archaeologists as volunteers during the survey. The impressive assemblage recovered from the orchard can in part be attributed to the dedication and experience of avocational enthusiasts. These volunteers were experienced in the operation of metal detectors, and many were also experts in the material culture of the Civil War. The inclusion of volunteers proved a success in the field and a benefit to the project as a whole. It is important to realize that, though traditionally at odds, professional archaeologists and avocational archaeologists or "collectors" have much to learn from each other. Without the time and dedication of these volunteers, the scope of the survey in the orchard could not have been as broad and successful. More importantly, without their expertise and knowledge, analysis of the artifact assemblage would have been less detailed. Working together offered volunteers an opportunity to observe archaeological methods of systematic excavation and recording. Archaeologists planning battlefield investigations would be well served to utilize the assistance of similar enthusiasts in their project plans.

Artifact Recovery at Antietam

During the four-year Antietam survey, more than 2,100 military and potential military artifacts were recovered. One of the most striking aspects of the artifact assemblage is the paucity of recovered military equipage and accoutrements other than bullets and artillery shot. Only a handful of military buttons, finials, a belt buckle, uniform accessories, and gun parts were identified. One possible explanation is that battlefields cover large expanses of landscape where the military presence, though intense, is relatively brief. At Antietam, the battle lasted a single day, with the majority of troops positioned on the fringes of the battlefield when not engaged. These locations were not within the scope of the archaeological survey.

The type of deposits left at a battlefield site can be contrasted with that of Civil War army encampments where more diverse artifact assemblages are present (Legg and Smith 1989). The Antietam battlefield, which was strewn with the bodies of the dead, was not favorable for army encampments; instead, those Union troops assigned to care for the dead and wounded established camps beyond the limits of the battlefield. No established military encampments were identified during the survey.

Another contributing factor to the dearth of militaria recovered is that much common military gear never made it to the battlefield. To be more effective and maneuverable in battle, infantry troops often jettisoned cumbersome supplies, which may partially explain the absence of larger artifacts recovered during the survey. At Antietam, James Dinkins of the 18th Mississippi Regiment recalled that Brigadier General Barksdale commanded that they "pitch everything except guns and cartridge boxes at this time" (Carman Papers, 1895–1902). The scene was the same for the 15th Virginia Regiment: "At daybreak on the march again, about 11 am we unsling knapsacks, pile them in a field and leave guard with them, every man fills up his canteen" (Leiter n.d.:6).

Any useful item that made it to the battlefield and was left with the wounded and dead could be requisitioned by soldiers under fire. According to Lieutenant Colonel Wilcox of the 132nd Pennsylvania Regiment: "when our ammunition gave out, the men stripped the dead and wounded of their cartridges. At length last of the ammunition was exhausted and we were ordered to fix bayonets and charge" (O'Brien 1965:63).

In the days following the battle, equipment and personal effects were buried along with the dead or were scavenged by soldiers and civilians. Many items salvaged from the field or turned out of the pockets of the dead and wounded had monetary value, such as coins, watches, weapons, shoes, uniforms, clothing, and horse tack (Griffith 1986:46). Relic hunters and farmers clearing their fields of debris removed larger military objects long before the arrival of metal detectors. What was left behind were less noticeable artifacts, shell fragments, grommets, buttons, and buckles, but mainly bullets—the most common items recovered during the survey. A local Civil War collector said that he rarely wasted his time collecting on battlefield sites because he mostly found bullets.

A large and varied number of metal artifacts were recovered that were not easily distinguished as relating to the battle. Many possible metal mili-

tary items could also be classified as farm related. These ambiguous artifacts included grommets, rivets, hooks, handles, straps, strap buckles,
horseshoes, and other tack. Certainly a portion of this collection is related
to the battle, but no specific artifacts can be distinguished as military ver-
sus agricultural. This dilemma is illustrated in the case of recovered horse
tack, which includes numerous horseshoes, and many of the buckles and
grommets. These can simply be remnants of long-term agricultural use or
can be associated with artillery horses or those used by officers. Historic
accounts after the battle relate that, "Dead horses were everywhere, and
the stench from them was horrible" (Hitchcock 1904:6). To further com-
plicate matters, many identical grommets and buckles were also part of
the infantry soldiers' military equipage on knapsacks, shoulder straps, and
so forth. Various density studies and comparisons of possible military
artifacts were conducted (both within and between survey areas) in an
attempt to distinguish between military and nonmilitary material. It was
anticipated that patterns could be discerned which related to battle conditions unique to each survey area. However, the results of these analyses
were disappointing and inconclusive.

Conclusion

Civil War battlefields have long been set aside as reminders of American
history and as vehicles for public interpretation. Archaeological research
on these battlefields is a new and ongoing process that offers a unique
opportunity for visitors, volunteers, and researchers to make a personal
connection with the past. The work at Antietam is one step in that process
that can be built upon through future studies.

One of the main objectives of this survey was to assess the effectiveness
of archaeological techniques on a large Civil War battlefield. Based on the
archaeological assessment at Antietam, it is clear that the use of traditional
archaeological methods, such as systematic shovel testing and surface collection, is completely ineffectual. The only effective means to retrieve significant data from a battlefield site is through the use of systematic metal
detector survey. The survey methods which attained a 25 percent sample
from parallel linear test transects were successful. However, there is compelling evidence that improvements can be made on these methods. A
larger sample size from transects aligned along the perpendicular axis of a
grid would provide more distinct distribution data for analysis.

Overall, the survey at Antietam was a success. The methods applied led
to the recovery of substantial and significant artifact assemblages, as well
as to the identification of a variety of discernible military features on the
landscape. The following two chapters present the interpretive results of
the research and analysis performed on small arms and artillery ordnance
recovered during the survey.

17

Archaeological Interpretations of the Battle of Antietam through Analysis of Small Arms Projectiles

Bruce B. Sterling

The American Civil War era was a period of dramatic social and political upheaval, as well as a crucial turning point in military technology. The decade preceding the conflict and the war years witnessed the most significant and rapid development of small arms and artillery weapons, or "firearms evolution," in history (Fuller 1958:1; Babits 1995:119). The development of projectiles and the weapons for which they were designed must be reviewed to appreciate the small arms assemblage recovered during the Antietam battlefield archaeological survey. This chapter will focus on the variety of projectiles, long arms, and pistols that saw action at Antietam. Following the discussion of small arms and projectiles, a detailed analysis will be presented on the significance of the bullet assemblage as a tool for interpreting the battle.

A History of Civil War Small Arms and Projectiles

Before 1855, the major tactical infantry weapon was the muzzle-loading smoothbore musket. One of the most notable achievements in weapons technology prior to the Civil War was the development of the rifled musket and expanding bullet to replace the less efficient smoothbore musket and round ball cartridge. Although rifled barreled long arms had been in use since the early 1700s, they were too cumbersome to load for use by the infantry in battle.

The advent of the expanding Minié bullet made the rifle practical for combat. The Minié bullet was invented in 1849 by Capt. Claude Minié of France. Minié replaced the round ball cartridge with an elongated conical bullet that was slightly smaller than the caliber of the rifle's barrel for easier loading. The bullet was designed with a hollow base cavity fitted with a metal wedge-shaped plug, or *culot*. Upon firing, the plug was forced deep into the base cavity, expanding the bullet to the size of the barrel and forcing the soft lead projectile to engage the rifling grooves.

This improvement decreased windage, increased velocity, and added spin to the bullet, resulting in greater range and accuracy. Minié's bullet design led to an increased effective range for the musket from a smoothbore's 100 yards to 400 yards for a rifled musket (Edwards 1962:9–16; Lewis 1956:116; Fuller 1958:4; Ommundsen and Robinson 1915:4–6, 47–48).

The American Minié ball (fig. 17.1)—the most common bullet type recovered at Antietam—was used by both armies during the war. It was developed at the U.S. Armory at Harpers Ferry following experimentation on the European Minié ball. All experiments and subsequent improvements to the bullet were made by Assistant Master Armorer James A. Burton, whose skills would later help the Confederacy's arms program at the Richmond Arsenal. The key American improvement to Minié's design was enlargement of the bullet's base cavity, which allowed the bullet to expand into the gun barrel's rifling without the use of a plug. The new bullet was also designed with three groves, or cannelures, to hold lubricant for easy loading. These grooves improved accuracy during flight and were responsible for the "solid deep toned bumble bee-like 'z-z-z-z-z-zip' that terminates in the echoing slap of the projectile at the target" (Edwards 1962:24), commonly referred to in battle histories.

Adoption and manufacture of the expanding .58-caliber conical rifle bullet necessitated development of a rifled musket for the U.S. Army. Experimentation and trials conducted at Harpers Ferry led to the U.S. Model 1855 rifle and rifle musket, commonly referred to as "Springfields." This crucial prewar program was initiated, tested, and approved by 1855, un-

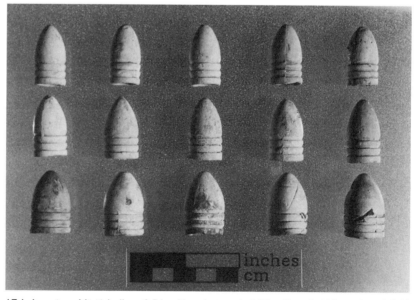

17.1. American Minié bullets: 0.54 caliber (*top row*), 0.58 caliber (*middle row*), and 0.69 caliber (*bottom row*) (courtesy of the National Park Service, National Capital Region, and URS Greiner Woodward Clyde).

der then Secretary of War Jefferson Davis (Edwards 1962:15–25; Coggins 1990:31–32; Fuller and Steuart 1944:41).

There is a dramatic difference between the battle effectiveness of the rifle musket (with a conical Minié bullet) and the smoothbore musket (with round ball). Since the 18th century, the infantry had used smoothbore muskets for close-range combat, up to 100 yards. The new rifle musket made Napoleonic tactics both obsolete and more deadly. The average Civil War infantryman suffered from the combination of technological improvements and the resistance of many field commanders to adapt tactics suited to the improved fire power and accuracy (Edwards 1962:13). This had a devastating effect on casualty rates, as illustrated by the 23,000 casualties at Antietam (Tilberg 1960:47).

In terms of weapons and supplies, both the North and South were unprepared for a protracted war. Southern governors prior to the war attempted to procure weapons for their militias, particularly new rifles. With the onset of the war, weapons procurement became crucial, and federal arsenals were seized by the Southern states. The diversity of weapons pressed into service for both armies was compounded by the growth of technological innovation. In 1863, the U.S. Army officially recognized 102 different models of long arms, as well as 19 models of pistols and revolvers (Peterson 1959:2). Many of these weapons were developed in the decade preceding the war and during the war years. The Confederates had a similar variety of weapons. Weapons diversity caused extreme pressure on ordnance and supply officers, who had to procure a variety of ammunition, since many weapons required specialized ammunition (Lewis 1956:154; Peterson 1959:1–2; Todd 1974 and 1983:734–937).

Both armies maintained ordnance and supply records, but documentation for the Union Army survived the war more intact. Like many Civil War era documents, military supply records tend to be "incomplete, contradictory, and frequently inaccurate" (Williams 1983:188, in Geier and Winter 1994:10–11). Inaccuracies in documentary records are magnified when one accounts for the unrecorded acquisition of military supplies and armaments during field campaigns. Soldiers scavenged battlefields for better guns to replace obsolete or damaged weapons. During McClellan's strategic retreat from Richmond, after the Seven Days Battle, the Union Army reportedly abandoned 30,000 small arms and 50 cannon, which were taken by the Confederates. During the first half of the war, the Confederates' battlefield successes, combined with the spoils of war, greatly contributed to their cause. By mid-1863, the Northern-produced Springfield rifle was probably the most common gun in the Southern army (Fuller and Steuart 1944:43).

The Union ordnance department worked throughout the war to supply its troops with modern weapons. In 1861, many regiments carried outdated smoothbore arms, but by 1863 almost all had rifles (McPherson

1988:475). Some historic accounts present a different situation. President Grant related in his memoirs that his troops exchanged old smoothbore .69-caliber, converted flintlocks for captured Confederate Enfield rifles at Vicksburg in 1863 (Fuller 1958:3). In July 1863, approximately 19 percent of Union soldiers at Gettysburg had smoothbore muskets, while the Confederate Army at Chickamauga in September had over 30 percent smoothbore (Griffith 1986:33).

Antietam Archaeological Bullet Assemblage

Recovering a significant assemblage of quantifiable military artifacts during the three-year archaeological survey of Antietam National Battlefield presented historical archaeologists with a unique opportunity to examine a moment in time relevant to military supply and the use of small arms by the Union Army of the Potomac and the Confederate Army of Northern Virginia. Four years of systematic metal detector survey at Antietam recovered 1,352 Civil War bullets, buckshot, and lead projectile fragments, constituting 65 percent of the identifiable military assemblage. This large bullet collection consists of 18 long arm and 6 pistol bullet types. Each bullet type and caliber can be associated with a variety of weapons. The discussion below will describe the bullet types and the most common small arms issued during the war for those bullets.

The American Minié Bullet

The most frequent bullet type recovered was the American Minié ball, which accounted for 57 percent of the bullet assemblage (fig. 17.1). Minié bullets were manufactured at a multitude of arsenals and private arms manufacturers in both the North and South. Archaeologically, distinctions between Confederate and Union Minié balls were determined by battlefield location and condition (dropped or fired).

The American Minié bullet was produced in three sizes, the most common being the standard .58-caliber, with fewer .54- and .69-caliber variants (fig. 17.1). The .58-caliber Minié ball was most commonly used in the Model 1855 and 1861 U.S.-issue rifle and rifle musket. The Springfield was the standard arm of the Union infantry, by which all other arms were judged. U.S.-issue .54-caliber muskets were also manufactured, while the .69-caliber long arms were originally manufactured as smoothbores. By Antietam, many old .69-caliber smoothbore muskets had been rifled and sighted. This conversion was accomplished either by replacing the barrels or by cutting rifling grooves into the original smoothbore barrels (Coates and Thomas 1990:11, 16, 83; Coggins 1990:31–32; Thomas 1981:20; Edwards 1962:20; and the West Point Military Museum).

The .577-caliber 1853 British Enfield rifle musket was second only to the Springfield rifle in quality, accuracy, and range (Peterson 1959:3) and was the most common foreign rifle musket imported by Union and Confederate forces. Although the Enfield rifle is a slightly smaller caliber than the standard .58-caliber rifle musket, the Minié ball could be fired from both .58- and .577-caliber guns. More than 400,000 English Enfields were imported for U.S. forces. The Confederates ordered approximately the same number, but only a portion actually made it through the Union blockade. The Enfield rifle was so popular that private arms manufacturers from the North and South reproduced it (Edwards 1962:31).

In addition to these popular arms, other American-made and imported weapons were employed by the Union and Confederate armies. These included the U.S. Model 1841 ("Mississippi") rifle, originally manufactured to fire a .54-caliber round ball; and the imported 1854 Austrian "Lorenz" rifle musket, the second most common imported long arm of the war, manufactured in both .58 and .54 calibers (Coates and Thomas 1990:21). Both weapons could fire the conical hollow-based expanding Minié balls.

The Round Ball Cartridge

At Antietam, cartridges for obsolete .69-caliber smoothbore muskets, most commonly the U.S. Model 1842 musket, were well represented by recovery of both single round ball and compound buck and ball cartridges (fig. 17.2). Both cartridges employed a spherical lead ball (measuring ap-

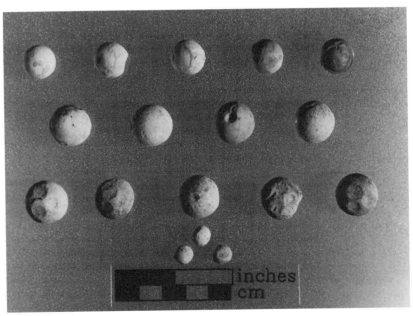

17.2. Round ball cartridges: 0.54 caliber (*top row*); 0.69 caliber single ball (*middle row*), and 0.69 caliber buck and ball with three buckshot (*bottom row*) (courtesy of the National Park Service, National Capital Region, and URS Greiner Woodward Clyde).

proximately .645–.65 inches in diameter), but the buck and ball cartridge contained an additional three smaller buck shot (measuring .31 inches in diameter) wrapped atop the larger round ball. The multiple shot buck and ball cartridge converted the smoothbore musket into a shotgun, and it was considered more effective and deadly than the single ball cartridge.

Dropped buck and ball cartridges are distinguished from single cartridges by three small marks left on the larger ball by the buckshot from the packaging. However, faint buckshot impressions are not always discernable, possibly masked by corrosion or patina on the ball. In the collection, fired buck and ball cartridges were more easily distinguished from fired single round ball cartridges because the buck and ball shot is uniquely disfigured when fired. The .69-caliber ball exhibits three exaggerated indents where the smaller buckshot is forced into the larger soft lead ball when fired. In addition, the fired buck and ball cartridge displays a distinct, impressed "firing ring" around the circumference of the larger round ball. The firing ring is evidence of the disfigured ball's tight passage through the musket barrel after the musket was fired. The ability to distinguish single round ball from buck and ball cartridges in the Antietam analysis did indicate a significant trend. A larger number of buck and ball cartridges were attributed to Union forces than to Confederate forces, suggesting that Union troops, although not as abundantly supplied with smoothbore muskets, were better supplied with the more efficient compound cartridges.

In addition to the .69-caliber cartridges, there were .54-caliber round balls originally intended for use in the U.S. Model 1841 Mississippi rifle prior to the development of the Minié cartridge. The smaller round balls could also be fired from .54- and .55-caliber foreign rifle muskets (Coates and Thomas 1990; Thomas 1993 and 1997).

The Williams Cleaner Bullet

Archaeological data and historic documentation indicate that the .58-caliber Williams Cleaner bullets recovered at Antietam were the only bullets employed solely by the Union Army (fig. 17.3). The cleaner bullet was developed and patented on May 13, 1862, by Elijah D. Williams in Philadelphia (Thomas 1997:211). The bullet was designed with a flat, solid base with protruding pin which held two or more zinc discs. Originally the disks were intended to "destroy" windage and add rotary motion to the projectile, giving the shot greater range and penetration than the standard ball. Ultimately, the Williams bullets gained a reputation as "cleaner" bullets. Upon firing, the discs were forced through the barrel, scraping the interior, freeing it of black powder build-up, or "fouling." Williams bullets were packaged with the standard .58-caliber Miniés, at least one to a bundle of ten cartridges (Thomas 1981:16 and 1997:211–25). Historic accounts suggest that the troops distrusted the cleaner bullet because they

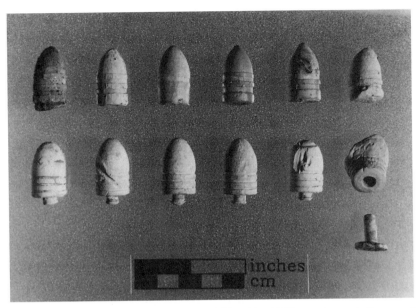

17.3. 0.52 caliber Sharps bullet (*top row*); 0.58 caliber Williams cleaner bullet type I (*bottom row*); type II with pin at far right (courtesy of the National Park Service, National Capital Region, and URS Greiner Woodward Clyde).

feared its odd construction would cause the gun to jam. This assertion is supported by archaeological evidence from the 1864 Battle of Franklin, Tennessee, where unfired cleaner bullets were found in disproportionate numbers at the location of Union positions (Samuel Smith 1994:70–73). However, based on the Antietam archaeological survey, there is no evidence that Union troops were prejudiced against the Williams bullets. No disproportionate concentration of dropped cleaner bullets was recovered from Union-held positions at the battlefield.

The Sharps Breech-Loading Bullet

Breech-loading weapons, popular with cavalry and sharpshooters, are advantageous for their ease and speed of loading without a ramrod (fig. 17.3). Civil War ordnance records indicate that more than 20 different brands of breech-loading carbines and rifles were available in September 1862. With few exceptions, each gun required its own unique ammunition. The only identifiable breech-loading cartridge recovered at Antietam was the .52-caliber Sharps bullet for the Sharps rifle and carbine (fig. 17.3). The Sharps system was developed by Christian Sharps and first issued to the U.S. Army in 1854 (Coates and Thomas 1990:34 and 45). The Sharps bullet, unlike the muzzle-loading Minié, was designed to be slightly larger than the gun barrel. Because breech-loading bullets fit tightly in the base of the barrel, there is no need for expansion, and a solid, rather than hollow, base design was used (Coates and Thomas 1990; Tho-

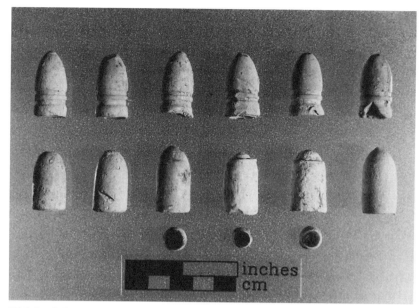

17.4. Confederate bullets: 0.58 caliber Gardner bullet (*top row*); 0.577 caliber Enfield with three boxwood plugs (*bottom row*) (courtesy of the National Park Service, National Capital Region, and URS Greiner Woodward Clyde).

mas and Thomas 1996:26–28). Sharps cartridges, found in limited numbers in all areas surveyed, were attributed to both Union and Confederate forces.

Confederate Bullets

Two distinct bullet types, the Gardner and the Enfield, were manufactured in the South and used solely by Confederates. Both Confederate bullet types were found during the Antietam survey.

The Gardner Bullet

The Gardner projectile, patented in the South on August 17, 1861, by Frederick J. Gardner, was of unique manufacture with a powder charge wrapped in paper crimped to the base of the bullet (fig. 17.4). Recovered in both .54 and .58 calibers, the bullet had a cylindro-conical form, similar to a Minié ball, with a hollow base that expanded without a plug and with only two wide flat rings encircling the base.

The Enfield Bullet

The .577 Enfield (often referred to as a Pritchett) is a smooth-sided, ringless conical bullet developed in England in 1853 specifically for the Enfield rifle. Although both sides imported Enfield rifles, only the Southern army purchased and produced the distinct smooth-sided ammunition. The main difference between imported and domestic Enfield bullets was that the British variety employed a boxwood plug and consequently utilized a large plug-shaped cavity, while the Confederate bullets were manufactured with a smaller base cavity without a plug (Thomas 1981:35; Thomas and Thomas 1996:69; Thomas 1993 and 1997).

Miscellaneous Bullets

The Antietam assemblage included several other imported bullet types, including three Italian-style "Carcanos," one French-style Minié with a triangular base cavity, one .69-caliber Belgian, and one Austrian-style Minié bullet. All of these examples were found in Confederate contexts and may have been imported or manufactured in the South with foreign molds (Thomas 1993, 1997; Dean Thomas, personal communication, 1998). In addition, two long, conical fired bullets of .44–.45-caliber attributable to Confederate fire may be "Picket" bullets, which were used in "Kentucky" or "Pennsylvania" rifles or in various sharpshooting rifles (Thomas and Thomas 1996:59).

Pistol Bullets

A small percentage of the bullet assemblage was identified as pistol bullets, indicating that most fighting at Antietam was conducted by infantry using muskets as their primary weapon. Pistols and revolvers were usually reserved for line officers and cavalrymen for defensive purposes during close combat. The pistol bullets can be divided into three general categories. The most common type was the .36-caliber round ball for single shot pistols. The remainder of the collection consists of .36- and .44-caliber conical pistol shot. As with breech-loading rifles, the conical pistol bullet was designed with a diameter slightly larger than the caliber of the barrel. Because these were not expanding bullets, they exhibit a flat base rather than a hollow cavity. The .36- and .44-caliber pistol bullets were most commonly used in the Model 1851 Colt "Navy" revolver (.36 caliber) and the Model 1860 Colt "Army" revolver (.44 caliber). However, all pistol bullet varieties could have been fired from a variety of handguns with the proper caliber.

Bullet Assemblage Analysis

Historical research indicated that many types of small arms were used during the Civil War period. However, the archaeological record from Antietam did not support this interpretation. The assemblage reflects a relatively uniform collection of arms and ammunition, with both armies largely dependent on standard weaponry. While the Union was better supplied with rifles, both North and South continued to use older smoothbore muskets. It is possible that many innovations in weaponry had yet to reach the Army of the Potomac and the Army of Northern Virginia by the time of Antietam. Ten months later, at Gettysburg, there was a greater diversity of weaponry present on both sides, including a larger number of breech-loading arms, as well as a greater variety of projectiles including sectional and exploding bullets (Thomas 1981).

Bullets recovered from archaeological work at Antietam are better understood when viewed within the context of the battle. In addition, it is important to assess the weapons reportedly issued to individual regiments engaged in each area of the battlefield. The remainder of this chapter will address the small arms assemblage from specific battlefield locations and weaponry documented as supplied to troops engaged in those locations.

The North Woods Assemblage

The North Woods, located at the battlefield's northern limits, functioned as a staging area for General Hooker's I Corps' advance against the Confederate left. Documentary evidence indicates Confederate troops did not occupy or pass through the woods. Based on the documentary record, it was surmised that unfired bullets recovered from the North Woods were attributable to Union forces and fired bullets ascribed to Confederate. Dropped bullets recovered from the survey area support this interpretation. No dropped bullets were of Confederate manufacture. The bullet assemblage derived from this distinct troop deployment allowed a comparison between dropped Union bullets recovered archaeologically with documentary evidence detailing the supply of weapons to units engaged in the North Woods. Together, supply documents and archaeology provide a test of the effectiveness of systematic metal detector survey.

Troop strength figures were compiled from regimental files at the Antietam National Battlefield library. To document weapons supply at Antietam, figures from the "Summary Statements of Quarterly Returns of Ordnance and Ordnance Stores on Hand in Regular and Volunteer Army Organizations 1862–1867" (for the Federal troops) were reviewed at the National Archives in Washington, D.C. Unfortunately, this source's earliest 1862 data are for the last quarter and represent regimental supply compiled more than two months after Antietam.

Nevertheless, supply estimates for Union troops engaged in the North Woods at the Sunken Road and Piper Orchard were calculated for comparative purposes. During the course of this investigation, it was noted that supply records list the small arms of each regiment, each regiment's ammunition stores, and the number and caliber of soldiers' cartridge boxes. For many regiments, ammunition varieties and cartridge box sizes reported in the records were not consistent with official regimental small arms inventory. Such discrepancies are a more likely indication of the small arms a regiment was actually carrying prior to filing fourth-quarter returns. This assumption is based on official reports of periodic resupply and from battlefield capture or scavenging of small arms. Since available Union quarterly returns are not complete for the early war period and do

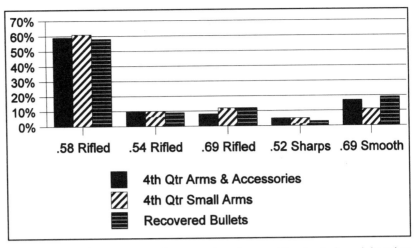

17.5. North Woods, comparison of recovered small arms with estimated supply based on 4th quarter ordnance records (courtesy of URS Greiner Woodward Clyde).

not correspond specifically to September 1862, a generalized comparison of supply estimates was warranted, one based on small arms and another on small arms and related equipment. Figure 17.5 presents the ratio of recovered, dropped Union bullets to two 1862 fourth-quarter regimental supply estimates.

Union Bullets

Comparing the three data sets for Union regiments reportedly engaged in the North Woods was astonishing. Figures for recovered dropped bullets from the North Woods are generally within 2 to 4 percent of the supply estimates for each bullet variety, except smoothbore .69-caliber round balls. Supply figures compiled from quarterly returns using only small arms weapons reported in December 1862 suggest a decline in smoothbore muskets after the battle. Estimates incorporating arms and related equipment are closer to the North Woods bullet assemblage, indicating a correlation with change of supply over time. This is consistent with expectations, through time, that veteran soldiers, who were initially issued smoothbore weapons, would upgrade to rifles through any official or unofficial means possible. The favorable results of this comparison indicate that the archaeological survey bullet assemblage is reflective of actual arms supplied to regiments in the field.

Confederate Bullets

It was not possible to conduct a similar comparison between fired Confederate bullets recovered from the North Woods with estimated Southern weapons supply. The reason is a lack of surviving Confederate regimental ordnance supply records and accurate regimental strength figures. In addition, it was impossible to determine, specifically, the Confederate regi-

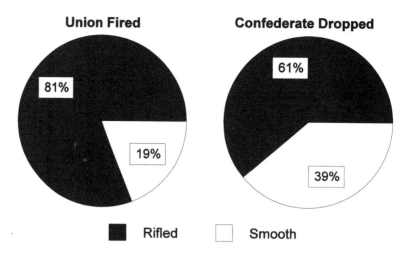

Union Fired

81%

19%

Confederate Dropped

61%

39%

■ Rifled   □ Smooth

17.6. North Woods, comparison of recovered Union and Confederate rifled to smooth-bore small arms (courtesy of URS Greiner Woodward Clyde).

ments positioned within range of the North Woods who were actively engaged against advancing Union troops.

Despite these obvious problems, a case can be made that the recovered, fired Confederate bullets from the North Woods are representative of general Confederate arms at Antietam. This assumption is based on a comparison of Confederate bullet assemblages from the North Woods and Piper Orchard; the two collections are nearly identical, with only a 2 percent differential in the ratio between rifled to smoothbore bullets. The similarity suggests that battlefield archaeological deposits are representative of original depositions. This is further substantiated by correlating Union supply estimates with the recovery of Union bullets in the North Woods.

Comparison between rifled arms and smoothbore muskets, demonstrated with the North Woods assemblage (fig. 17.6), suggests that Union forces were more adequately supplied with the superior rifled muskets than were their Confederate counterparts. The Union weapons ratio in the North Woods collection is four rifled to one smoothbore bullet. The Confederate ratio of rifled to smoothbore bullets, based on both archaeological assemblages, is three to two. These figures are consistent with a consensus among Civil War historians that Union troops were better supplied with modern weapons. Here, for the first time, is supporting archaeological evidence illustrating this disparity. It must be understood that this data reflects only the armies engaged at Antietam in September 1862. Further archaeological research conducted at other Civil War battlefields is likely to show variation in small arms supplies as the war progressed.

A closer look at the fired Confederate bullet assemblage recovered from the North Woods raises the question of how close the Confederate line or skirmishers advanced toward the woodlot. Numerous fired round balls were recovered deep within the confines of the original North Woods (fig. 17.7). Historic documentation indicates that the early morning Union advance through the North Woods toward the D. R. Miller farm and cornfield was under fire from Confederate forces located near the Miller house. However, the Confederate troops were forced to withdraw because of the superior numbers of the Union advance. The northernmost reported Confederate troop movement was to the Miller farmyard, approximately 400 yards south of the North Woods. This location is well beyond the 100-yard range of smoothbore muskets.

The recovery of six fired pistol bullets from the North Woods produces additional doubt about the accuracy of reported Confederate positions. The spent pistol rounds identified in the North Woods were unlikely to have been fired from the Miller farm. While six pistol bullets may not seem like many, they represent a disproportionate number compared with the remainder of the pistol bullets recovered from the battlefield. The fired North Woods pistol bullets represent nearly one-third of all identifiable pistol bullets (Union and Confederate, dropped or fired) recovered during the entire battlefield survey.

Pistols are generally carried by line officers and employed primarily at close range for defensive purposes when "tactical disintegration" occurs (Paul Chiles, personal communication, 1997). Do these recovered fired pistol bullets, combined with fired .69-caliber round balls, suggest a Southern incursion near the North Woods? Let us look at the various possibilities. It is feasible that the bullets are evidence of a brief fire fight which may have occurred in this area the evening before the battle as General Hooker's forces took their position. Brief flare-ups and picket fire were reported during the evening, alerting General Jackson of Hooker's

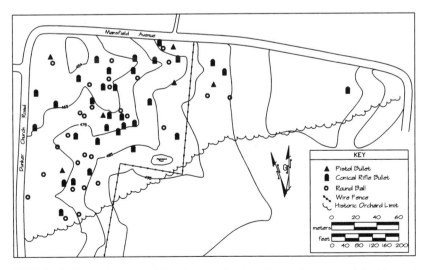

17.7. North Woods, location of Confederate fired small arms (courtesy of the National Park Service, National Capital Region, and URS Greiner Woodward Clyde).

presence (Longstreet 1896). However, accounts of these sporadic fire fights are vague and mostly associated with troops passing along the eastern edge of the East Woods. Any gunfire from the evening of the 16th was considered minor and not as likely to leave a distinct battle signature in comparison with the main battle. In order to evaluate evidence suggested by the archaeological assemblage in the North Woods, the historic documentation for this area bears closer examination.

The Carman-Cope battle maps (Carman and Cope 1904: 10:30 A.M.) indicate an incursion of Confederate troops, the 24th North Carolina, past Stuart's Artillery on Nicodemus Hill, approaching the North Woods from the southwest. This incursion, based on the maps, advanced to a point near the southwest edge of the North Woods, west of the Hagerstown Pike, well outside the archaeological survey area and beyond a range which could adequately explain the density of pistol bullets recovered during the survey. Movements and location of the 24th North Carolina at Antietam are vague. According to the brigade commander, Gen. Robert Ransom, Jr., the 24th Regiment, "on the extreme left, had come upon the enemy and opened fire" and thus became separated from the brigade. Ransom and the remainder of the brigade also engaged Union forces and drove them from the West Woods. However, they were soon engaged in a counterattack: "I now went to recall the Twenty-fourth, which had passed on and which had been directed, as I afterward learned, by General [J. E. B.] Stuart, to occupy a position near the extreme left, but, finding that it was far away, returned" (Jordan 1979:247–48). This general account does not offer specifics pertaining to the regiment's battlefield location or any possible engagement in or near the North Woods. In an attempt to further clarify the 24th North Carolina's position during the battle, the original Ezra Carman correspondence (1895–1902) with veterans was searched for accounts pertaining to the regiment's positions and movements in this portion of the battlefield.

The Carman correspondence, which includes his personal notes about specific troop positions, contains three separate accounts of the 24th North Carolina near Nicodemus Hill and the North Woods. It is unclear whether these separate accounts are from veterans' interviews conducted by Carman or interpretations of letters received by him. In short, these very similar accounts indicate that the 24th North Carolina marched with Semmes's Brigade (rather than Ransom's) and that they became separated from the brigade near the West Woods. As they marched north to Nicodemus Hill, they came under the command of General Stuart. The 24th North Carolina was ordered ahead to dislodge the enemy from a stone fence.

> From this point it [24th North Carolina] moved in same direction 400 or 500 yards beyond any other troops into a cornfield and was supported by a Petersburg battery.

Immediately north of this was a large grove. In our front the enemy had a battery from which was received a severe shelling late in the evening.

One account reports that the regiment "charged so far that it had to remain and come out under cover of the night." That evening, General Stuart is reported to have congratulated the regiment "on making the gallant charge of the war" (Carman 1895–1902).

Carman interpreted the 24th North Carolina's position on his maps as advancing past the Nicodemus farm to the southwestern edge of the North Woods (Carman and Cope 1904: 10:30 A.M.). This position is west of Hagerstown Pike, approximately 200 yards west of the North Woods survey area. Carman's interpretation of this advance is only half as far as the 400 or 500 yards described in the account. Carman makes a conservative interpretation of the Confederate regiment's northern advance. A more liberal interpretation might place the Confederate forces closer to the North Woods, and this could explain the concentration of short-range pistol and smoothbore musket bullets recovered. The 24th North Carolina is reported to have been supplied solely with .69-caliber smoothbore muskets (Todd 1974).

Further examination of the Carman papers uncovered a letter from an officer with Semmes's Brigade, the same brigade which the 24th North Carolina appears to have been attached to. In the letter, Lt. William L. Smith, 15th Virginia, states that he and his men were on the extreme left of General Lee's army, placing them near Stuart's artillery on Nicodemus Hill. His recollection of their participation in the battle recounts a northerly advance against enemy forces to the base of a wooded hill:

> After dislodging the yanks from the wall we drove them about 3/4 of a mile northwardly, they make numerous stands behind stone walls in the distance and a final stand in a body of timberland upon an elevated ridge or hill from which we could not dislodge them in our weak condition. We were protected by a stone wall that ran along this hill a little distance from the base. . . . Our hardest fighting came where the enemy made his third stand and about midway from the point of starting and this hill at which we were held in check.

Smith adds that they were supported by a battery (he believes Manly's North Carolina Battery) to his left about 200 yards that "kept up a fire upon the woods for some time" (Carman 1895–1902).

Although the Carman-Cope maps do not specifically indicate the location of the 15th Virginia or Manly's North Carolina Battery, Semmes's Brigade is shown advancing south of Miller's farm (Carman and Cope 1904: 9–9:30 A.M.) and falling back to positions north of the West Woods soon afterward (Carman and Cope 1904: 10:30 A.M.). Lieutenant Smith is unclear as to where his narrative begins. However, his description of engaging the enemy and pushing them back "northwardly" about 3/4 of a mile over numerous stone walls to a wooded hillside, suggests a location further north of where Carman placed Semme's Brigade. The wooded hillside held by the Union does not match a location near the Miller barn west of Hagerstown Pike. Rather, the wooded hillside might be interpreted as the edge of the North Woods. In fact, Lieutenant Smith returned a copy of the battlefield map Carman sent him to mark his position and movements. Smith's markings and notations indicate that he believed he and his company of the 15th Virginia crossed Hagerstown Pike and engaged the enemy on the southern edge of the North Woods. Smith notes that their furthest advance was to the southeastern corner of the North Woods. He also indicates their fallback position, where they experienced their "hardest fighting," near the point Carman interprets as their northernmost position on the battlefield.

All these accounts are supportive of the archaeological evidence of a northern incursion of Confederate forces near the North Woods beyond the Miller farm. A concentration of dropped Union bullets (and additional military material) located on a hill slope in the southwest corner of the North Woods survey area appears to add to this interpretation. The location of the bullet concentration appears to correspond with Smith's account of a skirmish between the 15th Virginia and Union forces on a wooded hill slope. If this dropped bullet concentration is evidence of a Union skirmish line, the location of the six fired Confederate pistol bullets recovered from the North Woods supports this interpretation. Four of the six pistol bullets were recovered along a straight line of trajectory from the southwest (the most likely position of a Confederate advance) through the Union concentration area. A fifth pistol bullet deviates only a fraction from that line, while the sixth is off the trajectory to the north.

The importance of battlefield archaeology is exemplified by findings in the North Woods. Individual lines of evidence, such as the historical record, fired pistol and musket bullets, and a concentration of Union military equipment, provide circumstantial evidence for a close engagement near the North Woods. Together, however, the historical and archaeological evidence provides a compelling case supporting this interpretation. To substantiate the existence of a Confederate incursion near the North Woods, an expanded archaeological metal detector investigation is necessary. The lack of any dropped Confederate bullets within the North Woods survey area indicates that Southern troops did not actually progress that far. Additional metal detector investigations, concentrated to the south and southwest, might produce irrefutable evidence of a Confederate advance. The identification of dropped Confederate bullets would indicate the exact location of Southern regiments near the North Woods.

The Piper Orchard Assemblage

On September 17, the Piper farmhouse was General Longstreet's headquarters, with the Piper Orchard to the north situated within the Confederate center. During the battle, the Piper Orchard was tactically opposite the North Woods. The orchard was under the sole control of the Confederates and served as a staging area for participants and reserves in the fight at the Sunken Road. A late Union advance through and past the Sunken Road stalled in the Piper cornfield because of a valiant Confederate rally. The Confederate center held, and Union troops were effectively kept out of the orchard. Piper dropped bullets were attributed to Confederates, while fired bullets were associated with Union forces engaged against the Sunken Road.

Union Bullets

Archaeological testing of the orchard recovered a total of 839 bullets and buckshot, by far the greatest collection of small arms projectiles from the battlefield. A comparison between Union bullets from Piper and those from the North Woods indicated a rise in the use of obsolete smoothbores. Nearly one-third of the fired shot from Piper Orchard were round shot (primarily buck and ball) compared with less than 20 percent Union round ball in the North Woods. Figure 17.8 demonstrates the difference between estimated arms supply to Union troops engaged against the Sunken Road (U.S. National Archives, Statements of Quarterly Returns 1862–67) and the same supply, based on archaeologically recovered bullets. Again there is a discrepancy—the large percentage of ordnance for smoothbore muskets does not fully correspond with the estimated supply figures. A partial explanation for this discrepancy is that supply estimates are based on all

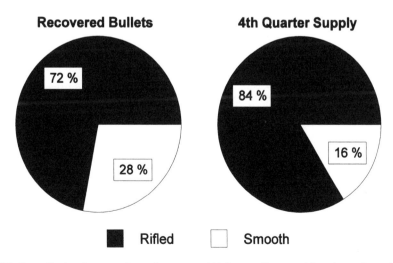

17.8. Piper Orchard, comparison of recovered Union small arms with estimated supply (courtesy of URS Greiner Woodward Clyde).

possible Union regiments engaged against the Confederates in the Sunken Road. Because of the length of the Union line, not all Union regiments would have fired directly against positions along the Sunken Road, with the Piper Orchard as a backdrop. Of critical interpretive importance is the question of which specific regiments would have been positioned to fire in the direction of the Piper Orchard.

The most plausible explanation for the high percentage of fired buck and ball cartridges in the Piper Orchard is the presence of Brig. Gen. Thomas F. Meagher's Irish Brigade in the struggle for the Sunken Road. The Irish Brigade was famous for its use of .69-caliber buck and ball cartridges. Unlike other regiments, the Irish Brigade used smoothbore muskets because the weapon was the preferred choice of its commander, General Meagher. The buck and ball cartridge had a distinct advantage over a single ball cartridge and the rifled musket in close range combat. A buck and ball cartridge is composed of a .69-caliber round ball packed with three smaller (.30-caliber) buckshot. Buck and ball are not necessarily more accurate, but when fired at close range, four balls have a better chance of hitting a target. While buckshot may not be as deadly as the larger round ball, any wound—no matter how small—increased the chances of disabling an enemy soldier. A red badge of courage, no matter how slight, can satisfy honor and permit a combatant to leave the front lines (Bilby 1995; Conyngham 1994; Goble 1997; Wright 1992).

The smoothbore musket loaded with buck and ball was best suited for General Meagher's style of battle; he expected his men to fight at "very close quarters" (Bilby 1995:182). The ultimate goal of Meagher's tactics was to push his brigade close enough to the enemy line to inflict enough casualties to allow for a bayonet charge, overwhelm the opposition, and take their position—classic Napoleonic tactics. Historic accounts place the Irish Brigade toward the left flank of the Union battle line within 30 yards of Confederates in the Sunken Road and nearly opposite the Piper Orchard. The high percentage of fired buck and ball shot in the Piper Orchard archaeological collection also pays tribute to the tenacity of the Irish Brigade during the battle at Antietam.

Confederate Bullets

Dropped Confederate bullets from the Piper Orchard were concentrated in the northern portion of the field on high ground overlooking the Sunken Road (fig. 17.9). During the battle, Confederate reserves (reinforcements from General Anderson's Division) were positioned in the orchard and cornfield. Here, reinforcements were fired upon by Union forces from General French's Brigade, reportedly in frustration over their inability to dislodge Confederate defenders from the Sunken Road (Sears 1983:241). Gen. Richard Anderson, who led the reinforcements, was mortally wounded and unable to place his division in position. Only one

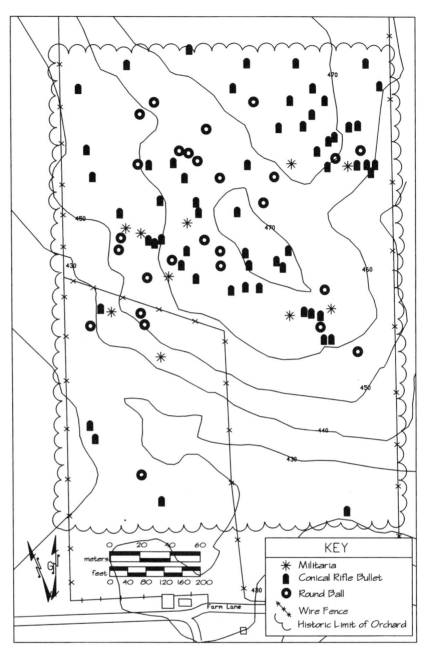

17.9. Piper Orchard, location of dropped Confederate small arms ordnance (courtesy of URS Greiner Woodward Clyde).

of Anderson's Brigades advanced to the Sunken Road, while the rest of the division was reportedly in disarray and without orders, scattered throughout the Piper Orchard and cornfield.

Dropped Confederate bullets in the Piper Orchard are concentrated on the northern hilltop with a commanding view of the Sunken Road. The dropped bullets are somewhat haphazardly distributed over the hilltop and represent no distinct battle line feature. The scattered arrangement of dropped Confederate bullets supports documentation of troops not in an organized battle formation. Confederate troops in the orchard likely took advantage of undulating terrain and natural "lines of cover" as protection from the rain of Union small arms and artillery fire. Any protection was short lived, as Confederate reserves made repeated attempts to join the defense in the Sunken Road and became targets of Union fire as they ran down the hill through the Piper cornfield. A Union soldier, who feared a Confederate bayonet charge from the crest of the hill, stated, "we did our best to kill them all before they could reach the ditch. It was truly pitiful to watch them tumble as they came down the slope" (Rownsdale n.d.:3). Union fire was directed at Confederate reserves not only as they came down the hill but also as they turned to retreat: "Many of the rebels when they had tried to leave the field, sometimes as many as twenty would spring to their feet and start to their rear then such another tumbling as would take place, was pitiful to see I am certain that not one of them ever got fifty steps away" (Rownsdale n.d.:5). When the Federals finally drove the Confederates from the Sunken Road, they advanced up the hill toward the orchard. One Union soldier recounted:

> We advance into the cornfield and up the ridge. We get to the crest. Over beyond the ravine is Sharpsburg, Lee's headquarters. Right in front of us, a mere stones throw away, is an orchard where Stonewall Jackson [probably General Hill] has been all day, and where he is now urging his men against us. But now as we look down the hill, which has a very gradual descent, we see two fresh lines of Confederates advancing towards us. We have but three rounds left to the man. The order is to retire slowly. (Galway 1961:44)

These early Union attempts to advance into the Confederate-held orchard failed.

The Charge of the 7th Maine

Confederates in Piper Orchard did not retain sole control of the orchard throughout the day. There was one brief Union intrusion into the orchard during the battle—the ill-fated charge of the 7th Maine. Around 5 P.M., after fighting at Bloody Lane died down and the Confederates fell back, the commander of the 7th Maine, Maj. Thomas Hyde, was ordered to "dislodge some of the enemy annoying our batteries . . . and drive them from the trees and buildings" at Piper farm (Scott 1887:412). Major Hyde was later to recount this order, "resultant from no plan or design from headquarters, but from an inspiration of John Barleycorn in our Brigade Commander alone" (Hyde 1894:104). In response, the 7th Maine quickly crossed the Piper pasture west of the orchard, reaching the haystacks by the Piper barn where they came under enemy fire. The regiment turned to retreat through a fence into the orchard. Once in the orchard, "the twigs and branches of the apple trees were being cut off by musket balls, and were dropping in a shower" around the men (Hyde 1894:102). The entire incident took only 30 minutes, but the 7th Maine suffered heavy casualties: only 81 of the original 181 officers and men survived what was described as the deepest incursion "into rebel lines than any Union Regiment that day" (Hyde 1894:104; Antietam Battlefield Board Map 1904: 5:00 P.M.).

Archaeological evidence of this incursion into Confederate-held Piper farm and orchard is apparent through the distribution of fired bullets. Three Confederate bullet types could be distinguished from the fired Union bullet assemblage: Enfield, Gardner, and Carcano bullets were attributed to Confederate fire. The distribution of these fired Confederate bullets follows the path of the 7th Maine through the orchard as described in historic accounts (fig. 17.10).

The archaeological imprint of Confederate fire is also represented by fired smoothbore round balls, not the compound buck and ball cartridges used by the Union. The differential ballistics between the two types of cartridges suggests that the buck and ball has superior range over the single round ball cartridge. A buck and ball cartridge is loaded into the musket with all three buck shot facing out. When fired, the force created pushes the smaller buckshot against the larger soft lead ball. Essentially, the buckshot performs the same function on the round ball as the base plug performs on the original European expanding bullets, expanding the larger ball and decreasing windage. With windage reduced, the tighter-fitting ball is shot through the barrel with greater force and distance than the loose-fitting single round ball cartridge. The same process that expands the ball also deforms it, making the ball less aerodynamic and more likely to stray from the intended trajectory.

Given the ballistics of the compound buck and ball cartridge, it was not surprising to find many examples in the orchard near the Piper farm, up to 600 yards from the main Union line and well beyond the reported effective range of the musket. The recovery of fired single shot round balls was a surprise. Typically, when fired from a smoothbore musket, at a height of 5 feet, on average the round ball would hit the ground after traveling only 120 yards (Fuller 1958:3). It is no coincidence that all fired single shot round ball cartridges in the southern half of the orchard were only retrieved among the fired Confederate rifle bullets (fig. 17.11), providing an enhanced representation of the retreat of the 7th Maine through the orchard. In this instance, the archaeological record is consistent with battle accounts. The resulting imprint reveals a trail of lead shot culminating in a concentration at the crest of the hill. This location is described by Major Hyde, who "marched the regiment by the left flank, formed them on a crest in the orchard, poured a volley into those who were endeavoring to

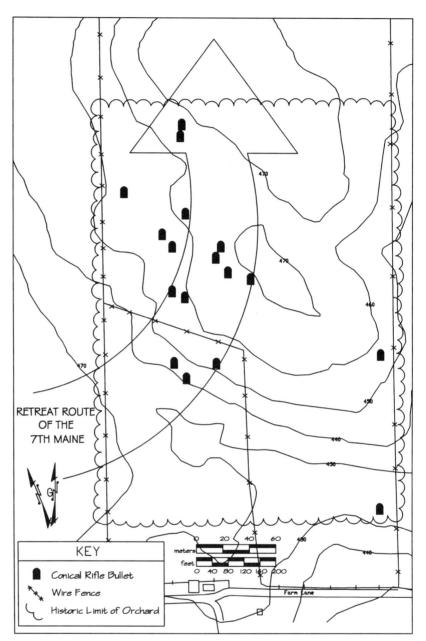

17.10. Piper Orchard, location of fired Confederate rifled small arms ordnance (courtesy of URS Greiner Woodward Clyde).

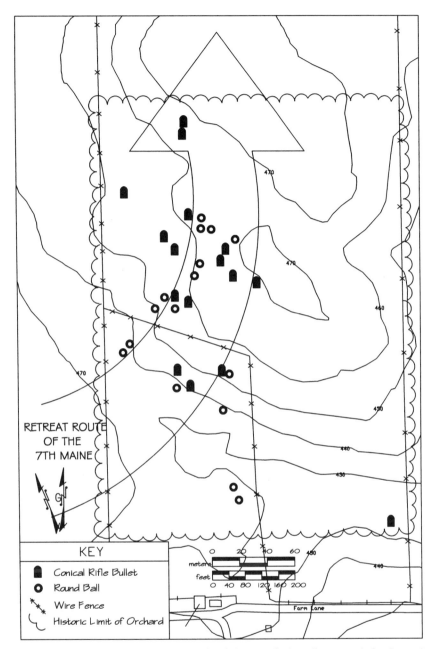

KEY

■ Conical Rifle Bullet
○ Round Ball
✕✕✕ Wire Fence
⌒⌒ Historic Limit of Orchard

RETREAT ROUTE
OF THE
7TH MAINE

Farm Lane

17.11. Piper Orchard, location of fired Confederate rifled small arms with fired round balls (courtesy of URS Greiner Woodward Clyde).

cut off our retreat, and faced those in front. Here we received a severe fire from three directions, and the enemy advanced in force" (Scott 1887:413). It is precisely this type of battle feature that can be detected archaeologically and then used to enhance or offer an alternate interpretation to battle events, especially in other, more poorly documented circumstances.

The Mumma Orchard Assemblage

The Mumma Orchard is located in the center of the battlefield south of the East Woods and the Miller cornfield. This section of the battlefield was under Confederate control early in the battle and passed into Union hands as troops moved through the area en route to the Sunken Road. A military feature in the orchard, encountered through archaeological study (chapter 16), offers a unique opportunity to analyze a specific collection of bullets (fig. 16.3). The military feature consists of a linear concentration of dropped Union small arms ordnance located in the northern third of the orchard survey area. This feature represents the location of three Union regiments of Sumner's 2nd Corps on the afternoon of the battle. These regiments from General Kimball's Brigade included the 14th Indiana, 8th Ohio, and 7th West Virginia (Carman and Cope 1904: 1–5:30 P.M.). The feature's location was a fall-back position for the brigade, which, low on ammunition, disengaged from the struggle against the Confederates in the Sunken Road.

With the linear military feature reasonably associated with elements of Kimball's Brigade, can the artifacts be linked to a specific regiment(s) through the use of military supply records? The artifact concentration consisted primarily of dropped bullets, two Union eagle buttons, and several miscellaneous military items. Because dropped bullets were the most prevalent and diagnostic artifact class of the feature, a comparison was made between the percentage of dropped rifle and smoothbore bullets and the estimated supply of Kimball's regiments. The Carman Cope battle maps indicated that the 7th West Virginia Regiment was positioned in the Mumma pasture to the east, outside the orchard survey area. The 8th Ohio and the 14th Indiana were placed along the southern orchard edge. The 7th West Virginia and the 14th Indiana carried solely .58-caliber rifles, while the 8th Ohio had a variety of weapons, including .58- and .69-caliber rifles and .69-caliber smoothbore muskets.

The recovered bullets closely match supply figures and the diversity of weapons associated with the 8th Ohio Regiment. This suggests that the feature may represent a location where the 8th Ohio Regiment was stationed in the Mumma Orchard rather than regiments armed only with rifles. As with the larger North Woods and Piper Orchard assemblages, there is a similarity between recovered bullets and the estimated supply.

Unlike dropped Union bullets in the North Woods, bullets from the Mumma Orchard feature include Williams Cleaner bullets, a distinctly

Union variety. The cleaner bullets, packaged with the standard .58-caliber Miniés, at least one to a bundle of ten cartridges, correlate well with the ratio (3:26) of recovered dropped bullets from the feature. This recovery ratio is another indication that, at the time of the battle at Antietam, Union troops had not developed any aversion to the use of the oddly shaped cleaner bullets (Samuel Smith 1994:70–73).

The analysis of dropped Union bullets in Mumma Orchard is subject to a greater degree of error because the assemblage constitutes a very small sample from a regiment which suffered heavy losses during the battle. Despite difficulties with sample size, the technique of comparing recovered small arms ordnance with the documented weapons supply shows promise in helping to identify a specific regiment associated with of an archaeologically documented feature.

Conclusion

The archaeological survey at Antietam resulted in the recovery of a substantial military small arms assemblage. Bullets, partly because they were the most commonly recovered artifacts, were determined to be the most informative for analysis. Bullets can be categorized as dropped or fired, which in some cases allows for a correlation with armies or a regiment from which they originated. When these distinctions are possible, meaningful evaluations of ordnance supply, military features, and battle signatures can be elicited through comparison of archaeological data with the voluminous historic record. More importantly, this allows a greater understanding of troop movements and activities and the use of the landscape during battle.

Distributional analysis of battlefield artifacts, when compared with historic documentation, can be used to test the effectiveness of systematic metal detector surveys on Civil War sites, including complex battlefields. If one goal of Civil War archaeology is, as Steven Smith (1994) claims, to collect information for a larger database to be used to help develop questions to better approach an understanding of Civil War archaeology, then this survey has been more than a success. Just as the bullets recovered at Antietam took on new meaning each year with comparative data from new survey areas, so this assemblage and its research value will gain relevance with additional data from other such surveys. It is hoped that the success at Antietam can help in interpreting data retrieved from Civil War sites not as well documented as the Battle of Antietam.

"Double the Cannister and Give 'Em Hell"

Artillery at Antietam

Jeffrey Harbison

On September 17, 1862, on farm fields north of Sharpsburg, Maryland, two armies met in an explosion of iron and lead. Gen. George B. McClellan and his Army of the Potomac clashed with Gen. Robert E. Lee's Army of Northern Virginia. The battle raged into the evening, and in the end, McClellan succeeded in arresting Lee's northward push, but with tremendous casualties incurred on both sides.

Over four years (1994–97), URS Greiner conducted systematic metal detector surveys for the National Park Service at Antietam National Battlefield Park. During the course of these surveys, a wide range of military artifacts were recovered. Among the assemblage was a collection of exploded artillery shells. At first, these heavily corroded pieces of iron and lead were unidentifiable beyond basic attributes. After electrolytic cleaning and analysis, specific types of ordnance were identified. In turn, the ordnance confirms the presence of various types of cannon used during the battle (fig. 18.1).

Documentation of Civil War military hardware is vast and varied, but much of it is riddled with conflicting information. Archaeological materials recovered from Antietam Battlefield provide a fresh look at the use of artillery for comparison with the historic record.

Project and Testing

Between 1994 and 1997, URS Greiner conducted fieldwork at Antietam National Battlefield, in Sharpsburg, Maryland, as part of the National Park Service's Systemwide Archeological Inventory Program (see chapter 16). Phase one focused on an intensive metal detector survey and shovel testing of the west woods and known farmsteads (fig. 16.1). As a result of the first phase, rich archaeological deposits were identified at a small farmstead called the Locher/Poffenberger site. Phase two operations involved an intensive archaeological investigation of the Locher/Poffen-berger farmstead. The third phase involved an intensive metal detector survey of the North Woods. The fourth phase called for investigation of the East Woods, Mumma Orchard, and the Piper Orchard. Each of these areas, including the North Woods, is scheduled for restoration to recreate the landscape as it was at the time of the battle.

Artillery at Antietam

The Battle of Antietam occurred at a point in history when armament technology was advancing at a rapid rate. In the 1850s, the U.S. military adopted rifled field artillery but refused to decommission smoothbore guns already in service. When the Civil War commenced in 1861, the demand for more advanced weaponry increased and led to the introduction of more types of rifled artillery as well as an extensive variety of explosive ordnance. Less industrialized Southern states, in an attempt to meet their own need for weaponry and munitions, imported rifled artillery from Europe (Johnson and Anderson 1995:5). Captured Union weaponry also helped outfit Confederate batteries.

At Antietam there was great variation in the types of artillery employed by both armies (fig. 18.1). There are two major classifications for cannon: smoothbore and rifled artillery. Smoothbore weapons were the military standard in the United States through the 1850s, after which rifled artillery was adopted in small numbers (Manucy 1949:14). In 1862, field artillery was generally named for the weight of the projectile it fired. A 6-pounder gun fired a 6-pound shot, and a 20-pounder Parrott rifle fired a 20-pound projectile. There are, however, exceptions to the rule. The 3-inch ordnance rifle was named for the diameter of its bore and not for the weight of its ammunition. Among the smoothbore muzzle-loaded guns at Antietam, there were 6-, 12-, 24-, and 32-pounders (Johnson and Anderson 1995:39, 47).

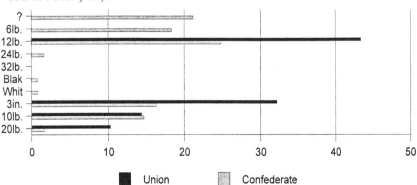

18.1. Artillery types, North and South (composed by the author after Johnson and Anderson 1995 and Priest 1989).

The howitzer was a variation of smoothbore cannon. It tended to be shorter and lighter than other guns of the same caliber. The howitzer was designed to throw a projectile in a lobbing arc at a high angle of elevation. It used less powder but tended to have a shorter range.

Both the Confederate and Union armies used guns that were in service before the war. Guns of the M1841 series were leftovers from the Mexican War. Three guns—the M1841 6-pounder, the M1841 12-pounder, and the M1841 12-pounder howitzer—were all employed by both sides, although documentary evidence shows that Union forces did not have 6-pounders in service at Antietam (Johnson and Anderson 1995).

The M1857 "Napoleon" howitzer was created in France and adopted by the U.S. military in 1861. It became one of the most popular and widely utilized artillery pieces of the Civil War (Johnson and Anderson 1995:21; Peterson 1969:92). Both armies employed the Napoleon, and at Antietam it was the primary smoothbore cannon in use by the Union forces.

Two more guns of the M1841 series were present in small numbers at Antietam. Documentary evidence shows that 24-pounder guns were employed by Southern forces in the field and that 32-pounders filled out the Company D, 1st New York Battery (Johnson and Anderson 1995:23). The 24- and 32-pounder guns were generally thought of as siege guns better suited for fixed emplacements. Their large size and weight were prohibitive to their use in the field.

Seven types of rifled artillery were used during the Battle of Antietam. These included 10- and 20-pounder Parrott rifles; the 3-inch ordnance rifle; the Dahlgren boat rifle; the James rifle; and two British rifles, the Blakely and the Whitworth. Rifling introduces spin to a projectile. This spin allows increased accuracy over longer distance. Long-range accuracy had its place, but the effective, and proven, anti-personnel tactics developed for smoothbore guns often proved more effective in hilly and wooded terrain (Manucy 1949:19; Coggins 1990:13). Each of the rifles required a specific size of ammunition, except for the 3-inch ordnance rifle, which could fire 10-pounder Parrott shells (Johnson and Anderson 1995:24; Thomas 1985:39).

The 10- and 20-pounder Parrott rifles were designed in the 1850s and adopted by the U.S. military in 1861 (Peterson 1969:92). About the same time, the 3-inch ordnance rifle was adopted. These three rifled weapons became standard U.S. field artillery. They were utilized by both Union and Confederate forces during the Battle of Antietam, although the Confederates had very few of the longer-range 20-pounder Parrott Rifles (Johnson and Anderson 1995:47).

The 12-pounder Dahlgren boat gun was a naval gun modified for field use. The Dahlgren saw limited use by both sides during the Civil War. At Antietam, five Dahlgrens comprised the armament for Battery K, 9th New York Artillery (Johnson and Anderson 1995:37).

Blakely and Whitworth rifles were British imports. Both had distinctly shaped projectiles. These guns were only used by Confederate forces at Antietam, and documentary evidence shows that only two of each were used in the battle (Johnson and Anderson 1995:47).

Another rifle that may have been used by Confederate forces at Antietam is the James rifle. The James was an early model rifle made by cutting rifling into an older model smoothbore gun. The bore diameter of the 12-pounder James rifle was the same as the 20-pounder Parrott, but James ammunition was shaped differently. Apparently, six James Rifles were captured at Harpers Ferry immediately preceding the Confederate push into Maryland, and they may have been used by Confederate forces at Antietam. However, James rifles do not appear on a list of the artillery put together by Johnson and Anderson in their book *Artillery Hell* (Johnson and Anderson 1995:47). They may be part of the 21.14 percent of artillery of unknown type used in the battle (Johnson and Anderson 1995:47).

The Artillery Collection

The artillery collection from URS Greiner's survey consists of 530 pieces. Artifacts were collected from four survey areas (fig. 16.1)—the North Woods, the East Woods, Mumma Orchard, and the Piper Orchard. These areas were all heavily bombarded during the battle. Among the several types of ordnance recovered there are fuses, canister balls, lead shrapnel, and shell fragments.

Iron ordnance fragments were identifiable as thick pieces of heavily corroded iron. Depending on the size of the piece, the inside and outside curves could be used to determine whether the fragment was part of a spherical or conical shell. Unfortunately, because of their heavily corroded state, identification beyond these basic attributes was difficult. In order to extract more information from the fragments, it was clear that extensive cleaning would have to take place. Electrolysis was used to remove the corrosion from the iron ordnance.

The diameter of the shell fragments was measured, allowing for the identification of specific caliber. Data was also generated by using calipers to record the thickness of individual shell fragments in an attempt to distinguish between exploding shell and case shot. By comparing data recovered from individual fragments to the specifications for a variety of shells, it was possible to identify 6- and 12-pounder shell and case shot, as well as 10- and 20-pounder Parrott and 3-inch ordnance rifle shell (fig. 18.2).

Rifle projectiles were initially identified by the cylindrical shape or the characteristic curve of the "ogive," or nose end. The 20-pounder Parrott shells were easy to identify because of their large caliber (3.63 inches). However, differentiating between 3-inch and 10-pounder Parrott shells

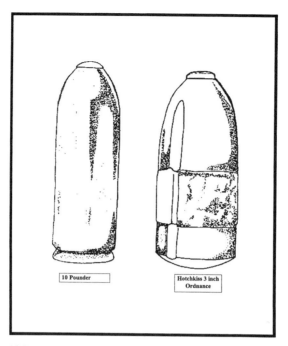

18.2. Ten-pounder Parrott (*left*) and 3-inch Hotchkiss ordnance (adapted from Melton and Pawl 1996; courtesy of URS Greiner Woodward Clyde).

was problematic. The 10-pounder Parrott shell had a diameter of 2.86 to 2.88 inches (fig. 18.2). This is only slightly smaller than the 2.9-inch diameter of the 10-pounder's bore.

Several variant 3-inch ordnance shell types were created by ordnance manufacturers. Each shell type proposed an improved ballistic feature. Three-inch ammunition was between 2.9 and 2.97 inches in diameter. Some projectiles had characteristic shapes, grooves, fuse seats, or bases that aid in identification. The majority of the fragments recovered from Antietam were from the body of the shell and exhibit no diagnostic attributes.

Two specific types of 3-inch ammunition were identified at Antietam: the Hotchkiss (fig. 18.2) and the Dyer. The Hotchkiss shell fragment was identified by a portion of the flash groove on the shell's side. The flash groove allowed flame from firing the rifle to ignite the fuse. The Dyer fragment came from the shell's base and was identified by a characteristic groove that held a sabot.

Explosive 6- and 12-pounder ordnance included exploding shell and case shot fragments. Exploding shell is a hollow, cast iron ball filled with a sulfur and gunpowder mixture linked to a fuse. When the sulfur and powder are ignited, the ball shatters, scattering ragged chunks of metal over a wide area. Case shot (fig. 18.3) carried the idea of the shell a step further. Developed by Lt. Henry Shrapnel, it incorporated lead or steel

18.3. Spherical case shot (adapted from Melton and Pawl 1996; courtesy of URS Greiner Woodward Clyde).

balls within the iron shell (Manucy 1949). The average 12-pound shot held about 78 lead balls, and a 6-pounder held around 38 (Coggins 1990:67). During artifact analysis, the lead case shot balls were differentiated from deformed musket balls by a characteristic flattening and dimpling. Case shot was manufactured for both rifled and smoothbore guns. Combined with a timed fuse system, it was a deadly anti-personnel weapon that exploded in the air and scattered lead balls like hail. These projectiles had a horrific effect on personnel and material:

A shell struck G company of the 107th New York. Captain H G Bringham (G Co.) watched helplessly as it shredded 11 of his men. Amid the smoke and carnage he heard 16 year old Willie Everts shrieking and wailing. The explosion had ripped the boys legs away.

Ezra Stickley (5th Virginia) went to mount as a federal battery rapidly walked three explosive rounds toward the brigade. The first struck about one hundred fifty yards to the south. The second fell seventy five yards closer. The third burst in Stickley's horse as he prepared to mount. The explosion violently hurled the aide to the ground and splattered the horse all over the field. Looking up from his gory puddle, the young man realized that what was left of his horse was going to fall on him. He immediately jumped up and stumbled into the horrified line of infantry, where two men caught him to keep him from collapsing. (Priest 1989:91, 37)

Fuse fragments were readily identified by their characteristic shape and size. Three types are represented in the collection. The first and most common is the Borman fuse. It was made of lead with an enclosed ignition channel that could be punched at various points along its length to expose a powder train. This allowed the fuse to be set for up to five seconds (Melton and Pawl 1996). When the cannon was fired, the blast would launch the ordnance as well as ignite powder in the ignition channel. In theory, the projectile would explode at the desired distance. Of course, things did not always work the way they were supposed to:

Matthew Hart lay very still, his knuckles white from their own grip. The big shell had come to a gentle stop against the souls of his feet. The fuse still sputtered. Within a moment it had burned itself into the casing. The nervous sergeant pushed his face closer to the ground and waited. Nothing happened. The shell was a dud. (Priest 1989:10)

The Borman fuse was produced by both Confederate and Union manufacturers for use in spherical exploding ordnance. The majority of examples recovered were highly fragmented with only the threaded edges remaining. A single piece, however, was still seated in a spherical 6-pound shell fragment. The characteristic punch plate was gone, but the brass underplug portion remained.

The second type of fuse represented in the collection is a zinc Parrott fuse. This fuse is threaded down its entire length and was screwed into place using a tool that fit into two holes on its top. Not as sophisticated as the Borman, the zinc Parrott was a cylinder that held a paper powder cartridge manufactured to burn at a measured rate. The fuses came in designated burn times or could be cut in the field so that the projectile would explode at the desired range.

A third type of fuse recovered resembles the zinc Parrott fuse. It is a lead cylinder that fits into the nose of a Parrott shell, but, unlike the zinc Parrott fuse, it is not threaded down its sides. Many examples of simple fuse plugs exist. They are made from a variety of materials, including wood (Thomas 1985:26; Melton and Pawl 1996). They would hold the same type of paper cartridge and were ignited in the same manner as the aforementioned types.

Canister shot (fig. 18.4) was one of the most deadly and effective antipersonnel weapons at the cannoneer's disposal. "The Four Napoleons unleashed a point blank barrage into the fence along their front. The 1st Texas received the full blasts of the canister. Fence rails flew through the air like straws in the wind. The cornstalks were flattened or sheered off and men thrashed about on the ground like beached fish" (Priest 1989:62). A tin can, resembling a coffee can, was filled with small iron balls. When fired, the can broke apart and the balls scattered, effectively turning the canon into a huge shotgun. Because of its wide dispersal, canister was used at short range, usually when the enemy was less than 150 yards away.

Thirteen canister balls were recovered, 12 of which measured 1 inch in diameter, and 1 which measured 1.5 inches in diameter. An 1862 ordnance manual states that canister balls for 12-pound howitzer should be about 1 inch in diameter (U.S. Ordnance Dept., *Ordnance Manual* 1862:36). Canister for the 6-pound gun should be about 1.1 inches in diameter, and canister balls for the 12-pound gun or 32-pound howitzer should be about 1.5 inches in diameter. Canister was produced for both rifled and smoothbore guns, although it was deemed more effective when fired from smoothbores.

18.4. Canister (adapted from Melton and Pawl 1996; courtesy of URS Greiner Woodward Clyde).

A large quantity of canister was expected, considering the amount fired during the battle. The low frequency of recovered canister balls is most likely related to relic collecting activities. The size of the canister shot makes them visible in plowed fields. Also, they are readily found by using a metal detector. These characteristics are shared with grape and solid shot projectiles, which, in part, accounts for their absence in the archaeological metal detector survey.

Another reason for the lack of canister is that, in some forms, it is not readily recognized: "In a pinch almost anything could be used for canister, and some Confederate ammunition consisted of canvas bags of scraps of metal, piece of trace chain, etc." (Coggins 1990:67). Scraps of iron and chain considered to be agricultural field debris may actually be expended ammunition. It appears that almost anything could be loaded into a gun as long as it fit down the muzzle. An anonymous Union officer stated: "The rebels must have been very short of missiles, when they fire off old sledges, horse shoes, old iron; and in one instance a mule of ours was struck with the leg of a cook stove!" (Wright 1992:9).

Artillery and the Battle

Each area tested by URS Greiner suffered intensive bombardment during the course of the battle. Union long-range artillery was deployed along a ridge east of Antietam Creek and fired on Confederate positions all over the battlefield. Their shelling supported field artillery keeping Confeder-

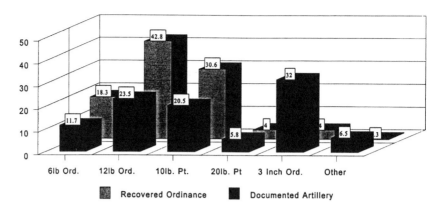

18.5. North Woods, percent ordnance compared to percent artillery (courtesy of URS Greiner Woodward Clyde).

ate guns at bay during Union advances. This served to keep the Confederate forces in the West Woods for most of the battle, massing their artillery to repel union assaults (Johnson and Anderson 1995:47–51; Priest 1989:29–110; Sears 1983:190–92).

At daybreak on September 17, the Union I Corps commanded by General Hooker massed in ranks in the North Woods and advanced southward. As they emerged from the woods they were met with deadly fire from Confederate batteries on Nicodemus Hill, and the cannon massed north and east of Dunkard Church. In total, ten batteries and a section from the Stuart Horse Artillery fired on Hooker's troops (Johnson and Anderson 1995:48; Priest 1989:28–42; Sears 1983:182).

When analyzing the North Woods collection (fig. 18.5) and comparing it to the types of cannon that might have fired into this area, certain trends and anomalies become apparent. First, a significant number of 10-pounder Parrott shells were recovered. They represent 30.6 percent of the North Woods collection. Then, over half of the collection is explosive ordnance case and shell from smoothbore muzzle-loaders. Case and shell from 12-pounder make up 42.8 percent, while 6-pounder fragments make up 18.3 percent. Few 20-pounder Parrott fragments were recovered.

The primary anomaly is the disparity between the number of 3-inch ordnance rifles represented on the field and the relative dearth of 3-inch ordnance present in the collection. Although the ordnance rifle was well represented on the field (32 percent of the participating guns), there are only 2 fragments of 3-inch Hotchkiss shell present in the collection.

The East Woods collection includes 3 fragments of 3-inch shell, a canister ball, a piece of 6-pounder shell, a single 10-pounder Parrott shell fragment, and two Borman fuse fragments. The lack of artillery-related artifacts from the East Woods is puzzling, because this area was under heavy fire from several locations. There are several accounts of troops

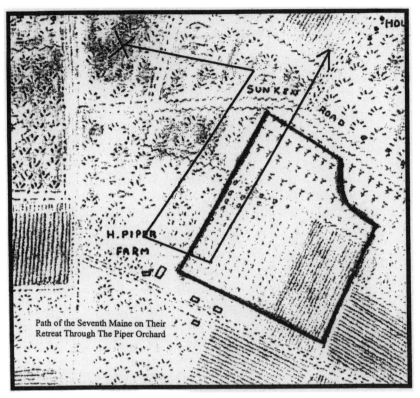

18.6. Piper Farm study area (courtesy of the National Park Service, National Capital Region, and URS Greiner Woodward Clyde)

witnessing large branches being blown off the trees and shells landing in the path of advancing troops: "The shelling temporarily undid the wet and inexperienced troops as they entered the East Woods. Huge branches showered them from above and round shot shrieked through the air"; and "Pvt. John D. Vautier (1 Co., 88th Pa.) barely escaped death when a branch, which a cannonball had severed, fell on his messmate Jess Tyson and killed him" (Priest 1989:59).

There is the possibility that the East Woods was heavily picked over by collectors, but the quantity of small arms ammunition found in the field does not support this theory. When interviewed, local collectors said that shell fragments were held in low regard and usually left behind.

The Mumma Orchard was inundated by artillery from both Federal and Confederate batteries. Considering the amount of fire power aimed at the Mumma farmstead and orchard, there was not a large amount of ordnance retrieved during the archaeological survey. A total of 38 artillery fragments were recovered. As with the East Woods, the low frequency of artillery artifacts severely restricts analysis and interpretation. More than half of the artillery artifacts were fired from smoothbore guns. Twelve fragments came from 12-pounder guns; four pieces of 6-pounder shell, attributable to Confederate batteries, were recovered. Two canister balls were recovered.

Among the rifled ordnance fragments recovered from the field, seven were 20-pounder Parrot fragments. These pieces were probably fired from General Hunt's Artillery Reserve positioned along the ridge east of Antietam Creek. The most probable target for these guns would have been the 3rd North Carolina posted on the south edge of the Mumma Orchard (Carman and Cope 1904).

The Piper Orchard (fig. 18.6) represents an area held by the Confederates. After Sedgewick's assault on the West Woods, the battle shifted south to the Sunken Road—known as Bloody Lane (Antietam Battlefield Board 1904; Johnson and Anderson 1995:50; Priest 1989; Sears 1983:235). This area saw intensive fighting as the rebels held the lane, repelling wave after wave of attack, before they fell back to the Piper Orchard.

In the North Woods and Mumma Orchard, the majority of the shell fragments were fired from smoothbore cannon. Of the identifiable shell fragments from the Piper Orchard collection, there is a dramatic rise in the percent of rifled over smoothbore projectiles. Almost 75 percent of the collection consists of rifled projectile fragments. This greater percentage is possibly because the Union artillery had far more rifled artillery at the time of the battle.

There is also a greater amount of canister in the Piper Orchard. This is not surprising. Here armies faced off at relatively close quarters. As Hill's infantry pulled back, their retreat was covered by Miller's Washington Artillery, positioned near the Piper house. He loaded his Napoleons with canister and fired into the advancing Union lines (Johnson and Anderson 1995:50).

The presence of 6-pounder explosive ordnance fragments in the Piper Orchard collection may be related to the charge and hasty retreat of the 7th Maine. Only Confederate artillery batteries were equipped with 6-pounder guns, and the men of the 7th Maine were the only Union targets to move through this area.

The 7th Maine was ordered to push the enemy from positions around the Piper outbuildings. Near the Piper barn, they met overwhelming numbers and were forced to retreat through the orchard. A barrage of artillery fire from numerous Confederate batteries pressed their retreat (Priest 1989:296, 297). When looking at distribution maps for 6-pound ordnance fragments in the Piper Orchard, the retreat of the 7th Maine can be traced as they fled to the safety of the sunken road.

Summary

The initial analysis of the artillery assemblage recovered from Antietam National Battlefield Park focused on trying to identify the individual fragments of ordnance. Electrolytic cleaning techniques proved to be an indispensable tool. Quantifiable information regarding individual attributes was collected from the artifacts and compared to Civil War era ordnance manuals. Using this information, it was determined that the artifacts did not degrade to any significant degree, and each artifact was readily identified and categorized as to the type of weapon that fired them.

The assemblages for each of the test areas show a relationship between the artifacts and particular events that took place during the battle. In particular, we see changes in the frequencies of various types of ordnance depending on who was firing into a particular area. Areas Confederate artillerists fired into were identified by the presence of 6-pound ordnance fragments, and in areas bombarded by Union artillerists there is a dramatic increase in the amount of rifled ordnance. In certain instances, these artifacts could be used to corroborate particular events that occurred during the battle, and they may help identify issues for further research.

Glossary

Borman fuse Circular disc threaded so that it could be screwed into an artillery shell. The top of the fuse was graduated in seconds and quarter-seconds (Coggins 1990). A special cutter was used to make a hole in the fuse corresponding to the length of time desired before the shell exploded. When the shell was fired, flames from the explosion lit the powder in the fuse, which, hopefully, burned for the appropriate time.

breech-loading A gun-loading system which allowed the cartridge to be loaded from the arm of the gun into the back end of the barrel. The breech-loading system allowed for easier and faster loading from difficult positions such as on horseback or prone.

cache An accumulation of material gathered and buried together, usually in storage for use at a later date or, in cases of ritual deposits, to influence fate, provide protection, or ward off malevolent intentions, both spiritual and secular.

caliber The inside diameter of a gun barrel (or bore) in inches. The caliber of a bullet refers to the barrel size of the gun for which the bullet is intended, not the diameter of the bullet.

caltrop Multi-pointed objects, generally of iron and measuring about two inches from point to point, that were thrown into roads and in front of defensive positions as a deterrent to cavalry attacks.

carbine The long arm employed by the cavalry. Because carbines were intended for use on horseback, the barrel length was shorter than an infantry musket and most carbines were breech-loading.

cartridge The lead shot (bullet) with gunpowder charge wrapped in paper, rubber, skin, or metal casing.

Colonoware A coarse, low-fired, handmade earthenware likely made and used by African Americans (Galke 1992b:12; Ferguson 1992:19). In 19th-century archaeology, the term refers to low-fired earthenware pottery believed to have been made and used by enslaved workers.

consumer culture An established set of ideas and objects which sets the standard for societal consumption during any given time period (Martin 1997:6–8).

cultural landscape The dynamic relationships between humans, nature, and artifacts of a particular place and their individual and collective relationships to the past and present (Martin 1997:5).

engine-turned Late 18th-century decorations composed of incised lines in wavy or angular patterns applied by means of an engine lathe (Harpers Ferry National Historical Park Ceramic Glossary 1989).

ethnicity The characteristics which define a particular ethnic group.

galena (or lead sulfide) A mineral that possesses a shiny, dull gray reflective surface. It forms naturally into a cube.

gaming pieces Objects used as tokens for games.

ideology The belief system of a particular culture as interpreted through material remains (Fagan 1996:339).

long arm (or shoulder arm) A firearm with a long barrel intended to be fired with the stock resting against the shoulder with the gun held in both hands. Long arms generally employed a larger bullet and stronger charge than pistols and thus had a greater range and accuracy.

mankala Generic name for a large family of board games derived from numerous regions of the Middle East, Arabia, Central Asia, South and Southeast Asia, and all parts of sub-Saharan Africa. Archaeologists recognize the transmission of mankala to America with gaming pieces identified at African American sites (Townshend 1979:794; Martin and Parsons 1998:7).

material culture The artifacts and ecofacts used by a group to cope with its physical and social environment (Thomas 1989:659).

minimum vessel analysis The identification of the minimum number of glass and/or ceramic vessels that exist in an assemblage in order to examine consumer and social behavior (Lucas 1990:1).

minkisi. See **nkisi.**

musket A generic term for the long arms employed by the infantry. At the time of the Civil War, "musket" referred to a smoothbore shoulder arm.

muzzle-loading A loading system in which the bullet and charge are loaded through the muzzle or front end of the barrel. The powder and shot were tapped into place at the rear of the barrel by a ramrod or rammer.

nkisi West African term which refers to an accumulation of objects gathered together for ritual purposes to influence destiny or for protection.

pearlware A refined earthenware developed by Josiah Wedgwood in England. To produce this "pearl white" ware, flint was added to the clay body, and a small amount of cobalt was mixed into the lead glaze to negate the earthenware's natural yellowish tint. Circa 1779–1890 (Harpers Ferry National Historical Park Ceramic Glossary 1989).

rifle A long arm in which the interior of the gun barrel has been set with grooves to guide the bullet through the barrel during firing. Rifling helped increase the range and accuracy of the gun.

rifle musket Prior to the Civil War, with the advent of the expanding conical bullet, the muskets manufactured for the infantry were rifles. The barrel of the gun was produced with rifle grooves.

rifled musket After 1855 and during the Civil War, many original smoothbore muskets were altered with rifle grooves cut into the barrel or by the original barrel being replaced with a rifled barrel.

shot The lead projectile or bullet fired from a gun.

small arms Firearms, such as pistols, muskets, and rifles, carried in hand by individual soldiers, as opposed to larger guns such as cannon.

smoothbore arm A firearm in which the interior of the gun barrel is smooth. Smoothbore arms generally fired a round ball, which was smaller than the gun barrel. Smoothbore arms have less range and accuracy than rifled arms.

torpedo An explosive device for use in water. During the Civil War, these were essentially floating mines, which exploded if hit by a boat or ship, or which were timed for explosion. Some were detonated by an electrical charge.

tradition The long-term customs of an ethnic group or community characterized by specific artifacts, clothing, and/or rituals.

transfer printed An indirect method of painted decoration in which the pattern is obtained from an engraving, lithograph, or silk screen print on transfer paper from which it is then applied to the ware by tissue paper, double paper, or wet slide transfer (Harpers Ferry National Historical Park Ceramic Glossary 1989).

Bibliography

Abrams, Elliot M.
1989   Architecture and Energy: An Evolutionary Perspective. In *Archaeological Method and Theory*, vol. 1, edited by Michael Schiffer, 47–87. University of Arizona Press, Tucson.

Adams, George W.
1961   *Doctors in Blue: The Medical History of the Union Army in the Civil War*. Crowell-Collier, New York.

Adams, James W.
1867   Letter. Ms. in possession of R. E. S. Adams, Bellevue, Washington. Photocopy on file, Handley Library Archives, Winchester, Va.

Albaugh, W. A. III
1975   *Union Armament in the Civil War*. North South Trader.

Albaugh, W. A. III, and Simmons, Edward N.
1957   *Confederate Arms*. Stackpole, Harrisburg, Pa.

Albert, Alphaeus H.
1976   *Record of American Uniform and Historical Buttons*. Bicentennial Edition. Boyertown Publishing Co., Boyertown, Pa.

Alberts, Robert C.
1986   *Pitt: The Story of the University of Pittsburgh, 1787–1987*. University of Pittsburgh Press, Pittsburgh.

Alexander, Ted
1997   ". . . Not a sight becoming a country that calls itself Christian . . .": The Impact of the Battle of Antietam on the Sharpsburg Civilians. Ms. on file, Office of the Park Historian, Antietam National Battlefield, Sharpsburg, Md.

Alexander, William A.
1902   The True Stories of the Confederate Submarine Boats. *New Orleans Picayune*, July 29.

Andrews, Susan C., and Paul R. Mullins
1989   Tableware and Bottle Glass Assemblages. In *The Hatcher-Cheatham Site (44CF258): A Multicomponent Historic Site in Chesterfield County, Virginia*, vol. 4, edited by Clarence R. Geier. 72–110. James Madison University Archaeological Research Center, Harrisonburg, Va. Submitted to Virginia Department of Transportation, Richmond.

Angle, Paul M. (editor)
1947   *The Lincoln Reader*. Rutgers University Press, New Brunswick, N.J.

Anonymous
1862   General Bird's-Eye View of Washington and Vicinity. *Harper's Weekly*, January 4. Print on file, Prints and Photographs Division, Library of Congress, Washington, D.C.

Antietam Battlefield Board (Carman-Cope Maps)
1904   Map of the Battlefield of Antietam. Andrew B. Graham, Photo-Litho. Washington, D.C.

Babits, Lawrence E.
1995   Bullets from the Maple Leaf. *Military Collector and Historian* 47(3):119–26.

Balicki, Joseph
1995   Archeological Resources. In *Historical and Archeological Survey for Fort C.F. Smith, 241 24th Street North, Arlington, Virginia*, vol. 2, edited by Charles D. Cheek and Peter Benton. John Milner Associates, West Chester, Pa. Submitted to Department of Community Planning, Housing and Development, Community Improvement Division, Arlington County, Va.

Balicki, Joseph, Charles D. Cheek, Stuart Fiedel, and Dana B. Heck

1999   *Phase I Archeological Investigations at Fort Monroe and Old Point Comfort (44HT27), Hampton, Virginia.* John Milner Associates, Alexandria, Va. Submitted to Directorate of Engineering and Housing, Fort Monroe, Va.

Ball, J. L.

1881   *West Branch Local Record,* March 10.

Barnard, George

1864   Civil War photographs. George Barnard Collection, Atlanta History Center, Atlanta.

Barnard, John Gross

1871   *A Report on the Defenses of Washington, to the Chief Engineers, U.S. Army.* Professional Papers of the Corps of Engineers, No. 20. Corps of Engineers, Government Printing Office, Washington, D.C.

Barry, Joseph

1988   *The Strange Story of Harpers Ferry with Legends of the Surrounding Country.* Reprint. Shepherdstown Register, Shepherdstown, W. Va.

Barry, William F.

1874   Report of Brigadier General William F. Barry, U.S. Army, Chief of Artillery, Military Division of the Mississippi. In *The War of the Rebellion: A Compilation of the Official Records of the Union and Confederate Armies.* Series I, vol. 38, part I: Reports. U.S. War Department, Government Printing Office, Washington, D.C.

Bartnik, George P.

1976   *A Cultural-Historical Overview of Camp Nelson, Concentrating on Its Main Line of Defense.* Kentucky Transportation Cabinet, Frankfort.

Barton, Keith C.

1997   "Good Cooks and Washers": Slave Hiring, Domestic Labor, and the Market in Bourbon County, Kentucky. *Journal of American History* 84:436–60.

Battles and Leaders of the Civil War. 1956. Vol. 1. Thomas Yoseloff, Inc., New York.

Baumgartner, Richard A., and Larry M. Strayer (editors)

1992   *Ralsa C. Rice Yankee Tigers: Through the Civil War with the 125th Ohio.* Blue Acorn Press, Huntington, W. Va.

Bearss, Edwin C.

1964   Battle Maps of the Battle of Atlanta. Maps on file, Kennesaw Mountain National Battlefield Park Library, Kennesaw, Ga.

1970   *Andersonville National Historic Site: Historic Resource Study and Historical Base Map.* National Park Service, U.S. Department of Interior, Washington, D.C.

1980   *Hardluck Ironclad: The Sinking and Salvaging of the Cairo.* Louisiana State University Press, Baton Rouge.

1981   *Battle of First Manassas and Engagement at Blackburn's Ford: Historical Report on Troop Movements.* Ms. on file, Manassas National Battlefield Park, Manassas, Va.

Beavins, William

n.d.   Diary. Southern Historical Collection, University of North Carolina, Chapel Hill.

Beck, Doreen

1973   *The Book of Bottle Collecting.* Hamlyn Publishing Group, London.

Beecher, Harris N.

1866   *New Record of the One Hundred and Fourteenth York.* J. F. Hubbard, Norwich, N.Y.

Bell, R. C.

1988   *Games to Play.* Michael Joseph, London.

Benton, Peter

1995   Planning Study. In *Historical and Archeological Survey for Fort C.F. Smith, 241 24th Street North, Arlington, Virginia,* vol. 5, edited by Charles D. Cheek and Peter Benton. John Milner Associates, West Chester, Pa. Submitted to Department of Community Planning, Housing and Development, Community Improvement Division, Arlington County, Va.

Betts, Edward E.

1892   Map of the Chickamauga and Chattanooga National Military Park. Prepared under the direction of Major S. C. Kellogg, 4th Cavalry. Map on file, Chickamauga and Chattanooga National Military Park, Chattanooga, Tenn.

1896   Map of the Battlefield of Chickamauga. Prepared under the direction of Daniel S. Lamont, Secretary of War, by the Chickamauga and Chattanooga National Park Commission. Map on file, Chickamauga and Chattanooga National Military Park, Chattanooga, Tenn.

Beverly, J. Howard, Jr.

1992   *Civil War Era Harpers Ferry, 1861–1865, an Examination for Public Interpretation: The Civil War Occupation Material Culture Recovered during Package 116 Archaeological Excavations.* M.A. project, Department of Anthropology, University of Maryland, College Park.

Bilby, Joseph G.

1995   Weapons of the Irish Brigade. In *The History of the Irish Brigade: A Collection of Historical Essays,* edited by Phillip Thomas Tucker, 181–85. Sergeant Kirkland Museum Historical Society, Fredericksburg, Va.

1998   *The Irish Brigade in the Civil War.* Combined Publishing, Conshohocken, Pa.

Billings, John D.

1887   *Hardtack and Coffee or The Unwritten Story of Army Life.* George M. Smith and Co., Boston, Mass.

1993   *Hardtack and Coffee or The Unwritten Story of Army Life.* Reprint. University of Nebraska Press, Lincoln.

Blanding, Stephen F.

1889   *In the Defenses of Washington or Sunshine in a Soldier's Life.* Freeman, Providence, R.I.

Blight, David W.

1989   "For Something beyond the Battlefield": Frederick Douglass and the Struggle for the Memory of the Civil War. *Journal of American History* 75(4):1156–78.

Bode, Frederick A., and Donald E. Ginter

1986   *Farm Tenancy and the Census in Antebellum Georgia.* University of Georgia Press, Athens.

Bond, Kathleen H.

1989   The Medicine, Alcohol, and Soda Vessels from the Boott Mills. In *Interdisciplinary Investigations of the Boott Mills, Lowell, Massachusetts,* vol. 3, *The Boarding House System as a Way of Life,* edited by Mary Beaudry and Stephen A. Mrozowski, 121–40. Cultural Resources Management Study, no. 21. North Atlantic Regional Office, National Park Service, Boston, Mass.

Bowen, James L.

1884   *History of the 37th Massachusetts Volunteers.* Clark W. Bryan and Co., Holyoke, Mass.

Bowen, William R.

1990   *An Archaeological Survey for the Proposed U.S. 27 Relocation. Georgia Department of Transportation Project MLP-813(1), Walker and Catoosa Counties, Georgia.* Georgia Department of Transportation, Atlanta.

Bowman, John S. (editor)

1989   *The Civil War Day by Day.* Dorset Press, Brompton Books Corporation. Greenwich, Conn.

Bowyer, Gary C.

1992   Archaeological Symbols of Status and Authority: Fort Hoskins, Oregon, 1856–1865. M.A. thesis, Department of Interdisciplinary Studies, Oregon State University, Corvallis.

Braley, Chad O.

1987   *The Battle of Gilgal Church: An Archaeological and Historical Study of Mid-Nineteenth Century Warfare in Georgia.* Southeastern Archeological Services, Athens, Ga. Submitted to Oglethorpe Power Corporation, Tucker, Ga.

Brawner, John C.

1871   Claim No. 1335, filed April 27. Commissioner of Claims, U.S. War Department, National Archives, Washington, D.C.

Brewer, David

1987 *An Archeological Overview and Assessment of Chickamauga and Chattanooga National Military Park, Georgia-Tennessee.* Southeast Archeological Center, National Park Service, Tallahassee, Fla.

Brinton, John H.

1914 *Personal Memoirs of John H. Brinton.* Neale Publishing Co., N.Y.

Brown, Jeffrey L.

1977 An Archeological Survey of the Proposed Highway 27 Relocation, Viniard-Alexander Connector. Ms. on file, Southeast Archeological Center, National Park Service, Tallahassee, Fla.

Brown, Jeffrey L., and E. Raymond Evans

1977 An Archeological Survey of Proposed Highway 27 Relocation Alternatives in Chickamauga and Chattanooga National Military Park. Ms. on file, Southeast Archeological Center, National Park Service, Tallahassee, Fla.

Brown, Kenneth L., and D. C. Cooper

1990 Structural Continuity in an African-American Slave and Tenant Community. In "Historical Archaeology on Southern Plantation and Farms," edited by Charles E. Orser, Jr. *Historical Archaeology* 24(4):7–19.

Brown, Kristine N., and Kenneth L. Brown

1998 Archaeology and Spirituality: The Conjure/Midwife and the Praise House/Church at the Levi Jordan Plantation. Paper presented at the 31st Annual Meeting of the Society for Historical Archaeology, Atlanta, Ga.

Bruce, Robert V.

1956 *Lincoln and the Tools of War.* Bobbs-Merrill, Indianapolis, Ind.

Brundage, W. Fitzhugh

1983 Slavery in Antebellum Rockbridge County. Ms. on file, Stonewall Jackson House, Lexington, Va.

Bullion, Brenda

1986 The Agricultural Press: "To Improve the Soil and the Mind." In *The Farm,* vol. 11, edited by Peter Benes, 77–94. Dublin Seminar for New England Folklife, Annual Proceedings. Boston University, Boston, Mass.

Burgess, James

1994 Transcription of the Robinson Papers. Ms. on file, Manassas National Battlefield Park, Manassas, Va.

Burk, Brett J.

1993 "Hotel De Stipes" Faunal Assemblage: A Civil War Boardinghouse in an Occupied Town. In *Interdisciplinary Investigations of Domestic Life in Government Block B: Perspectives on Harpers Ferry's Armory and Commercial District,* edited by Paul A. Shackel, 10.1–10.28. Occasional Report No. 6, Regional Archeology Program, National Capital Region, National Park Service, Washington, D.C.

Busch, Jane

1987 A Second Time Around: A Look at Bottle Reuse. *Historical Archaeology* 21(2):67–80.

Bushong, Carrie S.

1870 Letter to Frank Bushong, March 20. Bushong Collection, Archives, Preston Library, Virginia Military Institute, Lexington.

Campbell, R. Thomas

1996 *Gray Thunder: Exploits of the Confederate Navy.* Burd Street Press, Shippensburg, Pa.

Carman, Ezra A.

1895–1902 Correspondence between Brig. Gen. Carman and Antietam Veterans. National Archives, Washington, D.C.

1997 Carman Manuscript. In *"My Sons Were Faithful and They Fought": The Irish Brigade at Antietam. An Anthology,* edited by Joseph G. Bilby and Stephan D. O'Neill, 51–60. Longstreet House, Hightstown, N.J.

Carman, Brig. Gen. Ezra A., and Lt. Col. E. B. Cope
1904   Map of the Battlefield of Antietam. Complete series. Secretary of War, Washington, D.C.

Carpenter, Lt. Col. L. H.
1865   General Order 41. Record Group 393, part 4, entry 905. National Archives, Washington, D.C.

Castel, Albert
1992   *Decision in the West: The Atlanta Campaign of 1864*. University of Kansas Press, Lawrence.

Catton, Bruce
1962   *The Army of the Potomac; Mr. Lincoln's Army*. Anchor Books, Doubleday, N.Y.
1965   *A Stillness at Appomattox*. Pocket Books, Inc., New York.

Charleston Daily Courier
1862   September 11. Charleston, S.C.

Cheek, Charles D., et al.
1995   Management Summary. In *Historical and Archeological Survey for Fort C.F. Smith, 241 24th Street North, Arlington, Virginia*, vol. 1, edited by Charles D. Cheek and Peter Benton. John Milner Associates, West Chester, Pa. Submitted to Department of Community Planning, Housing and Development, Community Improvement Division, Arlington County, Va.

Civil War Watercolor Map Series
1994   *Antietam Battlefield, Sharpsburg, Maryland*. McElfresh Map Co., Olean, N.Y.

Clark, Col. Andrew H.
1864a   Letter to Major, May 23. Record Group 393, part 4, entry 902, p. 8. National Archives, Washington, D.C.
1864b   Letter to Lieutenant, May 31. Record Group 393, part 4, entry 902, p. 58. National Archives, Washington, D.C.
1864c   Order, June 18. Record Group 393, part 4, entry 902, p. 252. National Archives, Washington, D.C.

Clay, R. Berle
1990   Office of State Archaeology News. *Kentucky Archaeology Newsletter* 7(2):3.

Coates, Earl J., and Dean S. Thomas
1990   *An Introduction to Civil War Small Arms*. Thomas Publications, Gettysburg, Pa.

Coffman, Edward M.
1997   The Course of Military History in the United States since World War II. *Journal of Military History* 61:761–75.

Coggins, Jack
1990   *Arms and Equipment of the Civil War*. Reprint. Broadfoot Publishing Co., Wilmington, N.C.

Coleman, J. Winston
1935   *Stage-Coach Days in the Bluegrass*. The Standard Press, Louisville, Ky.

Confederate States Ordnance Bureau
1862–64 Records from Nashville and Atlanta Arsenals. Record Group 109, chapter IV, vol. 10, and vols. 78 and 79. National Archives, Washington, D.C.

Connor, Melissa, and Douglas D. Scott
1998   Metal Detectors and Their Use in Archaeology: An Introduction. *Historical Archaeology* 32(4):76–85.

Conyngham, David Power
1994   *The Irish Brigade and Its Campaigns*. Fordham University Press, N.Y.

Cook, Robert F., Assistant Deputy Attorney General of South Carolina
1996   Informal opinion to Glenn F. McConnell, State Senator, April 16.

Cooling, Benjamin Franklin
1989   *Jubal Early's Raid on Washington, 1864*. Nautical and Aviation Publishing Co., Baltimore, Md.
1991   *Symbol, Sword, and Shield: Defending Washington during the Civil War*. White Mane Publishing Co., Shippensburg, Pa.

Cooling, Benjamin Franklin, and Walton H. Owen

1988   *Mr. Lincoln's Forts: A Guide to the Civil War Defenses of Washington.* White Mane Publishing Co., Shippensburg, Pa.

Corbett, V. P.

1861   *Map of the Seat of War Showing the Battles of July 18th, 21st, and October 21, 1861.* V. P. Corbett, Washington, D.C. Map on file, Geography and Map Division, Library of Congress, Washington, D.C.

Cornelison, John E., Jr.

1995a Trip Report on Metal Detector Survey of Highway 27 at Chickamauga and Chattanooga National Military Park. Accession No. 1152, November 1994–January 1995, Trips 1, 2, and 3. Ms. on file, Southeast Archeological Center, National Park Service, Tallahassee, Fla.

1995b Research Design for an Archeological Survey of Selected Areas and Limited Site Testing at Stones River National Battlefield, Murfreesboro, Tenn. Ms. on file, Southeast Archeological Center, National Park Service, Tallahassee, Fla.

1995c Trip Report on Remote-Sensing Survey at Guilford Courthouse National Military Park, Greensboro, North Carolina. SEAC Accession No. 1189, Park Accession No. 56, 6/22/95–6/28/95. Ms. on file, Southeast Archeological Center, National Park Service, Tallahassee, Fla.

1997   The Application of Remote Sensing Technology to Aid in Locating Civil War Battle Lines as Demonstrated at Stones River National Battlefield. Paper presented at the 62d Annual Meeting of the Society for American Archaeology, April 1–6, 1997, Nashville, Tenn.

Cornelison, John E., Jr., and E. Carroll Hageseth

1995   Research Design for a Metal Detecting Survey of Selected Areas and Limited Testing to Locate Reported British Graves at Cowpens National Battlefield, Chesnee, South Carolina. Ms. on file, Southeast Archeological Center, National Park Service, Tallahassee, Fla.

Cornelison, John E., Jr., and Debbie Leslie

1996   Research Design for an Archeological Survey Prior to Installation of Utility Lines at Kennesaw Mountain National Battlefield, Cobb County, Georgia. Ms. on file, Southeast Archeological Center, National Park Service, Tallahassee, Fla.

Cotter, John L.

1959   Preliminary Investigations at Harpers Ferry: Harper House Garden and Building 23, Arsenal Area at Shenandoah and High Streets, April 8, 1959. Harpers Ferry National Monument. Ms. on file, Harpers Ferry National Historical Park, Harpers Ferry, W. Va.

Cox, Jacob D.

1895   *Atlanta.* Scribner's, New York.

Crass, David C.

1990   *Economic Interaction on the New Mexican Military Frontier.* Volumes in Historical Archaeology XIII, Stanley South editor. South Carolina Institute of Archaeology and Anthropology, University of South Carolina, Columbia.

Crouch, Howard R.

1978   *Relic Hunter: The Field Account of Civil War Sites, Artifacts, and Hunting.* SCS Publications, Fairfax, Va.

1995   *Civil War Artifacts: A Guide for the Historian.* SCS Publications, Fairfax, Va.

Cullen, Jim

1995   *The Civil War in Popular Culture: A Reusable Past.* Smithsonian Institution Press, Washington, D.C.

Cummings, Linda Scott

1993a Pollen and Macrofloral Analysis of Material for Package 116, the Late Nineteenth-Century Privies and Possible Garden Areas Associated with the Early Nineteenth-Century Old Master Armorer's House at Harpers Ferry National Historical Park. In *Interdisciplinary Investigations of Domestic Life in Government Block B: Perspectives on Harpers Ferry's Armory and Commercial District,* edited by Paul A. Shackel, 7.1–7.46. Occasional Report No. 6, Regional Archeology Program, National Capital Region, National Park Service, Washington, D.C.

1993b Diet and Prehistoric Landscape during the Nineteenth and Early Twentieth Centuries at Harpers Ferry, West Virginia: A View from the Old Master Armorer's Complex. In "An Archaeology of Harpers Ferry's Commercial and Residential District," edited by Paul A. Shackel and Susan E. Winter. *Historical Archaeology* 28(4):94–105.

Dabney, Virginius
1971 *Virginia, the New Dominion: A History from 1607 to the Present.* University Press of Virginia, Charlottesville.

Daily Dispatch
1862 Newspaper article, September 23. Richmond, Va.

Daniel, Larry J.
1991 *Soldiering in the Army of Tennessee: A Portrait of Life in a Confederate Army.* University of North Carolina Press, Chapel Hill.

Davis, Angela Kirkham
n.d. War Remembrances; A Letter to My Nieces. Ms. on file, Antietam National Battlefield, Sharpsburg, Md.

Davis, Maj. George B., Leslie J. Perry, and Joseph Kirkley (editors)
1895 *Atlas to Accompany the Official Records of the Union and Confederate Armies.* Compiled by Capt. Calvin D. Cowles. U.S. War Department, Government Printing Office, Washington, D.C.
1978 *Atlas to Accompany the Official Records of the Union and Confederate Armies.* Reprint. Arno Press and Crown Publishers, New York.

Davis, Julia
1945 *The Shenandoah.* Farrar and Rinehart, New York.

Davis, Maj. Murray
1865 Inspector General Report, May 13. Record Group 159, entry 15, file D-17. National Archives, Washington, D.C.

Deetz, James F.
1993 *Flowerdew Hundred.* University of Virginia Press, Charlottesville.

Dew, Charles B.
1994 *Bond of Iron: Master and Slave at Buffalo Forge.* W. W. Norton, New York.

Dickens, Roy S., Jr., and Timothy J. Crimmins
1982 Environmental-Impact Archaeology in the Urban Setting: A View from Atlanta. In *Archaeology of Urban America: The Search for Pattern and Process,* edited by Roy S. Dickens, Jr., 105–13. Academic Press, New York.

Dickens, Roy S., Jr., and Linda H. Worthy
1984 *Archaeological Investigations at Pickett's Mill Historic Site, Paulding County, Georgia.* Georgia Heritage Trust Program, Department of Natural Resources, Atlanta.

Dickey, Thomas S., and Peter C. George
1993 *Field Artillery Projectiles of the American Civil War.* Arsenal Publications II, Mechanicsville, Va.

Drickamer, Lee C., and Karen D. Drickamer (editors)
1987 *Harpers Ferry: On the Boarder of North and South with "Rambling Jour," a Civil War Soldier. The Civil War Letters and Newspaper Dispatches of Charles H. Moulton (34th Mass. Vol. Infantry).* White Mane Publishing Co., Shippensburg, Pa.

Du Bois, W.E.B.
1903 The Souls of Black Folk. In *W.E.B. Du Bois, Writings,* notes and selection of texts by Nathan Huggins. Literary Classics of the United States, New York.

Dudley, William
1862 Report of Co. B, 19th Ind. Vols. After the Battles of August 28th and 30th. *Richmond Palladium,* September 12, p. 2.

Dwight, Henry
1982 The Union Army Learns to Fight behind Fortifications. Reprint. In *The Blue and the Gray,* edited by Henry Steele Commager, 939–43. Fairfax Press, New York.

Dyer, Frederick H.
1959   *A Compendium of the War of the Rebellion.* Thomas Yoseloff, New York.

Early, Jubal
1867   *Memoir of the Last Year of the War for Independence.* C.W. Button, Lynchburg. Va.

Eby, Cecil D., Jr. (editor)
1961   *A Virginia Yankee in the Civil War: The Diaries of David Hunter Strother.* University of North Carolina Press, Chapel Hill.

Edgerly, Maj. H. C.
1864   Letter to Lt. McQueen, June 29. Record Group 393, part 4, entry 902, p. 313. National Archives, Washington, D.C.

Edmonds, William J., and James Stiegler
1981   *Soil Survey of Clarke County, Virginia.* Soil Conservation Service, United States Department of Agriculture, Washington, D.C.

Edwards, William B.
1962   *Civil War Guns.* Castle Books, New Jersey.
1997   *Civil War Guns.* Reprint. Thomas Publications, Gettysburg, Pa.

Ehrenhard, Ellen B.
1985   Archeological Resource Inventory, Prehistoric and Historic Sites, Andersonville National Historic Site, Georgia. Ms. on file, Southeast Archeological Center, Tallahassee, Fla.

Elkins, Stephen B., and Daniel S. Lamont
1874   *Map IV, Illustrating the Military Operations of the Atlanta Campaign, Embracing the Region from Pine, Lost and Kennesaw Mountains South to Include Atlanta and Its Environs, etc.* U.S. War Department, Government Printing Office, Washington, D.C. Map on file, University of Georgia Hargrett Library, Athens.

Emerson, Sir James
1864   *The Story of the Guns.* Longman, Green, New York.

Emory, Samuel T., Jr.
1964   The Economic Geography of Clarke and Frederick Counties, Virginia. Ph.D. dissertation, Department of Geography, University of Maryland, College Park.

Ensminger, Robert F.
1992   *The Pennsylvania Barn: Its Origin, Evolution, and Distribution in North America.* Johns Hopkins University Press, Baltimore and London.

Epperly, Marion
1861–65 Personal letters. Archives, Carrier Library, James Madison University, Harrisonburg, Virginia.

Ernst, Kathleen A.
1993   Broken Hearts Can't Be Photographed: The Social, Political, and Economic Impact of the 1862 Maryland Campaign on the Residents of Washington County, Maryland. M.A. thesis, Antioch University, Washington.

Evans, Clement (editor)
1987   Virginia. *Confederate Military History.* Extended edition, vol. 4. Reprint. Broadfoot Publishing Co., Wilmington, N.C.

Ewen, Charles R.
1984   Fur Trade Archaeology: A Study of Frontier Hierarchies. *Historical Archaeology* 18(1):15–28.

Eyles, William H.
1862   Letter. Robert W. Woodruff Library, Emory University. Photocopy on file, Manassas National Battlefield Park, Manassas, Va.

Fagan, Brian M.
1996   *The Oxford Companion to Archaeology.* Oxford University Press, New York.

Federal Agricultural Schedules
1860–80 Sharpsburg District, Washington County, Maryland. Maryland Hall of Records, Annapolis.

Federal Census Schedules

1860–70 Sharpsburg District, Washington County, Maryland. Maryland Hall of Records, Annapolis.

Federal Slave Schedules

1860 Sharpsburg District, Washington County, Maryland. Maryland Hall of Records, Annapolis.

Ferguson, Leland

1992 *Uncommon Ground: Archaeology and Early African America, 1650–1800.* Smithsonian Institution Press, Washington, D.C.

Fiske, Wilbur

1983 *Anti-Rebel, The Civil War Letters of Wilbur Fiske.* Emil Rosenblatt, Croton-on-Hudson, N.Y.

Fitts, Robert K.

1996 The Landscapes of Northern Bondage. *Historical Archaeology* 30(2):54–73.

1999 The Archaeology of Middle-Class Domesticity and Gentility in Victorian Brooklyn. *Historical Archaeology* 33(1):39–62.

Foote, Shelby

1958 *The Civil War: A Narrative.* Random House, New York.

Fox, Richard A., Jr.

1993 *Archaeology, History, and Custer's Last Battle: The Little Big Horn Reexamined.* University of Oklahoma Press, Norman.

Fox, Richard A., Jr., and Douglas D. Scott

1991 The Post–Civil War Battlefield Pattern: An Example from the Custer Battlefield. *Historical Archaeology* 25(2):92–103.

Franklin, Maria

1997 "Power to the People": Sociopolitics and the Archaeology of Black Americans. *Historical Archaeology* 31(3):36–50.

Frassanito, William

1978 *Antietam: The Photographic Legacy of America's Bloodiest Day.* Scribner's, New York.

Frederick County

1743 County Court Deed Books. Frederick County Courthouse, Winchester, Va.

1743 County Court Will Books. Frederick County Courthouse, Winchester, Va.

Frederickson, Fred

1863 Letter to his wife, May 7. Ms. on file, HFD 390, Harpers Ferry National Historical Park, Harpers Ferry, W. Va.

French, Samuel G.

1901 *Two Wars: An Autobiography of General Samuel G. French.* Confederate Veteran, Nashville, Tenn.

Friedlander, Amy

1985 Establishing Historical Probabilities for Archaeological Interpretations: Slave Demography of Two Plantations in the South Carolina Lowcountry, 1740–1820. In *The Archaeology of Slavery and Plantation Life,* edited by Theresa A. Singleton, 215–38. Academic Press, Orlando, Fla.

Friedman, Carol Drake

1987 Profile: Oswald Robinson. *Centre View,* August 29, pp. 1, 15, 21. Centreville, Va.

Fry, Brig. Gen. Speed S.

1864a General Order 11, July 26. Record Group 393, part 4, entry 905, p. 68. National Archives, Washington, D.C.

1864b General Order 15, August 10. Record Group 393, part 4, entry 905, page 74. National Archives, Washington, D.C.

1864c General Order 27, January 4. Record Group 393, part 4, entry 905, page 97. National Archives, Washington, D.C.

Frye, Dennis E.

1987 Stonewall Attacks! The Siege of Harpers Ferry. *Blue and Gray Magazine* 5(1):8–27, 47–54.

Fryman, Robert J.

1993a   The Last Redoubt: Archaeological Investigations at Fort Tyler, West Point, Georgia. Garrow and Associates, Atlanta. Submitted to Fort Tyler Association, West Point, Ga.

1993b   Mapping and Archaeological Reconnaissance of Johnston's Chattahoochee River Defense Line, Cobb County, Georgia. Garrow and Associates, Atlanta. Submitted to Cobb County Department of Transportation, Marietta, Ga.

1993c   Phase II Investigations at Loring's Position (9CO352), Barrett Parkway Extension Project, Cobb County, Georgia. Garrow and Associates, Atlanta. Submitted to Cobb County Department of Transportation, Marietta, Ga.

Fuller, Claud E.

1958   *The Rifled Musket.* Stackpole, Harrisburg, Pa.

Fuller, Claud E., and Richard D. Steuart

1944   *Firearms of the Confederacy.* Standard Publications, Huntington, W. Va.

Fulop, Timothy E., and Albert J. Raboteau (editors)

1997   *African-American Religion: Interpretive Essays in History and Culture.* Routledge, New York.

Gaff, Alan D.

1985   *Brave Men's Tears: The Iron Brigade at Brawner Farm.* Morningside Press, Dayton, Ohio.

Galke, Laura J.

1992a   *Cultural Resource Survey and Inventory of a War-Torn Landscape: The Stuart's Hill Tract, Manassas National Battlefield Park, Virginia.* Occasional Report No. 7, Regional Archeology Program, National Capital Region, National Park Service, Washington, D.C.

1992b   You Are Where You Live. Paper presented at the 25th Annual Meeting of the Society for Historical Archaeology, Kingston, Jamaica.

1992c   Brownsville: Archeology. In *Cultural Resource Survey and Inventory of a War-Torn Landscape: The Stuart's Hill Tract, Manassas National Battlefield Park, Virginia.* Occasional Report No. 7, Regional Archeology Program, National Capital Region, National Park Service, Washington, D.C.

1992d   Nash: Archeology. In *Cultural Resource Survey and Inventory of a War-Torn Landscape: The Stuart's Hill Tract, Manassas National Battlefield Park, Virginia.* Occasional Report No. 7, Regional Archeology Program, National Capital Region, National Park Service, Washington, D.C.

Gallagher, Gary W.

1996   How Familiarity Bred Success: Military Campaigns and Leaders in Ken Burns' "The Civil War." In *Ken Burns' "The Civil War": Historians Respond,* edited by Robert Brent Toplin, 37–59. Oxford University Press, New York.

Galway, Thomas Francis

1961   *The Valiant Hours: Narrative of "Captain Brevet," an Irish American in the Army of the Potomac,* edited by Col. W. S. Nye. Stackpole, Harrisburg, Pa.

Garcia-Herreros, Jorge

1998   The Interpretation of a Smith Cabin at the Levi-Jordan Plantation. Paper presented at the 31st Annual Meeting of the Society for Historical Archaeology, Atlanta, Georgia.

Garrett, Franklin M.

1954   *Atlanta and Environs: A Chronicle of Its People and Events,* vol. 1. University of Georgia Press, Athens.

Garrow, Patrick H., and Terry Klein

1984   Final Archaeological Investigations at the Wilmington Boulevard, Monroe Street to King Street Wilmington, New Castle County, Delaware. Delaware Department of Transportation Archaeology Series No. 29, Dover.

Gates, Arnold

1987   *The Rough Side of War: The Civil War Journal of Chesley A. Mosman, 1st Lieutenant, Company D, 59th Illinois Volunteer Infantry Regiment.* Basin Publishing Co., Garden City, N.Y.

Gates, Paul W.

1965   *Agriculture and the Civil War.* Alfred A. Knopf, New York.

Geier, Clarence R., Jr.

1994a   Toward a Social History of the Civil War: The Hatcher-Cheatham Site. In *Look to the Earth: Historical Archaeology and American Civil War,* edited by Clarence R. Geier and Susan E. Winter, 191–214. University of Tennessee Press, Knoxville.

1994b   Report of Findings from the Excavation of a Tent Platform at the Site of the Sheridan Military Field Hospital, Winchester, Virginia. Department of Sociology and Anthropology, James Madison University, Harrisonburg, Va. Submitted to Winchester Department of Parks and Recreation.

Geier, Clarence R., and Warren R. Hofstra

1992   An Evaluation of Cultural Resources at the Shawnee Springs Tract: Winchester Virginia. Department of Sociology and Anthropology, James Madison University, Harrisonburg, Va. Submitted to Winchester Department of Parks and Recreation, Winchester, Va.

Geier, Clarence R., and Susan E. Winter (editors)

1994   *Look to the Earth: Historical Archaeology and the American Civil War.* University of Tennessee Press, Knoxville.

Geier, Clarence R., Joseph W. A. Whitehorne, and Warren R. Hofstra

1993   The Sheridan Military Field Hospital Complex; A Preliminary Evaluation with Recommendations for Preservation and Management. Department of Sociology and Anthropology, James Madison University, Harrisonburg, Va. Submitted to Winchester Department of Parks and Recreation, Winchester, Va.

Geier, Clarence R., Joseph Whitehorne, and Ann McCleary

1995   The Cool Spring Battlefield District: A Report of Events Occurring July 16–20, 1864 Near Castleman's Ferry in Northeastern Clarke County, Virginia. Department of Sociology and Anthropology, James Madison University, Harrisonburg, Va. National Register Nomination prepared for the National Park Service, the Board of Supervisors of Clarke County, Va., and the Virginia Department of Historic Resources, Richmond.

Geier, Clarence R., et al.

1989   *The Hatcher-Cheatham Site (44CF258): A Multicomponent Historic Site in Chesterfield County, Virginia,* vol. 4, *Ceramic, Toys, Pipes, Glass, Buttons, Metal, and Faunal Analysis.* James Madison University, Archaeological Research Center, Harrisonburg, Va. Submitted to Virginia Department of Transportation, Richmond. Project #0288–020–102, PE-101.

Genovese, Eugene D.

1965   *The Political Economy of Slavery: Studies in the Economy and Society of the Slave South.* Pantheon Books, New York.

Gibbon, John

1978   *Personal Recollections of the Civil War.* Press of Morningside Bookshop, Dayton, Ohio.

Gibson, Col. H. G.

1864   Letter to Maj. Charles E. Smith, March 28. Record Group 393, part 2, entry 858. National Archives, Washington, D.C.

Gillespie, G. L.

1873   "Battlefield of Winchester, Va., September 19, 1864." In George B. Davis, Leslie J. Perry, and Joseph W. Kirley, eds., *Atlas to Accompany the Official Records of the Union and Confederate Armies.* U.S. Government Publication. Reprint 1978, Arno Press.

Gillett, Mary C.

1987   *The Army Medical Department, 1818–1865.* Army Center of Military History, Washington, D.C.

Gilmer, Maj. Gen. J. F.

1890a   Letter to Col. M. H. Wright, October 21, 1863. *The War of the Rebellion: A Compilation of the Official Records of the Union and Confederate Armies.* Series 1, vol. 31, pt. 3:575–76. National Historical Society, Harrisburg, Pa.

1890b Letter from Maj. Gen. J. F. Gilmer, Chief of Engineers Bureau (CSA) to Capt. L. P. Grant, August 11, 1863. *The War of the Rebellion: A Compilation of the Official Records of the Union and Confederate Armies.* Series 1, vol. 30, pt. 4:575–76. National Historical Society, Washington, D.C.

Ginn, Richard V. N.
1997   *The History of the United States Army Medical Service Corps.* Office of the Surgeon General and Army Center of Military History, Washington, D.C.

Glass, Joseph W.
1986   *The Pennsylvania Culture Region: A View from the Barn.* University of Michigan Research Press, Ann Arbor, Mich.

Glassberg, David
1990   *American Historical Pageantry: The Uses of Tradition in the Early Twentieth Century.* University of North Carolina Press, Chapel Hill.

Glatthaar, Joseph T.
1985   *The March to the Sea and Beyond: Sherman's Troops in the Savannah and Carolinas Campaigns.* New York University Press, New York.

Goble, William C.
1997   Irish Brigade Ordnance at Antietam. In *"My Sons Were Faithful and They Fought": The Irish Brigade at Antietam. An Anthology,* edited by Joseph G. Bilby and Stephan D. O'Neill, 61–66. Longstreet House, Hightstown, N.J.

Godden, Geoffrey A.
1964   *The Encyclopaedia of British Pottery and Porcelain Marks.* Schiffer Publishing, Exton, Penn.

Gold, Thomas D.
1914   *History of Clarke County Virginia and Its Connection with the War between the States.* N.p., Berryville, Va.

Gottschalk, Phil
1991   *In Deadly Earnest: The History of the First Missouri Brigade, CSA.* Missouri River Press, Columbia.

Gould, John M.
1871   *History of the 1st, 10th, and 29th Maine.* Stephen Berry, Portland, Maine.

Gould, Pamela
1993   Slavery, War Links Robinson to Family. *Potomac News,* February 13, p. A1. Manassas, Va.

Grant, James J.
1947   *Single-Shot Rifles.* William Morrow, New York.

Grant, Lemuel
1863–64 Lemuel Grant Collection. Atlanta History Center, Atlanta, Ga.

Grant, Ulysses S.
1985   Report of Lieutenant General Ulysses S. Grant, U.S. Army, Commanding Armies of the United States, of Operations, March 1864–May 1865, Washington, D.C., July 22, 1865. In *The War of the Rebellion: A Compilation of the Official Records of the Union and Confederate Armies,* vol. 38, part 1:1–51. Reprint. National Historical Society, Harrisburg, Pa.

Gray, Lewis Cecil
1941   *History of Agriculture in the Southern United States to 1860.* Reprint. Peter Smith, New York.

Grettler, David J.
1991   Farmer Snug and Farmer Slack: The Archaeology of Agricultural Reform in Delaware, 1780–1920. *Journal of Middle Atlantic Archaeology.*

Griffin, Col. Simon G.
1863   General Order 4, November 7. Record Group 393, part 4, entry 905. National Archives, Washington, D.C.

Griffith, Paddy
1986   *Battle in the Civil War: Generalship and Tactics in America 1861–65.* Fieldbooks, Mansfield, England.

1989   *Battle Tactics of the Civil War.* Yale University Press, New Haven and London.

Hacker, Charles M., and Jeffrey B. Mauck

1997   *On the Prairie of Palo Alto: Historical Archaeology of the U.S. Battlefield.* Texas A&M University Press, College Station.

Hagerman, Edward

1988   *The American Civil War and the Origins of Modern Warfare: Ideas, Organization and Field Command.* Indiana University Press, Bloomington.

Haines, Alanson A.

1883   *History of the 15th Regiment New Jersey Volunteers.* Jenkins and Thomas, New York.

Hains, Peter C.

1911   The First Guns at Bull Run. *Cosmopolitan* 51:391–92.

Hale, Laura V.

1986   *Four Valiant Years in the Lower Shenandoah Valley, 1861–1865.* Hathaway Publishing Co., Front Royal, Va.

Hall, E. M.

1855   *Practical American Cookery and Domestic Economy.* C. M. Saxton, Miller, New York.

Hall, Robert L.

1990   African Religious Retentions in Florida. In *Africanisms in American Culture,* edited by Joseph E. Holloway, 98–118. Indiana University Press, Bloomington.

Hall, Capt. Theron E.

1865   Letter to General M. C. Meigs, March 30. Record Group 92, entry 225, box 720. National Archives, Washington, D.C.

Hall, Wes, and Ralph Wilbanks

1995   Search for the Confederate Submarine H. L. Hunley off Charleston Harbor, South Carolina. National Underwater and Marine Agency. Submitted to Naval Historical Center, Washington Naval Yard, Washington, D.C.

Hamlin, Augustus

1866   *Martyria; or Andersonville Prison.* Boston, Mass.

Hammond, Maj. LaFayette

1865   Letter to General M. C. Meigs, March 30. Record Group 92, entry 225, box 720. National Archives, Washington, D.C.

Hanaford, Lt. George A.

1864   Letter to Captain J. S. Butler, May 6. Record Group 393, part 2, entry 1030. National Archives, Washington, D.C.

Harpers Ferry National Historical Park

1989   Harpers Ferry Division of Archeology Ceramic Glossary. Ms. on file, Harpers Ferry National Historical Park, Harpers Ferry, W. Va.

Harris, Charles S.

1987   *Civil War Relics of the Western Campaigns, 1861–1865.* Rapidan Press, Mechanicsville, Va.

Harris, Robert N.

1998   Shell Carving and Self-Reliance in an African-American Plantation Community. Paper presented at the 31st Annual Meeting of the Society for Historical Archaeology, Atlanta.

Harwit, Martin

1996   *An Exhibit Denied: Lobbying the History of the Enola Gay.* Copernicus Books, New York.

Hattaway, Herman

1998   *Shades of Blue and Gray.* University of Missouri Press, Columbia.

Haynes, E. M.

1870   *A History of the Tenth Regiment, Vermont Volunteers.* Regimental Association, Lewiston, Maine.

Heatwole, John L.

1998   *The Burning: Sheridan in the Shenandoah Valley.* Howell Press, Charlottesville, Va.

Henderson, G. F. R.

1955   *Stonewall Jackson and the American Civil War.* Longman, Green, New York.

Hennessy, John J.

1985   *Historical Report on the Troop Movements for the Second Battle of Manassas, August 28 through August 30, 1862.* National Park Service, Denver Service Center, Denver.

1993   *Return to Bull Run: The Campaign and Battle of Second Manassas.* Simon and Schuster, New York.

Henry, Susan L.

1987   Factors Influencing Consumer Behavior in Turn-of-the-Century Phoenix, Arizona. In *Consumer Choice in Historical Archaeology,* edited by Suzanne M. Spencer-Wood, 359–82. Plenum Press, New York.

Herald and Torchlight

1862   Newspaper article, September 24. Hagerstown, Md.

Herman, Bernard L.

1994   The Model Farmer and the Organization of the Countryside. In *Everyday Life in the Early Republic,* edited by Catherine E. Hutchins, 35–59. Henry Francis du Pont Winterthur Museum, Winterthur, Del.

Hern, Chester G.

1996   *Six Years of Hell: Harpers Ferry during the Civil War.* Louisiana State University Press, Baton Rouge.

Hernigle, Jacqueline

1991   Manassas National Battlefield Park Wayside Exhibit Installation Archeological Investigation and Clearance. Ms. on file, Manassas National Battlefield Park, Manassas, Va.

Hewitt, William

1892   *History of the 12th West Virginia Volunteer Infantry. The Part It Took in the War of the Rebellion, 1861–1865.* N.p., Berryville, Va.

Hibbard, Alma

1854–55 Journal. Ms. on file, Manuscript Department, William R. Perkins Library, Duke University, Durham, N.C.

Higgins, Thomas F. III, et al.

1995   *The Civil War at Gloucester Point: Mitigation of Site 44GL358 Associated with the Proposed Route 17 Coleman Bridge Project, Gloucester County, Virginia.* Technical Report Series No. 19. William and Mary Center for Archaeological Research, Department of Anthropology, Williamsburg, Va. Submitted to Virginia Department of Transportation, Richmond.

Hildebrand, John R. (editor)

1996   *A Mennonite Journal, 1862–1865: A Father's Account of the Civil War in the Shenandoah Valley.* Burd Street Press, Shippensburg, Pa.

Hill, Richard T., and Anthony, William E.

1978   *Confederate Long Arms and Pistols.* Hill and Anthony Publishers, Charlotte, N.C.

Hilliard, Samuel B.

1972   *Hog Meat and Hoe Cake: Food Supply in the Old South, 1840–1860.* Southern Illinois University Press, Carbondale.

Hinman, Wilbur F.

1897   The Story of the Sherman Brigade. *Daily Review,* Alliance, Ohio.

Hitchcock, Frederick L.

1904   *War from the Inside: The Story of the 132nd Regiment Pa. Volunteer Infantry in the War of the Suppression of the Rebellion 1862–1863.* Press of the J. B. Lippincott Co., Philadelphia, Pa.

Hodler, Thomas W., and Howard A. Schretter

1986   *The Atlas of Georgia.* The Institute of Community and Area Development, University of Georgia, Athens.

Hofstra, Warren R.
1986   *A Separate Place: The Formation of Clarke County, Virginia.* Clarke County Sesquicentennial Committee, White Post, Va.

Hofstra, Warren R., and Robert D. Mitchell
1993   Town and Country in Backcountry Virginia: Winchester and the Shenandoah Valley, 1730–1800. *Journal of Southern History* 59:619–46.

Hofstra, Warren R., and Joseph W. A. Whitehorne
1996   Report to Winchester Department of Parks and Recreation: Subject New York Public Library Sanitary Commission Holdings, March 6, 1996. Ms. on file, Winchester Department of Parks and Recreation, Winchester, Va.

Holcombe, Return I.
1916   *History of the First Regiment Minnesota Volunteer Infantry.* Easton and Masterson Printers, Stillwater, Minn.

Holley, Alexander L.
1865   *Ordnance and Armor.* Van Nostrand Co., New York.

Holtz, Wendy K., and Mark S. Cassell
1996   Images of Agriculture: Representations of Material Culture and Agrarian Production on the Farm in the 19th and Early 20th Century American North. Paper presented at the 29th Annual Meeting of the Society for Historical Archaeology, Cincinnati, Ohio.

Honerkamp, Nicholas, E. Raymond Evans, and M. Elizabeth Will
1982   Results of an Archeological Survey of Pistol-Range Hollow, Chickamauga and Chattanooga National Military Park, Walker County, Georgia. Ms. on file, Southeast Archeological Center, National Park Service, Tallahassee, Fla.

Hooker, Richard J.
1981   *Food and Drink in America.* Bobbs-Merrill, New York.

Horst, Samuel
1967   *Mennonites in the Confederacy: A Study in Civil War Pacifism.* Herald Press, Scottsville, Pa.

Hotchkiss, J.E.D.
1864   Engagement at Castleman's Ferry, July 18. In *Official Atlas of the Civil War.* Davis et al., editors [1978], Plate LXXXIV, Map 20.

Huelsbeck, David R.
1991   Faunal Remains and Consumer Behavior: What Is Being Measured? *Historical Archaeology* 25(2):62–76.

Huggins, Nathan Irvin (editor)
1995   *Voices from the Harlem Renaissance.* Oxford University Press, New York.

Hunt, Russell A.
1966   *The Ancestors and Descendants of John Henry Horine and Virginia Washington Overstreet.* Golden Rule Press, Griffith, Ind.

Hunter, Robert R., Jr., and George L. Miller
1990   *English Shell Edged Earthenware: Alias Leeds Ware, and Alias Feather Edge.* 35th Annual Wedgwood International Seminar, 107–36. Birmingham Museum of Art, Birmingham, Ala.

Hyde, Thomas W.
1894   *Following the Greek Cross or, Memories of the Sixth Army Corps.* Houghton, Mifflin, Boston and New York.

Inashima, Paul
1981   *Archeological Monitoring, Park Maintenance Repair: Lateral-Sag-Failure Section along the Northern Portion of the First Terrace "Harpers" Gardens' Wall.* National Park Service, Denver Service Center, National Capital Team, Washington, D.C.

Irish-American
1863   Corcoran's Irish Legion, August 1, p. 2. New York City.

Irwin, Richard B.

1985   *History of the 19th Army Corps.* Reprint. Elliot's Book Shop, Baton Rouge, La.

Isaac, Rhys

1982   *The Transformation of Virginia: 1740–1790.* University of North Carolina Press, Chapel Hill.

Jackson, Bruce

1997   The Other Kind of Doctor: Conjure and Magic in Black American Folk Medicine. In *African-American Religion: Interpretive Essays in History and Culture,* edited by Timothy E. Fulop and Albert J. Raboteau, 415–31. Routledge, New York.

Jessamine County, Kentucky

1816   Will Book B:287–89. Nicholasville, Ky.

1862–67 Order Books M:20, 210, 246, 250. Nicholasville, Ky.

Jewell, Thomas

1877   Southern Claims Commission Records, Claim No. 20709, General Records 1877 of the Department of the Treasury; claims allowed under special act of May 18, 1872. Washington, D.C.

Johnson, Curt, and Richard C. Anderson, Jr.

1995   *Artillery Hell: The Employment of Artillery at Antietam.* Texas A&M University Press, College Station.

Jones, Archer

1992   *Civil War Command and Strategy: The Process of Victory and Defeat.* Free Press, New York.

Jones, Gordon W.

1964   Sheridan's Medical Service in the Shenandoah. *Civil War Times Illustrated* 3:16–21.

Jones, Lynn Diekman

1995   The Material Culture of Slavery from an Annapolis Household. Paper presented at the 28th Annual Meeting of the Society for Historical Archaeology, Washington, D.C.

Jordan, Weymouth T. (editor)

1979   *North Carolina Troops 1861–1865,* vol. 7, *Infantry 22d–26th Regiment.* North Carolina Division of Archives and History, Raleigh.

Joseph, Maureen Delay

1994   *Cultural Landscape Inventory: Northeast Quadrant, Manassas National Battlefield Park, Manassas, Virginia.* National Park Service, Denver Service Center, Falls Church, Va.

Kellar, Herbert A.

1928   Rockbridge County, Virginia, in 1835: A Study of Ante-Bellum Society. In *The Crusades and Other Historical Essays Presented to Dana C. Munro by His Former Students,* edited by Louis J. Paetow, 321–65. F. S. Crofts and Co., New York.

Kelly, Dennis

1987   *Kennesaw Mountain and the Atlanta Campaign.* Kennesaw Mountain Historical Association, Marietta, Ga.

Kennett, Lee

1995   *Marching through Georgia: The Story of Soldiers and Civilians during Sherman's Campaign.* Harper Collins Publishers, New York.

Keyes, Charles M. (editor)

1874   *The Military History of the One Hundred and Twenty-Third Regiment Ohio Volunteer Infantry.* Register Steam Press, Sandusky, Ohio.

Kloeppel, James E.

1992   *Danger beneath the Waves: A History of the Confederate Submarine H. L. Hunley.* Sandlapper Publishing, Orangeburg, S.C.

Koons, Kenneth E.

2000   "The Staple of Our Country": Wheat in the Regional Farm Economy of the Nineteenth-Century Valley of Virginia. In *After the Backcounty: Rural Life in the Great Valley of Virginia, 1800–1900,* edited by Kenneth E. Koons and Warren R. Hofstra. University of Tennessee Press, Knoxville.

Laidley, T. T. S.

1861　*Ordnance Manual for the Use of the Officers of the United States Army.* J. B. Lippincott and Co., Philadelphia.

Larkin, Jack

1994　From "Country Mediocrity" to "Rural Improvement," Transforming the Slovenly Countryside in Central Massachusetts, 1775–1840. In *Everyday Life in the Early Republic,* edited by Catherine E. Hutchins, 175–200. Henry Francis du Pont Winterthur Museum, Winterthur, Del.

Larsen, Eric L.

1993　"That Trying Climate": Health and Medicine in Nineteenth Century Harpers Ferry. In *Interdisciplinary Investigations of Domestic Life in Government Block B: Perspectives on Harpers Ferry's Armory and Commercial District,* edited by Paul A. Shackel, 11.1–11.64. Occasional Report No. 6, Regional Archeology Program, National Capital Region, National Park Service, Washington, D.C.

Larson, Lewis H., Jr., and Morgan R. Crook, Jr.

1975　An Archeological Investigation at Andersonville National Historic Site, Sumter and Macon Counties, Georgia. Ms. on file, National Park Service, Southeast Archeological Center, Tallahassee, Fla.

Lathrop, J. M., and B. N. Griffing.

1991　*An Atlas of Shenandoah and Page Counties, Virginia, from Actual Surveys by J. M. Lathrop and B. N. Griffing.* G. P. Hammond Pub., Strasburg, Va. Originally published in 1885 by J. D. Lake & Co., Philadelphia, Pa.

Lee, Mrs. Hugh Holmes

1862–65　Civil War journal. Ms. on file, Handley Library Archives, Winchester, Va.

Leech, Margaret

1986　*Reveille in Washington.* Carroll and Graf Publishers, New York.

LeeDecker, Charles H., et al.

1987　Nineteenth-Century Households and Consumer Behavior in Wilmington, Delaware. In *Consumer Choice in Historical Archaeology,* edited by Suzanne M. Spencer-Wood, 233–59. Plenum Press, New York.

Lees, William B.

1992　Archaeology and the Interpretation of Civil War Battlefields: The Case of Mine Creek, Kansas. Paper presented at the Southeastern Archaeological Conference, Little Rock, Ark.

1994　When the Shooting Stopped, the War Began. In *Look to the Earth: Historical Archaeology and the American Civil War,* edited by Clarence R. Geier and Susan E. Winter, 39–59. University of Tennessee Press, Knoxville.

1996　The Impact of Metal Detectors: Preservation Lessons from the Battlefield. Paper presented at the 29th Annual Meeting of the Society for Historical Archaeology, Cincinnati, Ohio.

Lees, William B., and Kathryn M. Kimery-Lees

1992　Regional Perspectives on the Fort Towson Sutler's Store and Residence, Frontier Site in Antebellum Eastern Oklahoma. *Plains Anthropologist* 29:13–24.

Legg, James B., and Steven D. Smith

1989　*"The Best Ever Occupied . . .": Archeological Investigations of Civil War Encampment on Folly Island, South Carolina.* Research Manuscript Series 209, South Carolina Institute of Archaeology and Anthropology, University of South Carolina, Columbia.

Leiter, George T.

n.d.　*One of the Gamest of Modern Fights. 15th VA by Lt. Col. R. M. Morrison.* Ms. on file, Washington County Free Library, Hagerstown, Md.

Lewis, Berkeley R.

1956　*Small Arms and Ammunition in the United States Service.* Smithsonian Institution Miscellaneous Collections, vol. 129. Smithsonian Institution, Washington, D.C.

1959　*Notes on Ammunition of the American Civil War.* Smithsonian Institution, Washington, D.C.

Lewis, Ronald L.

1979　*Coal, Iron, and Slaves: Industrial Slavery in Maryland and Virginia, 1715–1865.* Greenwood Press, Westport, Conn.

Lincoln, William S.

1879　*Life with the Thirty-Fourth Mass. Infantry in the War of the Rebellion.* Noyes and Snow, Worcester, Mass.

Lippitt, Francis J.

1866　*A Treatise on Intrenchments.* John Wiley, New York.

Logan, George C.

1995　African Religion in America. In *Invisible America: Unearthing Our Hidden History,* edited by Mark P. Leone and Neil Asher Silberman, 154–55. Henry Holt, New York.

Logan, George C., et al.

1992　Archaeological Excavations at the Charles Carroll House in Annapolis, Maryland 18AP45. Ms. on file, Historic Annapolis Foundation, Annapolis.

Longstreet, James

1896　*From Manassas to Appomattox: Memoirs of the Civil War in America.* Indiana University Press, Bloomington.

Lord, Francis A.

1950　*They Fought for the Union.* Castle Books, N.J.

1957　Army and Navy Textbooks and Manuals Used in the North during the Civil War. *Military Collector and Historian,* pt. 1:61–67; pt. 2:95–101.

1965　*Civil War Collectors Encyclopedia,* 3 vols. Castle Books, N.J.

1969　*Civil War Sutlers and Their Wares.* Thomas Yoseloff, New York.

1995　*Civil War Collector's Encyclopedia,* 5 vols. Reprint. Blue and Grey Press, Edison, N.J.

Lucas, Marian B.

1989　Camp Nelson, Kentucky, during the Civil War: Cradle of Liberty or Refugee Death Camp. *Filson Club History Quarterly* 63:439–59.

Lucas, Michael T.

1990　Vessel Analysis: Procedure and Concerns. Ms. on file, Harpers Ferry National Historical Park, Harpers Ferry, W. Va.

1991　Nineteenth Century Ceramic Chronology. Ms. on file, Harpers Ferry National Historical Park, Harpers Ferry, W. Va.

1993　Late Nineteenth-Century Material Goods from Lower Town Harpers Ferry: The ceramic and glass evidence from Features 99, 132, and 21. In *Interdisciplinary Investigations of Domestic Life in Government Block B: Perspectives on Harpers Ferry's Armory and Commercial District,* edited by P. A. Shackel, 14.1–14.64. Occasional Report No. 6. Regional Archeology Program National Park Service, National Capital Region, Washington, D.C.

Luraghi, Raimondo

1996　*A History of the Confederate Navy,* translated by Paolo E. Coletta. Naval Institute Press, Annapolis, Md.

Luvaas, Jay

1959　*The Military Legacy of the Civil War: The European Inheritance.* University of Chicago Press, Chicago

Lynch, Charles H.

1915　*The Civil War Diary of C. H. Lynch, Eighteenth Connecticut Volunteers, 1862–1865.* Case, Lockwood and Brainard, Hartford, Conn.

Lynn, John A.

1997　The Embattled Future of Academic Military History. *Journal of Military History* 61:777–89.

Lyon, J. S.

1882　*War Sketches: From Cedar Mountain to Bull Run.* Lockwood and Co. Press, Buffalo, N.Y.

MacDonald, Rose M. E.

1983–84 Clarke County: A Daughter of Frederick. *Proceedings of the Clarke County Historical Association* 23:1–74.

MacGaffey, Wyatt

1991 *Art and Healing of the Bakongo Commented by Themselves: Minkisi from the Laman Collection.* Indiana University Press, Bloomington.

Madaus, H. Michael

1981 *American Longarms.* Main Street Press, New York.

Madden, David

1995 For the New Millennium: New Perspectives on the Civil War. *Phi Kappa Phi Journal* 77(3):24–30.

Mahan, Dennis H.

1836 *A Complete Treatise on Field Fortification.* Wiley and Long, New York.

1860 *A Treatise on Field Fortifications.* D. Van Nostrand, New York.

1861 *An Elementary Treatise on Advanced-Guard, Out-Post, and Detachment Service of Troops.* John Wiley, New York.

Mann, Franklin W.

1942 *The Bullet's Flight.* Standard Printing and Publishing Co. Huntington, W. Va.

Mann, T. H.

1890 A Yankee in Andersonville. *Century Magazine,* vol. 18.

Manning-Sterling, Elise, and Bruce B. Sterling

1997a *Draft Management Summary Part I and Part II of Third Phase of Archeological Investigations of the North Woods, Antietam National Battlefield, Sharpsburg, Maryland.* URS Greiner. Submitted to National Capital Area, National Park Service, Washington, D.C.

1997b Summary of Regiments and Batteries in and around the North and East Woods before and during the Battle of Antietam: Showing Locations and Weaponry Characteristics. Ms. on file, Antietam National Battlefield Park, Sharpsburg, Md.

Manucy, Albert

1949 *Artillery Through the Ages.* National Park Service, Division of Publications, Washington, D.C.

Marmion, Annie P.

1959 *Under Fire: An Experience in the Civil War,* compiled and edited by William Vincent Marmion, Jr., William Marmion, Harpers Ferry, W. Va.

Marrinan, Rochelle A., and Kenneth S. Wild, Jr.

1985 Soil Resistivity Survey of the Hospital Site Andersonville National Historic Site. Ms. on file, National Park Service, Southeast Archeological Center, Tallahassee, Fla.

Martin, Erika

1997 Cultural Landscape Report: The Nash Site, African-American Landscapes of Contention and Cultural Affinity. Ms. on file, University of Maryland, College Park, Md.

Martin, Erika K., and Mia T. Parsons

1998 Battling beyond First and Second Manassas: Perseverance on a Free African-American Farm Site. Paper presented at 31st Annual Meeting of the Society for Historical Archaeology, Atlanta, Ga.

Martin, Erika K., Mia T. Parsons, and Paul A. Shackel

1997 Commemorating a Rural African-American Family at a National Battlefield Park. *International Journal of Historical Archaeology* 1(2):157–78.

Martin, James J.

1868 Memorandom [*sic*] of Agreement with George Carter and Jacob F. Wiseman. Augusta County, Virginia. Ms. in private possession. Photocopy in possession of Kenneth E. Koons.

Martin, Mary E.

1987 Cobb County, Georgia in 1860: A Transcription and Index of the Federal Population Census. Ms. on file, Georgia Department of History and Archives, Atlanta.

Maryland, State of

1869   *A Descriptive List of the Burial Places of the Remains of Confederate Soldiers Who Fell in the Battles of Antietam, South Mountain, Monocacy, and Other Points in Washington and Frederick Counties in the State of Maryland.* Free Press, Hagerstown, Md.

Matheny, H. E.

1963   *Major General Thomas Maley Harris, 10th West Virginia Infantry.* McClain Printing Co., Parsons, W. Va.

Mauzy, George

1861   Letter to J. H. Burton, April 19. Ms. on file, HFD-388, Harpers Ferry National Historical Park, Harpers Ferry, W. Va.

McAulay, John D.

1981   *Carbines of the Civil War 1861–1865.* Pioneer Press, Union City, Tenn.

McBride, W. Stephen

1994   Civil War Material Culture and Camp Life in Central Kentucky: Archaeological Investigations at Camp Nelson. In *Look to the Earth: Historical Archaeology and the American Civil War,* edited by Clarence R. Geier, Jr., and Susan E. Winter, 130–57. University of Tennessee Press, Knoxville.

McBride, W. Stephen, and M. E. Esarey

1995   The Archaeology of the Ashland Privy, Lexington, Kentucky. In *Historical Archaeology in Kentucky,* edited by K. McBride, W. S. McBride, and D. Pollack, 265–95. Kentucky Heritage Council, Frankfort.

McBride, W. Stephen, and James P. Fenton

1996   *Phase II Testing of 15McL137 at the KY 81 Bridge over the Green River at Calhoun-Rumsey, McLean County, Kentucky.* Wilbur Smith Associates, Inc., Lexington, Ky.

McBride, W. Stephen, and William E. Sharp

1991   *Archaeological Investigations at Camp Nelson: A Union Quartermaster Depot and Hospital in Jessamine County, Kentucky.* Archaeological Report 241. Program for Cultural Resource Assessment, University of Kentucky, Lexington.

McCartney, Martha

1992a   Brownsville Plantation: Historical Background. In *Cultural Resource Survey and Inventory of a War-Torn Landscape: The Stuart's Hill Tract, Manassas National Battlefield Park, Virginia,* edited by Laura J. Galke, 47–63. Occasional Report No. 7, Regional Archeology Program, National Capital Region, National Park Service, Washington, D.C.

1992b   Nash: Historical Background. In *Cultural Resource Survey and Inventory of a War-Torn Landscape: The Stuart's Hill Tract, Manassas National Battlefield Park, Virginia,* edited by Laura J. Galke, 121–42. Occasional Report No. 7, Regional Archeology Program, National Capital Region, National Park Service, Washington, D.C.

McDavid, Carol, and David W. Babson (vol. editors)

1997   In the Realm of Politics: Prospects for Public Participation in African-American and Plantation Archaeology. *Historical Archaeology* 31(3).

McDonald, Archie P. (editor)

1973   *Make Me a Map of the Valley: The Civil War Journal of Stonewall Jackson's Topographer.* Southern Methodist University Press, Dallas, Tex.

McDonald, Cornelia

1934   *A Diary with Reminiscences of the War and Refugee Life in the Shenandoah Valley, 1860–1865.* Cullom and Ghertner, Nashville, Tenn.

McKee, W. Reid, and M. E. Mason, Jr.

1980   *Civil War Projectiles II, Small Arms and Field Artillery.* Moss Publications, Orange, Va.

McPherson, James M.

1979   *Ordeal by Fire,* vol. 2, *The Civil War.* Alfred A. Knopf, New York.

1982   *Ordeal by Fire,* vol. 2, *The Civil War.* Alfred A. Knopf, New York.

1988   *Battle Cry of Freedom: The Civil War Era.* Ballantine Books, New York.

Meaney, Peter J.
1979   *The Civil War Engagement at Cool Springs July 18, 1864.* N.p., Berryville, Va.
Medical and Surgical History. See U.S. War Department.
Meigs, Gen. Montgomery C.
1865   Letter to Secretary Edwin M. Stanton, October 5, 1865. Record Group 92, entry 225, box 720. National Archives, Washington, D.C.
1866   Letter to Secretary Edwin M. Stanton, January 12, 1866. Record Group 92, entry 225, box 720. National Archives, Washington, D.C.
Melton, Jack W., and Lawrence E. Pawl
1996   *Melton and Pawl's Guide to Civil War Artillery Projectiles.* Kennesaw Mountain Press, Kennesaw, Ga.
Meredith, Sol
1862   Colonel Meredith's Report of the Battle of the 28th of August. *Cincinnati Commercial Tribune,* September 12, p. 4.
Michael, Samuel
1862–65 Letters on file, Antietam National Battlefield, Sharpsburg, Md.
Miller, A. B.
1866   Map of Camp Nelson Showing the Locations of Buildings. Cartographic Section, Record Group 77, map 1.60. National Archives, Washington, D.C.
Miller, George L.
1980   Classification and Economic Scaling of 19th Century Ceramics. *Historical Archaeology* 14:1–41.
1991   A Revised Set of CC Index Values for Classification and Economic Scaling of English Ceramics from 1778 to 1880. *Historical Archaeology* 25(1):1–25.
Miller, George L., Ann Smart Martin, and Nancy S. Dickinson
1994   Changing Consumption Patterns: English Ceramics and the American Market from 1770 to 1840. In *Everyday Life in the Early Republic,* edited by Catherine E. Hutchins, 219–48. Henry Francis du Pont Winterthur Museum, Winterthur, Del.
Miller, Jacob
1862–65 Letters on file, Antietam National Battlefield, Sharpsburg, Md.
Miller, William
n.d.   Memoir. Typescript on file, Handley Library Archives, Winchester, Va.
Mills, J. Harrison
1887   *Chronicles of the Twenty First Regiment, New York State Volunteers.* Twenty-First Regiment Veteran Association, Buffalo, N.Y.
Mintz, Sidney W., and Richard Price
1976   *The Birth of African-American Culture: An Anthropological Perspective.* Beacon Press, Boston.
Mitchell, Mary Bedinger
n.d.   Shepherdstown after the Battle of Antietam. *Shepherdstown Register,* Shepherdstown, W. Va.
Mitchell, Robert D.
1977   *Commercialism and Frontier: Perspectives on the Early Shenandoah Valley.* University Press of Virginia, Charlottesville.
1995   The Settlement Fabric of the Shenandoah Valley, 1790–1860: A Preliminary Assessment. Paper presented at the conference "After the Backcountry: Rural Life and Society in the Nineteenth-Century Valley of Virginia," Lexington, Va.
Moore, Edward A.
1910   *The Story of a Cannoneer under Stonewall Jackson.* J. P. Bell, Lynchburg, Va.
Moore, Welton P.
1962   Union Army Provost Marshals in the Eastern Theater. *Military Affairs* 26:120–26.
Moore, William R.
n.d.   Reminiscences. Indiana Historical Society. Photocopy of ms. on file, Manassas National Battlefield Park, Manassas, Va.

Morgan, Otho Herron

1967   Home Letters, 1861–1864. Facsimile duplication of manuscript compiled and edited by the author in 1887. Ms. on file, Atlanta History Center Library and Archives, Atlanta, Ga.

Morton, Oren F.

1980   *A History of Rockbridge County, Virginia.* Reprint. Regional Publishing Co., Baltimore, Md.

Mullins, Paul R.

1996   The Contradictions of Consumption: An Archaeology of African-American and Consumer Culture, 1850–1930. Ph.D. dissertation, University of Massachusetts, Amherst.

Mumma, Samuel, Jr.

1888   Congressional Claim No. 334, submitted by Samuel Mumma, Jr., Executor of Samuel Mumma. Deceased v. the United States, filed May 29, 1885, in the Court of Claims. Commissioner of Claims, U.S. War Department, National Archives, Washington, D.C.

1906   Correspondence between Samuel Mumma and James F. Clark. Letters on file, Antietam National Battlefield, Sharpsburg, Md.

Munsey, Cecil

1970   *The Illustrated Guide to Collecting Bottles.* Hawthorn Books, New York.

Murfin, James V.

1965   *The Gleam of Bayonets: The Battle of Antietam and Robert E. Lee's Maryland Campaign, September 1862.* Thomas Yoseloff, New York.

1989   *From the Riot and Tumult: Harpers Ferry.* Harpers Ferry Historical Association, Harpers Ferry, W. Va.

Murphy, Larry E., Daniel J. Lenihan, Christopher F. Amer, Matthew A. Russell, Robert S. Neyland, Richard Wills, Scott Harris, Adriane Askins, Timothy G. Smith, and Steven M. Shope

1998   *H. L. Hunley Site Assessment.* A cooperative project of the National Park Service, the Naval Historical Center, and the South Carolina Institute of Archaeology and Anthropology, funded by the South Carolina Hunley Commission and the Department of Defense, Legacy Resources Program, Santa Fe, N.M.

National Park Service. *See* U.S. Department of the Interior

Neville, Ashley, Joseph S. White III, and Erick Voigt

1995   Phase I Cultural Resource Investigations for the Manassas Battlefield Park Transmission Line Corridor Relocation Project, Prince William County, Virginia. Gray and Pape, Richmond, Va. Submitted to Virginia Power, Richmond.

Newcomer, C. Armour

1895   *Cole's Cavalry or Three Years in the Saddle in the Shenandoah Valley.* Cushing and Co., Baltimore, Md.

Newlin, Keith

1987   Addendum to the Architectural Data Section on the Brawner Farm House. Ms. on file, Manassas National Battlefield Park, Manassas, Va.

New York, State of

1902a   Registers of the 88th, 89th, 19th, 91st, 92d, and 93d Regiments of Infantry. *Annual Report of the Adjutant General of the State of New York.* Serial No. 31. J. B. Lyon Co., Albany, N.Y.

1902b   Registers of the 63d, 64th, 65th, 66th, 67th, and 68th Regiments of Infantry. *Annual Report of the Adjutant General of the State of New York.* Serial No. 27. J. B. Lyon Co., Albany, N.Y.

Neyland, Robert S., and Christopher F. Amer

1998   Administrative History. In *H. L. Hunley Site Assessment,* edited by Larry E. Murphy, 21–34. National Park Service, Naval Historical Center, and South Carolina Institute of Archaeology and Anthropology, Columbia.

Nichols, G. W.

1898   *A Soldier's Story of His Regiment, 61st Georgia.* N.p., Kennesaw, Ga.

Noël-Hume, Ivor

1969   *Historical Archaeology.* Alfred A. Knopf, New York.

Nugent, James H.

1989   Letters reprinted in *Washington Post*, B1, B4–5, May 28.

O'Brien, Katherine

1965   The Seventh West Virginia Volunteer Infantry 1861–1862. M.A. thesis, West Virginia University, Morgantown.

Ommundsen, H., and Ernest H. Robinson

1915   *Rifles and Ammunition and Rifle Shooting.* Cassell, N.Y.

O'Neill, Stephan D.

1997   My Sons Were Faithful and They Fought. In *"My Sons Were Faithful and They Fought": The Irish Brigade at Antietam. An Anthology,* edited by Joseph G. Bilby and Stephan D. O'Neill, 3–33. Longstreet House, Hightstown, N.J.

Orr, David G.

1993   The Archaeology of Trauma: An Introduction to the Historical Archaeology of the American Civil War. In *Look to the Earth: Historical Archaeology and the American Civil War,* edited by Clarence R. Geier, Jr., and Susan E. Winter, 21–36. University of Tennessee Press, Knoxville.

Orser, Charles E., Jr.

1994   The Archaeology of African-American Slave Religion in the Antebellum South. *Cambridge Archaeological Journal* 4(1):33–45.

Osborne, Charles C.

1992   *Jubal.* Algonquin Books, Chapel Hill, N.C.

Otto, John S.

1977   Artifacts and Status Differences: A Comparison of Ceramics from Planter, Overseer, and Slave Sites on an Antebellum Plantation. In *Research Strategies in Historical Archaeology,* edited by Stanley South, 91–118. Academic Press, New York.

1980   Race and Class on Antebellum Plantations. In *Archaeological Perspectives on Ethnicity in America,* edited by Robert L. Schuyler, 3–13. Baywood Publishing Co., Farmingdale, N.Y.

1984   *Cannon's Point Plantation, 1794–1860: Living Conditions and Status Patterns in the Old South.* Academic Press, New York.

Park, Robert E.

1877   Diary of Robert E. Park, Captain 12th Alabama Regiment. *Southern Historical Society Papers* 1:370–86, 430–37; 2:25–31, 78–85, 172–80, 232–39, 306–15; 3:43–61, 123–27, 183–89, 244–54.

Parker, Kathleen A.

1989   An Archeological Assessment of the Brawner Farm House. Ms. on file, Manassas National Battlefield Park, Manassas, Va.

Parker, Kathleen A., and Jacqueline L. Hernigle

1990   *Portici: Portrait of a Middling Plantation in Piedmont Virginia.* Occasional Report No. 3, Regional Archaeology Program, National Capital Region, National Park Service, Washington, D.C.

Parry, Henry C.

1864   Civil War Diary. Ms. on file, Military History Institute, Carlisle Barracks, Pa.

Parsons, Mia T.

1995   Archaeological Investigation of the Harper Terraces: A Nineteenth-Century Domestic Yard and Garden. Ms. on file, Harpers Ferry National Historical Park, Harpers Ferry, W. Va.

1996   Archeological Investigations of the Robinson House, Site 44PW288: A Free African-American Farmstead Occupied from the 1840s to the 1930s. Ms. on file, Manassas National Battlefield Park, Manassas, Va.

Patten, Drake M.

1992   The Archaeology of Playtime: Artifacts of African American Games in the Plantation South. Paper presented at the 25th Annual Meeting of the Society for Historical Archaeology, Kingston, Jamaica.

Perkins, George

1911 *A Summer in Maryland and Virginia or Campaigning with the One Hundred and Forty-Ninth Ohio Volunteer Infantry.* School Printing Co., Chillicothe, Ohio.

Peterson, Harold L.

1959 *Notes on Ordnance of the Civil War, 1861–1865.* American Ordnance Association, Washington, D.C.

1969 *Round Shot and Rammers.* Bonanza Books, New York.

Phillips, Edward H.

1958 The Lower Shenandoah Valley during the Civil War: The Impact of War upon the Civilian Population and upon Civil Institutions. Ph.D. dissertation, University of North Carolina, Chapel Hill.

Phillips, Ulrich Bonnell

1946 *Life and Labor in the Old South.* Reprint. Little Brown, Boston, Mass.

Poe, Orlando M.

1874 Report of Captain Orlando M. Poe, Corps of Engineers, U.S. Army, Chief Engineer. In *The War of the Rebellion: A Compilation of the Official Records of the Union and Confederate Armies,* edited by Maj. George B. Davis et al. Series I, vol. 38, part I: Reports. U.S. War Department, Government Printing Office, Washington, D.C.

Poffenberger, Alfred

1864 Office of the Quartermaster General, Claims Branch, 1861–1889, Document File, Quartermaster Stores (Act of July 4, 1864) Rent, Services, and Miscellaneous Claims. Record Group 92, entry 812, file M917. National Archives, Washington, D.C.

Pollard, Thomas (compiler)

1878 Circular No. 11, Crop, Stock and Labor Report for June 1. Commissioner of Agriculture, Superintendent of Public Printing, Richmond, Va.

Pond, George E.

1883 *The Shenandoah Valley in 1864.* Scribner's, New York.

Pratt, Michael G.

1995 The Archaeology of the Fallen Timbers Battlefield: A Report of the 1995 Field Survey. World-Wide Web/Internet document by author. Heidelberg College, Tiffin, Ohio.

Prentice, Guy, and Marie Mathison

1989 Archeological Investigations of the North Gate at Andersonville National Historic Site. Ms. on file, National Park Service, Southeast Archeological Center, Tallahassee, Fla.

Prentice, Marie C., and Guy Prentice

1990 Archeological Investigations of the Southeast Corner of the Inner Stockade at Andersonville National Historic Site, Georgia. Ms. on file, National Park Service, Southeast Archeological Center, Tallahassee, Fla.

Pressly, Thomas J.

1965 *Americans Interpret Their Civil War.* Free Press, New York.

Priest, John Michael

1989 *Antietam: The Soldier's Battle.* White Mane Publishing Co., Shippensburg, Pa.

Prince William County, Virginia

1840 Deed Books, Prince William County Courthouse, Manassas, Va.

Memorandum of Programmatic Agreement

1996 Among the Dept. of the Navy, the General Services Administration, the Advisory Council on Historic Preservation, the South Carolina Hunley Commission, and the South Carolina State Historic Preservation Officer Concerning Management of the Wreck of the *H.L. Hunley,* August 6.

Raboteau, Albert J.

1978 *Slave Religion: The "Invisible Institution" in the Antebellum South.* Oxford University Press, New York.

Ragan, Mark K.
1995   *The Hunley: Submarines, Sacrifice, and Success in the Civil War*. Narwhal Press, Miami and Charleston.

Reardon, Carol
1997   *Pickett's Charge in History and Memory*. University of North Carolina Press, Chapel Hill.

Reitz, Elizabeth J.
1987   Vertebrate Fauna and Socioeconomic Status. In *Consumer Choice in Historical Archaeology*, edited by Suzanne M. Spencer-Wood, 101–7. Plenum Press, New York.

Resticaux, Capt. E. B. W.
1865   Letter to Gen. Robert Allen, March 20. Record Group 92, entry 225, box 720. National Archives, Washington, D.C.

Rhodes, Robert H. (editor)
1985   *All for the Union: A History of the 2d Rhode Island Volunteer Infantry*. Andrew Mowbray, Lincoln, R.I.

Richardson, Albert D.
1865   *The Secret Service, the Field, the Dungeon, and the Escape*. R. C. Treat, Chicago, Ill.

Ridgeway, W.
1862   Washington, D.C. and Its Vicinity. Print on file, Prints and Photographs Division, Library of Congress, Washington, D.C.

Riggs, David F.
1978   Robert Young Conrad and the Ordeal of Secession. *Virginia Magazine of History and Biography* 86:259–74.

Ripley, Warren
1970   *Artillery and Ammunition of the Civil War*. Promontory Press, New York.

Roberts, Ned H.
1944   *The Muzzle-Loading Cap Lock Rifle*. Clarke Press, Manchester, N.H.

Robert Smith Printing
1899   History of the Michigan Organizations at Chickamauga, Chattanooga, and Missionary Ridge. Robert Smith Printing, Lansing, Michigan.

Robinson, B. Oswald
1995   Oral communication with James Burgess, Manassas National Battlefield Park, November 1. Manassas, Va.

Robinson, James
1872   Claim No. 241, filed February 2, Commissioner of Claims, U.S. War Department. Photocopy on file, Manassas National Battlefield Park, Manassas, Va.

Robinson, Lillian
1993   Information sheet on James Robinson. Ms. on file, Manassas National Battlefield Park, Manassas, Va.

Rockman, Diana D. and Nan A. Rothschild
1984   City Tavern, Country Tavern: An Analysis of Four Colonial Sites. *Historical Archaeology* 18(2):112–21.

Roe, Alfred S.
1899   The Ninth New York Heavy Artillery. By author, Worchester, Mass.

Rovner, Irwin
1993   Phytolith Analysis: Archeological Soils from Lower Town Harpers Ferry, West Virginia. In *Interdisciplinary Investigations of Domestic Life in Government Block B: Perspectives on Harpers Ferry's Armory and Commercial District*, edited by Paul A. Shackel, 6.1–6.13. Occasional Report No. 6, Regional Archeology Program, National Capital Region, National Park Service, Washington, D.C.

Rownsdale, T. N.
n.d.   Story of Antietam: As Told to My Son (handwritten account, 14th Indiana Regiment). St. Bernice, Ind. Photocopy of ms. on file, Antietam National Battlefield, Sharpsburg, Md.

Rowntree, Lester, and Margaret Conkey

1980   Symbols and the Cultural Landscape. In *Annals of the Association of American Geographers* 70(4).

Ruger, Edward (compiler)

1895   Map Illustrating the Third Epoch of the Atlanta Campaign. In *Atlas to Accompany the Official Records of the Union and Confederate Armies,* edited by Maj. George B. Davis et al., Plate LIX. U.S. War Department, Government Printing Office, Washington, D.C. Copy in Wilbur Kurtz Collection, Atlanta History Center Library and Archives, Atlanta, Ga.

1983   Map Illustrating the Third Epoch of the Atlanta Campaign. In *The Official Military Atlas of the Civil War,* edited by Maj. George B. Davis et al., Plate LIX. Reprint. Fairfax Press, New York.

Runge, William H. (editor)

1991   *Four Years in the Confederate Artillery: Diary of Private Henry Robinson Berkeley.* Virginia Historical Society, Richmond.

Russell, G. Michael

1996   *The Collector's Guide to Clay Tobacco Pipes,* vol. 1. Russell Publications, Herndon, Va.

Russell, Isaac W.

1912   Personal Record. Typescript, Handley Library Archives, Winchester, Va.

Ryder, Robin

1991   Free African-American Archaeology: Interpreting an Antebellum Farmstead. M.A. thesis, College of William and Mary, Williamsburg, Virginia.

Samford, Patricia

1994   *African American Archaeology Newsletter* 12:1–3.

Sangston, Lawrence

1865   *Report of the Secretary of the Baltimore Agricultural Aid Society, December, 1865.* John Murphy and Co., Baltimore, Md.

Sauers, Richard A.

1987   *Advance the Colors! Pennsylvania Civil War Battle Flags,* vol. 1. Capitol Preservation Committee, Commonwealth of Pennsylvania, Lebanon.

Scaife, William R.

1992   *The Chattahoochee River Line: An American Maginot.* McNaughton and Gunn, Saline, Mich.

Schafer, Louis S.

1996   *Confederate Underwater Warfare: An Illlustrated History.* McFarland & Co., Jefferson, N.C.

Scharf, J. Thomas

1968   *History of Western Maryland; Being a History of Frederick, Montgomery, Carroll, Washington, Allegany, and Garrett Counties from the Earliest Period to the Present Day; including Biographical Sketches of their Representative Men.* 2 vols. Reprint. Regional Publishing Co., Baltimore, Md.

Schiffer, Nancy

1986   *Japanese Porcelain: 1800–1950.* Schiffer Publishing, Westchester, Pa.

Schildt, John W.

1997   *Roads to Antietam.* Burd Street Press, Shippensburg, Pa.

Schlebecker, John T.

1971   Farmers in the Lower Shenandoah Valley, 1850. *Virginia Magazine of History and Biography* 79:462–76.

Schmitt, Martin F. (editor)

1946   *General George Crook: His Autobiography.* University of Oklahoma Press, Norman.

Scott, Douglas D.

1989   An Officer's Latrine at Fort Larned and Inferences on Status. *Plains Anthropologist* 34:23–34.

Scott, Douglas D., and Richard A. Fox, Jr.

1987   *Archaeological Insights into the Custer Battle: An Assessment of the 1984 Field Season.* University of Oklahoma Press, Norman.

Scott, Douglas D., and W. J. Hunt, Jr.

1997   *The Civil War Battle at Monroe's Crossroads, Fort Bragg, North Carolina: A Historical Archeological Perspective.* Draft report on file, Southeast Archeological Center, National Park Service, Tallahassee, Fla.

Scott, Henry L.

1984   *Military Dictionary: Comprising Technical Definitions; Information on Raising and Keeping Troops; Actual Service, including Makeshifts and Improved Matériel; and Law, Government Regulation, and Administration Relating to Land Forces.* Reprint. Fort Yuma Press, Yuma, Ariz.

Scott, Robert N. (preparer)

1887   *The War of the Rebellion: A Compilation of the Official Records of the Union and Confederate Armies.* Series 1, vol. 19, part 1, Reports. Government Printing Office, Washington, D.C.

Sears, Richard D.

1986   *A Practical Recognition of the Brotherhood of Man: John G. Fee and the Camp Nelson Experience.* Berea College, Berea, Ky.

1987   John G. Fee, Camp Nelson, and Kentucky Blacks, 1864–1865. *Register of the Kentucky Historical Society* 85:29–45.

Sears, Stephen W.

1983   *Landscape Turned Red: The Battle of Antietam.* Ticknor and Fields, New Haven, Conn.

Secrist, Philip L.

1975   Historic Cobb County Bicentennial Project. Cobb County Commission and Cobb Landmarks Society, Marietta, Ga. Ms. on file, Cobb County Public Library, Marietta.

Seibert, Erika Martin

1998   Exploring the Consumerism of a Free African-American Family: From the Civil War through the Jim Crow Eras, a Minimum Vessel Analysis from Manassas National Battlefield Park. In *Archeological Investigation of the Robinson House, Site 44PW288: A Free African-American Domestic Site Occupied from the 1840s to the 1930s,* edited by Mia Parsons. Occasional Report series, Regional Archeology Program, National Capital Region, National Park Service, Washington, D.C.

Shackel, Paul A.

1994   Memorializing Landscapes and the Civil War in Harpers Ferry. In *Look to the Earth: Historical Archaeology and the American Civil War,* edited by Clarence R. Geier, Jr., and Susan E. Winter, 256–70. University of Tennessee Press, Knoxville.

1996   *Culture Change and the New Technology: An Archaeology of the Early American Industrial Era.* Plenum Press, New York.

Shackel, Paul A. (editor)

1993   *Interdisciplinary Investigations of Domestic Life in Government Block B: Perspectives on Harpers Ferry's Armory and Commercial District,* Occasional Report No. 6, Regional Archeology Program, National Capital Region, National Park Service, Washington, D.C.

Shackel, Paul A., Cari C. YoungRavenhorst, and Susan E. Winter

1993   The Archeological Record: Stratigraphy, Features, and Material Culture. In *Interdisciplinary Investigations of Domestic Life in Government Block B: Perspectives on Harpers Ferry's Armory and Commercial District,* edited by Paul A. Shackel, 4.1–4.85. Occasional Report No. 6, Regional Archeology Program, National Capital Region, National Park Service, Washington, D.C.

Sheffer, F. S.

1855   Receipt to J. J. Martin for purchase of negro slave named George. Ms. in private possession. Staunton, Va.

Shenandoah County, Virginia, Manuscript U.S. Census Returns (SCMCR)

1850a   Manufacturing Schedules.

1850b   Population Schedules.

1850c   Slave Schedules.

1860a Population Schedules.

1860b Slave Schedules.

1870 Population Schedules.

1880a Agricultural Schedules.

1880b Population Schedules.

Sheridan, Philip H.

1888 *Personal Memoirs of Philip H. Sheridan,* 2 vols. Charles L. Webster and Co., New York.

Sherman, William T.

1885 *Personal Memoirs.* Charles L. Webster and Co., New York.

Shewbridge, J.

1861 Letter to D. Shewbridge, April 23. Ms. on file, HFD-581, Harpers Ferry National Historical Park, Harpers Ferry, W. Va.

Shifflett, Crandall A.

1982 *Patronage and Poverty in the Tobacco South: Louisa County, Virginia, 1860–1900.* University of Tennessee Press, Knoxville.

Simmons, J. Susanne Schramm

1997 Augusta County's Other Pioneers: The African American Presence in Frontier Augusta County. In *Diversity and Accommodation: Essays on the Cultural Composition of the Virginia Frontier,* edited by Michael J. Puglisi, 159–71. University of Tennessee Press, Knoxville.

Simmons, J. Susanne, and Nancy T. Sorrells

2000 "Never a Stronghold?": Slave Hire and the Development of Slavery in Augusta County, Virginia. In *After the Backcountry: Rural Life in the Great Valley of Virginia, 1800–1900,* edited by Kenneth E. Koons and Warren R. Hofstra. University of Tennessee Press, Knoxville.

Simpson, Lt. Col. James H.

1864 Camp Nelson and Its Defenses, Jessamine County, Kentucky. Cartographic Section, Record Group 77, map 2.76. National Archives, Washington, D.C.

Singer, David A.

1984 Threshold of Affordability: Assessing Fish Remains for Socioeconomics. In *Consumer Choice in Historical Archaeology,* edited by Suzanne M. Spencer-Wood, 85–99. Plenum Press, New York.

Singer, Ralph Benjamen, Jr.

1973 Confederate Atlanta. Ph.D. dissertation, University of Georgia, Athens.

Singleton, Theresa

1987 The Archaeology of Slavery in North America. *Annual Review of Anthropology* 24:119–40.

Sivilich, Daniel M.

1996 Analyzing Musket Balls to Interpret a Revolutionary War Site. *Historical Archaeology* 30(2):101–9.

Slaughter, Bernard W., and Bruce B. Sterling

1998 Surveying the Civil War: Methodological Approaches at Antietam Battlefield. Paper presented at the 31st Annual Meeting of the Society for Historical Archaeology, Atlanta, Ga.

Smedlund, William S.

1994 *Campfires of Georgia's Troops, 1861–1865.* Kennesaw Mountain Press, Kennesaw, Ga.

Smith, Elmer

1973 *Patent Medicine: The Golden Days of Quackery.* Applied Arts Publishers, Lebanon, Pa.

Smith, Samuel D.

1994 Excavation Data for Civil War Era Military Sites in Middle Tennessee. In *Look to the Earth: Historical Archaeology and the American Civil War,* edited by Clarence R. Geier and Susan E. Winter, 60–75. University of Tennessee Press, Knoxville.

Smith, Steven D.

1994 Archaeological Perspectives on the Civil War: The Challenge to Achieve Relevance. In *Look to the Earth: Historical Archaeology and the American Civil War,* edited by Clarence R. Geier and Susan E. Winter, 3–20. University of Tennessee Press, Knoxville.

Smith, Theophus H.

1994   *Conjuring Culture: Biblical Formations of Black America*. Oxford University Press, New York.

Smithsonian Institution

1961   *Uniform Regulations for the Army of the United States 1861*. Publication 4467. Smithsonian Institution, Washington, D.C.

Sneden, R. K.

1864   Sketch of South Gate of Andersonville Prison. On file at National Park Service, Southeast Archeological Center.

Snell, Charles W.

1959   Harpers Ferry Becomes a Fortress, September 21, 1862–October 6, 1863. Ms. on file, Harpers Ferry National Historical Park, Harpers Ferry, W. Va.

1960a   The Fortifications at Harpers Ferry, Va., in 1861 and Jackson's Attack, May 1862. Ms. on file, Harpers Ferry National Historical Park, Harpers Ferry, W. Va.

1960b   Harpers Ferry Repels an Attack and Becomes the Major Base of Operations for Sheridan's Army, July 4, 1864, to July 27, 1865. Ms. on file, Harpers Ferry National Historical Park, Harpers Ferry, W. Va.

Snow, Dean R.

1981   Battlefield Archeology. *Early Man* 3(1):18–21.

Snyder, Daniel

1861–65 Personal letters. Ms. on file, Clarke County Historical Association, Berryville, Va.

Sommers, Richard J.

1982   *Richmond Redeemed: The Siege of Petersburg*. Doubleday, New York.

South, Stanley

1977   *Method and Theory in Historical Archeology*. Academic Press, New York.

Southern Agriculturalist

1837   *The Southern Agriculturalist, Horticulturist and Register of Rural Affairs, Adapted to the Southern Section of the United States*. A. E. Miller, publisher. Reprint. 1845, Miller and Browne, Charleston, S.Ca.

Southern Planter

1856   Harvesting Wheat. *Southern Planter* 16:237.

Spear, Donald P.

1970   The Sutler in the Union Army. *Civil War History* 16(2):121–38.

Speir, J. S.

1864   J. S. Speir Manuscript Collection. Atlanta History Center Library and Archives, Atlanta, Ga.

Spirit of Jefferson

1861   No title, May 4, p. 2. Charles Town, West Virginia. Ms. on file, Harpers Ferry National Historical Park, Harpers Ferry, W. Va.

Stach, Glenn Thomas

1996   *Historic Woodlot Restoration and Cultural Landscape Report: North Woods, Antietam National Battlefield Park, Sharpsburg, Maryland*. Report Submitted to Antietam National Battlefield Park, Oehrlein & Associates, Washington, D.C.

Stackpole, Edward J.

1959   *From Cedar Mountain to Antietam*. Stackpole, Harrisburg, Pa.

Stanley, David S.

1874   Report of Major General David S. Stanley, U.S. Army, Commanding the First Division. In *The War of the Rebellion: A Compilation of the Official Records of the Union and Confederate Armies*, edited by Maj. George B. Davis et al., Series I, vol. 38, pt. I: Reports. U.S. War Department, Government Printing Office, Washington, D.C.

Starobin, Robert S.

1970   *Industrial Slavery in the Old South*. Oxford University Press, New York.

Staski, Edward

1990   Site Formation Processes at Fort Fillmore, New Mexico: First Interpretations. *Historical Archae-ology* 24(3):79–90.

Staski, Edward, and Joanne Reiter

1996   Status and Adobe Quality at Fort Fillmore, New Mexico: Old Questions, New Techniques. *Historical Archaeology* 30(3):1–19.

Stern, Philip Van Doren

1961   *Soldier Life in the Union and Confederate Armies.* Indiana University Press, Bloomington.

Still, William N., Jr.

1985   *Iron Afloat: The Story of the Confederate Armorclads.* University of South Carolina Press, Columbia.

1987   *Confederate Shipbuilding.* University of South Carolina Press, Columbia.

Stillé, Charles J.

1864   *History of the United States Sanitary Commission: Being the General Report of Its Work during the War of the Rebellion.* J. P. Lippincott and Co., Philadelphia, Pa. Reprint 1997. Corner House Historical Publications, Ganesport, N.Y.

Stine, Linda France, Melanie A. Cabak, and Mark D. Grover

1996   Blue Beads as African-American Symbols. *Historical Archaeology* 30(3):49–75.

Storey, Henry W.

1907   *History of Cambria County,* 2 vols. Lewis Publishing Co., N.Y.

Stotelmyer, Steven R.

1992   *The Bivouacs of the Dead: The Story of Those Who Died at Antietam and South Mountain.* Toomey Press, Baltimore, Md.

Strong, Robert H.

1961   *A Yankee Private's Civil War,* edited by Ashley Halsey. Henry Regnery Co., Chicago.

Strother, David Hunter

1861   Ms. on file, Harpers Ferry National Historical Park, Harpers Ferry, W. Va.

1866   Personal Recollections of the War by a Virginian. *Harper's New Monthly Magazine* 33:1–25, 137–60, 409–28, 545–67.

1867   Personal Recollections of the War by a Virginian. *Harper's New Monthly Magazine* 34:172–91, 423–49, 714–34.

Stuart, A. Hulen

1947   Artillery Employed by the Union and Confederate Batteries in the First and Second Battles of Manassas. Ms. on file, Manassas National Battlefield Park, Manassas, Va.

Stuckey, Sterling

1987   *Slave Culture: Nationalist Theory and the Foundations of Black America.* Oxford University Press, New York.

Surgeon General. See U.S. War Department, Surgeon General

Sweig, Donald (editor)

1977   *Registration of Free Negroes Commencing September Court 1822.* Book No. 2, register no. 30, p. 22. Virginia Office of Comprehensive Planning, Manassas.

Switzer, Ronald R.

1974   *The Bertrand Bottles: A Study of 19th-Century Glass and Ceramic Containers.* National Park Service, Department of the Interior, Washington, D.C.

Sylvia, Stephen W., and Michael J. O'Donnell

1990   *Civil War Canteens.* Moss Publications, Orange, Va.

Taylor, James E.

1989   *With Sheridan up the Shenandoah Valley in 1864: Leaves from a Special Artists Sketch Book and Diary.* Western Reserve Historical Society, Cleveland, Ohio.

Taylor, Walter H.

1962   *Four Years with General Lee.* Introduction by James I. Robertson, Jr. Reprint. Indiana University Press, Bloomington.

Temple, Sarah Blackwell Gober
1989   *The First Hundred Years: A Short History of Cobb County.* 6th Edition. Agydo Publishers, Athens, Ga.

Tennent, Sir Joseph Emerson
1864   *The Story of the Guns.* Longman, Green, Longman, Roberts, and Green, London.

Thelen, David
1989   Memory and American History. *Journal of American History* 75(4):1117–29.

Thomas, Dean Hurst
1989   *Archaeology.* Holt, Rinehart and Winston, Chicago.

Thomas, Dean S.
1981   *Ready, Aim, Fire!: Small Arms Ammunition in the Battle of Gettysburg.* Thomas Publications, Gettysburg, Pa.
1985   *Cannons: An Introduction to Civil War Artillery.* 1st ed. Thomas Publications, Gettysburg, Pa.
1993   *Ready . . . Aim . . . Fire! Small Arms Ammunition in the Battle of Gettysburg.* Thomas Publications, Gettysburg, Pa.
1997   *Round Ball to Rimfire: A History of Civil War Small Arms Ammunition,* part one. Thomas Publications, Gettysburg, Pa.

Thomas, James E., and Dean S. Thomas
1996   *A Handbook of Civil War Bullets and Cartridges.* Thomas Publications, Gettysburg, Pa.

Thompson, Robert Farris
1983   *Flash of the Spirit: African and Afro-American Art and Philosophy.* Random House, New York.

Thorndike, Rachel Sherman (editor)
1892   *The Sherman Letters: Correspondence between General and Senator Sherman from 1837 to 1891.* Scribner's, New York.

Throne, Mildred (editor)
1957   Reminiscences of Jacob C. Switzer of the 22nd Iowa. *Iowa Journal of History* (October):319–47; (November):37–65.

Tilberg, Frederick
1960   *Antietam.* Historical Handbook No. 31. National Park Service, Department of the Interior, Washington, D.C.

Time-Life Books
1987   *Echoes of Glory: Arms and Equipment of the Confederacy.* Time-Life, Inc., Alexandria, Va.
1996a   *Voices of the Civil War: Antietam.* Time-Life, Inc, Alexandria, Va.
1996b   *Voices of the Civil War: The Battles for Atlanta.* Time-Life, Inc, Alexandria, Va.
1998   *Echoes of Glory: Arms and Equipment of the Union.* Time-Life, Inc, Alexandria, Va.

Todd, Frederick P.
1974   *American Military Equipage, 1851–1872.* Company of Military Historians. Providence, R.I.
1978   *American Military Equipage 1851–1872.* Scribner's, New York.
1980   *American Military Equipage 1851–1872.* Scribner's, New York.
1983   *American Military Equipage,* vol. 2, *State Forces, 1851–1872.* Chatham Square Press.

Toplin, Robert Brent
1996   Ken Burns' "The Civil War" as an Interpretation of History. In *Ken Burns' "The Civil War": Historians Respond,* edited by Robert Brent Toplin, 17–36. Oxford University Press, New York.

Townshend, Philip
1979   African Mankala in Anthropological Perspective. *Current Anthropology* 20(3):794–96.

Turner, Charles W. (editor)
1979   *The Diary of Henry Boswell Jones of Brownsburg (1842–1871).* McClure Printing Co., Verona, Va.

Turner, Ronald Ray
1993   Prince William County, Virginia, Death Records 1853–1896. Ms. on file, Bull Run Library, Manassas, Va.

Tyler, Mason W.

1912   *Recollections of the Civil War, 37th Massachusetts.* G. P. Putnam's Sons, New York.

Tyree, Marion Cabell

1879   *Housekeeping in Old Virginia.* John P. Morton and Co., Louisville, Ky.

United States Army Military History Institute

1865a   Photograph of Company K of the 2nd New York Heavy Artillery in front of the Fort C.F. Smith bombproof, August. Photograph on file, U.S. Army Military History Institute, Carlisle Barracks, Pa.

1865b   Photograph of Company I of the 2nd New York Heavy Artillery, view to the south showing powder magazine and south flank of Fort C.F. Smith, August. Photograph on file, U.S. Army Military History Institute, Carlisle Barracks, Pa.

n.d.   *Civil War Times Illustrated* Collection: Diary of Unidentified Soldier (170th Ohio).

U.S. Bureau of the Census

1854   *Statistical View of the United States, . . . Being a Compendium of the Seventh Census.* Government Printing Office, Washington, D.C.

1860a   Manuscript Returns of the Eighth Census of the United States, Population Schedule. Microfilm on file, Georgia Department of Archives and History, Atlanta.

1860b   Manuscript Returns of the Eighth Census of the United States, Agricultural Schedule. Microfilm on file, Georgia Department of Archives and History, Atlanta.

1864   *Population of the United States in 1860: Compiled from the Original Returns of the Eighth Census.* Government Printing Office, Washington, D.C.

1872   *A Compendium of the Ninth Census (June 1, 1870).* Government Printing Office, Washington, D.C.

1885   *Compendium of the Tenth Census (June 1, 1880).* Government Printing Office, Washington, D.C.

U.S. Congress

1879   *Senate Executive Document 37: The Proceedings and Report of the Board of Army Officers in the Case of Fitz-John Porter,* part 2. Government Printing Office, Washington, D.C.

U.S. Department of the Interior

1992   Study of Civil War Sites in the Shenandoah Valley of Virginia. National Park Service, Interagency Resources. U.S. Department of the Interior, Washington, D.C.

U.S. Department of the Interior, Census Office

1885   *Report on the Productions of Agriculture as Returned at the Tenth Census (June 1, 1880).* Government Printing Office, Washington, D.C.

U.S. National Archives

1861–1917 U.S. Army General's Reports of Civil War Service, Papers of the Adjutant General's Office, Record Group 94. Washington, D.C.

n.d.   Records of the Surgeon General's Office, Record Group 112. Washington, D.C.

1862–67 Summary Statements of Quarterly Returns of Ordnance and Ordnance Stores on Hand in Regular and Volunteer Army Organizations of 1862–1867. Office of the Chief of Ordnance, Record Group 156. Washington, D.C.

1863–66 Quartermaster Records. Record Group 92, entry 225, box 720. Washington, D.C.

U.S. Ordnance Department

1862   *The Ordnance Manual.* 3d edition. J. B. Lippincott and Co., Philadelphia, Pa.

U.S. Quartermaster Department

1865   Plan Showing Quartermaster Property at Fort C.F. Smith, Defenses of Washington, South of Potomac, May 10. Map on file, National Archives and Records Administration, Cartographic Division, Record Group 77, College Park, Md.

U.S. Sanitary Commission, New York Public Library (U.S.S.C.)

1861–65 Various numbered reports on clinical and medical service procedures.

1864–65 Bulletins. September–December 1864, January 1865.

1864–65 Correspondence Files, Shenandoah Valley.

U.S. War Department (W.D.)

1861   *Revised Regulations for the Army of the United States.* J.G.L. Brown, Philadelphia, Pa.

1880–1905 *The War of the Rebellion; A Compilation of the Official Records of the Union and Confederate Armies* (O.R.). Series I, 128 parts in 70 vols. Government Printing Office, Washington, D.C.

1980   *Revised Regulations for the Army of the United States.* Reprint. National Historical Society, Harrisburg, Pa.

U.S. War Department, Surgeon General

1870–88 *Medical and Surgical History of the War of the Rebellion.* 11 vols. Government Printing Office, Washington, D.C.

Vandiver, Frank E.

1952   *Ploughshares into Swords.* University of Texas Press, Austin.

1969   The Confederacy and the American Tradition. In *The Civil War,* edited by William R. Brock, 148–56. Harper and Row, New York.

1977   General Hood as Logistician. In *Military Analysis of the Civil War,* edited by T. Harry Williams, 141–51. KTO Press, Millwood, N.Y.

Wagner, Mark J., and Mary R. McCorvie

1992   *The Archaeology of the Old Landmark.* Center for American Archaeology, Kampsville, Ill. Submitted to Illinois Department of Transportation, Springfield.

Waird, Norman

1862   *Facts about Ordnance.* Washington Chronicle, Washington, D.C.

Walker, John W.

1989   Archeological Investigations of the Northwest Corner of the Inner Stockade of Andersonville Prison, Andersonville National Historic Site, Ga. Ms. on file, National Park Service, Southeast Archeological Center, Tallahassee, Fla.

Walker, Mark, and John Bedell

1993   Archaeological Investigations at the Mumma Farm House, Antietam National Battlefield, Sharpsburg, Md. Engineering-Science, Washington, D.C. Submitted to Oehrlein and Associates Architects, Washington, D.C.

Walker, William C.

1885   *History of the Eighteenth Regiment Connecticut Volunteers in the War for the Union.* Gordon Wilcox, Norwich, Conn.

Wall, Cheryl A. (editor)

1995   *Zora Neale Hurston: Folklore, Memoirs, and Other Writings.* Library of America, New York.

Wall, Diana diZerega

1994a   *The Archaeology of Gender: Separating the Spheres in Urban America.* Plenum Press, New York.

1994b   Family Dinners and Social Teas: Ceramics and Domestic Rituals. In *Everyday Life in the Early Republic,* edited by Catherine E. Hutchins, 249–84. Henry Francis du Pont Winterthur Museum, Winterthur, Del.

1999   Examining Gender, Class, and Ethnicity in Nineteenth-Century New York City. *Historical Archaeology* 33(1):102–17.

Walsh, Lorena S.

1993   Slave Life, Slave Society, and Tobacco Production in the Tidewater Chesapeake, 1620–1820. In *Cultivation and Culture: Labor and the Shaping of Slave Life in the Americas,* edited by Ira Berlin and Philip D. Morgan, 170–99. University Press of Virginia, Charlottesville.

1997   *From Calabar to Carter's Grove: The History of a Virginia Slave Community.* University Press of Virginia, Charlottesville.

Ward, Joseph

1985   Civil War letters of J. F. Ward, 34th Regiment, Massachusetts Volunteers, Company B. Ms. on file, Harpers Ferry National Historical Park, Harpers Ferry, W. Va.

Warder, T. B., and James M. Catlett

1862   *Battle of Young's Branch or Manassas Plain.* Enquirer Book and Job Press, Richmond, Va.

Warville, Brissot de

1964   *New Travels in the United States of America, 1788,* edited by Durand Echeverria. Harvard University Press, Belknap Press, Cambridge, Mass.

Wayland, John Walter

1907   The German Element of the Shenandoah Valley of Virginia. Ph.D. dissertation, University of Virginia, Charlottesville.

1957   *Twenty-five Chapters in the Shenandoah Valley; to Which is Appended a Concise History of the Civil War in the Valley.* The Shenandoah Publishing House, Strasburg, Va.

Webster, Albert

1873   A Jaunt in the South. *Appleton's Journal* 10(234).

Weigley, Russell F.

1968   Philip H. Sheridan: A Personality Profile. *Civil War Times Illustrated* 7:5–9.

1983   *History of the United States Army.* Indiana University Press, Bloomington.

Weinert, Richard P., Jr., and Robert Arthur

1989   *Defender of the Chesapeake: The Story of Fort Monroe.* White Mane Publishing Co., Shippensburg, Pa.

Wellman, Manly W.

1956   *Rebel Boast: First at Bethel—Last at Appomattox.* Henry Holland Co., New York.

Wert, Jeffrey

1978   The Snickers Gap War. *Civil War Times Illustrated* 17(4):30–40.

Westlager, C. A.

1969   *The Log Cabin in America from Pioneer Days to the Present.* Copyright Rutgers University, Quinn & Boden Co., Inc., Rahway. N.J.

Westmacott, Richard

1990   *African American Gardens and Yards in the Rural South.* University of Tennessee Press, Knoxville.

Wetherbee, Jean

1981   *A Look at White Ironstone.* Wallace-Homestead Books, Des Moines, Iowa.

Wheaton, Thomas R., and Patrick H. Garrow

1985   Acculturation and the Archaeological Record in the Carolina Lowcountry. In *The Archaeology of Slavery and Plantation Life,* edited by Theresa A. Singleton, 239–59. Academic Press, Orlando, Fla.

Wildes, Thomas F.

1884   *Record of the One Hundred and Sixteenth Regiment Ohio Infantry Volunteers in the War of the Rebellion.* March and Brothers, Sandusky, Ohio.

Wiley, Bell Irvin

1952   *The Life of Billy Yank.* Louisiana State University Press, Baton Rouge.

1971   *The Life of Johnny Reb.* Doubleday, Garden City, New York.

Williams, Susan R.

1987   Introduction. In *Dining in America, 1850–1900,* edited by Kathryn Grover. University of Massachusetts Press, Amherst

Williams, T. Harry

1965   *Hayes of the Twenty-Third: The Civil War Volunteer Officer.* Alfred A. Knopf, New York.

Williams, Thomas J. C.

1968   *A History of Washington County, Maryland, from the Earliest Settlements to the Present Time,* 2 vols. Reprint. Regional Publishing Co., Hagerstown, Md.

Wills, Mary Alice

1975   *The Confederate Blockade of Washington, D.C. 1861–1862.* McClain Publishing Co., Parsons, West Virginia.

Wills, Richard

1998   Historical Context. In *H. L. Hunley Site Assessment*, edited by Larry E. Murphy, 21–36. National Park Service, Naval Historical Center, and South Carolina Institute of Archaeology and Anthropology, Columbia.

Wilshin, Francis F.

1970   *Mumma Farm "Spring House," Piper Farm "Slave Quarters," Sherrick Farm "Smoke House," Historic Structures Report, History Data Section, Antietam National Battlefield, Sharpsburg, Maryland.* Division of History, Office of Archeology and Historic Preservation, National Park Service, Washington, D.C.

Winchester Times

1866   Dedication of the National Cemetery, April 8. Winchester, Virginia.

Winter, Susan E.

1994   Civil War Fortifications and Campgrounds on Maryland Heights, the Citadel of Harpers Ferry. In *Look to the Earth: Historical Archaeology and the American Civil War,* edited by Clarence R. Geier, Jr., and Susan E. Winter, 101–29. University of Tennessee Press, Knoxville.

Wise, Stephen R.

1988   *Lifeline of the Confederacy: Blockade Running during the Civil War.* University of South Carolina Press, Columbia.

Wood, W. Dean, and Karen G. Wood

1990   *Soldiers and Citizens: Civil War Actions around Latimer's Farm, Cobb County, Georgia.* Southeastern Archeological Services, Athens, Georgia. Submitted to Marietta County Club, Marietta, Georgia.

Wood, William N.

1956   *Reminiscences of Big I,* edited by Bell I. Wiley. Jackson, Tennessee.

Worsham, John H.

1989   *One of Jackson's Foot Cavalry.* Broadfoot Publishing Co., Wilmington, North Carolina.

Wright, Steven J.

1992   *The Irish Brigade.* Steven Wright Publishing, Springfield, Pennsylvania.

Wyckoff, Martin A.

1984   *United States Military Buttons of the Land Services 1787–1902: A Guide and Classificatory System.* McLean County Historical Society, Bloomington, Illinois.

Wynne, Lewis N., and Robert A. Taylor (editors)

1993   *This War So Horrible: The Civil War Diary of Hiram Smith Williams.* University of Alabama Press, Tuscaloosa.

Yoder, Paton

1969   *Taverns and Travelers: Inns of the Early Midwest.* Indiana University Press, Bloomington.

Young, Daniel J.

1863   21, OCO, file W.D. 387, Report of U.S. Agent Daniel J. Young to Colonel H. K. Craig. Photocopy of ms. on file, Harpers Ferry National Historical Park, HFD 677. Harpers Ferry, West Virginia.

Zelinski, Wilbur

1972   *The Cultural Geography of the United States.* Prentice-Hall, Englewood, New Jersey.

Contributors

Susan C. Andrews is a historical archaeologist with Wilbur Smith Associates, Lexington, Kentucky. She received a Master of Arts in anthropology at the University of Tennessee, Knoxville. Her current research interests include frontier and 19th-century farmsteads, tavern life, and Civil War encampments.

Joseph Balicki is a graduate of George Washington University and holds a Master of Arts degree in anthropology. He is a principal archaeologist with John Milner Associates, Inc., and has been active in military site archaeology. In addition to his work at Fort C.F. Smith, he has participated in extensive research at Fort McHenry in Baltimore. He has conducted field investigations at Possum Nose, an 1862 Confederate battery blockading the Potomac River, at Trench Hill, a Confederate field fortification used during both the Battle of Fredericksburg and Wilderness, and at Rose Hill, the site of the First Battle of Kernstown.

John E. Cornelison, Jr., has a Master of Arts in anthropology from the University of Southern Mississippi. Since 1992 he has served as an archaeologist for the National Park Service and as project archaeologist at Stones River National Battlefield, at Fort Donelson National Battlefield, and at Chickamauga and Chattanooga National Battlefield.

Sean P. Coughlin is a Ph.D. candidate in anthropology at the University of Tennessee, Knoxville. He specializes in faunal analysis and has completed studies of prehistoric and historic collections from the southeastern United States.

Marian C. Creveling has a Master of Arts from the University of Maryland, College Park. She is currently archaeological collections manager for the National Park Service, National Capital Region. Focusing primarily on historical archaeology, her experience in the field and lab includes the excavation, processing, and long-term management of objects recovered from prehistoric and historic sites spanning the 17th to the 20th centuries, including significant work on Civil War–period sites in the area of Washington, D.C.

Susannah L. Dean is an archaeologist with the National Park Service, National Capital Region. She holds a Master of Arts degree in anthropology from the College of William and Mary and has five years experience examining Civil War–era archaeological sites in the Middle Atlantic region. Her research interests include faunal analysis and interpreting archaeological sites to the public.

Robert J. Fryman received his Ph.D. from the University of Pittsburgh where he specialized in the historical archaeology of 19th-century North America. Since 1992, he has conducted archaeological research on Civil War sites of the Atlanta Campaign, including the Chattahoochee River Line fortifications and entrenchments associated with the Lost Mountain Line. He is on the faculty of the Shiloh Middle School, Gwinnett County, Georgia, where he teaches social studies.

Laura J. Galke has a Master of Arts degree from Arizona State University and serves as the assistant archaeologist for the Southern Maryland Region. Her experience with Civil War–era archaeology includes work at Manassas Battlefield, Virginia, Monocacy Battlefield, Maryland, Point Lookout Hospital, Maryland, and Pamplin Park near Petersburg, Virginia.

Clarence R. Geier has a Ph.D. in anthropology from the University of Missouri–Columbia. He is a professor of anthropology at James Madison University, Harrisonburg, Virginia. His Civil War interests have concentrated on the Shenandoah Valley, including work at the Cool Spring, Third Winchester, and Cedar Creek battlefields. His most recent research has been at Fort Edward Johnson, a Confederate earthwork and associated encampment complex in Augusta County, Virginia. He is coeditor, with Susan Winter Trail, of *Look to the Earth: Historical Archaeology and the American Civil War*, published in 1994.

Jeffrey Harbison has a Bachelor of Arts degree in anthropology from the University of Delaware. He has worked on numerous 19th-century agricultural and entrepreneurial sites in the Middle Atlantic region and in the northeastern United States. He was introduced to battlefield archaeology while working for URS Greiner at the Antietam Battlefield National Park.

Warren R. Hofstra has a Ph.D. in history from the University of Virginia–Charlottesville and is professor of history at Shenandoah University in Winchester, Virginia. He directs the Community History project for Shenandoah University that provides him with opportunities for pursuing public programming, research, and writing in the local and regional history of the Shenandoah Valley.

Kenneth E. Koons has a Doctor of Arts in history from Carnegie Mellon University and is a professor of history at Virginia Military Institute. His research and writing focus on the history of society and economy in the Pennsylvania and Virginia sections of the Great Valley during the 19th century.

Elise Manning-Sterling has a Master of Arts in historical archaeology from the College of William and Mary, with an emphasis on faunal analysis. In addition to her work at Antietam Battlefield, she has been part of historic and prehistoric excavations in the eastern United States. She now works at Williamsburg and Jamestown, Virginia, and in Dutch Albany, New York. She is involved with archaeological research at Hubbardton Battlefield in Vermont and Fort Ticonderoga in New York.

Erika K. Martin Seibert is a Ph.D. candidate in American studies at the University of Maryland, College Park, where she studies historical archaeology and material culture. She works for the National Park Service and has worked at several Civil War parks, including Manassas National Battlefield and Harpers Ferry National Historical Park.

W. Stephen McBride is a senior historical archaeologist at Wilbur Smith Associates, Lexington, Kentucky. He holds a Ph.D. from Michigan State University and has been involved in Civil War archaeology, planning, and interpretation for over ten years.

Douglas W. Owsley has a Ph. D. from the University of Tennessee and is curator and division head for physical anthropology at the National Museum of Natural History, Smithsonian Institution. His studies include examinations of the remains of Civil War soldiers from several battlefields, including Antietam, Brandy Station, Gettysburg, and Port Hudson. In his 1994 monograph, *Bioarchaeology on a Battlefield: The Abortive Confederate Campaign in New Mexico*, he describes the skeletons of 31 Confederate soldiers killed during the 1862 Battle of Glorieta Pass.

Mia T. Parsons has a Bachelor of Arts in sociology and anthropology from St. Mary's College of Maryland. She has been an archaeologist with the National Park Service for six years, working on projects at Harpers Ferry National Historical Park, Manassas National Battlefield Park, and the George Washington Memorial Parkway.

Stephen R. Potter has a Ph.D. in anthropology from the University of North Carolina–Chapel Hill and is regional archaeologist, National Park Service, National Capital Region, which includes parks in portions of Maryland, Virginia, West Virginia, and the District of Columbia. His research interests include both the prehistoric and historic archaeology of the eastern United States, the 17th-century Chesapeake frontier, the southern Algonquian Indians, and the archaeology and history of the American Civil War. Since 1985, he has directed 14 major projects at Civil War–era sites.

Guy Prentice received his Ph.D. from the University of Florida and has been project director for the National Park Service's Southeast Archeological Center, where he has supervised several multiyear archaeological programs conducted at various parks throughout the region. Included among these are investigations at a number of Civil War–era sites, the most notable of which is Andersonville Prison.

Marie C. Prentice (née Mathison) has a Master of Arts degree from the University of Tennessee–Knoxville. She joined the staff at the Southeast Archaeological Center, where she participated in the excavation and analysis of archaeological remains at Andersonville Prison.

Paul A. Shackel received his Ph.D. from the State University of New York and is a professor of history at the University of Maryland, College Park. He was park archaeologist at Harpers Ferry National Historical Park and has become a scholar-spokesman for the history and historical archaeology of that important Civil War–era town. As a student of personal discipline and material culture, he has written on the historical archaeology of Annapolis and the Chesapeake Bay areas of the Middle Atlantic Region.

Bernard W. Slaughter received his Bachelor of Arts in sociology and anthropology from Eastern Illinois University. After postgraduate studies at Southern Illinois University, Carbondale, he has taken part in and directed excavations on prehistoric and historic sites throughout the United States and the U.S. Virgin Islands. He is employed by URS Greiner Woodward Clyde, where he was involved with fieldwork and research pertaining to a multiyear study at Antietam National Battlefield.

Steven D. Smith has a Master of Arts degree from the University of Kentucky, Lexington, and is head of the Cultural Resources Consulting Division at the South Carolina Institute of Archaeology and Anthropology, University of South Carolina. In the past 12 years he has conducted archaeological excavations at Civil War sites in South Carolina, North Carolina, and Louisiana, and historical research on the Civil War in Louisiana, Tennessee, and Missouri.

Robert C. Sonderman received a Masters of Arts from Illinois State University and is senior staff archaeologist, National Park Service, National Capital Region. Trained with an emphasis in historical archaeology, he has directed excavations at a variety of sites spanning the 17th through the 20th centuries, including such Civil War–era sites as the battlefields of Manassas and Antietam and the fortifications that provided the defense of Washington, D.C.

Bruce B. Sterling has 14 years of experience as a historic archaeologist, having excavated at sites dating from the 18th and 19th centuries in the Northeast and Middle Atlantic regions. As a field supervisor for URS Greiner he participated in a three-year survey of Antietam National Battlefield. He is involved with archaeological research at Hubbardton Battlefield in Vermont and Fort Ticonderoga in New York.

Joseph W. A. Whitehorne was educated at the University of Pennsylvania and holds a doctorate from George Mason University. He is professor of history at Lord Fairfax Community College, Middletown, Virginia. In addition to his numerous articles in military history, he is the author or coauthor of 13 books dealing mostly with 19th-century military history. Within the Shenandoah Valley he has conducted research at the New Market Battlefield, Cedar Creek, and the Battlefield of Third Winchester.

Index